Religion, Orientalism and Modernity

Edinburgh Historical Studies of Iran and the Persian World

Published in association with Elahé Omidyar Mir-Djalali, Founder and Chair, Roshan Cultural Heritage Institute

Series General Editor: Stephanie Cronin, Elahé Omidyar Mir-Djalali Research Fellow, University of Oxford

Series Advisory Board: Professor Janet Afary (UC Santa Barbara), Professor Abbas Amanat (Yale University), Professor Touraj Atabaki (International Institute of Social History), Dr Joanna de Groot (University of York), Professor Vanessa Martin (Royal Holloway, University of London), Professor Rudi Matthee (University of Delaware) and Professor Cyrus Schayegh (The Graduate Institute, Geneva)

Covering the history of Iran and the Persian world from the medieval period to the present, this series aims to become the pre-eminent place for publication in this field. As well as its core concern with Iran, it extends its concerns to encompass a much wider and more loosely defined cultural and linguistic world, to include Afghanistan, the Caucasus, Central Asia, Xinjiang and northern India. Books in the series present a range of conceptual and methodological approaches, looking not only at states, dynasties and elites, but at subalterns, minorities and everyday life.

Published and forthcoming titles

The Last Muslim Intellectual: The Life and Legacy of Jalal Al-e Ahmad
Hamid Dabashi

The Persian Prison Poem: Sovereignty and the Political Imagination
Rebecca Ruth Gould

Religion, Orientalism and Modernity: Mahdi Movements of Iran and South Asia
Geoffrey Nash

Remapping Persian Literary History, 1700–1900
Kevin L. Schwartz

Muslim–Christian Polemics in Safavid Iran
Alberto Tiburcio

edinburghuniversitypress.com/series/ehsipw

Religion, Orientalism and Modernity

Mahdi Movements of Iran and South Asia

Geoffrey Nash

EDINBURGH
University Press

Edinburgh University Press is one of the leading university presses in the UK. We publish academic books and journals in our selected subject areas across the humanities and social sciences, combining cutting-edge scholarship with high editorial and production values to produce academic works of lasting importance. For more information visit our website: edinburghuniversitypress.com

© Geoffrey Nash, 2022

Edinburgh University Press Ltd
The Tun – Holyrood Road
12 (2f) Jackson's Entry
Edinburgh EH8 8PJ

Typeset in 11/15 Adobe Garamond by
IDSUK (DataConnection) Ltd

A CIP record for this book is available from the British Library

ISBN 978 1 4744 5168 0 (hardback)
ISBN 978 1 4744 5171 0 (webready PDF)
ISBN 978 1 4744 5170 3 (epub)

The right of Geoffrey Nash to be identified as author of this work has been asserted in accordance with the Copyright, Designs and Patents Act 1988 and the Copyright and Related Rights Regulations 2003 (SI No. 2498).

Contents

Acknowledgements	vi
Notes on Transliteration	viii
1 Introduction	1
2 Contexts and Issues	25
3 Race and Religion in Gobineau's Persia	45
4 Ernest Renan's Search for a Religion of Modernity	69
5 Edward Granville Browne and the Writing of Babi Narratives	96
6 Empire and Orient: Baha'is in Russian Transcaspia and Palestine	123
7 Orientalism and Modernity in Baha'i and Ahmadi writings	156
8 Muslim Responses and a Future for Mahdi Movements	212
Notes	237
Bibliography	296
Index	320

Acknowledgements

Since Richard King's excellent study *Orientalism and Religion* opened up postcolonial readings in the field of religious studies, to my knowledge his approach has yet to be applied to the three movements from the Islamicate world under review here. I began to collect the materials incorporated into the present book for a seminar entitled 'Can Religions make Peace?' held at Goldsmith's, University of London in 2002. However the gestation period for the issues it debates stretches back a further twenty years to the time when, as a post-doctoral researcher, I published a short book on the persecution of the Baha'i community of Iran. Six years after this appeared, Dr Denis MacEoin referred to it in an article dealing with a similar topic, pointing out my representation of Shi'i Islam as typical of 'the way in which the Baha'is themselves have adopted an essentially orientalist vision of their own community and of Iranian society'. It is to Denis that I owe much in terms of the development of my thought on the subject on which this book is based. That is not, however, to lay the blame on his shoulders for some of my views on the modern Middle East over which he and I are now likely to diverge. Nonetheless, Denis's work on the Iranian Babis and Baha'is, substantively present in his collection of essays *The Messiah of Shiraz*, has to be the foundation on which any critical evaluation of the topic area covered in my work would still need to build.

Similarly, but for different reasons, the scholarship of Dr Moojan Momen has also been vital to my work. From his readings of Baha'i history I also diverge but for my part there is nothing lost when it comes to the respect I hold for the honesty behind the positions he holds. His painstaking accumulation of detailed and extensive knowledge on Baha'i and Shi'i history and their major themes is indispensable for any researcher on these topics. I also owe a great debt of thanks to Dr Stephen Lambden and Dr Seena Fazel both as scholars and for the seminars in Baha'i studies which they have organised and which I have attended in Newcastle and Oxford, respectively.

Portions of this book have been delivered as papers at these seminar series. Part of Chapter 4 was published as 'Aryan and Semite in Ernest Renan and Matthew Arnold's Quest for the Religion of Modernity', *Religion and Literature*, 46.1 (2014), pp. 25–50.

To the library staff at the School of Oriental and African Studies, University of London where I spent many hours researching this book I owe thanks, and I am very grateful too to Dr Amina Yaqin for her collegiate spirit in helping me during my period as Research Associate at SOAS.

I would also like to thank Dr Reza Zia-Ibrahimi, an outstanding representative of a younger generation of scholars of Iranian cultural history, who gave his support at the proposal stage and whose perspectives have been of great help to me.

To Daniel O'Donoghue for his fine translations of Gobineau and the special insight he has brought to the Frenchman's thought-world, I am greatly indebted. Thanks are also due to Dr Peter Shambrock and Dr Moya Tönnies for supplying material on, and helping me to improve my understanding of, Britain's role in Palestine during the Mandate period.

To my dear friend Dr Khalil Rashidian formerly of Durham University, I am greatly indebted for the hours and years during which I have been able to share his insights and imbibe his deep love of Iran and its culture.

Lastly, all my love goes to Mina, for her longsuffering endurance of my engagement in a project of which she, in her innate state of enlightenment, is beyond the need.

Durham, England
May 2021

Notes on Transliteration

Arabic words feature in large numbers in Persian and Urdu. In the main, spellings of proper names are used as they commonly appear in the literature, for example, *Khwaja Kamaluddin, Bashiruddin Ahmad, Maulana Muhammad Ali, Mohammad Reza, Quratul Ayn, Rashid Rida, Abdul Hamid, Al-e Ahmad, Nizam-i Nau, Ahmadiyya, Suleymaniya, taziya*. Diacritics are largely omitted, so *'Abdu'l-Baha* is written *Abdul Baha*; *'Ali Shari'ati* is *Ali Shariati*; but they are retained in *Baha'i, Shi'i*, and a few other cases. Transliterated words are italicised only when unfamiliar to the general reader, for example, *mashriq al-adhkar, mazhar-i ilahi, mubahala, risalih*, but jihad not *jihad*; ulama not *ulama*; umma not *umma*.

Nothing can be less philosophical than to apply semi-criticism to narratives conceived [of as] beyond all criticism.

Ernest Renan, *The Future of Science*, pp. 42–3

For 'Orientalism' consists of those Western knowledge practices in the modern era whose emergence made possible for the first time the notion of a single world as a space populated by distinct civilizational complexes, each in possession of its own tradition, the unique expression of its own forms of national 'genius'.

Aamir Mufti, *Forget English! Orientalisms and World Literatures*, p. 24

Fundamentalists are not, however, very receptive to the notion of limitations, nor to their belief system having to be updated to take account of historical change.

Stuart Sim, *Fundamentalist World: The New Dark Age of Dogma*, p. 165

1

Introduction

When in the early 1980s Ronald Reagan spoke up for the persecuted Baha'i community of Iran he most likely lacked an understanding of the resonance such an intervention by a United States President would have for a religious animosity deeply rooted in nineteenth-century Iranian history. The issue had its origins in the radical millenarian movement known as Babism whose claims surrounding the appearance of the expected Imam Mahdi threatened alike the upper echelons of the Shi'i religious hierarchy and the Qajar monarchy in mid nineteenth-century Iran and led to a trail of sectarian division and oppression that is still with us to this day. Some pundits of the Reagan era were even ready to compare Babism with the revolution inspired by Ayatollah Khomeini.[1]

In this study I argue that in addition to the clash of theological truth claims that polarise Shi'i Muslims and the Babi movement's offshoot the Baha'i faith, the divergence which shaped their continuing animosity in the twentieth century has in part been written in terms of orientalism and modernity. Both Shi'a and Baha'is have adopted the tool of religious othering. The former condemn Baha'is as a political grouping and agents of Western imperialism, while Baha'is have employed orientalist vocabulary that casts Muslims in the role of backward fanatics. Such an intersection of religious, social and political elements makes the Shi'i Muslim/Baha'i antipathy a particularly instructive example of mutual othering in the modern world.

Studies on responses to modernity from within the Islamicate world have largely focused on different branches of revivalist Islam, Islamist and latterly jihadist movements focusing on their social and political goals.[2] Attention has also been paid, but in a more limited way, to other movements centred on *mujaddid* figures arising at a key period of encounter between Islamic societies and the Western world in the nineteenth and early twentieth centuries.[3] This book presents a specific analysis of three mahdi movements, the first two comprising the Babis and the Baha'is of Iran, and the third, the Ahmadiyya, a movement of a slightly later epoch emerging in late nineteenth-century India. Christian missionaries in the early twentieth century were among the first to compare the Ahmadiyya with the two Iranian movements, and the triumvirate was revived later in the century as embodying a particular form of deviance by Sunni antagonists in Pakistan and Shi'a in Iran. A comparative analysis will facilitate viewing mahdi movements in terms of geographical variation: not only are Iran and northwest India spatially removed, the configuration of the respective branches of Islam in the two countries, and variance in historical timeframes, means the politics and governance are distinctive as well.[4] The comparison is consistent with Christopher Bayly's call to 'reemphasize the proposition that national histories and "area studies" need to take fuller account of changes occurring in the wider world'.[5] Writing during the Islamic revival of the 1970s John Voll made a point which is equally valid for the charismatic millennial movements of the previous century:

> It is important to understand the specific conditions out of which particular groups emerged rather than simply view them as examples of some abstract model. At the same time, if these experiences are simply viewed in isolation, their broader significance in world history can be missed and even their specific aspects can be misunderstood if they are separated from the broader patterns and experiences of which they are a part.[6]

According to the late Andrew Rippin the major issue around which these movements was constructed was their response to a perceived need for change and a concomitant renewal of religious authority: 'if the questioning of the authority of the past is taken far enough in the desire to be able to accommodate or compensate for changes of the modern period, there is need for a new source of authority'. Babis, Baha'is and Ahmadis each came up with variant encodings of this authority. For the latter 'the correct interpretation of Islam has been invested with the authority of revelation . . . The situation is quite different for the Baha'is who do not wish to consider themselves Islamic but rather proclaim themselves to be members of a new "World Faith" which supersedes Islam'.[7]

The term 'mahdi', as indicated above, is one that is called into use relatively infrequently to qualify new movements from the Islamicate world of the previous two centuries. *The Shorter Encyclopaedia of Islam* offers a varied repertoire of definitions of the term including an etymology of the Arabic root-word, *h-d-y*, a discussion of its application in significant historical figures to whom the name 'Mahdi' is given (such as Muhammad ibn al-Hanafiyya), and follows the term's diachronic trajectory as it 'gradually hardened from being a general honorific into a special designation, and even a proper name, for a restorer of the Faith in the last days'.[8] Lists of movements belonging within the mahdi category invariably include Babism, its offshoot Baha'ism, and chronologically the latest, the Ahmadiyya. Acolytes draw from the term meanings specific to their own movement in connection to relevant religious, temporal and geographical contexts. What becomes apparent from scrutiny of these is that the term undergoes slippage and may be displaced or substituted by further signifiers, either of clarification or of extension, depending among other things on the claimant's own consciousness, immediate recipients, and the broader reception of his message.[9] Mahdi movements are not so much generic as self-defining, concerned with an urgency to fulfil spiritual needs and accomplish long-held religious expectations, but emerging from within straightened sociopolitical contexts that often leave an indelible mark on their future orientation. While each of the movements concerned are commonly viewed by their adherents as possessing mahdi characteristics, in the case of the Baha'i faith these are in effect no more than a point of departure in the sense that apart from the religion's scholars its followers, especially those from non-Muslim backgrounds, today mostly see very little continuing relevance in its Islamic origins. One scholar has pointed out that even among his colleagues working with Persian and Arabic texts the history of their faith begins with its founder Ali Muhammad the Bab, or at a push, with the Shaykhi leaders Shakyh Ahmad Ahsai and his successor Sayyid Kazim Rashti who propelled the search for the imminently appearing Imam Mahdi.[10]

This study is not specifically concerned with giving detailed accounts of the historical progression of any of these movements beyond providing the background historical context necessary for situating the issues and themes under scrutiny or analysing religious concepts. This study is interpretative rather than descriptive or centred on archival research, and it is written from the broader premise that European empires impacted upon 'the Muslim World' in ways that were instrumental in the formation of the mahdi movements.[11] Evidence for this will be drawn from narratives inscribed by their founders and followers, and by allowing for the ways in which their development affected the position of the majority who did not accept their claims and who, for want of a better distinguishing feature, we must continue to call Muslims. To suggest that they remained as they had been before the new movements appeared, or that their development was arrested or entered into decline as a result of their refusing to accept the innovators and the innovations they proffered, is a standpoint which will be found embedded within the mahdi narratives, but which can hardly be allowed to go uncontested. Beyond the foundational phase, owing largely to their proselytic activities in the West, the mahdi movements constructed narratives preponderantly in English (with, in the Ahmadi case, translations from Urdu) and to a lesser extent French, while Muslim counter-narratives late into the twentieth century continued to be composed in oriental languages.

Early studies of the chief actors, their prominent followers, and the movements they created employed the philological techniques current in nineteenth-century orientalism. In the 1920s Soviet orientologist M. S. Ivanov used a Marxist approach to explain the social construction and role of Babism in Iran in the 1840s. Standard methodological frameworks utilised in the sociology of religion started to be applied with what Peter Smith calls 'the first proper sociological study of the Babi and Baha'i religions' conducted by the young Peter Berger in the 1950s.[12] Later, western Baha'i scholars, Smith included, have tended to employ Weberian conceptualisations such as routinisation of charisma and the use of motifs. Missing thus far is application of a theory that might insightfully take into consideration the religious movements' transmission of messages and ideas, particularly narratives, across cultures. As Richard King puts it in his study *Orientalism and Religion*,

> both philosophy and the history of ideas should take more seriously *not only the social location* of the concepts under examination *but also their involvement in a wider cultural field of power relations*, or what has become know as 'the politics of knowledge'.[13]

The task taken up here is to ascertain how the development of the mahdi movements intersects with the two recurring concepts and patterns, orientalism and modernity. From a theoretical-philosophical perspective, I set out to address the question as to whether movements with a reform agenda and messianic orientation, in the process of emerging from the East during the period in question, adopted/adapted orientalist discourse(s) and if so, why. This perspective defines the main objectives of the study: to situate the rationale for deployment of orientalist discourses and to scrutinise their utilisation by Western and Westernised Eastern authors according to categories of religion, empire and race. This will in turn be linked to the revival of religion in the Islamicate domains and beyond, the relationship between religion and modernity, and in particular the way in which European colonial powers conceived of the 'backwardness' of Muslim states in relation to their indigenous minorities.

* * *

A movement of millennial expectation and social protest deeply embedded within Iranian Shi'ism, Babism was the creation of Sayyid Ali Muhammad Shirazi (1819–50) who claimed to be the gate (*bab*) to the Hidden Imam, then the Imam Mahdi himself, and finally the revealer of a separate religion to Islam. Shirazi's claims led to confrontations with state and ulama in Qajar Persia. The violent erasure of his most active followers occurred around the time of his execution in July 1850 and after an assassination attempt on the shah two years later leaving the few surviving Babi leaders to be moved to Ottoman domains. They spent ten years in Baghdad followed by a brief period in the capital of the Empire. For a further five years they were accommodated in Edirne in western Turkey where the movement split into two factions. Mirza Husayn Ali Nuri, Baha'ullah (1817–92) head of the majority was banished to Akka, Palestine, where he spent the last two decades of his life. The minority retained allegiance to the Bab's appointed successor Subh-i Azal (1831–1912) who was sent to Cyprus. In Edirne, Baha'ullah extended the bounds of Babism by proclaiming his own 'divine manifestation' (*mazhar-i ilahi*) and thus transformed the Babis into Baha'is, promoting a new message of world peace.[14] In Akka the Baha'i leaders, though initially kept in strict confinement later established contact with other reformers notably members of the Young Ottomans who were also in exile. Subh-i Azal continued a conservative Babi anti-Qajar stance, however later figures from the Azali faction would make a significant contribution to the Iranian Constitutional Revolution of 1906–11. Collectively, therefore, the different factions that sprang out of the Bab's initial impetus developed along variant chiliastic and reformist pathways.

In 1883 Mirza Ghulam Ahmad (1835?–1908) announced his mission as *mujaddid* (the renewer expected by Sunni Muslims in every century) and in 1889 assembled a group of followers in Ludhyana, Punjab where these proffered him an oath of allegiance (*bay'a*). A year later a conference held in Qadian that attracted five hundred people saw the formal inauguration of the Ahmadiyya community. In 1891 Ghulam Ahmad went even further in his claims adopting the title Promised Messiah and declaring himself a prophet, albeit not a law-giving one such as Muhammad. Initially, no importance was given to Ahmad's claims until against a background of several years' opposition raised by 'sectarian' ulama in 1903 he pronounced the separation of the Ahmadi community from Sunnism.[15] After Ahmad's death in 1908 his close disciple Hakim Nuruddin held the position of the community's first khalifa until his death in March 1914.

Babis, Baha'is, and Ahmadis should each be understood to be followers of a mahdi figure responding to pressures exerted by his surroundings. In Ghulam Ahmad's case these related to Muslim decline in India as the Mughal rulers who had once held sway over most of the subcontinent succumbed to British colonial control. This situation demarcates Ghulam Ahmad's claim to be the Mahdi quite significantly from Ali Muhammad Shirazi's. As a Sunni, albeit with sufi predilections (as was commonly the case for emergent Muslim sects in nineteenth-century India), Ahmad did not graduate, as the Bab did, from a milieu of Shi'i expectancy, nor from an autonomous Muslim territory. In addition, of the figures who laid claim to the title of 'Mahdi' he adopted a specifically *masihi* stance in appropriating the Christianised title 'the Promised Messiah', combining his claims in such a way as to collapse the discrete messiah and mahdi roles into one and the same designation. Ahmad also invited controversy in his engagement in public religious debates (*mubahala*) against Christian missionaries and prominent figures from the Hindu Arya

Samaj. His ingenious re-imagining of a later career for Jesus in Kashmir and advancement of his personal claim to be the return of Christ unsurprisingly antagonised the missionaries. Initially admired by Indian Muslims for his aggressive defence of Islam he began to involve himself in *mubahala* with Muslim ulama, apparently genuinely unfazed by the inevitable excoriation he attracted for diminishing the *khatim al-nabiyyin*, Muhammad's title as last ('seal') of the prophets. 'Whereas British missionaries opposed him because of his insistence on Jesus' natural death, Indian Muslim scholars excommunicated him on the grounds that he contradicted the Koran'.[16] Ahmad knew, however, that the varied religious landscape of imperial India and the religiously neutral government of the British insulated him from wholesale persecution.

According to the Frenchman Arthur Gobineau, who was the first to relay an extended version of the Bab's story to Europe, the Bab instructed his followers to stage uprisings and a semi jihad.[17] Around him accumulated a narrative of legendary dimensions, in which followers were initially drawn to him as a charismatic fulfilment of Shi'i prophecy, but like Ghulam Ahmad he extended his claims producing a new religious book, the *Bayan*, to supersede the Quran. In contrast to Ghulam Ahmad's adversarial but non-violent relations with Christians and Muslims in India, the execution of the Bab, the prophet-martyr of Shiraz, was seen by Muslims, including Ahmad, as a sign of violent rebellion and of his being a false prophet. However, encouraged by Gobineau's account, Westerners came to view his short messianic career as a kind of simulacrum of Christ's ministry and crucifixion.

As a follower of the Bab, initially making his claim neither to Muslims nor Christians but to his fellow Babis, Baha'ullah declared himself in 1863 not to be the Mahdi but 'he whom God will make manifest' (*man yuzhiruhu 'llah*), who the Bab had said would follow in his stead at an undetermined time within the next thousand years. As a Babi leader and then claimant to divine manifestation in his own right, what made the theatre of Baha'ullah's operation distinctive was his exile beyond the borders of Iran. He was for several years a visitor to a sufi *tekke* in Suleymaniya in what is now Iraqi Kurdistan. Qajar and Ottoman statesmen and functionaries, nervous of his influence, sought to eclipse both his person and his claims by a series of banishments to the western Asiatic/eastern European boundaries of the Ottoman

Empire. Few Europeans came into direct contact with him (though more than who met the Bab). The orientalist E. G. Browne, however, was able to visit Baha'ullah in his mansion near Akka shortly before he died, where he enunciated a message of hope and renewal for the world. All three mahdi/prophet figures enacted traditional performances of Islamic signs in their revelations. In the Bab and Baha'ullah's cases the recitation of holy verses, the litmus test of a revelator's credentials, was the key factor. Ghulam Ahmad tended to apply his pen to writing newspaper articles and papers which were read out for him at *mubahala* contests. In addition to writing his multi-volume *Barahin-i Ahmadiyya* he also spent time drumming up the money to get his pamphlets printed. Receiving his revelations in dreams he popularly excelled in the exercise of prophecy against opponents and enemies, in several cases correctly foretelling their deaths.[18]

Transmission to, and Reception in, the West

The focus now turns to the impact of the three movements outside of Iran, Ottoman West Asia and India, tracking their respective development beyond the Islamicate world as Baha'i and Ahmadi missionising grew indigenous communities in the West.[19] Moshe Sharon suggests like the Mormons in North America, Baha'is 'also sustained persecution and exile and also experienced the movement of the centres of their religion *westward* from the Iranian domains to the Ottoman Empire, and then to Europe and America'.[20] As Rippin stated, both Baha'ism and Ahmadism were formed around new revelatory claims causing the founders of each to take up innovatory positions with respect to their links with Islam, but each movement was offering different things to potential converts. The conversion of Westerners is one of the most striking features of both movements, and recent work has tended to assess the separate impacts of both Baha'i and Ahmadi proselytising activities in Europe and America during the early twentieth century.[21] When it came to sending out Muslim missionaries to Europe in the early years of the new century, a significant impact was made by Ahmadis, particularly in Britain and Germany. Converts were attracted in the name of Islam rather than of Ghulam Ahmad, the new messiah. How the mahdi movements enlisted Western interest and support vis-à-vis the hostile response of mainstream Muslims, and the ways in which this feeds into larger debates concerning Islam and the Western world more generally, is the main focus of the present study.

Information on these movements filtered back to Europe in the form of diplomatic reports, articles and books transmitted by Western diplomats, travellers, missionaries and orientalists who encountered them in the lands of their birth. The diplomatic record, though quite extensive and sustained, was necessarily restricted with respect to dissemination. From the 1890s onwards Iranian, Central Asian and Levantine theatres of Baha'i activity began to feature in European literatures. Since the mid-nineteenth century, European diplomats and travellers in Iran had been alerted to the Babi 'episode' and their notes and dispatches amounted to a varied portrait of the Bab and his movement in fragments.[22] The figure of the Bab, according to MacEoin, 'remains elusive in the absence of detailed contemporary material', though he cites a rare European witness, Dr. William Cormick, an Irish doctor called in to treat him after he had received the bastinado in Tabriz in 1848, who described him as 'mild and delicate looking'.[23] However, the Bab and his followers were introduced to European audiences in an important way by Arthur Gobineau's extensive narrative account in *Religions et les philosophies dans l'Asie centrale* (1865). This stimulated educated inquiry in Russia by orientalists Mirza Kazem Bek and Baron Rozen, the latter influencing a group of younger scholars, and in England by Cambridge professor of Persian and Arabic Edward Granville Browne.[24] Given the later date of its emergence, Ahmadism necessarily began to attract attention in the new century. In the work of missionaries, such as H. A. Walter's *The Ahmadiya Movement* (1918), the later entrant to the mahdi arena was often compared to the Babi and Baha'i innovations.[25] It was on the above mentioned sources that the reception of the mahdi movements mainly depended until their own missionaries were dispatched and converts began to be made in the West.

By the early 1900s, having established itself in Iran as a modern movement of change attracting Jewish and Zoroastrian converts in addition to Shi'a Muslims, Baha'ism entered on a successful period of proselytisation outside of Iran. In the process it shed its links to Shi'i Islam. At the 1893 World Parliament of Religions in Chicago, Baha'ism first received public mention and Baha'ullah's eldest son and successor Abbas Effendi/Abdul Baha (1844–1921), attracted his first group of Western pilgrims while still in detention in Akka in 1898. The small stream of wealthy pilgrims from North America continued. In North America, as well as in Britain and France, 'Bahai' was recognised as the name of a movement of 'the new age', to which acolytes of esotericism, New Thought and liberal Christianity were drawn. For a seminal moment, between 1911 and 1912, the line of division between East and West was erased with Abdul Baha's journeys to Europe and America. This was a time when Eastern savants were arriving and finding audiences in Western capitals. However, they came mostly as visitors from the colonised Orient, not from limited self-governing Muslim-majority lands (which were fast disappearing!) like Iran. In point of fact, although on his Western visits he promoted Muhammad alongside other 'divine manifestations', Abdul Baha and his supporters succeeded in decoupling his own spiritual aura and message of peace and unity from the traditionally negative image Westerners held of Islam.[26] Regarding Abdul Baha's journeys in the United States, one Protestant critic noted the,

> fanatical devotion with which he was hailed by American zealots. Wherever he appeared, someone in the crowds claimed that a glance from him had an electrical effect. Women came forward to kiss his hands. One enthusiast said that she 'had seen God!' A minister, feeling the touch of Abdul-Baha's hand, said that his heart melted to tears, that his voice choked in his throat and that he could not have spoken a single word had his life depended on it. America was being initiated to a hypnotic spiritual power.[27]

Recent attention paid to Ahmadi missionising style and activities in both Europe and America in the first four decades of the twentieth century focuses the sect's role in the promotion of a modern form of Islam. Distinguishing his own movement from that of the Babis and Baha'is, Ghulam Ahmad made the interesting claim that Baha'i teachers used different tactics in the East to the West:

> ... the missionaries of this religion pose to be Muhammadans among Muhammadans and under the guise of Islam instil their secret teachings into the heart of men quite imperceptibly. But to ensure success of the movement in the West that attitude could no longer be maintained and among the Christians this movement is associating itself with Christianity. While,

therefore, in the West it is plainly acknowledged that the religion of Bab or Bahaullah has nothing to do with Islam, the Bahai missionary in the East still gives the public the impression his creed is an offshoot of Islam under the guise of a profound respect for the Holy Prophet and the Holy Quran . . .[28]

However, following Ghulam Ahmad's death, Ahmadi missionaries had to balance their own velleities with respect to whether and how his messianic claims should be handled vis-à-vis the delivery of the 'pure' message of Islam. After several years these tensions could no longer be contained and the split into Lahori and Qadiani branches of Ahmadiyya began to impact upon missionising work in Europe.[29] Nonetheless, hostile mainstream Muslim opponents of the Ahmadis found great difficulty in 'tracing any doctrinal influence of Mirza Ghulam Ahmad in the European Lahori propaganda and . . . only at the very end of the inter war period . . . [did] their anti-Ahmadi arguments gain ground'.[30] In the Baha'i case, a significant proportion of American converts were initially attracted by the esoteric teachings filtrated into the Baha'i message by Ibrahim Kheiralla, a Syrian Christian who had converted to Baha'ism in Egypt. He soon fell out with Abdul Baha and aligned himself with the dissident half-brother Mirza Muhammad Ali creating a potential schism.[31]

There was at least one moment when Baha'i and Ahmadi trajectories intersected in the West. On 17 January 1913 Abdul Baha and the dynamic leader of the Ahmadi mission in London Khwaja Kamaluddin (1870–1932) encountered one another on the occasion of the opening of the Woking Mosque. Abdul Baha was surrounded by an entourage of liberal-universalist Christians who may have seen his religion 'as an "entrée", closer on an accepted grid of worldviews and which could serve to blanche out problematic vertices of Christian attitudes to Islam'.[32] Kamaluddin challenged Abdul Baha to perform the *salat al-zuhr*, which he did together with his companion, Kamaluddin reported, according to the Sunni rite.[33] Brendan McNamara notes a subtle convergence of Kamaluddin's method of teaching would-be English converts and the similarly placatory way of Abdul Baha:

> Contacts with sympathetic middle- and upper-class figures were cultivated, every effort made not to cause disaffection, and British cultural norms were readily adopted. Kamaluddin was eager to connect with those engaged in religious enquiry and spoke at meetings of Theosophists and Spiritualists.[34]

While the connection of each to messianic figures operated on different scales with respect to their relationship to Islam, the Baha'i and Ahmadi leaders fished in similar waters in the West, speaking to audiences looking for something more than the standard Christian orthodoxies. They both attracted acolytes and sympathisers at the higher end socially, propounding a similar modernist message of progress, rationality and spiritual generosity that elided the 'unreformed' aspects of Islam that could otherwise have been a turn off to European truth seekers.[35]

Proselytism and Polemic

The present study attempts to evaluate Western interest in Baha'is and Ahmadis in line with investigation of key thematic concerns employed in contemporary postcolonial scholarship: the politics of empire, modernity, and orientalism. Both movements presented an unmistakable determination not only to eschew anti-colonial confrontation with the West, but to enlist the protection and support of European agencies, and later on specifically to engage in missionary activity within Western domains. Both heterodox movements were charged by their adversaries with being instruments of British, and in the case of the Babis and Baha'is, Russian colonial projects. Cringingly loyal to British power in India, Ghulam Ahmad did not hesitate to 'appropriate central Christian claims and widen the function of charisma as he went along'. An argument has been made that Ahmad's 'project was not to attack British colonial administrators with weapons but to attack their religion'.[36] On the other hand, in India, Ahmadi propagandising against the Christian missionaries was never anti-colonial and in actuality it never arose above the level of parochialism, an affair in which 'fair dealing' allowed religions to clash with one another so long as this was conducted under the aegis of the secular, religiously neutral, all-powerful British Empire. Between the two World Wars, in Europe and North America, Lahori Ahmadi missionising was transformed into an operation that was both Islam-rich and in its message of interracial brotherhood appealing to Western converts. In England however, in spite of Khwaja Kamaluddin's statement 'sedition and anarchical movements are *haram*, and strictly prohibited in Islam',[37] the Woking Mosque came closest to dissent and pan-Islamic alignment over the issue of Ottoman entry at the start of the Great War. British converts and fellow travellers Lord Headley and Marmaduke Pickthall took up opposing Empire loyalist and pro-Ottoman stances, respectively, but security sources reported the Ahmadi mission itself to be politically benign.[38]

Clinton Bennett believes the attention given the Ahmadi movement in the West (largely by Christians) has tended to overestimate its relevance in comparison to the notice vouchsafed it in the country in which it grew up and in the Islamic world generally. The cause of this Bennett suggests, is Ghulam Ahmad's proselytism and aggressive intervention in the territory of Christianity, specifically his doctrine of Jesus' non-crucifixion and relocation to Kashmir, which engaged serious attention among missionaries. On this basis Ahmadis were considered objects worthy of study and contestation.[39] A similar factor was in operation in Iran where the missionaries' initially high estimation of Baha'is led them to draw incorrect inferences from their apparent flexibility, shedding of Muslim doctrinal fixity, and openness toward Christianity.[40] Once disabused of their potentiality as converts, the missionaries did not miss the opportunity to inveigh against Baha'is with cynical invective.[41] Overall, the attitudes the two mahdi movements displayed toward Christianity were in keeping with their respective missionising projects, an early commentator seeing Baha'is as 'go[ing] out of their way to speak well of Christianity and to make the transition easy for Christians. Yet the Ahmadis, though rather better treated by Christians than by Moslems, retain the typical Moslem scorn for the Christian'.[42]

For their part, nineteenth-century Babis penned works vehemently denouncing the corruption of both the Qajar monarchy and the Shi'i ulama, and later, Baha'i writers contemptuously dismissed the latter in the name of reform and modernity. Shi'i and secular polemic in Iran has in turn tarred the Babis and Baha'is with collaboration with Western imperialism. The aim is to assess these crossed lines dispassionately, addressing both sides of the argument where for the most part the dispute has been written about from entrenched positions, both religious and political. While the links European governments had with followers of all three movements is of interest, the main focus will be contextualising the reception of Babis and Baha'is in nineteenth and early twentieth-century Western discourse, notably in the work of travellers and orientalists, this being substantially larger and more significant than orientalist interest in Ahmadism. The aim is to ascertain the extent to which an orientalist discourse impacted on the manner in which Baha'i authorities and influential leaders of thought conceived of the character, role and place of their religion in the modern world. The hypothesis is that the Babi and Baha'i movements (which Baha'i sources tend to conflate into the Baha'i faith) were enabled in their presentation not only by their story passing through the hands of orientalists, diplomats and executors of empire, but more specifically in the way 'Babi-Baha'i history' was in its formative stage conceived of in orientalist terms in writing produced by Baha'is themselves. Taking place over a period of roughly the first half of the twentieth century, the Baha'i discourse may be said to coincide with a process whereby from the 1890s,

> a fortuitous combination of factors led to conversions in the United States and Europe, and the Baha'i leadership soon adopted a conscious policy of proselytization outside the Middle East. As new communities emerged and consolidated themselves in the West, a modified presentation of Baha'i history, law, and doctrine evolved to suit the tastes and preoccupations of a membership mentally and culturally divorced from the movement's Islamic background and character.[43]

This process led to 'a deracinated, Westernized Baha'ism, and its promulgation over an ever-expanding geographical area as a "new world faith"' embedded within which was a discourse of Baha'i orientalism of the movement's own originating.[44]

In the case of the Ahmadiyya, Ghulam Ahmad's project, which we have already seen was founded upon sectarian controversy, spilled into attacks upon *maulvis* over the dogma of jihad which he abrogated in a manner that appeared to tie his claim of Mahdi-Messiah with support for the British government. A discourse that within northwest India developed adversarial positions vis-à-vis Christian missionaries, also had a strong in-built tendency in the same area and in a similar context to proliferate into *mubahala* against mainstream Muslims, and following the martyrdom of several followers in Afghanistan in the early 1920s, grew 'the general perception among Ahmadis that non-Ahmadi *mullas* are the enemy'.[45] It would, however, be straining the Ahmadi position of accommodation to Western norms which in some ways parallels that of the Baha'is, to link it to orientalism. Orientalism features, if at all, in a less overt manner in Ahmadism than in Baha'i narratives. For the reasons stated above it is difficult to employ the type of orientalism that others modern Muslims while still sharing the majority of their beliefs. However, by the time they were legally categorised as non-Muslims in Pakistan in 1984, Ahmadis had developed their own discourse privileging their exceptionality and accenting the Islam of all other Muslims as the embodiment of corruption and disorder in the modern world. In post-colonial contexts, 'the Ahmadis' desire to present themselves as exceptional while casting mainstream Islam as defective, has thus unsurprisingly led to them being celebrated by groups and individuals who are often accused of hostility to Islam'.[46] There seems to be a discrepancy between the Ahmadiyyat's self-presentation as a religion of peace and tolerance in English language media, as per their slogan 'Peace for all, Hate for none', while statements in Urdu or Arabic made by Ghulam Ahmad contain attacks upon his opponents replete with colourful, 'fierce imagery'.[47] However, the fact that Ahmadis claim to be followers of the movement that is the only true expression of Islam, the one set out by the Mahdi Messiah, but nonetheless maintain traditional practises such as purdah, polygamy and the Hanifite code of law, and hold conservative positions on sensitive issues such as homosexuality, has made their endorsement by some anti-Muslim groups in the name of tolerance and democracy more complex than it first appears on the surface.[48]

Orientalism and Modernity: Key Motifs

The formative years of the Babi and the Baha'i movements coincide with the period addressed in two Baha'i sources, the first of which is *God Passes By*, a faith-history of the first century of the Babi and Baha'i dispensations covering the period 1844 to 1944 and written by Shoghi Effendi Rabbani, Guardian of the Baha'i faith between 1922 and 1957.[49] Baha'i scholar Moojan Momen's valuable, extensively researched sourcebook, *The Babi and Baha'i Religions, 1844–1944: Some contemporary Western Accounts* is the second. The period these two texts cover and the material they contain form the major part of the subject area on which academic work on Baha'ism has so far concentrated. Over the last forty years this has mainly been conducted within the area of Islamic, and specifically Iranian Shi'i, studies notably by Abbas Amanat, Todd Lawson, Denis MacEoin, and Moojan Momen. Juan Cole, Oliver Sharbrodt and Necati Alkan have situated Baha'ism within contexts of Islamic modernism. Stephen Lambden and Christopher Buck have studied Biblical connections to Islamic, Babi and Baha'i scripture, and Sen McGlinn has initiated the beginnings of Baha'i theology.[50] Taking up the component of modernity, recent work on Ahmadiyya has focused on international networks within the broader context of the proselytisation of Islam in the West. Weberian principles in the field of the sociology of religion especially the notion of the routinisation of charisma have been applied by Peter Smith and MacEoin to both Babi and Baha'i developments.[51] Antonio Gualtieri and Nicholas Evans have written ethnographical studies demonstrating how in Ahmadism charisma is specifically regularised (though not diluted) through the construction of a modern administration and bureaucracy.[52] Peter Smith's description of progressive 'dominant motifs' within the Baha'i faith, 'social reformism, modernization and the millennium' afterward taken up by Cole, are imbricated in the Baha'i programme itself and its self-image as a modern religion. Cole's *Modernity and the Millennium* arguably took the approach as far as it could go in identifying Baha'ullah's statements from the 1860s to the 1880s as bringing 'the nascent Baha'i movement into the mainstream of modernist thought in the Middle East'.[53] Cole's work certainly set out to find a place for Baha'ism in modernist narrative, one as it happens the Baha'i institutional authorities did not take kindly to, even though it took as its point of departure conceptualisation of the Baha'i faith as a modern, reforming religion that had been maintained by Western Baha'i intellectuals from the early 1900s. For its part MacEoin's groundbreaking research showed consistent awareness of E. G. Browne's arguments and the specific cases he adduced concerning a process of Baha'i rewriting of earlier Babi narratives, and of conflation of Babi purposes and axioms within later Baha'i ones. He also reiterated the charge raised by Browne concerning the Baha'is' suppression of information in the form of documentation.[54] Other criticisms of Baha'i narratives refer to rearrangement of prophecies, and still others, the adaptation of narrative slant to suit different recipients/audiences in a specifically Baha'i form of *taqiyya*.[55] To apply critical readings of Baha'i narratives demonstrating how they are weighted in these various ways, using previous criticism would, however, say little that is new. These issues have been sufficiently aired although recalling them can still be useful, in specific instances, for advancing certain rational explanations. Existing research in the above areas produced by scholars of Babism, the Baha'i faith, and also Ahmadism, is therefore taken as read.[56]

Adapting in particular Smith's discussion of key religious concepts in a modern context, the study will further probe the place of the Baha'i faith and Ahmadiyyat within discourses of religion and modernity looking at their respective reconceptualisations and extensions of the Islamic notion of the succession of prophets and modernising of traditional eschatological components. Millenarianism with respect to Islamic figurations of the Mahdi and eclectic incorporation of ideas about the return of Christ that are dogmatically unorthodox in Islam will be considered particularly in Ahmadi contexts, as well as Baha'i understanding of the return of the Jews to Palestine. Review of readings of nineteenth and twentieth-century world history as prophecy made by Baha'ullah, Abdul Baha and Ghulam Ahmad will be conducted as they arise. Shoghi Effendi's articulation of a systematic periodicity in which a predefined historical process achieves fulfilment in a new world order will be compared with similar concepts applied by Bashiruddin Mahmud Ahmad (Ghulam Ahmad's son and the second Qadiani khalifa). To these conceptual narratives will be added analysis of discourse that represents more generalised functionalities such as the exercise of authority/power, coherence and adaptation, and changes through time.

Importantly, since the research on Babi-Baha'i topics outlined above, new perspectives have emerged by looking at the existence and functionality of non-Western modernities. This perspective might be said to date from the 1990s, one example being Partha Chatterjee's assertion of the agency of the postcolonial nation 'to fashion a "modern" national culture that nevertheless is not Western'.[57] More recently, Dietrich Jung has argued: 'contrary to classical modernization theory, the concept of multiple modernities assigns religious and other premodern traditions a general role in shaping different forms of modernity'. He also points out the rise of multiple modernities within the asymmetrical power relations of colonialism: 'modernity itself has implied imposition, resistance, appropriation and renovation and borrowing in Europe and the Orient'.[58] In recent times some work on Ahmadi conversion of Afro-Americans in the 1920s has seen this as a version of an alternative Muslim modernity. Richard Brent Turner assesses the Ahmadiyyat as 'unquestionably one of the most significant religious movements in the history of Islam in the United States in the twentieth century, providing as it did the *first multi-racial model* for American Islam' stressing its 'adversarial relationship with the American media and with mainstream Christianity'.[59] This is one example of the way Islam and modernity in Muslim societies and communities can, and has started to be, reviewed; it also constitutes a stretching of the areas where older Baha'i narratives can now be seen to be reductive and outmoded. These may have been more than ready to discern in the Babi and Baha'i revelations what Amanat calls 'indigenous modernities', but less ready to extend this to other 'reformists of all shades – freethinkers, revolutionaries, state officials, and dissidents'. Baha'i narratives are much more likely to encode 'the Qajar period as an age of defeat and decadence' as did twentieth-century historiography 'influenced by condescending European attitude'.[60] It will be argued in this study that Baha'i positioning within modernity as evidenced by much twentieth-century writing by Baha'is, including despite its ambiguity toward the modern world Shoghi Effendi's, was linked to the classic Weberian view of modernity. Although this has been noted by Baha'i scholars they have not considered it problematic and likely to benefit from recalibration.[61] Accordingly, the Baha'i faith has remained tied to a superseded Westo-centric view of modernity with strong accompanying overtones of orientalism. While constructive rereading would potentially benefit current Baha'i thinking, given the scriptural authority accorded to Shoghi Effendi's writings in particular this might be difficult to perform.

Orientalism and modernity are needless to say correlatives. Here the major theoretical approach is centred on orientalism, first viewed as an unreconstructed scholarly discipline and descriptive tool, and second, as a way of configuring and controlling 'the East' in the manner set out in Edward W. Said's *Orientalism*. Said's theorisation of orientalism in certain respects remains invaluable as a tool for analysing western European interaction with eastern movements during the period under consideration. Arif Dirlik points out how, in orientalism, so-called oriental societies may appear at once objects of admiration for their civilizational achievements, but also relegated to the past as fossilized relics because, with culture substituted for history they have no 'real historicity' . . . their presents are but simple reproduction of their pasts.[62]

Ali Mirsepassi has elucidated how while China and India were denied a place in Hegel's schema of the history of civilisations, Iran was granted a dubious presence but only as a beginning long since surpassed by an ascendant Europe.[63]

Although Said wrote very little about religion per se, a major concern of *Orientalism* was the manner in which Islam and Muslims were represented by Westerners, specifically missionaries like William Muir. Zachary Lockman accents the part played by orientalist historiography in writing off Muslim societies, according to which:

> Islam grew increasingly rigid, inflexible, tyrannical, intolerant, and hostile to outside influences, and thus proved unable to absorb and keep up with dynamic new ideas and techniques first developed elsewhere, in the West. As the West surged ahead, Islam slipped into social and cultural stasis and political despotism.[64]

In this domain, however, Islam was only part of a Western Christian sense of superiority. For 'such a cultural discourse to function, the prejudicial image of an irreligious and barbaric other – the Orient – is essential to the affirmation of the virtuous and civilized Victorian cultural identity'.[65] Andrew Wilcox probes the utilisation of orientalist discourse by American and British Christian missionaries in northwest Iran with the aim of testing the assumption that missionaries were invariably 'archetypal Orientalists and arch-imperialists'.[66] His work demonstrates that whether we consider the missionaries to be motivated by altruism or as agents of imperialism depends on one's definition of imperialism. However the Anglican missionary George Percy Badger's discourse on the 'withering influence of Mohammedan despotism' and 'Mohammedan bigotry and oppression' was echoed in others who frequently invoked the 'darkness' of Persia and condemned it as 'A land of Muslim fanaticism and misrule'.[67] In reporting their activities in this manner the missionaries broadly condemned Islam without distinction as to Shi'i and Sunni, a position also maintained in later Baha'i texts which use similar language and close off Islamic practice in both Qajar and Pahlavi Iran.[68] Admiration for Confucianism may have partially tempered Protestant missionaries' deployment of orientalist discourse in China in the 1840s.[69] However, such admiration almost never penetrated the 'obscurantism' ascribed to Islam.[70]

A feature of orientalism which was, however, far less condemnatory can be seen in the way it was applied to India's religious heritage by Westerners who attached positive meanings to Hinduism and Buddhism lending or associating them with an 'Aryan' character. In his pioneering work, *Orientalism and Religion*, Richard King traces how the type of orientalism that validated eastern spirituality triumphed over orientalism of the kind that inscribed the East as backward, mired in tradition, irrational and prone to fanaticism,

> it operated as what Clifford calls a 'sympathetic, nonreductive Orientalist tradition'. Richard Fox refers to this strand as 'affirmative Orientalism', and has in mind such Western apologists for Indian culture as the Theosophist Annie Besant, Hindu convert Sister Nivedita, and apostle of non-violence Leo Tolstoy . . .[71]

King scrutinises the ways in which orientalism functioned in articulating Indian 'spirituality', paying particular attention to both the colonial context and the ways in which orientalism was applied to India's religions. This involves him in reassessing the well-known debate between 'orientalists' and 'Anglicists', which Said has been criticised for ignoring. King proposes a differentiation between the type of colonialist agenda implicated in orientalist discourse delineated by Said, and the type which informed an essentialist notion of Indian 'spirituality' that was later incorporated into anti-colonial Hindu nationalism by reformers like Rammohun Roy, Dayananda Saraswati, Swami Vivekananda and Mohandas K. Gandhi.[72] This reciprocal valorisation stretches to the spell the coloniser's culture had upon the colonised elite:

> Even when the anglicised Indian spoke a language other than English, 'he' would have preferred, because of the symbolic power attached to English, to gain access to his own past through the translations and histories circulating through colonial discourse. English education also familiarised the Indian

with ways of seeing, techniques of translation, or modes of representation that came to be accepted as 'natural'.[73]

I shall show how a similar mindset can be applied to Shoghi Effendi's accumulation of material for a canonical history of Babism whereby the writings of European orientalists are used to validate his English translation of a Persian text for the reception of an educated Western audience. In practice, as will be argued below, different types of orientalism applied by Western observers of the Babi and Baha'i movements were taken up by Baha'i leaders and converts in their initial descriptions of the oriental background within which the Baha'i faith emerged. Baha'i thinking of the first half of the twentieth century, along with Ahmadism, as I have already remarked, rarely raised a word against colonialism. In claiming to be concerned with purely spiritual matters it confined itself to directing the Baha'i faith's message of moral condemnation against the corruption and materialism of the West in a similar mode to the Romantic orientalism King observes functioning in Indian Hindu and Buddhist polemics of the same epoch.

The contexts and features discussed above confirm the importance of Saidian *Orientalism* as a standard against which other 'orientalisms' as we have just seen, can be codified. Perspectives consistent with postmodern antifoundationalism have tended to produce multi-orientalisms which when applied to complex situations in the East are particularly germane to the topic under consideration. In the forty years or so since *Orientalism* new applications have come to the fore resulting in the simple binaries Said deployed being muted so as to allow for greater flexibility particularly with respect to orientalism being appropriated within modernising societies in the East. Through discourse analysis-led readings Baha'i and Ahmadi narratives can be assessed for intertextual traces of Western discourses current at the period of their composition. The chief application of the theoretical approach is through analysis of Western orientalists' writings and twentieth-century Baha'i and Ahmadi narratives which are mainly of a discursive type but also include promotional material and expository writing. In postcolonial theory 'discourse' is applied in Foucault's sense 'to denote language and statements through which disciplines delimit what is "in the true" . . . "it is in discourse that power and knowledge are joined together"'.[74] Said applied

Foucault's conception of discourse to orientalism, which is a discipline that accumulates expertise, '[t]he authority of academics, institutions, and governments . . . Most important, such texts [applying orientalist discourse] can *create* not only knowledge but also the very reality they appear to describe'.[75] Other modes of theorising writing will also be applied including approaches taken from postcolonial translation theory, particularly in the sense of what Andre Lefevere called 'rewriting', narrative theory in which 'narrative [is] a form not only of representing but of constituting reality'. Authors' construction and rewriting of texts is scrutinised in particular for the manner in which they construct orientalism and modernity.[76]

Orientalism was involved in both the construction and transmission of the Babi and Baha'i movements in the West. However, apart from some significant interventions by Denis MacEoin the relationship between orientalism and the Baha'i faith has hardly been explored.[77] In the case of the Baha'i faith, scrutiny will be brought to bear on the part orientalism played, to use Shoghi Effendi's seminal phrasing, in 'transforming a heterodox and seemingly negligible offshoot of the Shaykhi school of the Ithna-'Ashariyyih sect of Shi'ah Islam into a world religion'.[78] A framework is established for probing the relationship of orientalism and modernity in Baha'i understanding by laying out the roles nineteenth-century orientalists played in establishing knowledge about the Babi and Baha'i movements and encoding within them particular versions of 'modernness'. The question is posed: do these orientalists conform to Said's paradigms of Western orientalist writing on eastern societies, and if so to what extent? Do their writings confirm orientalist ways of seeing of the kind Said discusses? Were their visits to Persia, Transcaspia and the Caucasus underwritten by ulterior motives (spying/reporting on, connected to the interests of their governments)? Were their interests in Babis and Baha'is of an instrumentalist kind, that is, did they see these sects as of use to British, French, Russian or other imperial strategies?

This study argues that Baha'ism in particular was comprehended into the discourse of orientalism by European authors such as Arthur Gobineau, Ernest Renan, Matthew Arnold, Edward Granville Browne and George Curzon for a variety of reasons linked to nostrums attached to race, religious quest, and the politics of empire. In Chapters 3, 4 and 5 diverse varieties of orientalism, connected to modernist and anti-modernist discourses, are explored in these writers' work, and sections of each chapter discuss the uses of their ideas and nostrums were put to in Baha'i writing, mainly in Shoghi Effendi's compositions, editing and translations. Also, the same chapters will scrutinise how European racial thought which was clearly inflected by orientalism was not above valorising Babism as a product of Aryan Persia, as can be seen in the work of Gobineau and thence passed on to the others named. Having surveyed the interest taken in the Babis and Baha'is by Western orientalists, Chapters 6 and 7 proceed to discuss the Baha'i movement's interaction with orientalism in the context of its leaders' desire to explore greater opportunities for its growth and further dissemination. Evidently, the Bab, Baha'ullah and Abdul Baha knew no Western languages, and they must each therefore be exonerated from having come under the direct influence of orientalism. However, in their interrogation of modernity they were not unaware of aspects of Western thought current at the time. Orientalism's influence, which implies knowledge of European languages, enters Baha'ism via the movement's connections with Western orientalists, the influx of early Western converts, and the assumption of leadership by a Western-educated oriental. One of the main arguments of this book is that, as such, the combination of orientalism, a self-orientalising oriental leader, and Western converts impacted seriously on the creation of an 'official' Baha'i narrative or series of narratives. Chapter 6 probes how Christian Zionist ideas and textual hermeneutics impacted on Baha'i narratives at the Baha'i World Centre in Palestine.[79] In addition to staging a critical assessment of these an implied counter-narrative applied in a manner consistent with postcolonial methodology gestures toward what was excluded. In Chapter 7 orientalism is redefined and a typology produced by reviewing a number of its spin-offs in which eastern voices feature. The Aryan tendency also returns. Drawing upon the work of Iranian scholars the chapter reviews orientalist influences on the writing of Iranian racial nationalism, in particular those absorbed in Aqa Khan Kermani's work. Despite his connections to the – from a Baha'i point of view – hated Azali-Babi faction, entertaining ideas of a common provenance unsurprisingly Kermani is seen to share features with Baha'i orientalist forays. These common axioms are probed further in the context of early twentieth-century American Baha'is' endorsement of Pahlavi dynastic nationalism with its vaunting of a pre-Islamic Iran.

With the exception of Chapter 3, comparative analysis of Babiyya, Baha'iyya and Ahmadiyya as mahdi movements runs through each of the chapters. The question as to whether Ahmadi writing bears a similar orientalist imprint to Baha'i writing is addressed, while at the same time there is discussion of how in their anti-Baha'i narratives Ahmadi scholars and writers put to use orientalist sources on Babism and Baha'ism to condemn, as they saw it, both movements' ideological extremism and unorthodoxy. In the field of cross-cultural dissemination Ghulam Ahmad, having no knowledge of English, relied upon his lieutenants Khwaja Kamaluddin and Muhammad Ali who were both trained lawyers and recipients of an English language education and flexible in their negotiation of Western norms. Although the Lahoris were not as inclined to compromise vis-à-vis Western attitudes to Islam as was Shoghi Effendi, Bashiruddin Mahmud Ahmad and the succeeding khalifas of the Qadian branch amplified Ghulam Ahmad's condemnation of contemporary non-Ahmadi Islam, moving the Ahmadiyya Jama'at along a similar route of othering to Baha'ism. Comparable efforts were made to promote Ahmadism as a modern, reforming movement to VIPs, and an administrative apparatus alongside a model for a new world order of Islam was articulated.

2

Contexts and Issues

Orientalism and Inter-cultural Exchange

There have, of course, been serious criticisms of Said's *Orientalism*, some declaring his thesis flawed and, more recently, some announcing its demise. Others see it as a line that must be negotiated before it can be crossed. In *Beyond Orientalism* Fred Dallmayr proposes, using Said's own words, 'to undertake studies in "contemporary alternatives to Orientalism", this is, to inquire how one can study other cultures from a "nonrepressive and nonmanipulative perspective", something which would demand a rethinking of "the whole complex problem of knowledge and power"'.[1] Beginning, symbolically, with the westward voyage of Christopher Columbus in 1492, Dallmyr shows how asymmetries of power came to operate through violent conquest with Cortes's Spanish mission to the Americas and the planting of colonialism and Catholicism on the Amerindians. According to Tzvetan Todorov, in this context a situation of dialogue between cultures was set up based on two types of intense cross-cultural or self-other engagement: the cases of radical conflict and of dialogical reciprocity. While the former is particularly relevant in situations of insurgency against imperial (or class) domination, the second type provides the chief avenue for attempts at fostering 'nonviolent or non-manipulative ways of cultural interaction'.[2]

Orientalism can be seen as operative when asymmetries between dominant and subordinate cultures give rise to conflict and preclude reciprocal dialogue. Dallmayr begins with the violence inbuilt in the spread of Western global dominance which began in the Renaissance and looks forward to a future where his 'preferred option [is] the notion of a "deconstructive dialogue" or a "hermeneutics of difference" where dialogical exchange respects otherness beyond assimilation'. Arguing that 'cross-cultural inquiry and exegesis today is no longer the monopoly of Europe or the West' he confirms the process whereby at the end of the last century 'non-Western voices have increasingly come to infiltrate the "conversation of humankind", thus correcting (at least in part) the monological privilege chastised by Said'.[3] It is of course still possible to deny the validity of the set of conditions Dallmayr outlines which he argues were the conditions under which orientalism 'infused asymmetrical cross-cultural contact'; but if one does so, conflict is likely to go unchallenged and meaningful dialogue prove less fruitful. Referring to Heidegger's warnings about the need for Europe to accord to the rest of the world the unity in diversity it has itself achieved, Dallmayr asserts: 'by the accelerated pace of globalization proceeding under the banner of Western science, technology and industry; as an antidote to facile "one-world" formulas, dialogue and cross-cultural encounter have acquired both intellectual and political urgency'.[4]

Several points here are significant for the domain covered by the present study. The mahdi movements under consideration emerged within conditions of asymmetry in which the dominant powers of the West were acting in multiple ways – economic, political, military and cultural – upon the Islamicate world. Dallmayr and his philosophical sources conceptualise the difficulties of self-other correspondence within asymmetrical dialogues as a form of 'agonism'. The mahdi movements each found themselves inserted within the cross-cultural encounter between European and Muslim-majority lands (or post-Mughal India) where conditions for dialogue reciprocity were straightened to say the least. In a manner of speaking, one could say that these movements' respective projects each embodied the hope of promoting cross-cultural reciprocity. However, as we shall see, the dangers of the kind of religious intra-cultural conflict which the emergence of the mahdi sects engendered within their respective societies meant they were not so much drawn into agonistic awareness of the power/culture asymmetries between Islam and Europe as led to take sides in them. In practice, this conflict made them incline toward the dominant powers to who they would address specialised forms of favourable enunciation in discourses that endorsed Western notions of modernity. While unfettering their aim of establishing reciprocity with Europe, this form of activism also appeared to attract them toward its monological privilege tempting them to acculturate with it. Such a position is observable within the following frustrated outburst of Abdul Baha:

> A thousand years must elapse before Persia can, by aid of material power, rise to the height of the peoples and governments of Europe . . . But for his chains and prison, Baha'u'llah by this time would have gained absolute ascendancy over the minds and thoughts of the peoples of Europe . . . Had he appeared in Europe, its people would have seized their opportunity, and his Cause, by virtue of the freedom of thought, would by this time have encompassed the earth.[5]

The mahdi movements' urge toward dialogic reciprocity with a culturally dominant Europe in the late imperial period was expressed not only in the form of the occasional semi-official démarche for government reception but in steps taken toward paying homage to, and assimilating aspects of, the West's Christianity. As we shall discuss below, symbolic but also substantive assimilations in both Baha'ism and Ahmadism resulted in the abrogation of the key Islamic doctrine of jihad and resetting of the relationship between religion and politics in line with St Paul's doctrine of God and the State. This was no mere concession to Christian sensibility: Baha'ullah and Ghulam Ahmad who both laid claim to be the return of Christ were obviously interested in Christian eschatology as well. The latter's relationship with Christian teaching can be characterised as aggressive and appropriative but there is no denying his conversance with it, a fact in itself unsurprising given that *mubahala* contests had been taking place in India between Muslims and Christian missionaries for several generations. Baha'ullah's first encounter and engagement with oriental Christians dates from his period in Baghdad (1853–63) but he did not have access to Arabic translations of the Bible until his post-Iraqi period.[6] On the other side of the exchange, Christian missionaries did initially enter into dialogue with Baha'is in Iran, but it is fair to say that until Abdul Baha started a correspondence with Christian universalists in the early 1900s relations were largely hostile on the ecclesiastical side. However, the relationships with Western orientalists are our primary focus. The extent to which their writings constitute, and are proof of, genuine exercises in intercultural inquiry/exchange, or whether they proffer evidence of 'infused asymmetrical cross-cultural contact' is the main subject of this study.

Mahdi Movements in the Colonial/Post-colonial Middle East and South Asia

Having presented a model dynamic in which founders of the mahdi movements and those in authority after them were drawn toward the imperialist power overshadowing the Islamicate lands, we must now turn to the issue as it is embedded in historical contexts. Movements like Baha'ism and Ahmadiyya emerged in the age of colonialism either within weak notionally independent or colonised eastern nations or societies in which Muslims for the most part found themselves embattled and resistant to imperialist powers. Nineteenth-century Iran 'endured within its shrunken borders while many countries in the non-Western world gradually succumbed to colonial rule'.[7] Abbas Amanat's classic study, *Resurrection and Renewal: The Making of the Babi Movement in Iran*, shows awareness of the economic power imbalance introduced by British commercial penetration in the south of Iran in the 1840s, the decade that saw the rise of the Babi movement. That there is a connection between the Babi revolution and the growing influence of British commercial power may be assumed, although it requires spelling out more clearly.[8] At present we cannot say for sure whether Babism was predicated on an attraction to modernising methods of trade brought in by the British, or hostility. Charges and counter charges in the polemic surrounding the emergence of Babism in Iran from the nineteenth century onwards may have in time significantly shifted focus, but the proposition that both Babi and Baha'i movements were assisted if not created by outside powers is a twentieth century crystallising of anti-colonial politics advanced by both Shi'a and secular Iranian nationalists. Dabashi's work implies that the fact that Babism doubled as both a mahdi and a potentially revolutionary movement has proven difficult for Iranians to appreciate, or at least those following the Shi'a *usuli* line that the Bab was a false Imam Mahdi figure and his movement the creation of Russia. Equally, Baha'i rewriting of the movement's history has been anachronistic and too obsessed by prophetology. Penetration of Islamicate societies by Western powers in the later nineteenth century certainly coincided with the growth of nationalist and mahdi movements in North Africa. Setting aside the much-studied mahdist episode surrounding Muhammad Ahmad in Sudan, and the Senusiyya movement in Libya, Babism invites comparison with the Urabi nationalist awakening that took place four decades after the Babi insurrection. J. R. I. Cole argues that 'both the Egyptian revolution of 1882 and the Islamic revolution in Iran of 1978–9 constituted social revolutions against states characterised by informal imperial hegemony. Both possessed an indigenous state that lacked complete sovereignty'.[9] In the Sudanese case the mahdi response was both defensive and militant whereas the Baha'i development was inspired by a perceived need for change and acceptance of modernisation. In the case of Ahmadiyya, an amalgam of defensiveness and resistance toward missionary and Hindu pressure and endorsement of modernisation brought about by the colonising British were clearly at play.

In the stages that followed we may question to what extent the mahdi movements developed favourable stances toward imperial powers, and *ipso facto*, how imperial powers came to regard them. Said's statement: 'standing near the centre of all European politics in the East was the question of minorities, whose "interests" the Powers, each in its own way, claimed to protect and represent' has relevance for both Baha'ism and Ahmadism.[10] Following the aborted revolutionary struggle of the Babis, the Baha'i leaders took a path notable for the absence of fear of outside intervention in Iran's affairs. The movement's friendliness toward the broader non-Islamicate world and the universalism of its message opened up wider possibilities for encounter with the West. At the same time as their heterodoxy placed them in a vulnerable position vis-à-vis the mainstream Muslim majority, as a strategy of survival which was largely ad hoc Baha'is sometimes sought the protection of the imperial powers, petitioning them to intervene on their behalf within Iran and the Ottoman domains. Ahmadis were beneficiaries of British protection from the inception of their movement up until India and Pakistan achieved independence. Both Baha'i and Ahmadi sources present an open book in so far as their celebration of Great Britain is concerned. In return for their pledges of loyalty the Ahmadis courted protection from the Government of India and also in several countries outside the subcontinent.[11] Having established excellent relations with the British in Palestine in 1918 Abdul Baha accepted a knighthood from King George V in 1920. Later, Shoghi Effendi lobbied the mandated power to exert influence on successive Iranian governments to protect endangered co-religionists in Iran.[12]

At the point at which the pendulum began to swing away from autochthonous cultures and peoples in the Islamicate world toward invasive Western influences we need to consider the extent to which the Baha'i/Azali elite were conscious of leaning toward the new Western modes. In the 1860s, a decade in which, initially at the behest of Iran, the leaders were sent to various destinations in the Ottoman Empire, if they had any grand strategy of separation from 'the Muslim world' this was very much kept under wraps.[13] The Ottoman officials, weighing up the threat of the new movement, viewed its leaders as a local or, at most, a regional danger. It was too early for Ottoman ministers Ali Pasha and Fuat Pasha to think of themselves as players in an incipient clash of civilisations.[14] Cemil Aydin stresses:

> The distinction of the Muslim world and the Christian West began taking shape most forcefully in the 1880s, when the majority of Muslims and Christians resided in the same empires. The rendering of Muslims as racially distinct – a process that called on both 'Semitic' ethnicity and religious difference – and inferior aimed to disable and deny their demands for rights within European empires.[15]

A swap, albeit an unequal one, entailed Muslims from Asian lands colonised by Western empires coming to identify with the Ottoman Empire as the last world Muslim power, while the European empires concerned themselves more and more with Christian minorities within the Ottoman domains.

Baha'ullah's writings during this period began to place stress on his own messianic claims which he announced in messages to world leaders along with statements concerning the necessity for a demilitarised, unified world. While still inhabiting Muslim lands (as he did throughout his life) the author of these messages was aware he was situated in a part of the world that was in decline. If he still felt any connection to the Islamic domains, the idea began to take shape in his writings during this period that Christians – pre-eminently individuals in European consulates – had at times been more sympathetic to his plight than Muslims. The turning point for the Baha'is came at the close of the First World War. At the moment when Abdul Baha's erstwhile allies, that is, the Young Turks were on the point of being defeated by the British, military leader and Governor of Syria Jamal Pasha may have had reason to single him out for plotting with the British when it became clear Turkish power in Palestine was melting away. For the Baha'i community which was mainly settled in, and around, the Akka-Haifa area, this transfer of power initiated a quarter-century of friendship and at a number of levels close collaboration with the British. In the case of the founders of the Baha'i faith, that is both Baha'ullah and Abdul Baha, it is clear that their 'Anglophilia' was never intended to subvert Iran or Islam. However, their absence of concern toward Britain as an imperial power (as inspired religious figures, of course, they feared no one); as well as their understanding of Western Christianity as a benign missionising entity (see below); and, in Abdul Baha's case, alertness to the emerging world significance of the United States; could all be said to be factors moving the Baha'i faith beyond quietism in the Islamicate context into the province of positive approbation of, and reciprocity with, the modern Western order.[16]

In the post-colonial Middle East (excluding Israel) and in Pakistan, both Baha'i and Ahmadi movements found themselves at the mercy of the same hostile entity, the Muslim ulama. According to Margit Warburg (quoting Denis MacEoin), 'a source of perpetual tension between the ulama and the Baha'is is that the Baha'is pursue the visions of messianic Shi'i Islam, but on their own religious premises'.[17] However, we can see how the religious debate is occluded in favour of politics by an Iranian mujtahid in a book in which Baha'ism and Ahmadism are defined as,

> pseudo-religions invented by western (British, French) and eastern (Russian) imperialism ... These are two cancerous glands which the colonial powers have placed inside the Islamic world in order to produce differences and disunity among the Muslim community ... in Iran and India.[18]

While it is important to point out here the change in tactics in substituting a political for a religious pretext, such charges directed against both Baha'is and Ahmadis possess plausibility when viewed from the perspective of politically-oriented Islamism emerging in the twentieth century. According to Ismail Kara the religious and political issues are interwoven:

> [T]he idea of Islamism started to emerge at a time when the Islamic world was politically weak, defeated, and overwhelmed, and it continued like that.

According to [the Islamists'] interpretation, the reason for this negative situation of decline did not originate in religion and in Islam. It was a result of misunderstanding Islam, the inadequate practice of Islam in daily life, and the incomplete implementation of Islam. At the same time there was a strong notion that the survival and empowerment of the Muslim state (whether empires or nation-states) was necessary to defend the rights of Muslims, and it depended on a true understanding of religion. This idea of the Muslim state's preservation from the hostile assaults of the Christian, imperialist Western powers (*or their domestic collaborators*) necessitated the search for a new strength, power, and potential in politics and foregrounded this as normal for the political arena.[19]

Having once belonged to 'those societies that are Christianity's traditional antagonists',[20] both Baha'is and Ahmadis were treated sympathetically by Western governments (though not always by Christian missionaries), not least because they represented developments in the Muslim world which did not trouble the age-old Christian antipathy to Islam as opponent, competitor, and intransigent antagonist. Formerly, this was an orientation the West shared with eastern Christians and non-Muslim or tendentiously Muslim communities.

The protection of religious minorities such as Druzes, Maronites, Jews, Armenians and Baha'is became a central prop for European politics in the Middle East; such groups were 'studied, planned for, designed upon by European Powers improvising as well as constructing their Oriental policy'.[21]

Having ceased to belong within mainstream Islam, the Baha'is, and later on the Ahmadis, had no reason to fear for the coherence and continuing stability of their forefathers' religion and the communities that preserved it, which presumably they would have had if they had stayed within its compass.

In the post-colonial period Middle East and South Asia politics often turns on the parties concerned adopting variant positions of acceptance or resistance with regard to power, or acquiescence or realignment. It is clear with regard to these considerations that movements such as, on the one hand the Baha'is and Ahmadis, and on the other resurgent Islamist ones, have to all intents and purposes moved along antipodal tracks. The case levelled against the Baha'is in Iran in the twentieth century was reoriented from a base in Shi'i religious polemics to a political one that charged them with acting as agents of imperialism. This may have been opportunistic but it accorded with a worldview in which Shi'a in the modern period saw themselves as the victims of imperialism, thus corresponding to a perceived post-colonial reality. Writing during the decade following on from the Iranian revolution of 1978–9, MacEoin considered that in Iran the Baha'is, having initially been condemned on religious grounds were now arraigned on political ones which continued to be the official position of the Iranian regime.

> A marked feature of the Iranian perspective has been its continuing concern with Babism and, more particularly, its offshoot Baha'ism, as the favourite tools of first Russian, then British, and, eventually, American and Zionist policies within Iran. Exposure of the Dolgorukov memoirs has not prevented polemicists, even in recent years, from either retaining a residual faith in them or looking for alternative evidence that the Babi-Baha'i movement has been a central agency of foreign disruption in Iran. More tragically, accusations, supported by exceedingly flimsy evidence, of subversion on behalf of foreign powers, have been levelled at Baha'is executed by the present regime. It is undeniable that the British and Russians were seriously interested in the Babis (as they were in any movement of potential significance in the Middle East at this period) and that later contacts between Baha'is and British and Russian government officials or missionaries were often cordial and of mutual benefit, but the sort of evidence that would lead to the far-reaching conclusions of the polemical literature is lacking.[22]

In the case of the Ahmadis, though they still today continue to proclaim themselves members of the umma and consider it their religious duty to perform hajj to Mecca, the process of leave-taking has been longer drawn out than for the Baha'is. The minority Lahoris have not even considered separation from Islam. But as their leader Maulana Muhammad Ali put it, the far more numerous Qadianis put themselves on the horns of a dilemma following the declaration of the second khalifa, Bashiruddin Mahmud Ahmad, 'that anybody who does not accept Mirza Ghulam Ahmad as a prophet is a *kaf[i]r* and outside the pale of Islam'.[23] Ahmadis contributed a battalion in Pakistan's 1946 war in Kashmir and, in the figure of Chaudhry Muhammad Zafrullah

Khan, provided the foreign minister of the first government of Pakistan.[24] However, their ejection from the umma accruing from climactic incidents beginning with the 1953 anti-Ahmadi riots, culminated in the 1970 legislation that defined Ahmadis as non-Muslims and in the 1984 law that forbade them to call themselves Muslims or engage in overt worship. In the same year the relocation of the khalifa and Ahmadiyyat headquarters to London was both a practical and symbolic marker of their departure.

Baha'is and Ahmadis on Government and Politics

Yohanan Friedmann began his study of the Ahmadiyya movement by reviewing Ghulam Ahmad's ancestry. He traced it to the fabled Central Asian city of Samarqand, from whence his ancestors settled in North India in the beginning of the sixteenth century, acquiring wealth and estates in Punjab under the patronage of the Mughal dynasty. By the nineteenth century, although there was some restitution under Ranjit Singh, under Sikh rule the family's land and wealth had been eroded (1780–1839). Their British successors may only have awarded an annual pension to Ghulam Ahmad's father but the son claimed they were responsible for restoring his family's status and prosperity.

> In numerous places in his works [Ghulam Ahmad] pays tribute to the British on this account. He also reminds his readers time and again that his father . . . did not forget the just kindness of the British and stood by them during the uprising of 1857.[25]

This pro-British attitude 'is frequently stressed in Ghulam Ahmad's writings and adumbrates the future loyalist policies of the Ahmadi movement'.[26]

Mirza Husayn Ali Nuri, Baha'ullah, was from a noble family in the province of Mazandaran, his father being known in royal circles as Mirza Buzurg. 'His family was wealthy and distinguished, many of its members having occupied important positions in the Government and in the Civil and Military Services of Persia'.[27] Moreover, Iranian Baha'i hagiography has identified him as descended from Zoroaster and the Sassanian kings of Persia and therefore of 'pure Persian lineage'.[28] Baha'ullah's favourable attitude to Great Britain is expressed in his letter to Queen Victoria dating from the first year of his banishment to Akka (1868). In it he praised her personally for abolishing the slave trade and 'congratulated her on having entrusted the reins of counsel into the hands of the people'.[29] In the cases of both Baha'ullah and Ghulam Ahmad, aristocratic or high birth and privileged background seem to have signified a disinclination to turn the world upside down in political or social terms. Ghulam Ahmad vehemently rejected a claim made at one point that his movement was attracting a following among sweepers.[30] Baha'ullah was responsible for turning round the militancy of the Babi movement in favour of obedience to the Iranian monarch Nasir al-Din Shah and so established in principle future Baha'i political quietism.

The leaderships of the Baha'is and the Ahmadis demonstrated great willingness to engage with colonial power. When writing about the state of Persia, Baha'i writers adopted self-orientalising strategies. Ghulam Ahmad positioned his movement in a way that not only ingratiated it with the British rulers but also connected his status as a prophet with the providential role Britain exercised in India. He recalibrated Islam in a form which was not threatening to imperial power at a time (1890s) when the Muslim community in India was drawn in several directions by competing religio-political narratives.[31] In return for their loyalty Ahmadis gained from Great Britain implicit protection from religious persecution within British ruled territory in India and British possessions in Africa, as did Baha'is in mandated Palestine.[32] Each movement published its representations to power and proudly posted what official or diplomatic responses came their way from representatives of the colonial ruler.

> Ghulam Ahmad ... invested the British rule in India with unquestioned legitimacy ... [H]e went so far as to consider British rule as a 'God-given' favor. His son and second successor Mahmud Ahmad went even further when he compared the British takeover of India with Muslim occupation of the country: 'if the Muslim occupation had been legal, why should the British takeover be regarded differently?'[33]

Obviously a departure from conventional Muslim views on Islam's historical expansion, this understanding reverses embedded assumptions in the Islamic tradition about the abodes of war and peace. Such a position enabled Ghulam Ahmad 'to develop the idea that Muslims must be loyal to the British Government'.[34]

In doctrinal terms, Ahmadism politicised and personalised jihad by connecting it with Ghulam Ahmad's authority as a peaceful (non-*ghazi*) mahdi-messiah:

> The advent of one who receives revelation from God, has the characteristics of the Messiah, and brings a message promoting peace was necessary for the reformation of these people. Did this age not need the *avatar* [second coming] of Jesus the Messiah? Of course it did. Currently, millions of Muslims are ready to kill other people under the pretense [*sic*] of *jihad*. Indeed, some are unable to truly love a benevolent government even while living under its protection. They are unable to reach the highest levels of sympathy, and cannot cleanse themselves of affectation and pretence. There was therefore a dire need for the *avatar* of the Messiah. So I am that very promised *avatar*, who has been sent in the spiritual likeness, personality and temperament of Jesus the Messiah.[35]

In Punjab the British Government had liberated Muslims from Sikh rule, allowing the call for prayer and providing conditions in which Muslims could debate ideas free from fear of persecution. Although a Christian power Britain ruled without bias toward any religion, but in Ghulam Ahmad's conjoining of the roles of mahdi and messiah we might infer in no small measure the Indian context in which after 1857 Muslims inhabited an ambiguous situation with regard to British rule, and Christians and non-Ahmadi Muslims were the main objects of his polemic. In his writing on the issue of jihad, Mahmud Ahmad stressed the life of the Muslim community in Mecca and its initial non-violent response to oppression. The Prophet's establishment in Medina is represented as an act of self-defence on behalf of the Muslim community. Jihad was therefore only a temporary measure and not part of the Islamic creed. In the modern context (and this has again specific reference to India post-1857) incitements to violence by maulvis were strongly condemned.[36] In the lexicon of twentieth-century Islamist movements jihad might be construed as social activism and a (perhaps *the*) key indicator of faith.[37] It is significant that in contrast, Ghulam conjoined statements on loyalty to the British government with a strong apologetic for his abrogation of jihad which he linked in turn to his authority as Mahdi-Messiah.[38]

Like Ahmadism, Baha'ism also veered toward a Christian vision of worldly and spiritual dispensations in which civil and religious powers are distinct if not separate. Baha'ullah's interpretation of the separation of state and religion drew upon Christ's maxim to deliver to Caesar what is Caesar's and to God what is God's, and he quoted St Paul's axiom that 'there is no power but of God; the powers that are ordained of God. Whosoever therefore resisteth the power, resisteth the power of God'.[39] Baha'ullah's abrogation of jihad was part of his attempt 'to reconcile the Babis with the Qajar authorities, condemning the Babi attempt on the life of [Nasir al-Din] Shah and explicitly rejecting the Islamic and Babi doctrine of *jihad*'.[40] It can be seen as part of what Abbas Amanat refers to as Baha'ullah's 'call for moderation in the nascent Baha'i doctrine', particularly after his exile to Akka. It 'came to represent a moral ethos increasingly disengaged from political involvement as it fits his essentially mystical worldview. Nasir al-Din Shah never recognised the sincerity of Baha'ullah's disclaimers and his doctrinal dissociation from the still politically active Azali-Babi minority'.[41] Baha'ullah also praised British constitutional monarchy and monarchical power in general and prophesied that a future Baha'i monarch would arise in Iran. In the official Baha'i narrative that developed in Baha'ullah's later years, notably Abdul Baha's *A Traveller's Narrative written to illustrate the Episode of the Bab*, the Babi insurgency was declared to have been entirely peaceful in intent and the shah was exonerated of all blame for the Babi casualties. Smith's summary of Abdul Baha's views on Christian missionising underlines the extent to which an imagined Christian idealism (harkening back to the 'early Christians' rather than the militant colonisers of Cortes's age) was a suitable model to replace present-day Iran's degraded Islamic war ethic:

> In place of *jihad* Baha'is were bidden to engage in non violent teaching (*tabligh*) to spread their religion ... For 'Abdul-Baha Christian missionary enterprise clearly demonstrated the efficacy of non-violent propagandizing. Christianity had 'encompassed the whole earth', and yet its early adherents had never used violence to counter the terrible persecutions from which they suffered.[42]

In his *Treatise on Governance* (Risalih-yi Siyasiyyih), Abdul Baha reasserts the division of society into religious and secular domains; with respect to religious leadership he stresses 'the complementarity of religious teachings and the social order' at the same time warning clerics against getting involved in politics beyond 'explaining the implications of religious teaching to the government, when the government asks for their opinions'.[43] Sen McGlinn sees Abdul Baha's text partly as a challenge to the Shi'i clergy looking forward to the *mashrutih*, the Constitutional Revolution which broke out in Iran in 1905 and beyond that to Ayatollah Khomeini's creation of a clergy-dominated state post 1979. For a number of academics and scholars of Baha'ism (e.g. MacEoin, Cole, Alkan, Sharbrodt, Momen) the *mashrutih* is indeed a defining moment (but we could equally take the discussion further back to the Babi revolution of 1848–52, or forward to the Iranian revolution of 1978–9 and its aftermath.) Baha'ullah, had weened his followers away from the militancy of the Babis. The next crucial moment for laying down the principle of Baha'i abstinence from practical politics occurred within a year of the commencement of the *mashrutih*, when having been initially keen for Baha'is to engage on the side of reform, Abdul Baha withdrew them from any direct involvement. Momen suggests that Abdul Baha's withdrawal from politics happened after the death of Muzzafar al-Din Shah when the constitutional movement (which had been thus far united) began to break up.[44] As Momen notes, the Azalis had been particularly active in the constitutional movement and this would have been a factor in Abdul Baha's decision. MacEoin however, argues that Abdul Baha consistently upheld the monarchy whether the shah facilitated the constitution as did Muzaffar al-Din, or whether he opposed it as did the succeeding shah Muhammad Ali. Rather than being concerned with political principles, Abdul Baha's criteria with regard to political affairs boiled down to whether or not a ruler would protect the Baha'is.[45] From the time of the *mashrutih* Baha'is disassociated themselves from political parties though a number of individuals held high posts in the political administration.[46] In the long term the price they paid for being forbidden political involvement was having no voice in contemporary affairs.[47]

In spite of their orientation toward Christian quietism however, both Baha'i and Ahmadi teachings predict a future when their respective messages will gain world ascendancy (and by implication govern a world in which conflicts are resolved).[48] In the interim it is clear that although Baha'is and Ahmadis envisage close engagement with power for the time being the non-political, non-militant ethic operates. Each religious organisation is centred on the institution of a spiritual and administrative order built around the authority of a descendant of the prophet. The Qadiani khalifa presides over followers who have paid *bay'a* (sworn allegiance) to him in a ceremony that has been compared to sufi practice in which the adepts declare obedience to the shaykh. In the Baha'i order, following the Shi'i notion of *wilaya*, guardianship and authority over the community is to be exercised by blood descendants of the Manifestation of God, supplemented by an elected governing body or house of justice (*bayt al-'adl*). Shoghi Effendi assumed the role of the first Baha'i Guardian.[49] As regards secular affairs Baha'ullah endorsed a representative system of government, legislating in his holy book the *Kitab-i Aqdas* for houses of justice to be set up in every city. Ahmadis too have their 'New World Order' (*nizam-i nau*) based upon Bashiruddin Mahmud Ahmad's interpretation of Ghulam Ahmad's early plan defining the prophet's relationship with the believers in terms of economic allegiance which morphed into a blueprint for world economic justice.[50] According to a Danish scholar: 'The global-scope of both religions and their messages of world-unification, are at least superficially identical and have the same origin in a vision of perfecting a global-reaching Islam'.[51]

For a long while Baha'i thought has tended to eschew drawing any linkage between the teachings of the founders and the politico-historical environment with which they interacted. For example, until recent research uncovered it, there was silence over the temporary relations of Baha'ullah and Abdul Baha with Ottoman reform groups. However, different scholars emphasise different tendencies within the Baha'i leadership's orientation toward political authority during the time of Baha'ullah and Abdul Baha. Overall, MacEoin stresses a conservative orientation to power in general pointing out a clearly anti-clerical but consistent pro-monarchical stance with respect to Iran in the first instant but elsewhere too. In the context of the nineteenth-century Middle East, Cole valorises Baha'i ideals as constitutional, modernising and reformist.[52] In sum, the Baha'i faith's declared preference for limited forms of constitutional government and for consultative forms of organisation in society in general, and its orientation with respect to governments and political authorities, is largely notional and obscure, as Wendy Momen admits: 'The

Baha'i teachings are curiously silent on the organization of national and local political institutions (accept as they refer to the Baha'i organization itself.)'[53] Directions given to Baha'is to disengage with specific (effectively all?) aspects of political processes reflect this. A wider ranging more coherent explication of both the Babi and Baha'i movements in the light of political history and present-day definitions of politics as a category of social behaviour is clearly lacking. Reflecting Baha'ullah's aristocratic background and 'his essentially mystical worldview' Baha'i political theory might be said still to hover at the level of 'the ideal relationship between religion and politics' set out by Abdul Baha in his *Treatise on Governance*.[54] It would, though, be naïve to imagine that any group purporting to hold social values and a desire to implement them could consistently remain aloof from politics or from implicitly holding political orientations, however amorphous.[55] When complete dissociation from centres of power and influence under a particular regime is compromised, unequivocal obedience to government authority of whatever hue can leave the door open to charges of self-interest. During the later years of the reign of Mohammad Reza Pahlavi a period of flirtation with public profile on the part of individual Baha'is in economic, if not overtly political realms, led to (perhaps unfair) charges of elitism being laid against the Iranian Baha'i community as a whole.

Mahdi Movements: Religious Communities in a Modern World

Both Baha'ism and Ahmadism in key respects started as self-constructing modern movements developing out of Islamicate contexts, their modernist aspects functioning alongside their mahdi-messianic presumptions. Before looking at their respective modern self-images we might clarify both their assimilation to, and divergence from, more mainstream Muslim responses to modernity. H. A. R. Gibb's view of Islamic modernism stressed its defensive response to 'European influences and Christian attacks' and saw it as 'primarily a function of Western liberalism'.[56] Wilfred Cantwell Smith accounted for Islamic modernism in colonial India wholly within the terms of British imperialism as 'the working out of a liberal Islam compatible with the nineteenth-century West, similar to it in general outlook, and, especially, in harmony with its science, its business method, and its humanitarianism'. In order to make this alignment principles had to be separated out from legalism, 'disengaging the religion from its feudal manifestations and especially (here paralleling the "*Wahhabis*") from the corruptions of recent decadence ... stressing the while the similarity of the fundamentals of all religions, specifically Islam and Christianity'.[57] Nikki Keddie considered the Babi movement contained 'two "modern" notions': its '"Protestant"' message against clergy and interpreters; and its 'idea of progress' according to which mankind progresses in maturity and understanding and religion presents a new message in accordance with its maturity.[58]

To situate this developing modernism in terms of chronology, it needs to be emphasised that almost a half-century separates 1844, the year of the Bab's declaration, and 1891, the year of Ghulam Ahmad's orientation of the Ahmadi community in alignment with his mahdi-messiah claims. Whereas Babism was revolutionary Ahmadism, or for that matter Sayyid Ahmad Khan's form of pro-British Islamic modernism, was not. The Babi experiment dated from the mid-1840s and occurring within Iran at that time it was peripheral to Western penetration. As a purely religious doctrine, its concept of the cycles of revelation deriving from a mystical Shi'i re-envisioning of the Islamic doctrine of the succession of prophets and traditional conceptions of the Day of Judgement, was carried forward by Baha'ullah. According to Amanat: 'The Babi endeavour ... was striving to build in its own esoteric language an indigenous concept of modernity that relied on historical progression rather than the sanctity of the past'. Baha'ullah's *Kitab-i Iqan* (Book of Certitude) is a masterly exposition of the concept mixing allegory and rationalism. According to Amanat it was significant 'that the movement emerged just before Iran's full exposure to imported models of modernity in the second half of the nineteenth century'.[59] Later Baha'i interpretation would attribute to Babism a tolerance that occluded its radical Shi'i mahdism. A popular example of Baha'is misreading the modern in Babism is the case of the Babi poetess Quratul Ayn who they elevate to the rank of the East's first proponent of the rights of women. While Tahirih, as she is also known, was undoubtedly 'modern' in terms of her orientation toward her Shi'i background, she was hardly a Mary Wollstencraft-type forerunner of feminism and never invoked the emancipation of women as many Baha'is claim.

W. C. Smith's emphasis on the business method and the 'bourgeois' component as essential to Islamic modernism should certainly be considered applicable to Babis, Baha'is and Ahmadis, for all of whom capitalism, the obvious shaper of nineteenth-century modernity, was a development with which they most definitely engaged. Soviet orientologist Vladimir Minorsky pointed out how the preaching of Babism 'was addressed definitely to the middle classes, to the petty bourgeoisie, the lesser clergy and the traders. The Bab himself belonged to a family of merchants'.[60] Later at the *fin de siècle* a Baha'i community grew up in Ashkhabad in the Transcaspian part of Russia's expanded empire in western Central Asia. Flourishing in this haven of protection, a short-lived model of economic achievement emerged that would be seen as a model of the modern developmentalist religious movement Baha'ism aspired to be (see Chapter 6). This economic achievement coincided with the growth of Baha'i schools and hospitals during the last years of Qajar and the early years of Reza Shah's rule. Baha'is are happy to view these activities as markers of the difference between an emerging community responding to the impetus of the revelation of Baha'ullah, and a stagnant larger entity which comprised their Shi'a fellow countrymen.[61] Lapidus confirms that under the pressure of Western-led modernity the old Islamic hierarchies broke up, and a 'vast cultural gap opened between elites and the common people; elites adopted a Western style of living while the common people persisted in traditional mores'. Ironically, since their heterodoxy raised serious, if not insuperable, problems with respect to their status and hence acculturation within the new national states, the mahdi movements were nonetheless identifiable as filled by members of the modern elites more than by bazaaris, teachers, clerks and common people who were more likely to be attracted to revivalist (*tajdid*) movements.[62]

As stated above, an important body of scholarly work has accumulated in the last twenty years mapping Baha'i engagement with the development of modernity and the different religio-political reform tendencies in the later nineteenth-century Middle East.[63] In particular, Abdul Baha's primer on political reform in Iran, *The Mysterious Forces of Civilization*, has been scrutinised and seen to demonstrate an indigenous engagement with modernity. The work predates the anti-colonial turn Oliver Scharbrodt identifies with the aftermath of the Urabi revolution in Egypt in 1881–2 and the subsequent raising of a campaign against British imperialism by Jamal al-Din 'Afghani' and Muhammad Abduh in the *Al-'Urwa al-Wuthqa* society and publication.[64] However, Cole proposed an 'interaction between Iranian millenarianism, Ottoman and Qajar reformism and European modernity' in which 'Young Ottoman' reformers joined Baha'i leaders with their messianic claims to explore social teachings able to fit the Middle East with the modern world. Cole's earlier work also set out relationships between Abdul Baha and Egyptian reformer Muhammad Abduh and between Baha'i scholar Abul Fazl Gulpaygani and liberally minded students at al-Azhar in Cairo, a tack also discussed by McCants and Sharbrodt.[65] In developing his research topic comparing Abdul Baha and Abduh, and on the relationship of the Baha'i leadership to other Middle East reform groups, Scharbrodt agrees 'the encounters of the Baha'is with the reformist discourse in the Ottoman Empire affected the doctrinal formation of the new religious movement'. However he also considers 'tracing back [such] channels of influence . . . to be a rather futile task' and believes Baha'is were not above the practice of *taqiyya* in interacting with Muslim reformers.[66] Amanat, however, thinks it likely that,

> Baha'ullah did not remain impartial to some ideals propagated by some leaders of the Young Ottomans – his co-prisoners – and to the reforms of the Tanzimat era. His approach to such social notions as universal peace, racial and gender equality, economic justice, and the rudiments of a democratic model were groundbreaking though mostly inspirational.[67]

In so far as they could access the Baha'i teachings in the limited translations available to them, Western Baha'is at the beginning of the twentieth century, sustained by the liberal ecumenical climate that preceded the Great War, emphasised the coincidence of Baha'ism and modernity, stressing the former's progressive social teachings and universality.[68] Frenchman Hippolyte Dreyfus (who *was* able to read oriental languages) and American Horace Holley accented Baha'ism as a modern religion of science and rationality replacing the domination of the Persian mullahs and the 'medieval' barbarism of their land. However, in the post-war environment these principles suffered eclipse. In consolidating an official Baha'i voice Shoghi Effendi took a conservative turn adopting an ambivalent and ambiguous stance toward modernity. Praising on the one hand programmes of Kemalist Westernisation, secularisation and campaigns against the Islamic orders, Shoghi Effendi more broadly condemned modern trends as well as leaders political and religious, and ruled out all hopes of enduring peace and reform in the world outside of Baha'ullah's revelation.[69] Despite regularly asserting the values of modern civilisation as Holley and others in *Baha'i World*, the Guardian steadily distanced the Baha'i faith from Western ideas of liberalism and progress, inveighing against America's corruption and materialistic hedonism as evidence of humanity's moral decline. With Baha'ullah's 'New World Order' at the centre, this condemnation of the state of an errant world in apocalyptic terms – not a difficult proposition in the 1930s – continued into the Second World War and the decade after. For a moment it had looked as though the Baha'i faith fitted perfectly Weber's model of a rational religion 'shorn of most of its magical and mystical properties and anchored in an ethical code, thus promot[ing] political development'.[70] But retreating into eschatology and a Manichaean construction of the future, under the guardianship, Baha'i orientation entered into what in some respects was an anti-modern phase.

3

Race and Religion in Gobineau's Persia

A cosmopolitan writer and diplomat who counted among his friends aristocrats like Alexis de Tocqueville, and a great artist like Richard Wagner, Arthur Gobineau's reputation as an originator of racist theory has largely obscured recognition of his versatility in other areas of French literature such as the novel, the short story, literary criticism, political journalism, and travel writing. As an orientalist his status has been even less secure; in his lifetime his work was entirely overlooked by professional orientalists. In *Orientalism* he makes but a brief appearance, when Said juxtaposes the 'great Orientalist works of genuine scholarship' by bona fide orientalists Silvestre de Sacy and Edward Lane against 'the racial ideas' of Renan and Gobineau which 'came out of the same impulse, as did a great many Victorian pornographic novels'.[1] Said most likely did not read any of Gobineau's writing about the East and was aware only of his reputation as a racist when he placed him along with Renan within the category of 'scientific' orientalism accusing them both of being core contributors to European racial chauvinism. In key respects Gobineau is too complex and individual a figure to be neatly fitted into Edward Said's orientalist schema, but there is a case for situating him alongside writers such as Gèrard de Nerval and Gustav Flaubert who were engaged by orientalism at the level of imagination and who in Said's book are assigned to the category of *imaginative* orientalism.

One of the questions raised in the previous chapter concerning Westerners who wrote about the Babis and Baha'is of Iran was whether they did so for instrumentalist, political reasons. In the case of Gobineau, who was completely innocent of manipulating Iran in the interests of his own country or any other, the answer has to be firmly in the negative. In the last analysis though, as this chapter will attempt to demonstrate, distinctive and individual as Gobineau's writing on Persia/Iran was, it undeniably impacted on its varied readerships in ways that contributed to the purveyance of an orientalist image of the land and its Shi'i version of Islam. Race was not programmatically embedded in *Religions et Philosophies dans l'Asie centrale* (hereafter cited as *Religions and Philosophies*) the book which incorporates a lengthy narrative of the birth and suppression of Babism together with a European presentation of the *taziya* form of religious theatre. However, the work invites reading in parallel with *Essai sur l'inégalité des races humaines* (Essay on the Inequality of the Human Race – hereafter cited as *Essay*) as its author's Aryan predilections can be traced in his portrayal of the Bab.[2] In a fascinating manner, in Europe Gobineau's portrayal of the Bab was accepted in the Aryanised and Christianised forms he undoubtedly gave him at one and the same time, laying open the question both of the author's intentionality and the degree to which later on, consciously or unconsciously, some Baha'is may have manipulated these linkages.

Gobineau was born on Bastille Day, 1816, in uncertain times and into a highly unstable family. His parents, Louis de Gobineau and Anne-Louise Madeleine de Gercy, were doomed to be an unhappy couple. Their only son, christened Joseph-Arthur, inherited his father's Bourbon legitimism and impecunious living. When his parents separated, the boy was forced to accompany his mother and younger sister Caroline in their wanderings in France and Switzerland, where he acquired an education in German language and culture. In 1834, when his mother started a relationship with his tutor and embarked upon a career of criminal deception, Arthur rejoined his father who was living in a town aptly named Lorient. Temperamentally unable to follow him into a military career, he left for Paris the following year. Financially hard-up and afforded only grudging recognition by his rich uncle, Thibault-Joseph, the young Gobineau performed lowly jobs working for the post office and a gas company. Controversial though he was to become, he was nonetheless a man of his age. Through his unstable childhood he had nurtured a desire to belong elsewhere and the same Romantic orientalism that was fashionable among the educated elite supplied an object for this need. He gravitated to circles opposed to the bourgeois July Monarchy, writing poorly paid articles for legitimist publications which helped finance classes in Persian at the Collège de France. He also became a founder member of a literary club, Société des

Scelti (Society of the Chosen Ones), a group of young men similarly disenchanted and mixed-up as himself. In search of a living, he found writing the popular *roman-feuilleton* a useful source of income, especially after his marriage to Clémence Monnerot in 1846, and the birth of their first child Diane in 1848. At the same time he was writing literary criticism extolling George Sand and Stendhal, and political articles including one on Greece where he would later hold a diplomatic post.

Gobineau's big break came in April 1843 when he was introduced to Alexis de Tocqueville at the salon of Charles de Rémusat. Tocqueville enlisted the younger man's assistance in researching the political and social morals of the nineteenth century with special attention to Germany and Britain, and when in 1849 he briefly became foreign minister, he made Gobineau his chief of cabinet. Although by no means a supporter of Louis Napoleon, who seized power soon after his appointment, Gobineau nevertheless continued on a diplomatic career path which would supply him with time and material for literary composition as well as the opportunity to realise his childhood fascination for the Orient. During diplomatic postings in Berne, Hanover (1851) and Frankfurt (1854), Gobineau found the time to write the *Essay* which initially attracted a tiny readership. In 1854 he left for a tour of duty as first secretary to the French mission in Tehran, where he stayed until 1857. There followed a second diplomatic mission to Iran between 1861 and 1862, this time as first Minister. The two visits resulted in the publication of *Trois Ans en Asie* (Three Years in Asia) and *Religions and Philosophies* – probably Gobineau's best books. Further periods as French diplomat in Greece, between 1864 and 1868, and later in Brazil and Sweden, stimulated Gobineau's prowess as a short story writer. *Souvenirs de voyage* (Memories of Travel) and *Nouvelles asiatiques* (Asiatic Short Stories), as well as the novel, *The Pleiads* were the fruit. After his retirement in 1877, and the breakdown of his marriage, Gobineau returned to the impecunious state of his youth, emotionally sustained in his final years by his love for Countess Mathilde de la Tour, before dying in Turin in 1882.

Taint of Racism

The thinking behind the *Essay* inspires all of Gobineau's writing and incorporates his personal alienation from nineteenth-century Europe, especially

France. '[H]e finds in the physical nature of men themselves inherent race factors that explain men's mind and institutions'. His race theory,

> boils down to three ideas: special race-characteristics, mixture of blood, and decadence ... [It] starts with the three-fold division of mankind into white, yellow, and black ... It is only when two races mix ... that civilization occurs ... But civilization leads to more mixing of 'inferior blood' with that of the ruling caste, so that the 'great race' is inevitably bastardized and decadence follows.[3]

Race was one of the mastercodes of the age and it has been argued that Gobineau was unjustly charged with originating views that were widely held at the time. Initially, the *Essay* won him few admirers in France, where Tocqueville (someone we would today consider an Islamophobe) criticised it for its racial determinism and potentially dangerous appeal to Germans. Though the work continued to remain unacknowledged during Gobineau's lifetime it articulated positions that stimulated the mid-century interest in biology and human origins and influenced some of the key thinkers of the age, including Renan, Taine and Nietzsche. (Gobineau felt his racial theories had been purloined by Renan without a word of acknowledgement.) Contrary to the right-wing nationalist ideologues who later misappropriated it, Gobineau's race theory was founded on the negative conclusion that in modern times no nation or people should be singled out as superior on account of its racial purity. While he frequently employed the term *germanique* (German) to single out the European branch of the Aryan race he so admired as the force behind all great civilisations, Gobineau never intended that this accolade be applied to modern Germany where between 1894 and the outbreak of the Great War, his first German biographer, Ludwig Schemann was instrumental in promoting his legacy. Gobineau's reputation flourished among the Bayreuth Circle, but it was only in the decades after his death that extremists like the proto-Nazi racist thinker Houston Stewart Chamberlain, who intentionally misread Gobineau, accorded him the dubious credit of having discovered the truth of Aryan-German racial supremacy.

Through association the *Essay*, even until today, has tainted Gobineau with a racist stain. It spread his name abroad early on: an abridged translation was published in the United States by southern white supremacists Josiah Nott and Henry Hotz in 1856.[4] A century later, Raymond Schwab accorded Gobineau a place among those Europeans who discovered in 'the Orient' a font for rebirth, but disparaged him for playing his part in perpetrating the distortion of the Aryan myth that led to Nazism. Writing immediately after the Second World War, Schwab's attitude toward a fellow Frenchmen who many believed had joined the enemy is perhaps understandable.[5] In 1970 Michael Biddiss edited an English version of the *Essay*, which is largely a reissue of the 1915 translation of Book One, in which he declared the 'Father of racism' sobriquet an oversimplification of the origins of right-wing ideology, but opined: 'it is nevertheless proper that this versatile, brilliant but infuriating Frenchman should have a central place in the history of that pernicious brand of political thinking which culminated in the excesses of the Nazi era . . .'[6] Yet, as Robert Young has pointed out, Gobineau,

> admits that the notion of a pure white, Aryan race is an ideal that has never existed historically, and though he continues to use the three categories of white, black and yellow, [he] concedes that even the white race is today a 'hybrid agglomeration'.[7]

Nonetheless, although there have been dissenters, Gobineau's notoriety has shown little sign of diminishing in the over one century and a half since the *Essay*'s first appearance. In the last two decades of the twentieth century, however, Gobineau's race theory became of interest to the field of postcolonial studies, notably in works by Tzvetan Todorov and Robert Young, and his two key works on the East, *Religions and Philosophies* and *Three Years in Asia*, previously untranslated, appeared in abridged form in English in 2009.[8]

Gobineau's Persia: Creation of an Orientalist Image

As we have said, Gobineau lived his later years aggrieved that he had not received the recognition he felt was his due. Although admired by his peers, his literary criticism which had only occupied a brief decade (the 1840s) and his fiction were largely forgotten. Ironically, given his subsequent inclusion in Schwab and Said's books, his credentials as an orientalist were also obscure, although as we shall see he helped sponsor several key ideas about the Near East. Nonetheless, when alive his aspiration, held since childhood, to be accounted an orientalist seemed to founder. At one level his knowledge of the East amounted to that of an enthusiastic, unsystematic, untrained amateur. Scholars of eastern languages, history and culture were largely silent over his claim to have deciphered the cuneiform language found in inscriptions in northwestern Iran. Some condemned his methods as deranged occultism. Gobineau's command over oriental languages, specifically Arabic and Persian, has also been contested. He claimed to have made Persian translations, including of a work by the Bab that appears as an appendix to *Religions and Philosophies*, but most likely this was done by Iranians overseen by him. Then why call Gobineau an orientalist at all? In France his editors and biographers have argued Gobineau's greatest achievement was his imaginative exploration of an East that was passing. 'It was above all an elsewhere, a surviving reality European modernity had abolished'.[9] The preferential treatment the Frenchman received in Iran alleviated pains of a troubled ego and eased the sense of deracination that was the root cause of his racial speculation and fantasising. His two stints in the French Legation in Tehran caused Gobineau to become enamoured of the Iranian nation, and among other things, he developed a fascination for the recently emerged and peremptorily suppressed Babi movement. He found among the servants of the French legation two Azali-Babi informants, and they, together with consulting the court historians' accounts, enabled him to write a narrative of the movement which would in later nineteenth-century Europe prove widely influential. In contrast to his work on the inscriptions, the validity of his narrative of Babism was attested by professional orientalists of the ilk of Browne and Rozen, and by Lord Curzon, an 'authority' on the East. Moreover, contemporary Persianists like Nikki Keddie frequently quote Gobineau as a commentator on Iran, and it is now agreed that he transmitted some crucial ideas about the country and its people that have succeeded in forcing an entry into orientalism. In Robert Irwin's words: 'Gobineau's chief importance lies in the fact that he was a pioneer in various aspects of Persian studies and in the inspiration he gave to others who came after him'.[10]

Beyond the frame of his diplomatic career the activities in which Gobineau engaged in Persia helped produce the distinctive, idiosyncratic orientalism which Said misconstrued. In literary terms his Asiatic short stories, employing settings stretching from the Aegean eastwards to the Iranian plateaux, were composed during his period in Stockholm and project the Iranic world Gobineau had encountered a decade and a half earlier. In the backgrounds to the stories the reader encounters a different perspective to the ideas on race floated by the *Essay* where the primacy of Aryan blood in the advance and decline of civilisations was promoted. In some respects a response and (in terms of imaginative sympathy) an improvement on Morier's *Hajji Baba of Isphahan*, the short stories include a medley of characters from different peoples and strata of 'Asia', the Persianate countries situated between Mesopotamia and Afghanistan that had once fallen within the orbit of the core Persian empire. Gobineau saw the Persians as 'semitized' and 'melanized' and in racial terms the stories show (as do his non-fictional pieces on Iran) 'a love ... inconsistent with his written profession of faith'. That is, his race theory in no way detracts from his fascination for his oriental characters. In few, if any, do we find incarnations of the Aryan ideal. 'The Shamakhi Dancer' for example, which was especially singled out by Henry James for its 'vivid representation of a passionate Tartar maiden' depicts the eponymous protagonist's attempt to enlist her cousin in deeds of revenge against her people's Russian conquerors, only to be thwarted by his dipsomania and her hopeless passion for a Spanish mercenary.[11] Gobineau's acute consciousness that the mixing of races diluted notions of racial supremacy and was ultimately a delusion is made clear in *Three Years in Asia*, especially in the early chapters comprising his account of a sea journey from Suez to Bushehr on the Persian Gulf taking in ports along the way. Racial and cultural distinctiveness among African and Indian Lascars, Goans, Arabs, Arab-Jews and Parsees is intently observed, and there is an implied hierarchy base on business prowess. While the Parsees, whose business sense consistently outwits the British, rank highest in his esteem and the Africans the lowest, his pro-eastern attitude is epitomised by the difference he sees between the 'Asiatic' lower classes and the European ones.[12]

According to Albert Hourani, writing before Said's *Orientalism*, Gobineau together with Renan contributed to 'the racial theory ... so old-fashioned now that it is difficult to understand the force of its impact' which pronounced that,

> [t]he great age of Islamic thought had been the Abbasid, but the Abbasid caliphs themselves were scarcely believers. The culture of their court and empire was a revived Sassanian culture, produced by men who were not deeply Muslim and were in inner revolt against the religion they were forced to profess ... Islam was created by the Arab race because it could not be absorbed into the civilisations already existing. In the same way, other races were never really absorbed into Islam: they remained true to themselves, and in the end reasserted their own culture.[13]

The implied distinctiveness of a Persian genius was an idea Gobineau and Renan both shared; the historical calibration and disabling of Islamicate culture as a crude Arab (read 'semitic') hybridised concoction is more Renan's than Gobineau's. Robert Irwin, however, is correct in stating Gobineau 'was the first to espouse the notion that Shi'ism was the revolt of the Aryan Persians against the Islamic Semites, an expression of the Persian national spirit and of Persian supernaturalism and a rejection of pure monotheism'.[14] The germ of the idea is to be found in *Mémoire sur l'état de la Perse actuelle* (Memoir on the Social Composition of Present-Day Persia) a piece commissioned by Tocqueville and written in 1856 soon after Gobineau's arrival in Iran on the first period of his diplomatic residence. The contours of his argument about Persian uniqueness and resistance to the Arab invaders and the religion they brought with them are present here at an early point in their gestation. Accompanying them is an idea which also permeates *Religions and Philosophies* which was published in the next decade: in Persia nothing is as it seems on the surface. Gobineau passed on to later European travellers the idea that varieties of race and racial mixing correlated in some way with variations of belief. 'Little wonder that for many centuries this confusion of blood has allowed no dogmatic idea to take root too deeply in their midst'.[15] The Zoroastrian Sassanians, become worn out and decrepit, had been ruthlessly conquered by the vigour and energy of the barbarian Arab armies who, in exception to their usual practice with conquered peoples, aimed totally to wipe out all traces of

Magianism. However, contrary to notions of single-race superiority, racially mixed as they were Persians were inherently flexible, naturally intelligent and philosophical. That is why, though forced to accept Islam, they were the first among heretics and introduced all shapes of heterodoxy, mysticism, and new religions, renewing ancient dogmas, even espousing atheism. Typically carrying the idea to extremes, Gobineau goes on to make the outlandish claim that every educated Persian was a deist at heart – or worse. He was, however, among the first to draw attention to Shi'i sects like the Ali Ilahis, and in emphasising their exalting of Ali, he exemplified the idea that the creation of Shi'ism was the epitome of Persian resistance to Arab conquest. (It is interesting that at this point Gobineau mentions Babism as a movement from the upper echelons of Persia favourable to European ideas, which carries an implied hostility.)[16]

Gobineau and the Messiah of Shiraz

We will now interrogate in more detail Gobineau's account of Babism which in *Religions and Philosophies* appears as a series of cataclysmic events surrounding the Babi insurrection. Still very fresh in the minds of Iranians, the story as mediated by the French diplomat would have a significant impact on intelligentsias across Europe, from Britain to Russia. The focus will be trained on the method by which the he tailored his Persian sources for a European readership. The Islamicate context is important but does not exert an overbearing influence on Gobineau's writings on Babism, which were underwritten by considerations of race and power. The important distinguishing factor is that his emphasis on the Bab as a messiah advancing a claim of a higher order than that of an Imam Mahdi divested the Babi movement of its Shi'i milieu in order to rewrite it into a European context.

In general terms, it may be stated that Gobineau's account foregrounded two, on the surface opposed, readings of Babism. The first turned on the collision between the Babis and the state. Here the historian makes no effort to downplay the ferocity of conflict, particularly the slaughter, emphasising how both sides committed excesses that we would nowadays consider to be massacres. The main difference between the two parties was that the Babis were motivated by a mostly unfailing religious zealotry which enabled them repeatedly to defeat their adversaries despite the latter's superior numbers. The various struggles between the Babis and the mix of army and militia forces sent by the rulers to suppress them amounted to a watershed for the Qajar state. The country, Gobineau opines, was in danger of being lost to the dynasty. Likewise, had the Bab given his followers the licence to stage a general uprising, the prize might equally have been a Babi state. This opinion leads to the second narrative facilitating an image of the Bab as a Persian martyr/messiah that might effectively appeal to Western audiences. It is especially evident in Gobineau's accounts of the disputation between the Bab and the mullahs of Shiraz, and in his trial and punishment in the last days before his execution in Tabriz. These episodes could not fail to resonate with a Christian audience for the implied parallels to the arrest and trial of Jesus. The scene below, the final parade of the Bab and his two disciples around Tabriz pursuant to their execution, obviously echoes the last hours of Christ at the hands of the rabble and the Jewish religious authorities:

> They were promenaded through the town, through all the streets and all the bazaars, continuously insulted and beaten. The crowd thronged the thoroughfares and people climbed on each others' shoulders to get a better look at the man everybody had been talking about. Well distributed, the Babis and half-Babis tried to excite commiseration or some other feeling they could take advantage of to save their master. The indifferent, the philosophers, the Shaykhis, the Sufis, turned away from the procession in disgust and returned home, or, on the contrary, waiting on the street corners, contemplated the scene with silent curiosity and nothing more. The ragged, turbulent, impressionable masses screamed vulgar abuse at the three martyrs; but they were only too ready to change their ideas if only some circumstance would arise that would push their spirits in another direction. Finally, the Muslims, lords of the day, continued to insult the prisoners, trying to break through the escort to hit them on the face or head, and when they had not been beaten back in time or when a bottle thrown by a child hit the Bab or one of his companions in the face, the escort and the crowd burst out laughing.
> . . . Around him people were crying: 'he admits his crimes!' and they beat him! 'He is afraid!' and they slapped him. In the name of the law, the three mujtahids [high priests] of the town did not neglect to ratify, in the presence of the Bab, the death sentence adjudged to him. That formality had a great effect on the crowd, which probably deduced from it that the novator was even guiltier than they had thus far supposed.[17]

Here Gobineau's emphasis falls on the Bab as a messiah in the Christian mode (and elsewhere, as a default position, a non-Muslim.) The 'Muslims' control the day as had 'the Jews' in Jesus' passion, thus obscuring the discussion that has continued to exercise scholars, often with reference to an historical Magian context, concerning the scale and range of the claims made by the Bab, claims that were almost routine in Asia but remained embedded within Shi'i terms of reference.[18] Gobineau's argument – which was to be assiduously incorporated into Baha'i promulgation – was that such a manifestation as the Bab's could be considered either as nothing less than the appearance of a new faith (throwing off the yolk of an old one which Persians had no hand in birthing), or a renewal of the ancient spirit of the Persian race in a new form. In whichever way it was regarded, 'in our own age, only yesterday so to speak, the highest manifestation of the modern Persian spirit succeeded in founding a new religion'.[19] By projecting the Bab beyond the 'narrow' locus of Iranian Shi'ism, and relocating him as a universal prophet connected to th Aryan race (the Aryans were bearers of universal civilisation as he had argued in *Essay*), Gobineau produced a variant of the European nineteenth-century penchant for discerning 'universalistic religion, genuinely Aryan in . . . origin, arising quite independent of Semitic monotheism'.[20] Just as Christianity needed to be purged of its Semitism by the Aryan input of Europe, Iran is separated from Islam first in the form of Shi'ism and, potentially more universally, with the appearance of Babism. Baha'is would take note.

A further area of orientalist wishful-thinking transference to Baha'i sources is Gobineau's image of the Bab as a reader of the Bible. This notion, which appears to have been transmitted by Christians, allows Gobineau to transform the Iranian Imam Mahdi into an exponent of comparative religion or advocate of ecumenicalism among the Peoples of the Book; it has certainly added to the myth-making that obfuscates the Bab's actual embedding within Shi'ism.

> Not content with fulfilling religious duties or with professing orthodox doctrines, he threw himself with a passion into seeking and examining all that was new. All indications point to his having had a natively open and bold spirit. It is established that he read the Gospels in translations brought by Protestant missionaries, he often conferred with Jews of Shiraz, he sought out the knowledge of Guebre doctrine . . .[21]

In a chapter on Biblical influences on Ali Muhammad in which he reviews the Bab's writings in detail, Stephen Lambden presents the Bab, for whom the Islamic revelation and his own were the sole criteria and scope of his mission, as immersed in Shi'i Islamic tradition. The Injil (Christian scripture), despite being the Book of God, was 'superseded or abrogated by the [Quran] and the *Bayan* which are more excellent and complete divine revelations'.[22] E. G. Browne filtered a report which came from Christian missionaries that Armenian carpenters had seen the Bab reading a Persian translation of the Bible. Lambden opines that, while such an event cannot be disproved:

> Concrete evidence in the primary sources for the Bab's knowledge of the Bible/N[ew] T[estament] is wholly lacking. There is not a great deal that presupposes either Jewish or Zoroastrian influence either. He never directly cites the H[ebrew] B[ible] in Arabic, Persian or any Jewish writers or literatures of any period . . .[23]

Gobineau might perhaps be exonerated for adding another facet to his Christianising-of-the-Bab project on account of his limited knowledge of Persian and the Babi scriptures. However, the lapse of discerning Christian scriptural influence for the Bab's writings is less easy to forgive when proposed by E. G. Browne or Baha'is literate enough in Arabic and Persian to read the Bab's writings. Lambden finds no evidence for Browne's assertion of *isra'iliyyat* (Jewish/Christian), or specific 'signs of the influence of the Gospel on the Persian Bayan'[24], but he has a lot to say about 'a Gospel informed speech of the Bab' inserted by Shoghi Effendi into the *Dawn-Breakers*, which will be discussed below.

Witnesses for the Baha'i Faith: The Role and Function of Gobineau and other Orientalists in Baha'i Narratives

In the development of a European perception of the Babis of Iran Gobineau once had a status that, in some ways ironically, matched his reputation as 'the Father of racism'. For European audiences, particular the avant-garde, as a result of his narrative the Bab achieved a brief cult status in France in particular where he was held to have been a kind of second Christ.[25] With its primary tenet of the unity of mankind, on the face of it Gobineau's reputation as a racist made him an unlikely sponsor for the Baha'i faith. (Like many western commentators of the time Gobineau did not distinguish Baha'is as separate from Babis.) Educated Baha'is who are aware of his narrative of the Bab and also know of this other reputation as a racist consider there was a good and a bad Gobineau.[26] Writing in *God Passes By*, Shoghi Effendi had no reservations in qualifying him as 'the noted diplomat and brilliant writer'. He quotes his remarks on the force of the Babi spirit and the impact a similar sect might have made had it appeared in Europe, the breadth of Babism's scope among the different classes in Persia, and the memories it evoked of the birth of the great religions of the past.[27] Though noting the disconnect between the Frenchman's role as racial theorist and his testimonial on behalf of the Bab and his followers Shoghi Effendi does not attempt to reconcile the two, but allows them to stand together, we might say, as a species of paradox or divine fiat.

A. L. M. Nicolas, a Babi enthusiast like Gobineau, was another writer on Babism who Shoghi Effendi summoned to act as an orientalist witness to the 'Baha'i Revelation' which encompassed the Babi episode. Born in Gilan he worked in the French consular service in Iran for much of his life and his family had a connection with Gobineau whom his father had clashed with at the French legation. Nicolas complained: 'Gobineau's book swarms with errors; its historical part is no more than a translation of *Nasikh-i Tavarikh* ... all the calumnies of Muslims against the Bab are found in it'.[28] It is, as Nicolas points out, actually strange to realise that his compatriot's narrative of the Bab which excited so much sympathy for him in Europe was so closely structured around the hostile account of court historian, Lisan ul-Mulk Sipihr, author of *Nasikh-i Tavarikh*. Browne acknowledges this too, but insists:

> Though largely based on the Lisanu'l-Mulk's account ... it embodies also many statements derived from Babi sources; and not only are the facts thus obtained sifted with rare judgment and arranged with consummate skill, but the characters and scenes ... are depicted in a manner so fresh and vivid that the work ... must ever remain a classic.[29]

Of varied character and, to say the least, quite distinct as orientalists, Gobineau, Nicolas and Browne, each in their own ways identified with Ali Muhammad Shirazi with an ardour that transcended mere scholarship. As we have seen, Nicolas certainly did not have the unassailable belief Browne had in the veracity of Gobineau's *Religions and Philosophies*, but he veered toward Subh-i Azal's designation as the Bab's successor as upheld by Gobineau's work.[30] Browne's relationship with the Baha'is was more than significantly affected by the same issue. All three had been directly informed by Azalis, and Gobineau seems not to have known any Baha'is. Nicolas and Browne did, however, and so they might equally have accepted the Baha'i position on the succession. In sum, when we consider a notional narrative of the 'martyr-prophet of Shiraz', it must be stated at the outset that as far as these three European orientalists were concerned, it was Babism that held primacy, not the emergent Baha'i faith. In Shoghi Effendi's writing the sequence is obviously reversed. Browne himself did admit that as a new religion with potential world significance, it was Baha'ullah's version that was more likely to attract followers than the Bab's original. Yet for these western European orientalists (though not perhaps the Russians who interacted with Baha'is more closely at first hand) it was the Bab who mattered above all others. Either way, the heat generated by debate over what is the 'right' understanding of the relationship of the Babi and Baha'i faiths runs through both Nicolas and Browne's work.

So, although the two Frenchmen and the Englishman had chequered careers as far as concerns the standard Baha'i narrative of the Babi movement, each was enlisted by Shoghi Effendi as an expert witness in the footnotes he added to his edited work on the Babis, *The Dawn-Breakers*, and also in the main text of *God Passes By*. The orientalists' expertise is appropriated in such a way as to smooth out any differences they might have had with his authoritative Baha'i narrative. Subtitled 'Nabil Zarandi's Narrative of the Early Days of the Baha'i Revelation', *Dawn-Breakers* is nominally Shoghi Effendi's translation or, as Andre Levefere would have termed, 'rewriting' of a text locked away in the archive of the Baha'i World Centre in Haifa. *Dawn-Breakers* is purported to be a translation of the first part of *Tarikh-i Zarandi*, an ur-text by the Baha'i poet and historian Nabil-i Zarandi (d. 1892). For a long time no one, neither Baha'i nor non-Baha'i, has been allowed to see this unpublished, original manuscript. Obviously excluded from *Dawn-Breakers* are the defunct Babi narratives and revisionist Azali perspectives. This summative Baha'i narrative assimilates earlier Baha'i accounts of Babism such as Abdul Baha's *A Traveller's Narrative* and H. M. Huseyn's *Tarikh-i Jadid* (*New History*) and it draws heavily upon orientalists' accounts in its footnotes. Gobineau's *Religions and Philosophies*; Browne's articles on the Babis in the *Journal of the Royal Asiatic Society*; Nicolas's two volumes on Shaykhism, his biography of the Bab, and translations of *The Seven Proofs*; and the *Bayan* in both Arabic and Persian versions, all feature significantly.[31] As we have already pointed out, Shoghi Effendi elides aspects that might diverge from the orthodox view about to be established and substantively re-casts the original *Tarikh-i Zarandi* in what Lambden calls a 'selective English translation and thorough reworking of parts of the first portion of Zarandi's history of the Bab and Babism'. Lambden also points out how at one point the volume 'occupied a central place in Babi-Baha'i salvation history' and was considered a model for self-sacrificial evangelism.[32] From the product, the reader can derive what MacEoin calls a 'somewhat romanticized image of a band of inspired reformers systematically killed and persecuted by the forces of Islamic obscurantism and oriental despotism – an image fostered by Gobineau and numerous writers after him'.[33]

Gobineau's *Religions and Philosophies*, as seen from the evidence presented earlier in this chapter, can be considered to initiate a process whereby a reclothing of Babism to suit a Christian audience was set in train. Accompanying it was an orientalist representation of Persia. In both *God Passes By* and *Dawn-Breakers* additional passages from sources such as Curzon's *Persia and the Persian Question*, Valentine Chirol's *The Middle East Question* and from the writings of T. K. Cheyne and J. Estlin Carpenter, liberal theologians who had met Abdul Baha, are inserted to 'give weight' to the narrative, but their presence moves both texts further in an orientalist direction.[34] *Dawn-Breakers* is saturated with footnotes carrying Westerners' observations, though for the most part they were untrained in oriental languages. However, by their bulk and variety they were presumably meant to impress the reader with the sense that, though dense with unfamiliar oriental terms, titles, personal names and place names, the text must be conveying an amplitude of significance.

The orientalism is announced in an apparently innocuous way in the third paragraph of the Introduction:

> The main features of the narrative – the saintly heroic figure of the Báb, a leader so mild and so serene, yet eager, resolute, and dominant; the devotion of his followers facing oppression with unbroken courage and often

with ecstasy; the rage of a jealous priesthood inflaming for its own purpose the passions of a bloodthirsty populace – these speak a language which all may understand. But it is not easy to follow the narrative [i.e., the new one being constructed] in its details, or to appreciate how stupendous was the task undertaken by Bahá'u'lláh and His Forerunner, without some knowledge of the condition of church and state in Persia and of the customs and mental outlook of the people and their masters. Nabíl took this knowledge for granted. He had himself travelled little if at all beyond the boundary of the empires of the Shah and the Sulṭan, and it did not occur to him to institute comparisons between his own and foreign civilizations. He was not addressing the Western reader. Though he was conscious that the material he had collected was of more than national or Islamic importance and that it would before long spread both eastward and westward until it encircled the globe, *yet he was an Oriental writing in an Oriental language for those who used it, and the unique work which he so faithfully accomplished was in itself a great and laborious task.*[35]

The paragraph as set out above stretches to sixteen lines consisting of only three sentences, each with a distinct purpose. The first sets up the soon to be familiar dichotomy of the 'somewhat romanticized image of a band of inspired reformers' and the 'forces of Islamic obscurantism and oriental despotism' arrayed against them. The active persecutors, 'the jealous priesthood', whip up 'the passions of a bloodthirsty populace' in a way 'every reader can understand', that is, a Western, Christian reader who is able to grasp universal narratives and has encountered the same or almost the same story before. The next sentence begins with a disclaimer: universal though the narrative is it cannot be appreciated in its fullness without a qualified author to mediate an alien oriental society with its peculiar 'condition of church and state' which we are told in the third sentence has only local 'national or Islamic' importance. An effective rendering of the story cannot be delivered to the 'Western reader' by 'an Oriental writing in an Oriental language', namely, Nabil, who nonetheless, did 'faithfully accomplish a great and laborious task' as best he could as an 'Oriental'. Therefore, the problem has been transferred into the hands of the author who displays his authority by quoting Western experts and conveys the seriousness of the subject in heavy, ornate prose.

It might be argued that as a religious text *Dawn-Breakers* is above politics, that it deals in the categories of belief/unbelief and in delivering a divine message parallels the figurative and symbolic discourse of other religious narratives such as those found in the Old and New Testaments and the Quran. The modern life and times of the holy messenger, or 'manifestation' in Baha'i parlance, can replicate features found in the missions of former prophets and their revelations. Some might even see here an intertextual parallel in which St Mark's early semitically-oriented Gospel is reworked and brought by an admixture of the Aryan-Greek philosophical mind up to the level of sophistication of the Gospel of St John. (That would have been a topic to exercise Renan.) However, the passage goes out of its way to draw attention to an unavoidable distinction, the one that separates a universal – Western, Christian – understanding and a local – national, Persian, Islamic – mode of perception in which the latter is subordinate. In *Dawn-Breakers* as a whole it is not just that the Bab's story is in parts amplified into a modern Persian re-enactment of the mission of Jesus Christ; the orientalist inflection adds an encoding that Shi'i Muslim Iran, illiberal and paralysed in a way that made development impossible, is the other of the enlightened West which alone can apprehend the Bab's message in its full significance. Shoghi Effendi is here addressing the work's intended Western readers. What he has to relate is much more than a mahdi narrative (which would only be parochial), but nothing less than the overture to the appearance of the World Saviour. In its proportions this is going to be a narrative similar, if not superior, to-the-greatest-story-ever-told, which explains why it could not be left in the hands of a mere oriental, insightful though he might have been concerning the spiritual power unleashed by the events he was describing. Someone was required with knowledge of other domains that stretched far 'beyond the boundaries of the empires of the Shah and Sultan'.[36]

The Christianising of the Bab and his story, first begun by Gobineau, is marked at key moments in *Dawn-Breakers*. Gobineau and Nicolas come into their own when the narrative arrives at the Bab's execution and martyrdom, footnoted extracts from their works supplying strong parallels to Christ. Gobineau is brought in to describe what happened to the Bab's corpse, but it is Nicolas who (fittingly, perhaps, as a European Babi) is the most explicit in comparing the Messiah of Shiraz with his Judean original:

> He sacrificed himself for humanity, for it he gave his body and his soul, for it he endured privations, insults, torture and martyrdom. He sealed, with his very lifeblood, the covenant of universal brotherhood. Like Jesus he paid with his life for the proclamation of a reign of concord, equity and brotherly love. More than anyone he knew what dreadful dangers he was heaping upon himself. He had been able to see personally the degree of exasperation that a fanaticism, shrewdly aroused, could reach; but all these considerations could not weaken his resolve. Fear had no hold upon his soul and, perfectly calm, never looking back, in full possession of all his powers, he walked into the furnace.[37]

Interpolation, Rewriting and Narrative Intent: Shoghi Effendi's Christianising of *Dawn-Breakers*

The most overt textual device signalling a Christian parallel is embedded in the speech the Bab delivers to his first followers, the 'Letters of the Living', as he sends them out to win converts. Addressing them as Christ did his disciples, he urges:

> Ponder the words of Jesus addressed to His disciples, as He sent them forth to propagate the Cause of God. In words such as these, He bade them arise and fulfil their mission: 'Ye are even as the fire which in the darkness of the night has been kindled upon the mountain-top. Let your light shine before the eyes of men . . . You are the salt of the earth, but if the salt have lost its savour, wherewith shall it be salted? . . . Nay, when you depart out of that city, you should shake the dust from off your feet'.[38]

The passage is part of a larger speech replete with Christian overtones which, according to Lambden, led even a scholar of the eminence of Abbas Amanat to ascribe Christian influences to the Bab where there were none. Lambden diplomatically focuses his rebuttal of this inauthentic interpolation into the Bab's story on Nabil, who he says might have accessed the overt Christian subject matter and language through living in 1880s Palestine.[39] However, it is more than likely that Shoghi Effendi himself is responsible for the insertion and this would be consistent with my argument that he did not produce a translation according to the interlingual method but provided instead an orientalist rewriting of *Tarikh-i Zarandi*.

For Lefevere there are two types of translator: the 'conservative faithful' translator and the 'spirited' translator. The former works at the level of 'word or sentence', the latter at the 'level of the culture as a whole'.[40] Here I do not wish to enter the debate about the domesticating and the foreignising styles of translation raised by Lawrence Venuti other than to assert that *Dawn-Breakers* must fit into the first category if we take the insertion of Christianised passages into an oriental text as evidence of domestication per se. As such, it confirms Venuti's point that translation is 'an asymmetrical act of communication, weighted ideologically towards the translating culture'.[41] Lefevere's argument that translation can take place at the level of culture is certainly apposite in the case of Shoghi Effendi's editorial mediation of Nabil's text to a Western readership of Christian background. However, we can go further and say that the composition of *Dawn-Breakers* though much larger in scale (certainly it contains orientalists' notes that are far more extensive in number and range), could be compared in method to Edward FitzGerald's version of Khayyam's *Ruba'iyyat*, a text frequently discussed for the way in which the indigenous Persian culture is subsumed into an exotic European imaginary on the understanding that: 'For many Europeans, any non-European cultures were automatically "anthropologised" and their cultures studied and evaluated as "other". The norm was European'.[42]

We know Persian chroniclers were fond of putting imaginary speeches into the mouths of historical figures, in *Dawn-Breakers* however the invention transcends even FitzGerald's insertion of quatrains of his own into the *Ruba'iyyat*. (In a(n) (in)famous remark made in a letter to Cowell he writes: 'It is an amusement for me to take what liberties I like with these Persians who (as I think) are not Poets enough to frighten one from such excursions, and who really do want a little Art to shape them').[43] Applied to Nabil's narrative this is a quotation that takes some teasing out. Shoghi Effendi we should not forget was himself an oriental. Yet, if we consider the Bab's 'Christian' speech to be his own insertion then the act extends beyond an eastern redacteur's licence to create imaginary speeches. Further, in this case the 'translator' is not simply using 'a little Art' to shape an original text that may not have possessed the organisation with which he has invested the translated text. A serious project is in play. Though we cannot go so far as to suggest that Shoghi Effendi's position vis-à-vis Nabil's text is patronising in the same way as FitzGerald's toward Persian poetry is, it is nonetheless the case that it is enacted on the basis that the original culture is in key respects deficient and must be mediated and improved in order to meet the Western reader's horizons of expectation.

Finally, there are the notes to *Dawn-Breakers*, which line up very much in the same mode as orientalist translation. Detailed, explicatory footnotes were always an orientalist affectation as can be seen in Richard Burton's self-indulgent creation of lengthy footnotes which he considered the mark of his erudition. Perhaps for this reason, as well as his failure to accommodate the painstakingly literal style of his translation to his readers' tastes (no domesticating strategy in this particular) Burton's *One Thousand and One Nights* was unsuccessful 'once the scandal surrounding its appearance had died down'.[44] In the case of *Dawn-Breakers* it proved necessary to reduce on the luxury and pretension of the original 1932 edition, with later editions almost entirely shorn of footnotes (an improvement?) and minus also the valuable photographic illustrations contained in the original (too costly?). Leaving aside its function as a gift to VIPs, and its accommodation to Western susceptibilities in its Christianising tendencies, one can only suppose the form *Dawn-Breakers* acquired had a lot to do with Shoghi Effendi's belief in a need to repackage the oriental original. He made a similar assumption to many Western publishing houses today about 'the incompatibility of the poetics of the European and the Islamic systems', going some way toward allowing the readership to 'make the acquaintance of Islamic literature, but strictly on the basis of a dominant/dominated relationship'.[45] Certainly, in relation to *Tarikh-i Zarandi*, Shoghi Effendi was acting well beyond the competence of an eastern translator/compiler. Rewriting across cultures, and adopting the role of an orientalist translator, his aim was to win over a non-oriental Judeo-Christian audience for the Babi part of a Baha'i narrative destined to conquer the West. Despite this huge domesticating effort though, and Lambden's comment on the iconic importance Baha'is attribute to *Dawn-Breakers*, there is still a sense that the Persian milieu incorporated in the volume and other such offerings of the pen of Shoghi Effendi represents a cultural overload that may inhibit the spread of the Baha'i faith. MacEoin notes:

Practising Baha'is, at least those who aspire to some serious knowledge of their origins and beliefs, will say that they do not feel alienated by these elements in their faith. But many Western Baha'is find long Persian names, or historical accounts set in the alien world of 19th century Iran, or even Shoghi Effendi's impossibly long periods difficult to read and digest.[46]

The principle of interpolation of later material into an earlier text, which as we shall see in Chapter 5 preoccupied orientalist Edward Granville Browne, had an afterlife in the battles Denis MacEoin faced in the 1980s in his attempt to establish the factual veracity behind the development of Babism.[47] It shows that, in spite of the claims made on its behalf, the Baha'i faith is a modern rational religion and bears the mark of practises not dissimilar to those employed by the early Church. A basic understanding of form criticism would establish the inauthentic character of this rewriting by taking as an example the *Sitz im Leben* (lit. 'life situation') of the Bab's missionary speech to his followers, that is to say, 'its social setting or circumstances ... which explains how a story has been adapted to fit changes in the development of the Church'.[48] Further,

> [i]t will be clear that the *Sitz im Leben* allotted to any particular unit of tradition is of the utmost importance: if this can reasonably be seen as belonging to the life of Jesus, the unit concerned may be authentic; if it appears to have owed its origin to the [early Christian] community, it seems it must be at least in some respect unhistorical.[49]

In the gospels the evangelist might introduce a saying 'meaningless within Judaism but significant in Rome where [he] probably wrote ... There are no doubt many such additions to sayings explicable by the *Sitz im Leben* in which they are used'.[50]

The implausibility of the Bab's speech deriving from an original Shi'i context can be noted at several levels. Even if the Bab spent his spare time reading the New Testament (for which we've already seen there is no evidence), we can be ninety-nine per cent sure his disciples, the Letters of the Living, like himself immersed in a world of Shaykhi conceptualisations and expectations, did not. Why then would he adopt a Christian paradigm to address such a vital message to them? In paralleling the sending out sermon to the Apostles in Matthew 10 the passage employs some of Jesus's sayings, for example, 'you are the salt of the earth', and mimics his use of the phrase 'heavenly father'. This at once points to the passage's domestication for a target audience of the Baha'i church of Western converts and VIPs. It is hard to believe that any scholar would give any more than a moment's reflection to the possibility that this was an authentic speech of the Bab, even allowing for the disclaimer that 'apart from quotations from the Writings of the Bab, speeches attributed to Him or to anyone else in these pages must not be taken as exact reportage of words spoken at the time'.[51] Of course, a sophisticated approach toward these matters would preclude the need to be defensive about upholding the precise historical truth of a text such as *Dawn-Breakers*, on the understanding that historical research can, and should, be separated from concern over the vindication of religious faith. But that is the paradox this piece of text represents: many Baha'is will believe it to be 'true' simply because the Guardian included it in a canonical narrative of the beginnings of the Baha'i faith. What is clear from the discussion so far is that Shoghi Effendi carried forward Baha'ullah and Abdul Baha's Christianising tendencies, expanding their implications for the Baha'i faith by reaffirming and bolstering Gobineau's Christianising account of the Bab and his martyrdom and introducing further Christian embellishment. In addition, the passage I have quoted from the beginning of *Dawn-Breakers* raises further issues concerning aspirations toward universalism contained in the Baha'i message through its alignment to Christian models. In a similar way to how Jesus had been decoupled from his static, fanatical 'narrow' Jewish locus and refitted for the universalism of the Roman Empire, the Bab's story is raised above its Shi'i Muslim locale and, in a bid to underwrite the universality of the Baha'i faith, rearranged and addressed to a Western readership implicitly understood to be more embracing in its vision than an oriental one.

Conclusion: Gobineau's Persian Master Narrative

The thrust of my argument in this chapter has been that Gobineau the orientalist, in the process of Christianising Babism alienated it from its Shi'i roots, and helped provide a Baha'i leader like Shoghi Effendi with the authority to present it as a prelude to a new world religion. The Christianising and orientalising of the story of the Bab began with Gobineau's portrayal of the Iranian mahdi in *Religions and Philosophies*; his formulation and connection of the

Messiah of Shiraz to broader observations about the distinctiveness of Persia is underpinned by the formational notion of Aryan race theory. These elements, it could be argued, are the product of a complex mind struggling with a profound personal disorientation caused primarily by family background, but also a dark intuition of the neuroses of the European nineteenth-century. Nonetheless, in his writing on Babism an orientalist narrative-in-the-making can be discerned which, while it is inflected by his own idiosyncrasies and emphases, fed into archetypal notions about Islam such as are to be found in orientalism more generally. While Gobineau was not at all inclined to undermine Muslims as the enemies of Christianity, and did not access the more usual semantic field applied to Islam in orientalism whose key lexis is dominated by terms such as 'darkness', 'barbarism', 'stagnation' and 'fanaticism', through his implicit understanding of Persia as a land set apart, not seriously embedded in Islam but more given to speculation, heterodoxy and *taqiyya*, he provided the materials that could usefully be appropriated by those who *did* consider Muslims and their faith as inferior and a bar to progress. This prejudice, combined with an unconscious desire for religious renewal which he construed as the prerogative of the East joined to a facility to powerfully articulate these ideas and clothe them in Christian forms, accounts for the way in which Gobineau's portrayal of Babism, and to a lesser extent Persian *taziya*, travelled through European savants and orientalists like Renan, Matthew Arnold, E. G. Browne, R. A. Nicholson and others.

For Iranians, these race-emphases answered an embedded yearning for an essentialised, ancient Persia that might be revived and realised anew. A form of orientalism specially tailored to contain Persia as a key constituent could perhaps not have failed to activate a trend among the elite of educated Westernised Iranians. Gobineau was not the only contributor to this tendency. Other orientalists who had picked up on and indulged the revival topos impacted upon the range of modernisers and religious innovators who wanted to erase Iran's recent past and move on toward some brave new world. For such Iranians – myth-making nationalists, modernisers, Azali-Babis, Baha'is, Pahlavis, even avant-garde Shi'a – disparate in their positionings and often mutually antagonistic though they might be, there was plenty of aliment in the Western-originated ideas of renewal to nourish their variant projects. For Baha'is in particular, Gobineau was simply the foundational

European figure who had announced the advent of the Bab and his heroic followers to the West as practitioners and performers of a new religion for modern times. They responded to the idea of a new Iran in the belief that it would be brought about through recognising the dual manifestations of Ali Muhammad Shirazi and Husayn Ali Nuri. Few Baha'is were interested in the *taziya* nor were they especially exercised by Aryanism, and if they looked deeply enough (which Shoghi Effendi's writings did not encourage them to do), they might have been repelled by the Azali virus that successive orientalists contracted from Gobineau either directly or indirectly. For their ideas about Persia, the land that gave birth to their faith, early Western Baha'is variously drew inspiration from Renan, Huart, Browne or even Nicolas, though the last named was, before Shoghi Effendi showcased his work in his notes to *Dawn-Breakers*, an obscure figure and, as we have seen, a conservative Babi with Azali leanings. The British, notably Curzon and Chirol, who Shoghi Effendi and later Baha'i authors like George Townshend and Hasan Balyuzi liberally quoted whenever they wanted to dilate upon the decadence of the country prior to the miraculous arrival of Reza Shah, had foregrounded a valorisation of modernity against which they contrasted Shi'i Persia as its backward Other. Into this clash of cultures they even gratifyingly inserted Baha'is on the side of the modern. As for the Other sunk in medievalism and plagued by such recidivistic practises as arbitrary rule, fearful torture and killing of enlightened visionaries and of peace-loving votaries, into it could perfectly be fitted those who wished to quench the light of the new revelation of Baha'ullah. There was enough evidence of these practises in Iranian Baha'is' experience of persecution for the image to filter though to their Western co-believers, amply backed up by 'expert' condemnations drawn from the codex of orientalism.

4

Ernest Renan's Search for a Religion of Modernity

The relationship between Arthur Gobineau and Ernest Renan was friendly but not always frank. Gobineau resented the fact that Renan never acknowledged the influence of the *Essay on the Inequality of the Human Races* on his own theory of race. In another area Renan's perspective on what he considered to be a vital ingredient in the history of the Christian Church was also crucially inflected by a cognate topic trail-blazed by the orientalist manqué, that is, Gobineau's account of the Bab's life and sacrifice in *Religions and Philosophies*. Renan's *Vie de Jesus* (The Life of Jesus), the first title in his seven volume series, *Origins of the History of Christianity*, appeared in 1863 to be followed in 1866 by volume two, *The Apostles*, published one year after the first edition of *Religions and Philosophies*. *The Apostles* closed with a discussion of martyrdom as a feature of the oriental scene, and as an illustration of his theme Renan took an incident lifted from Gobineau, an account of the deaths of those called by Babis and Baha'is 'the seven martyrs of Tehran'. It was a topic Renan would return to in later volumes of *Origins*. Like Gobineau, Renan was also a traveller to the Middle East. He had written much of his biography of Christ in the hills above Beirut, where his sister Henriette nursed him of fever before dying of it herself. In 1864, this time with his new wife, Renan returned to Beirut after taking a tour down the Nile. From Lebanon the couple went on to Damascus to visit the site of St Paul's conversion which Renan was researching for the third volume in the *Origins* series. Old and New Testament studies were his area of specialism; but though he was not an Arabist he had written his doctoral thesis on the Andalusian philosopher Averröes (Ibn Rushd). The world of Islam held a specific significance for Renan's work; if in his mind it did not exactly intersect with Christianity, it possessed a radical complementarity with Jewish history and rooted his views on race and civilisation. His fascination for the enduring significance of martyrdom and its reappearance among the Babis of Persia, and his stretching of ideas on race into a wholesale attack on Islam intermesh to form the major discussion points of this chapter. Each theme is integral not only to Renan's work but informs the European reception of a mahdi movement from a standout sector of the Islamicate world.

Following Gobineau, Renan and Matthew Arnold each descried in the Babi phenomenon a manifestation of religious feelings embedded in traditional practises and recent episodes in the Near East. They saw in them solvents for the agnostic scientism of Europe, even while their observations remained meshed into the Victorian conflation of race and modernity. Renan incorporated into his study of religion the nineteenth-century's linkage between language, race and culture, in particular the Semitic–Aryan binary. Islam and Judaism were united in *sémitism*, a narrow religiosity that represented a bar to progress and modernity. Judaism and Islam were disparaged as twins in upholding a tyrannical religious law with fanatic fixity. Islam in particular was marked as a debased continuation of Semitism into the modern world. Indo-Europeans, in contrast, had brought to the collective history of mankind the spirit of flexibility and the unfettered use of reason that had triumphed in the modern age.

Renan and Arnold's search for a suitable religion for modernity found a focus in Gobineau's writings about Persian Shi'ism. Taking his cue from Gobineau, in his essay 'A Persian Passion Play' Arnold instances Shi'ism as a blending of strict Semitic monotheism with a more generous, spiritual tenderness characteristic of an Aryanised Christianity. Gobineau's account of Shi'ism's mid nineteenth-century offshoot Babism exemplified Persia's putative Aryan genius. The quality of sacrifice its followers evinced in the face of fierce opposition and repression especially moved Renan and Arnold as a modern manifestation of the leaven of martyrdom.

The question as to what would constitute a suitable religion for modernity was an issue not infrequently discussed in the nineteenth century by liberal thinkers and scholars of religion, pre-eminent among who was Ernest Renan.

Renan's writings on religion are shot through with apparently conflicting prognoses concerning religion's status in his own time and the prospects for its continuance into the future. From his writings on this theme emerged a picture that was admittedly sketchy, but which might be said to contain several key elements. The hallmark of modern religion always remained for him freedom of belief of the kind generated in Protestantism, more specifically in its Unitarian form. Also central was his personal desire for a spiritual renewal that would be the re-embodiment of the ethic and élan of the Christianity of Jesus. The French thinker's concerns ran in key respects parallel with those of Matthew Arnold in England. While Arnold also clearly valued freedom of thought, he laid stress on amplification of both the ethical and an emotional colouring that might render palatable to popular minds the otherwise austere reality of humanity's existential modern predicament. Allied to the latter was one further prized ingredient in a modern religiosity, which Renan also espoused: the leaven of martyrdom. Rarely discussed, this important factor in their thought on religious renewal is the focus of this chapter. Proof that such a vital aliment to religion had not died out in modern times was supplied by diplomat and traveller to the Orient, Gobineau, whose account of the brief and cataclysmic appearance in nineteenth-century Iran of Babism, a millenarian religious movement, projected a creed that embodied a sacrificial spirit lacking in the religious composition of the West. Renan and Arnold responded to Gobineau's valorisation of this contemporary Near Eastern re-enactment of the phenomenon of religious martyrdom partly because they saw it supplying the extra element missing from their rational exposition of a modern religion.

This key ingredient in Renan's religion of modernity is also linked to the larger categorisation of religions according to race, which although it was hardly of Renan's invention, he continually – and influentially – reiterated. Written into his discussion is a strand of thinking which became influential for nineteenth-century European thought. Debating the place of religion in modern society, Renan stresses the negative type of religion that held society back. Central to this discussion, in the nineteenth century and today, as the putative epitome of opposition to secularity and the spread of democratic values, narrow-minded religion is secular modernity's Other. In Renan's writings Islam and Judaism are united in *sémitism*, a category he derived from his study of Semitic languages. Semitism, as it related to Judaism and Islam, had once been a strong factor in the growth of monotheism, but in course of time its rigidity caused these faiths to atrophy. In Renan's redaction, Islam represented (and for some still represents) the persistent embodiment of a narrow religiosity that is a bar to progress and modernity. Renan would have agreed with a recent polemicist against religious dogmatism that 'the most important resistant culture and religion is that of Islam'.[1] On the other hand, as I intend to show later in the chapter, Babism, supposedly emerging from 'Aryan' Persia, is constructed as a product of the malleable, adaptable Aryan spirit Renan celebrated almost as frequently as he denigrated the Semitic.

To begin with we need to see how Renan came to adhere to ideas on Indo-European and Semitic race and culture that advanced dubious Eurocentric nostrums which he however wholeheartedly embraced. We shall observe his privileging of 'Aryan' Persia from among the rest of the Islamic nations, and how this may have influenced his reception of Babism, both as a recent manifestation of religious innovation and a confirmation of Persia's putative Aryan spiritual genius. Arnold's response to Babism will also be seen to operate in a similar light, showing how it connected to the nineteenth-century European intellectual struggle over the troubling effects of agnosticism on those who still possessed a residual religious bent.

Race and Philology

Albert Hourani pointed out how Renan's work functioned within a field emerging in the first half of the nineteenth century by which the study of languages was connected to the study of religion. The Germans combined philology with speculation on the mythological/cultural development of peoples based on the notions of Indo-European and Semitic root languages. Hourani also made a connection between Renan's loss of religious faith and his philological study: he gave up his inherited Catholic faith but,

> retained a basic seriousness in his search for truth. The method by which this search should be conducted, he believed, was that of philology. He even spoke of the 'religion of philology', the faith that a precise study of texts in their historical context could reveal the essential nature of a people, and of humanity.[2]

Race forms an inescapable dimension to Renan's work as it does in that of so many nineteenth-century European thinkers. The linguistic division of root languages was accompanied by the speculative reconstruction of religio-cultural histories of the Indo-European and Semitic peoples.[3] Maurice Olender accounts for the Aryan–Semitic binary through a trajectory that begins with the linguistic discovery of Sanskrit and the West's search for a common Indo-European ancestor. Accepted by the Church as the first 'secular science', philology became a tool by which secular humanism adopted the providential role vacated by Christianity. Thus, 'the discourse of Aryan and Semitic ... revived the old conflict between monotheisms', in which 'the Christian tradition, even in a secularized form, sought to distinguish itself from Judaism and Islam'.[4] However, Renan's study of Semitic languages was not only a substitute means of arriving at truth where religion had failed as Hourani suggests; as Edward Said argued, his 'ambition was to carve out a new Oriental province for himself, in this case the Semitic Orient ... and ... to do for Semitic languages what Bopp had done for the Indo-European'.[5]

The crucial linkage between language, race and culture had been made several generations before Renan by the German thinkers Friedrich Schlegel and Wilhelm von Humboldt. Of the cultural systematisers who sought to extrapolate characteristics of an Indo-European spirit from the language divisions, von Humboldt, according to Lawrence Conrad, was pre-eminent: 'in the wake of the connections between Sanskrit and European languages [he] promoted the notion of a language as an organic manifestation of the particular character of those who speak it'.[6] Language for von Humboldt was, Tomoko Masuzawa points out, 'an accomplishment of a people, an expression of their intrinsic nature' – in Humboldt's own words 'the outer appearance of the spirit of a people'.[7] In her excellent resumé of this intertextual field, which formed one of nineteenth-century Europe's master narratives, Masuzawa separates out what she terms the 'technophilological' thrust of scientific linguists like Franz Bopp, whose work on comparative grammar sustained the hypothesis of an Indo-European category of language first intuitively hit upon by the Indologist Sir William Jones, and the speculative dogmas of the likes of Schlegel and von Humboldt.[8] Science, in Renan's lexicon, meant the discipline of philology, his mastery of which was essential to his self-esteem as a savant and connection to the guild of orientalists, as can be seen in his acknowledgement of his debt to Bopp in the dedication of *General History of the Semitic Languages*.[9] But it was from Humboldt, and also perhaps Schlegel, that Renan derived the high estimate of the Sanskrit family of languages and denigration of the non-Indo-European ones that informed his commentary in that work and many subsequent ones. Schlegel's ideas on the superiority of Indo-European language over Semitic language were recycled – such as the axiom that,

> the notorious 'rigidity' of the Semitic language structure directly corresponded to the limitation of the Semites' mental capacity and to their intellectual flexibility. Lacking the inherent power of creativity characteristic of Sanskritic peoples they would not generate original ideas of their own. And whatever they 'borrowed', they might contain but not assimilate; nor could they foster its further growth and efflorescence.[10]

Humboldt's redaction of this principle was to declare the Arabs incapable of 'erecting the edifice of science and art' which the West had performed 'today' upon the foundations of Greek scientific inquiry.[11] Renan inscribed this dictum into his pronouncements on Arabian Islam, going so far as to decouple the scientific achievement of the Abbasid period from the Arabs: Arabic philosophy and science were Arabic only in language, in spirit they were Greco-Sassanian.[12]

Raymond Schwab, whose exposition of the oriental renaissance accepts the seminal contribution of Friedrich and Wilhelm Schlegel to this project, nevertheless believed in a fatal corruption of the linguistic discovery of Bopp. Initiated by the German orientalist Klaproth when he 'awarded his Indo-European fatherland the appellation Indo-Germanic', it would be followed by Gobineau, who 'had previously demonstrated how a dangerous ethnic innuendo could arise from a misused linguistic graph'; and Schopenhauer, 'who sanctioned a fundamental dispute between a spirituality born of India and carried on through a long Aryan tradition which was allegedly pure and wholesome, and a corrupting Semitic exploitation of this spirituality which was the cause of all evil'.[13] Interestingly, Schwab did not include Renan in this perversion of the idyllic fantasy of European and Indian Aryan brotherhood which he saw leading to Houston Chamberlain and Nietzsche. Renan's contribution to the Aryan–Semite discussion seems largely to have lain in his repetition of ideas regarding the incomparably advanced contribution the Indo-Europeans had brought to the collective history of mankind, his disparagement of the Semites, and his emphasis on Islam as a debased continuation of Semitism into the modern world.

Judaism, Islam and 'Le sémitisme'[14]

The first thing to note about Renan's articulation of the Semitic is that it is a trans-historical category, an essentialism deriving from language extended to race and culture that comprehends both Jews and Arabs and the religious traditions of both Judaism and Islam. The term *le sémitisme*, following 'the English scholars of Calcutta, and the philologists of Germany, M. Bopp in particular', is placed in linguistic opposition to the *indo-germanique* or *indo-européen*.[15] Together the Semitic and Indo-European form the two rivers into which have flown all others in the history of civilisation. The direct association of Arabs and Jews begins in Renan's early philological writings and is never far from the surface in the two great projects that occupied him in his maturity: the *History of the Origins of Christianity* and the *History of the People of Israel*. His doctoral thesis and first scholarly publication, *Averroës and Averroism* (1852), pronounces on the barren soil of Arab and Muslim culture, in particular its incapacity to produce flourishing philosophy. 'Philosophy, with the Semites, had been nothing but a purely exterior imprint, without great fecundity, an imitation of Greek philosophy'.[16] In this respect Islam manifested an 'irremediably narrow spirit', the kind that he would later invariably argue, was cognate to its Semitic relative Judaism.[17] Renan claimed a licence to speak on such matters from the 'scientific' work he was pursuing in philology. However, the gaps in knowledge opened up by this labour gave him the opportunity, in the vacuum of authority created by the retreat of religion, to deliver grand dogmatic pronouncements on race and culture. Through a careful, 'reserved' excavation of the linguistic record supplied by the Semitic family of languages, he claims in the preface to his *General History of the Semitic* Languages that he is able to recover the external history (*l'histoire extérieure*) delineating the idioms, chronology, order and character of its 'written monuments'; and also (what the Aryan languages sadly lacked) an interior history of organic development, in particular, a comparative study of grammar. Rather than providing for richness, the availability of such data for the Semitic languages signified a lack; they were relatively easy to study and their history was reducible to a skeleton with all that implied of deadness or ossification. The absence of an interior history in the Aryan languages, on the other hand, connoted to a marked degree a progressive, developmental, re-birthing character. Thus, in the breaks of evidence Renan found the space to expatiate on the limited nature of the Semitic in contradistinction to the protean, inventive character of the Aryan. The essay ends by making the crucial extrapolation from language to race. Though judgements on race must be hedged by caveats, including acknowledgement that modern conditions demonstrated a more complex assimilation of influences, the 'immense part played in the movement of humanity' by the 'primordial factor of race' (*l'influence primordiale*) was still worth enunciating.[18] In his first chapter, Renan makes the connection explicit by claiming:

> the Semitic languages must be envisaged as corresponding to a division of human kind . . . the character of the peoples we are speaking of is marked in history by traits as original as the languages which have served to formulate and delimit their thought.[19]

As well as in *General History*, Renan's statements on Semitism are to be observed in his review articles of the 1850s, collected in 1857 as *Etudes d'histoire religieuse* (citations below are from the English translation, *Studies of Religious History and Criticism*). A major context to these pieces, which he discusses in his preface, is the climate of religious criticism in the mid-nineteenth century that from a personal point of view would break out into bitter confrontation between Renan himself and the forces of religious orthodoxy on the publication of his *Life of Jesus* in 1863. In them he also foresees that 'the unity of the Indo-European race as opposed to the Semitic, a unity recognised in religions as well as languages' would henceforth structure the writing of religious history, especially the religions of antiquity.[20] Renan's main focus of study is the Semitic religions Judaism, Islam and Christianity. 'Now these three grand religious movements', he says, 'are three Semitic facts, three branches of the same trunk, three versions, unequally fine, of the same idea. From Jerusalem to Sinai, from Sinai to Mecca, the distance is but a few leagues'.[21] Compared with the Aryan mood of pagan Greece (on which Renan was no authority) the Semitic spirit had 'sprung from the desert and [was] insistent upon the unity of God'.[22] This marked form, an unquestionable, absolute monotheism, was the root of Semitic intolerance, making Semitism incapable of liberty of thought, in stark contrast to the Aryans who were able to embrace it because they never ascribed absolute truth to their religions. On this account, having been almost single-handedly responsible for giving mankind the consciousness of one God, Semitism exhausted its contribution to human civilisation and 'was destined in the paths of secular existence, not to pass mediocrity'.[23]

The respective articles on Judaism and Islam in *Studies of Religious History* amplify a Semitic–Aryan binary that Renan would never tire of repeating. However, what is also significant for this discussion is how they cement Judaism and Islam together in an idiom that, strangely enough, almost seems to prioritise Arab over Jew. This can be accounted for, I suggest, by Renan's construction of race and culture along axes that allow for intersections of the synchronic and diachronic in a peculiarly orientalist manner. In spite of the location of its origins in a remote past, Semitism functions as an essentialised trans-historical category. Or, as Ignaz Goldziher judged, 'Renan's theory amounts to an assertion that Judaism and Islam had not developed from or into anything – they were just "there", like a person who had no childhood or adolescence, but simply sprang into being as an adult'.[24] To admit its dissolution in the Jewry of modern civilisation as Renan does in *General History* is not to consign Semitism's narrow fanatical monotheism to the dustbin of history. This is because its most recent embodiment Islam, though now surpassed by European civilisation, still maintains a tenacious hold on large sections of humanity. In another sense, Judaism is reducible to the nomadic patriarchal society of the Arab tribes: 'Arab life in its full perfection; such, in effect, is the spectacle which Israel still presents to us during the whole period of the Judges, and previous to its organization as a monarchy'.[25] The history of Israel represents for Renan a continual battle between the conservative, exclusivist prophet (assigned the dual Hebrew/Arabic term *nabi*) and the pragmatic king. David, who in his person joins the dual function of prophet and statesman, displays 'the odd mixture of sincerity and of mendacity, or religious exaltation and of egoism which strikes us in Mahomet'.[26]

Renan's most forthright exposition of the Semitic–Aryan dualism is to be found in his inaugural lecture to the Collège de France on 21 February 1862, *De la part des peuples sémitiques dans l'histoire de la civilisation*. Affected as this was by the controversy that intensified around the *Life of Jesus*, and in its assertion of the scientific pre-eminence of philology, the lecture proclaims nothing less than a *Kulturkampf* between the Semitic and Aryan principles. Together they represented opposite poles supplying the dialectic tension needed to produce civilisation. Nevertheless, the Aryan-European principle is proclaimed triumphant in the modern age, incorporating the spirit of flexibility and the unfettered use of reason that anti-philosophic, anti-scientific Semitism cannot admit.[27] In cultural terms no less significant was the Aryan Indo-European (that is Germanic, Celtic, Greek, Indian) aptitude for poetry and imagination. Christianity had broken out of the Semitic mould, flourished in Aryan lands, and was destined to grow increasing less Jewish.[28] Judaism, especially the Pharisaic branch, had espoused a narrow formalism and was fanatically disdainful of contact with foreign elements. Outside of France, Jews continued to form a separate society; their contribution to medieval philosophy had been entirely Arab.[29] However, the carrier of Semitism and therefore the embodiment of fanaticism in more recent times was Islam: 'the Semitic mind is especially represented in our times by Islam'. As such it represented a disdain for science and suppression of civil society – in short, 'the complete negation of Europe'.[30]

Having laid a ground plan for the study of religion, and having identified the Semitic religions, establishing the particular association of Judaism and Islam, from the 1860s onwards Renan launched into an exemplification of these ideas in his multi-volume histories of Christianity and Judaism. The latter was completed barely a few years before his death. Though Arabic and Islamic studies were not in his area of expertise, he continued to include references to both in these writings, usually adopting the mix of diachronic and synchronic perspectives outlined above. In *The Life of Jesus* Renan uses 'Semitic' as a racial categorisation to connect both Jewish 'responsibility' for the persecution and death of Jesus, and persisting manifestations of Muslim obscurantism. The book is especially inflected by a synchronic engagement with Islam as it was composed under the influence of Renan's visit to the Middle East in the spring–summer of 1861. There he had endeavoured to 'raise the mantle of aridity and mourning with which it [northern Palestine] has been covered by the demon of Islamism'.[31] He cites, for example, the Arabic names of villages in the environs of Lake Tiberius, blames history for having the design of concealing the traces of Jesus, then declares: 'It is Islamism, and especially the Mussulman reaction against the Crusades, which has withered as with a blast of death the district preferred by Jesus'.[32] These Islamic manifestations, which he saw around him in Palestine, recalled for Renan the Judaism of Christ's time. 'Islamism' was 'a sort of resurrection of Judaism';[33] its diachronic foil was 'Pharisaism' (*le Pharisaisme*), the Jewish sect he associated most with Semitic intransigence. The Pharisees were the main antagonists of Jesus, who had started as a religious reformer but became a 'destroyer of Judaism'.[34] Toward Paul, who arguably performed this role more actively even than Jesus, Renan was ambivalent. In proselytising Christianity he displayed the fanatical characteristics Renan associated with Pharisaism, and becomes the object and personification of the Frenchman's perhaps most shocking anti-Semitic outburst. In his arguments with the Greeks on the Acropolis, 'surrounded by so many things he did not understand', Paul demonstrated according to Renan, 'the prejudices of the iconoclastic Jew', perceiving Greek culture and religion as idol-worship: 'The fatal words had gone forth: "Ye are idols!" The error of that pitiful little Jew was your [i.e., Aryan Greece's] death warrant!'[35] In Renan's mind the conflict between the Semite and the Aryan was diachronically doubled: the Jews of the first century, epitomised by Paul, in their narrowness and ignorance looked down on Greek culture; in the nineteenth century the Islamic world rejected European civilisation. But as he would write in his last great effort in describing the religion of the Semites: 'The simultaneous apparition in the Greek race of all that which goes to compose the honour and the pride of the human intellect impresses me far more than the passage of the Red Sea or of the Jordan'.[36]

Aryanism and a Persian Revelation

When it came to the study of religion, Renan's insights are marred by ideas about race unfortunately endemic to European thought of the period. He was of the opinion that 'religions are what the races who adopt them make them'. While his writings on Judaism and Christianity demonstrate a refreshing awareness of their origins and context in the Near East, he brands Judaism and Islam twins in upholding a tyrannical religious law with rage and fanaticism, and generally displays a prejudice against all manifestations of Muslim expression.

> Islamism, falling as it did on ground that was none of the best, has, on the whole, done as much harm as good to the human race; it has stifled everything by its dry and desolating simplicity. Christianity escaped this danger solely because the Semitic element in it has always been resisted, and at last has been nearly banished.[37]

While Renan's articulation of the Aryan–Semitic dichotomy was fully formulated as we have seen, the work of Arthur Gobineau, though Renan never acknowledged it, clearly influenced his view of at least one Muslim country – Iran. Said conflated both Frenchmen's orientalism in terms of a common interest in philology and racial attitudes, emphasising Gobineau's *Essay* as a decisive factor though, as Ahmad Gunny points out, he said nothing of Gobineau's other writings.[38] Putting aside the fact that Gobineau's assessment of Islamic culture was not the same as Renan's, his *Religions and Philosophies*, a major articulation of his ideas on the factors that defined the Orient's separation from Europe, made it clear Gobineau did not establish his assessment of the Near East solely, or even largely, on premises derived from racial theory. Disenchanted with Europe and possessing a horror of America, Gobineau's predilections were engaged by what he argued were intuitive, speculative, and syncretistic oriental ways of thinking as opposed to what he considered to be the rigidity of European approaches fixated upon the pursuit of a single truth. Gobineau's divergence from Renan and the scientific orientalists of France and Germany was objectified in his idiosyncratic *Treatise on Cuneiform Texts* published in 1862. In this he deciphered the cuneiform inscriptions discovered a generation earlier by Henry Rawlinson and Austin Layard in Mesopotamia and Iran by recourse to the esoteric methods of native religious scholars. Unsurprisingly, Gobineau's ideas were ridiculed by the French orientalist establishment.[39]

While he disregarded Gobineau's esoteric explanations of the cuneiform inscriptions, and was sceptical about the latter's fantastic renditions of ancient Persian history, Renan concurred with his friend's Aryan predilections and responded positively to his descriptions of Babism. He subscribed to a belief in the superiority of the Persian race that Gobineau had himself been instrumental in disseminating. Both single out the 'Aryan' Persians from amidst the sea of races, predominantly African and Semitic, which constitute the Muslim world. Gobineau was instrumental in passing on the myth as to an ancient Iranian racial type that had withstood the Islamic tide and presented its enduring character beneath the Islamic faith system:

> But in Persia, intelligence plays, on the contrary, a very big role. The customs, habits, national honour of a nation that considers itself as the most ancient in the world imposes a respect, as a kind of point of honour, even on the government itself.[40]

Gobineau marked Shi'ism as a specifically Persian response to the invading force of Arab Islam, discerning within it and the Iranian forms of sufism, ideas, beliefs and rituals that pre-dated Islam. Fascinated, however, as he was by the style and varieties of exegesis of the Quran, Gobineau did not denigrate Islam as a Semitic creation per se, as did Renan. He saw nineteenth-century Iran as heterogeneous in terms of the wide variety of its religious practice and its racial make-up: the land's 'confusion of blood . . . allowed no dogmatic idea to take root deeply'.[41] In contrast Renan's estimate of the Persian contribution to Arab/Muslim civilisation is far more dualistic in the absolute qualities he ascribes to both. He denigrates the contribution of Arabs, Africans and other eastern races to Islam in order to exalt the Iranian. He sees Islam and its influence upon the races that had embraced it acting as a cumbrous chain denying all opportunities for progress and development. The one race excluded from this Manichaean state of affairs is the Persian: 'Persia alone is the exception; she has protected her genius; that's why within Islam Persia is set apart; she is at bottom more Shiite than Muslim'.[42]

From Renan's perspective it was therefore adventitious that it should be from within Iran that a movement emerged which both he and Gobineau took to be a modern instance of religious renewal. In *Religions and Philosophies* Gobineau had stressed precisely that sense of being present at the kind of events which attended in the past the birth of the great religions.[43] The Babi movement, started by Ali Muhammad of Shiraz in mid nineteenth-century Iran, to which is devoted a long narrative in *Religions and Philosophies*, attracted Renan's attention judging from the references he makes to it (directly and indirectly), on account of its manifestation of a quality of sacrifice in the face of fierce opposition and repression. The Babi episode constituted an historical series of events that helped emphasise Renan's criticism of miracle and the supernatural. In *The Apostles* (1866), he sustains this by inscribing the events surrounding the foundational episodes of Christianity according to rational (if imaginative and sympathetic) codes. Though his account was anathema to traditional orthodox understanding, Renan was concerned to demonstrate the verity of the grand sentence of his penultimate paragraph: 'Religion is not a popular error; it is a great instinctive truth, imperfectly seen by the people'.[44] His attempted closure of the space between the contending signs of criticism and belief was in part facilitated by the exemplum of martyrdom of which the most pertinent was offered in Gobineau's account of Babism. Renan closely follows Gobineau's characterisation of the founder of Babism, Ali Muhammad Shirazi:

> A gentle and unpretentious man, a sort of modest and pious Spinoza, has found himself almost against his own will raised to the rank of miracle worker, of incarnation of the divine; and has become the leader of a numerous, ardent and fanatical sect, which has very nearly brought about a revolution comparable to that of Islam. Thousands of martyrs have run to him with joy before death. A day unequalled perhaps in the history of the world was that of the day of the great butchery which was made of the *babis* of Teheran.[45]

The circumstances attending the birth and development of the Babi sect, specifically its violent suppression and the heroic martyrdom of many of its followers, constituted more than merely an example of religious fanaticism on the part of persecutors and acolytes. They provided testimony to the enduring character of religious faith in an age that could no longer support the supernatural framework of the creed. 'Absolute faith is for us wholly out of the question'. Western man tested and reformulated his opinions many times, and as a result his strength of conviction was enfeebled. The oriental, on the other hand, being narrow, obstinate and unreflective, was apt to behold truth in simple categories of black and white. But this fact also enabled heroic acts of self-sacrifice such as those manifested by the Babis. 'For an opinion thus embraced a man will allow himself to be killed'.[46] For Renan the fascination of Babism was that, more than Mormonism in the West, it proffered an example of the continuity of religious faith into the scientific world of the nineteenth century. 'Absolute devotion is, for simple natures, the most exquisite of joys and a species of necessity . . . It is so sweet for a man to suffer for something, that in many cases the thirst for martyrdom causes men to believe'.[47] Thus ended *The Apostles*; but Renan would return again to the topic of martyrdom in later volumes of *Origins*, and to show that the Babis were not simply a passing image, he referred to them again, usually in the context of spiritual struggle or martyrdom.[48]

Some observations might also be made concerning the extent to which Renan saw the Babi movement as analogous to Christianity. Once again, Gobineau's redaction of the Babi story was highly influential on the way Renan (and indeed other Europeans such as Matthew Arnold and orientalist Professor E. G. Browne) saw the Bab. The episodes illustrated above and the explication Gobineau gave them certainly captured Renan's attention and made him ponder, if only for a while, the possibilities of religious renewal, a subject that had engrossed him from the early days. Since *The Future of Science*, written on the eve of the 1848 revolutions, his early enthusiasm for the energy and abandonment of self-sacrifice – 'magnificent outbursts of the grand instincts of human nature' – is expressed with a romantic brio not out of step with the time. Those who despaired that religion was a thing of the past were referred eighteen hundred years back to the birth of Christianity, and told that humanity, however dire its situation, had always resurrected itself.[49] As Wardman pointed out: 'The "new religion" was a romantic version of the first revolution, preached and believed in by numerous thinkers and writers of the time – Lamartine, George Sand, Pierre Leroux and others'.[50] Against Renan's progressively more complicated attitude toward what he considered the inevitable decline of orthodox religion in modern Europe, can be set his claim that man has a natural intuitive and self-sacrificing bent. Nothing was supernatural.[51] Martyrdom may not prove the truth of a doctrine, but it proved the impression that it had made on men's minds, and that was all that was needed for success.[52] The critical study of religion affirmed it as 'an integral part of human nature', and 'in its essence true', despite its variations in form. Though 'frequently deceived', humanity 'in the object of its worship [was] not mistaken'.[53] At the end of *Life of Jesus*, Renan asked his readership: 'Will great originality be born again, or will the world content itself henceforth by following the ways opened by the bold creators of the ancient ages? We know not'.[54] A few years later, fired by Gobineau's account of the Babi episode, with its construction of an Iranian messiah that appealed to a Christian European audience, Renan might for a moment have felt a little more optimistic.

Revitalising Religion: Arnold's Programme in 'A Persian Passion Play'

Matthew Arnold's writings on religion have been victim to the twentieth and early twenty-first century's sharp divergence away from the Victorian Age's interest in this topic. As James Walter Caufield puts it, 'Arnold's religious ideas generally, like his notion of "renouncement" particularly, receive little or no critical attention today, although this neglect is hardly new'.[55] Even in his own time, Arnold's particular stance in bringing a literary hermeneutic to the critique of Christianity was misunderstood. '[M]odernist and demythologizer though he was in doctrine, he . . . loved [the] poetry of [the Church and its liturgy] [and] loved them as being at the very heart of religion, and indispensable to its life'.[56] In tracing Arnold's affinity with Renan, Donald D. Stone sees the Frenchman's writings on Christianity as representing, in a similar way to the project Arnold nurtured, 'simultaneously an attack on the dogmatism and institutions of Christianity and an affirmation of the power of the ideal'. The adeptness of *Life of Jesus* at translating the German Biblical criticism of the type done by David Strauss into an historical context suited to the mid-nineteenth century constituted one of Renan's main attractions for Arnold, embodying the 'kind of religious criticism that [he] found lacking in England, a criticism that allowed for both an objective examination of Christianity and an affirmation of its symbolic value'.[57]

However, Basil Willey may have been taking an overly Christocentric view of Arnold's desire for religious reformation when he conceived of him not only rejecting 'new religions' like Comtism, but also counselling 'not [to] look outside Christianity for guidance – say to other world-religions or ethical systems'.[58] Pointing out in Arnold's *Note-Book* references to the Vulgate New Testament, a Buddhist text, and passages from Confucius, Spinoza and George Sand, Ruth apRoberts opined: 'the mere fact of the eclecticism indicates Arnold is himself working toward definition of the nonsectarian ground of religious thought'.[59] Arnold's eclectic bent enabled him to trawl exotic waters. 'A Persian Passion Play', which appeared in *Cornhill Magazine* in December 1871, five years after *The Apostles*, and was later added to the 1875 edition of *Essays in Criticism*, takes its cue from the concluding section of *Religions and Philosophies*, where Gobineau discusses and presents episodes from Persian *taziya*, a form of Shi'i religious theatre that ritually re-enacts martyrdom among the family of the Prophet's grandson, Imam Husayn. Growing to fruition in the nineteenth century, and thus concurrent with the events surrounding the emergence of Babism, the *taziya* was for Gobineau further proof of the superiority of Persia, and he went so far as to compare the theatre produced in this form with the great tragedies of Ancient Greece. It was a riddle that as an oriental race, when they ought (according to much European nineteenth-century race-history) to have been in their dotage, Persians as a people and a nation were able to produce such a creation as the *taziya*: 'It is the spirit of Antiquity, it is the eternal spirit of mankind, it is the work of development of one of the great forms of human thought that Persia today offers us the opportunity to examine in full flight'.[60]

Arnold's essay extracts several scenes adding a sympathetic commentary that, characteristically, demotes Gobineau's presentation in favour of a sermon of his own:

> No doubt there is much truth in what Count Gobineau . . . says; and it is certain that the division of Shiahs and Sunis [sic] has its true cause in a division of races, rather than in a difference of religious belief.
>
> But I confess that if the interest of the Persian passion-plays had seemed to me to lie solely in the curious evidence they afford of the workings of patriotic feeling in a conquered people, I should hardly have occupied myself with them at all this length. I believe they point to something much more interesting.[61]

Placing the *taziya* on a par with the Christian passion play performed annually at Ammergau, Arnold appears to demote a race and revelation thematic; the *taziya* is made to yield a larger truth of which Christianity's was the original, 'carrying into these hard waters of Judaism a sort of warm gulfstream of tender emotion'. Islam ('Mahometanism'), however, 'had no such renewing. It began with a conception of righteousness, lofty indeed, but narrow, and which we may call old Jewish; and there it remained. It is not a *feeling* religion'.[62] Nevertheless, the Prophet's grandson, Husayn, and his followers accomplished a kind of simulacrum of Jesus' sacrifice. 'Now, what are Ali, and Hasan, and Husayn and the Imams, but an insurrection of noble and pious natures against this hardness and aridity of the religion around them?'[63] Receiving passing acknowledgement at the beginning of the piece, the story of the Bab is also shown to confirm the sacrificial motif. Gobineau had identified the Bab's visit to the mosque of Imam Ali in Kufa as the moment of spiritual crisis when he conceived of his mission. This he knew would result in his death, as Ali's path had led to his. 'His followers say that he then passed through a sort of moral agony which put an end to all the hesitations of the natural man within him'.[64]

Conjoined with the stories of Imam Husayn and Jesus, the Bab's story declared the conduct of religion rather than its mythology. As such it qualified to fill the vacuum left by modernity's excision of the mythological and supernatural from religion, what Arnold would elsewhere call the *Aberglaube*, or '*extra-belief*, belief beyond what is certain and verifiable'.[65] In its dramatisation of the great sacrificial theme in religion, as seen in the Bab's spiritual struggle at Kufa, it added to the imagination and poetry that was the very fibre of religious feeling. In Arnold's exegesis the Christ-like status of the Bab is implicitly understood. The English critic takes as his point of departure Gobineau's influential but erroneous portrayal of a complex spiritual innovator who had read the Christian scriptures, knew Jewish traditions through contact with the Jewish religious doctors of Shiraz, and had studied the ancient religion of Persia, Zoroastrianism.[66] In this way, Arnold appropriated Gobineau's orientalist narrative for his own purposes making it serve his preoccupation with spiritual practice denuded of dogma, though ultimately operating within what he conceived to be a Christian frame.

However, we should not be deceived into upholding Arnold's underplaying of the underlying race assumptions of Renan and Gobineau. For all three the Persian *taziya* and its connection with the Babi movement coheres around a complex of ideas in which race plays no small part. Despite dismissing Gobineau's foregrounding of race with respect to the *taziya* by arguing this brand of Shi'i religious theatre pointed to 'something much more interesting', Arnold in fact only reaffirms Gobineau and Renan's fascination with Persia's spiritual genius as seen in the Shi'i cult of martyrdom of the first three Imams and that land's capacity for giving birth to a movement of religious renewal (Babism).[67] All three authors balanced similar preoccupations. Though totally uninterested in Christianity except in so far as it contributed to the aristocratic civilisation of the Middle Ages, Gobineau, as we have seen, was no less aroused by religious renewal in an oriental context than Renan and Arnold. It had after all been his researches with respect to the richness of Aryan religious expression and in particular the Babi manifestation in Persia that had stimulated his colleagues' imaginations in the first place. Arnold too was not disinclined to go in for the type of conflations of race and culture which Renan counselled against but which, as we have seen, was himself prone to pronounce on. Under the influence of Renan, Arnold tried out the Aryan–Semitic binary in a well-known passage from *On the Study of Celtic Literature*, and incorporated it into his sermon on the Hellene–Hebrew division in Victorian England in *Culture and Anarchy*. Moreover, we have seen already at the heart of the message of 'Passion Play' sits Renan's argument concerning Aryan Europe's spiritual transformation of the 'hard waters of Judaism':

> The crowning anomaly for Renan was the fact that Europe had adopted as the basis of her spiritual life a work least adapted to her spirit, the Bible, product of an alien race and a different soul ... Right reason would have dictated the Vedas as the holy book, for they at least were the work of the racial ancestors of Europe. Fortunately, however, modern Christianity tended to return to the Indo-European heritage, to separate itself more and more from Judaism. Eventually, he felt, it would become the religion of the heart, substituting delicacy and nuance for dogmatism, the relative for the absolute. To anyone acquainted with Arnold's works most of these opinions have a familiar ring.[68]

In some aspects 'Passion Play' is weak as an essay on comparative religion. According to Ruth apRoberts, it shows Arnold writing 'as though Christianity were later, more *developed* than Islam, when of course Islam arose later as a kind of reformation of the Judaeo-Christian line'.[69] Moreover, in spite of what he implies is Gobineau's narrow racial interpretation of the *taziya*,

Arnold also quite clearly aligns himself with the notion of the primacy of Iranians as a subtle aristocracy within Islam,

> The conquered Persians, a more mobile, more impressionable, and gentler race than their concentrated, narrow, and austere Semitic conquerors felt the need of [a tender and pathetic side in Islam] most, and gave most prominence to the ideals which satisfied the need.[70]

In its articulation, seen above, of the division of human culture into Semitic and Aryan parts, 'Passion Play', as we have said, consolidates a theme that runs through *Culture and Anarchy* and the major essay *On the Study of Celtic Literature*. Shi'ism and Babism, Persia's most recent charismatic manifestation, are demonstrated as blending strict Semitic monotheism with a more generous, spiritual tenderness characteristic of an Aryanised Christianity. This was the kind of religiosity Arnold wanted to advocate, and the discovery that it had been only very recently manifested in a religious movement in Persia confirmed its verity. Therefore, though largely considered a minor essay in Arnold's *oeuvre*, 'Passion Play' can be seen as central to his thinking about religion. In the context of the religious criticism of Arnold's later prose period, it holds major importance when read as an integral part of his broader message concerning the essentiality of religion in the modern world. The essay also demonstrates the outreach of Arnold's ideas on religion to spiritual elements outside Christianity while still maintaining the original centrality of its message. Renan, Gobineau and Arnold's religious and cultural criticism, and the interest they entertained in manifestations of religious feeling observed in traditional practises and recent episodes in the Near East that served as solvents for the agnostic scientism of Europe, was meshed into the Victorian conflation of race and modernity. For Renan, exalting the principle of unfettered thought and the faculty of subtle imagination that came from Europe's Aryan inheritance involved objectifying his hatred of fanaticism, bigotry and intolerance in Europe's Other.[71] Semitism fitted this role because, as Olender has argued, Renan's project had all along been to exalt Christianity over Judaism and Islam. Jesus the Jew – *Jeshua* the Aramaic speaking spiritual healer of first century Galilee in northern Palestine – is a figure Renan could well have imagined but cared not too closely to envisage.

The same might be said of Arnold, whose espousal of the Indo-European in the form of Greek sweetness and light may have modulated his distaste for Hebraic Puritan Protestantism, but amounted to an over-determined argument staged around not only religion, but also culture and class. Arnold's search for a modern religiosity encapsulated in a core of renunciation that extended from Marcus Aurelius to the Bab has sunk almost without trace. We could say that the various attempts made by nineteenth-century agnostics to replace the traditional, largely literalist religion of their age by a reformed, rational religion of modernity, suffered the same fate.

Modern Refractions: Renan, Science, Rationalist Method and the Baha'i Faith

For scholars of the great Muslim radical Jamal al-Din 'Afghani', his 1883 debate with Renan on the topic of Islam and science provides an opportunity to discuss his orthodoxy. However, with respect to Renan the debate also epitomises a number of the key issues I have been discussing in this chapter. Keddie summarises Renan's argument as follows: it 'has two major points. One is . . . racial: the Arabs by nature and temperament are hostile to science and philosophy . . . The second is that Islam is essentially hostile to science'. [72] For our purposes, the debate begins by summarising the Frenchman's ideas on the 'golden' period of Muslim civilisation, when he argued the flowering of a rational, scientific culture should be attributed neither to Islam as a religion, nor the Arabs as a race, but to the Aryans, specifically Persians and Greeks, who were the real source of cultural renaissance during the reign of the Abbasids. The most complete rational culture produced under the auspices of Islam, in spite of the fact of its being composed in Arabic, was the product of Greco-Sassanian civilisation.[73] Afghani, on the other hand, makes the perhaps surprising admission (from the point of view of a Muslim thinker) that Islam had tried to stifle philosophy, but argues this is the situation wherever and whenever religion gets the upper hand. 'As long as humanity exists, the struggle will not cease between dogma and free investigation, between religion and philosophy'.[74] Keddie assesses Afghani's argument as 'evolutionary' and forward-looking, and more original than Renan's. It does seem that he epitomised Renan's struggle (going back to the 1840s) to assert the primacy of criticism above religious orthodoxy in all its systemic guises; however, he excluded Renan's race arguments and campaign against Islam as the quintessence of reaction barring the way to progress in modern times. Responding with admiration to the subtlety of Afghani's reasoning, Renan according to Keddie 'appears, under Afghani's influence to retract his singling out of Islam for dispraise, although his prior remarks reflect a continued anti-Muslim prejudice'.[75] The irony, however, is that while he may seem to have made concession to the Muslim intellectual, Renan's covering explanation for Afghani's brilliance is still inveterately wedded to the recidivism of race: 'Sheikh Jemmal-Eddin is an Afghan entirely divorced from the prejudices of Islam; he belongs to those energetic races of Iran, near India, where the Aryan spirit lives still so energetically under the superficial layer of official Islam'.[76] Nowadays it is considered that Jamal al-Din adopted the title 'Afghani' for tactical reasons and that he was actually known as Sayyid Jamal al-Din Asadabadi. Renan would, no doubt, have felt satisfied to know that his interlocutor was actually Iranian. The *Kulturkampf* against Islam that Renan had inaugurated in his public lecture of 21 February 1862 continued at least up to his debate with Afghani in 1883. The latter exchange confirmed Renan's arrogation of the province of scientific and rational culture to one race and, in modern times, to one culture: Europe/the West. The debate itself moves us into the later twentieth century to the argument between Islam and modernity crystallised by the Iranian revolution.

The major shift the Babi movement underwent in the latter half of the nineteenth century resulted in the split in which the minority Azali-Babis had a significant input alongside Jamal al-Din 'Afghani' in the agitation for the Persian revolution of 1905–11.[77] In Baha'i narratives the violence and fanaticism of Babism was quietly abrogated reconfiguring the Babis as primitive forerunners of the new, modernist creed. Toward the end of the nineteenth century and at the beginning of the twentieth, Baha'is embarked on missionary activity in the West. In their proselytising material in America they may be said to have adopted features of the Unitarianism that Renan so admired in their promotion of openness and freedom from dogma.[78] Presenting a subtle modernist demythologising of traditionalism in its various Judeo-Christian and Islamic formats, Baha'ism appeared at the beginning of the twentieth century to represent the kind of 'new religion' to which Renan and Arnold might have given their endorsement. Recognising the same projection but speaking from a conservative Christian perspective, a report of an American missionary in Persia from the early 1900s observes:

> [Baha'is] are not more open to the gospel than the Moslems. In fact, many consider them less so, for although they profess to accept the whole Bible, yet by their allegorical interpretation and denial of all miracles they effectually change its meaning. Having incorporated into their books some of the moral precepts of Christ and having adopted a semi-Christian vocabulary, they delight to discourse at great length on love, on a tree being known by its fruits, and on kindred themes; but having left out Christ, the centre, they have missed the essential thing, and now in Persia are notorious as being religious in word rather than deed. In fact many of them are simply irreligious rationalists.[79]

In the West, in the first decade of the twentieth century, Baha'ism, not unlike the Islam of the Ahmadiyya missionaries at Woking, was becoming known as a modern religion of science and rationality claiming to replace sectarianism. In a sense, both were parallel developments of the rationalist tendencies the missionaries had already met and, according to some accounts, had been worsted in the 'colonially-conditioned Muslim-missionary confrontation' in North West India between Muslim ulama and Christian missionaries.[80] In Agra in the 1850s Muslims shocked the intellectually limited evangelicals by using Biblical criticism against them.[81] This was a prelude to the later Muslim apologetics raised in print by modernists such as Chiragh Ali and Sayyid Amir Ali, but sophisticated as their argumentation was, as Moadell points out, it faced the daunting discrepancy between 'European civilization and the Islamic nations [which] naturally gave rise to a pervasive consciousness of decadence among the modernists, which necessitated an account of Muslim decline'.[82] Here was where the Baha'is stepped in: they had no decline to account for since their claim was to be a new movement which (in the West at least) had thoroughly disentangled itself from Islam. Hauling themselves into the modern world did not present the difficulties it did for those still rooted in the umma – hence the respect accorded to Abdul Baha by Christian liberals and universalists like T. K. Cheyne and J. Estlin Carpenter. This too was possibly the period when a Baha'i influence crossed over into the Muslim mainstream as Sharbrodt and Cole have sketched out in their studies of Abdul Baha's relations with Muhammad Abduh and Abul Fazl Gulpaygani's short period at the Azhar seminary in Egypt.[83] Also to come was the celebrated Abdullah Cevdet case in post-Ottoman Turkey in the 1920s.[84]

Baha'i interest in Renan was almost entirely limited to his recycling of Gobineau's account of the Babi martyrs of Tehran in *The Apostles*. However, in an important sense his influence runs through the early stage of Baha'ism's presence in the West not only because of this endorsement but also due to his pre-eminence, which has been clearly established in this chapter, as a conveyer of the nineteenth-century project of the criticism of religion to which Baha'i thinking of the time was partially attuned. Renan pointed out that European scholarship, in an inevitable process which was however a cause of sadness, had moved on from secular objects of inquiry such as Homer and Aristotle to the holy of holies, that is, criticism of the Bible:

> So profound an instinct impels man to search for truth, at the price of his dearest beliefs; this instinct constitutes for noble natures so imperious a duty, that the criticism of the beginnings of a religion is never the work of free thinkers, but of the most enlightened followers of the religion . . . [85]

Here, of course, Renan was referring to himself; from a position of unbelief in the forms and creed of Catholic Christianity he had set out to rescue religion from the incubus of superstition and myth. This was a programme to which Baha'is could confidently join. In his presentations in the West, Abdul Baha promoted the requirement of independent search for truth and an end to *taqlid* which he took to mean imitation of superstitious, worn-out traditions and prejudices. His utilisation of rationalism was never brutal and was anyway accompanied by the Baha'i penchant for allegorising religious ideas and doctrines that were otherwise so steeped in crudity or literalism as to be barely recuperable to the modern intellectual mind. Nonetheless, the sense that Renan was on the right track in removing past superstitions (including the dethronement of Jesus as the incarnate Son of God) might have sufficed for any Baha'i intellectual who had attempted to penetrate the Frenchman's thought-world. However, very few Baha'is would have properly understood Renan's stance on the criticism of religion; it is unlikely they would have reflected very deeply on whether this criticism had gone so far as to endanger belief in the concept of divine revelation itself.[86]

As has been seen from our discussion of *Dawn-Breakers*, problematic aspects of the thinking of the Western experts cited was invariably elided. That Baha'ism incorporated rationalist and demythologising approaches toward Biblical themes and doctrines and so was among the first new religious movements to seek to build into its hermeneutic a modern consciousness did not mean questioning traditional ideas of revelation, as is borne out by the practice of one of its soi-disant proponents of rational methodology. Abul Fazl Gulpaygani, whose 'clerical education was wide ranging, including rational and gnostic philosophy as well as the mainstream Islamic sciences [and whose] intellectual interests included European science and Buddhism',[87] obtained a reputation as a forward-looking scholar on Islamic topics while at Cairo's al-Azhar. Here his rational approach to texts and Averrovian method in interpretation of religious history cut the mustard sufficient for him to make converts to Baha'ism. On the basis of his calls upon Averroës to support his own rationalist method of interpreting myth in Biblical stories, Gulpaygani might have laid claim to a tangential connection to Renan, who had written his thesis on the great Arab humanist philosopher and whose methods in appraising historical religious texts were of course in line with wider Biblical criticism. Gulpaygani promoted Averroës' ideas to support his argument that the prophets were not sent as historians but knowingly indulged the myths and stories current at the time.[88] Whether this idea would have won Renan's assent is doubtful, since it is not clear that he considered Jesus' own understanding as transcending the *Weltanschauung* of his age. Moreover, although he advocated advanced thinking and rationalist hermeneutics of a kind, Gulpaygani had clearly not traversed the period of uncompromising rationalist treatment of miracles performed by eighteenth century and early nineteenth-century agnostic European Biblical scholars that Renan would have.[89] In Amin Banani's opinion, Gulpaygani 'combines the best – and vast – advantages of his traditional knowledge with an open, critical and questioning mind'. His traditionalism was to be found in the style of religious scholarship that looked beyond literal meanings to 'figurative interpretations which differ from the understanding that might be gained from their external sense'.[90]

Although he lacked the subtlety of investing myth with human meaning which Renan achieved in his *Life of Jesus*.

On the question of the 'scientific' approach to the writing of history Abul Fazl adverted to his own *sira* of Baha'ullah claiming that although he believed in the Baha'i faith he had 'not been unduly influenced in the writing of this history by my love or faith. My devotion to Baha'u'llah has not deflected me from the path of fairness'. This was because according to his terminology 'the station of a historian' was,

> beyond that of love and devotion and too sacred to be defiled by bias and prejudice. A historian must put to one side his love or hate for various groups when writing about historical events and must with the utmost justice and equity record what he knows.[91]

However, earlier in the same essay Gulpaygani outlines a methodology he devised for producing *The New History*, an account of Babi history supplementary to Abdul Baha's *Travellers' Narrative*. This involved its untrained editor Mirza Huseyn Hamadani collating material from an early manuscript by one of the martyrs of Tehran, Haji Mirza Jani, 'a religious man' who 'transmitted correctly the events he saw and heard' but having lacked any skill as a historian had 'left out the dates'. By supplying these dates from those given in the court histories, and finally checking the manuscript over with another Baha'i who had lived through the period, Hamadani is bidden to work with 'meticulous care' to 'produce a correct history'. In a manner that stresses 'correctness' and witnesses' religious credentials, confusing veracity with 'the will of God', Gulpaygani undermines his own claim to adopt a scientific methodology.[92] In effect, he was leaving open a space that would attract the writing of Baha'i faith-history to the critical attention of a later generation of scholars. Peter Smith must have had this issue in mind when he wrote in 1983: '[i]t is not yet possible to say whether [the Baha'i Faith] will escape the tensions engendered by the application of "scientific" principles in what, from a Baha'i point of view, are the more sensitive areas of historical analysis and textual criticism'.[93]

Renan's own modernism, of course, was not limited to the criticism of religion, as we have seen it connected him to an orientalist colonialist view of Islam as well. His condemnation of Arabic culture for its negation of Averroës and rational thought in favour of al-Ghazali's mysticism (and hence rejection of philosophy) was known to nineteenth-century Arab thinkers, though it does not appear to have penetrated the consciousness of eastern Baha'i writers.[94] But it is possible, perhaps likely, that Shoghi Effendi, though he could not have accepted his essentialist ideas about Islam or the racial bias that underwrote his dogma concerning Islam and science, might well have been influenced by Renan's forcible reiteration of the orientalist idea that in the nineteenth century Islam 'must everywhere and always be a hindrance to progress and an enemy to reason'.[95] One senses that this notion had sunken into the minds of some (though not all) of the Western Baha'is of the early twentieth century whose writings will be analysed for their orientalist articulations in Chapter 7.

Renan's place in European thought is not what it once was, and the cachet of 'claiming' him as some sort of sponsor, which is what he became for Baha'is from his death in 1892 to the publication of *God Passes By* over fifty years later, tells us a lot about the modern epoch (what Hourani in his overview of modern Arabic thought dubbed 'the liberal Age') when to be rational and progressive was to be at the forefront of modernity. As Hourani's book demonstrated, easterners during this period found the influence of the West desirable to imitate but at the same time troubling, a predicament Edward Said later recalibrated as the gap between 'filiation' and 'affiliation'.[96] Paradoxically, that was a position Baha'ism or as it came to be known, the Baha'i Faith, also needed to negotiate. For while the Baha'i revelation figures in the writing of Shoghi Effendi as the towering fact of the age, indeed of the coming millennium, it nevertheless emerged in the period of late Western colonialism. In order to make its way, as the Church had understood during the hundreds of years of Roman ascendancy, it was necessary in part to pay homage to the dominant power. This the Baha'i leadership did at the time when its locus of origin, the Islamicate world, along with the rest of the non-West was registering Western hegemony not only as political, but also as cultural and spiritual subjugation.

5

Edward Granville Browne and the Writing of Babi Narratives

Gobineau's principal disciple, Edward Granville Browne was integral in bringing the skills of a professional orientalist (which the Frenchman demonstrably lacked) to relaying the detail of the history and tenets of the Babis to a late Victorian and early twentieth-century audience. Working on his own but in parallel and sometimes in collaboration with Rozen and his disciples, Browne occupies an influential link in the chain of orientalist transmission of the Babi movement after Gobineau, Kazem Bek and Bernhard Dorn.[1] Before taking up his college fellowship at Cambridge, in 1887 Browne set off for a year's travel in Persia where he encountered Persians from all walks of society. His report was simultaneously inflected by two parallel considerations, both embedded in his outlook as an orientalist. The first underwrote Babism as a remarkable modern development in the spiritual renewal of the East, while the second stressed in orientalist terms the pristine purism of the Bab's mysticism and his insurrectionary movement against the Qajars which Browne valorised over the modernising but quietist Baha'i development that succeeded it. In later years, disillusioned by the direction the Babi and Baha'i movements had taken, Browne switched his allegiance to Iranian nationalism, which he again articulated in partly orientalist terms, in alliance with some Azali-Babis who were reviving the revolutionary trajectory of Babism in the new direction of the *mashrutih* (Iranian Constitutional Revolution). In his pursuit of pristine Babism, Browne's intervention in the formational Baha'i/Azali succession dispute caused him to play an ambiguous role in an emerging Baha'i narrative. While this involvement reduced and diverted the orientalist's putative scopic powers, his style of narrative, particularly his encapsulation of the ideas of Gobineau concerning the significance and originality of the Bab and his revelation, are nonetheless partly incorporated by Shoghi Effendi into the narrative of *Dawn-Breakers* and *God Passes By*.

A Peculiar Style of Orientalism

Browne's social position as the son of a wealthy Tyneside industrialist together with his medical qualifications were the background to a radical change of vocation when as a young man of twenty-five he started out for Persia in 1887. An early youthful espousal of the cause of the Turks in the Russo–Turk War of 1877–8 followed by individual tuition in oriental languages led him to declare a mission to connect with the East. Under the influence of Gobineau he did so in the committed fashion of an unashamed self-proclaimed pro-Babi. Given his later public profile as an opponent of the Persian policy of the Liberal Government of 1906–14, and his position as Sir Thomas Adams's Professor of Arabic at Cambridge where he trained a generation of career diplomats, quite astonishingly Browne has not as yet been the subject of a full-length biography. His entirely self-directed career has often been accounted for in terms of his 'personal position in the world'. As G. Michael Wickens puts it:

> He was bred to wealth and status and was (particularly in his mature years) a very rich man in his own right. This meant that his time was largely his own . . . and that he could please himself in virtually everything that he did and said.[2]

As such, it is difficult to place Browne within a guild of orientalists potentially at the bid and call of government, like the ill-fated and impecunious E. H. Palmer who was killed as a British agent in Egypt in 1882; or servant of empire and Christian evangelism, William Muir.[3] Their individualism and non-identification with establishment imperatives, as Robert Irwin rightly points out, disqualifies Browne and Gobineau from inclusion within the type of orientalism Said dilated upon. Said, in fact, only mentions Browne once in a list of academic orientalists 'who followed directly in the line of descent from [Edward] Lane'.[4] Those on the list provide a scholarly cohort against which to measure others like Gertrude Bell, T. E. Lawrence and Harry St John

Philby who, posturing as 'Oriental experts', acted as 'agents of empire' and were in a position to formulate oriental policy because of their 'knowledge of the Orient and of Orientals'.[5] Browne is assigned to a category that includes several notorious antagonists of Islam most notably William Muir and eccentric Jewish convert to Christianity D. S. Margoliouth. Margoliouth subscribed to the general view among Christian scholars that Muhammad had authored the Quran out of 'floating stories and traditions largely picked up from hearsay ... his over-wrought mind ... his only teacher'.[6] Given that Margoliouth was one of the critics who disparaged Browne's work on Babism as a topic unsuitable for an academic orientalist to engage in, Said's listing of Browne alongside him is ironic to say the least. Orientalists, no doubt, disagreed and fell out as people in professions will do, but Browne was no antagonist of Islam nor stereotyper of its Prophet. Moreover, as a supporter of the Persian revolution, the trainer of sympathisers in the Tehran embassy, and correspondent with other like-minded sources in the British consular service, he was clearly no agent of the British government either.[7] In fact, in certain ways Browne was a peculiar type of orientalist; consigned by the exposer of orientalism's biases in an uncritical and homogenising manner to a group from which he diverged in fundamental respects, it is not simply that Browne was someone Said found it difficult to account for, he was actually an orientalist who countermanded some of his key arguments.

What then can we say about Browne's orientalism in the context of his study of the Babi movement which is the main focus here? As already noted above, a personal interest in the Babis first led him to travel to Persia where he met a cross-section of society, including members of the movement who were now re-aligned into Baha'i and Azali factions. In his first published essay, 'The Babis of Persia', which appeared in the *Journal of the Royal Asiatic Society* in 1889, Browne paid homage to Gobineau who shared and had originally inspired his enthusiasm for the Bab: 'from [his] graphic and vivid description [in *Religions and Philosophies*] of the first beginnings and early struggles of the Babis I derived more pleasure than I can describe'.[8] Browne's first article on the Babis starts in the form of a narrative which sets a precedent for his treatment of the topic in future publications. It concerned his clandestine meeting with some Baha'is of Isfahan and related the recent martyrdom of two of their number in a shocking quasi-judicial murder contrived by the leading mujtahid of the city. *A Year Amongst the Persians* was published in 1893, by which time Browne had already begun to adopt a pro-Azali attitude, nevertheless it preserves a genuine sense of the awe in which he held the 'grave faces, illuminated with the light of inward conviction, and eyes gleaming with unquenchable faith' of the Baha'is he had encountered in Isfahan and Shiraz.[9] The travelogue gives further support to the contention that few orientalists can have packaged their work in quite so personal a way and to the same intensity as Browne did. Unlike many of the canonical nineteenth-century oriental travellers he eschewed disguise even though his object in travelling to Persia to make contact with 'a proscribed sect' was a highly sensitive one.[10] What does link him to many orientalists, however, is his motivation to be first. Not as discoverer of an untrodden terrain, but as he openly admits, to become the first custodian of documentary evidence about the Babis, a feat to be compared with the work of Anquetil du Perron 'unlocking the secrets of the Zoroastrian religion by going among those who professed it'.[11]

After his visits to Famagusta and Akka in 1890 where he met Subh-i Azal and Baha'ullah respectively, Browne's narrative-line challenged. He already knew from the Baha'is he had met in Persia that Azal had ceased to be 'universally acknowledged by [the Babis] as the Bab's successor, the sole head to whom they confessed allegiance' and, worse still, that the majority 'spoke only of Beha as their chief and prophet . . . that the Bab was merely his herald..'.[12] By 1893, in which year he published *Tarikh-i-Jadid or New History of Mirza Ali Muhammad the Bab*, Browne had enlisted on the side of Subh-i Azal in the Baha'i/Azali schism. His argument was that the Baha'is had suppressed the true history of the Bab and his heroic supporters. This he dressed up as an orientalist issue: the need for 'the earliest records' of the founder's religion to be saved from 'mutilation or . . . embellishment at the hands of his later followers', by passing 'into the hands of strangers, who, while interested in their preservation, have no desire to alter them for better or worse'.[13] The decision Browne made to take on the role of the disinterested 'stranger' is a disingenuous one for it turned out that he was completely won over by the Azalis, notably Shaykh Ahmad Ruhi, who among other things passed off on him a manuscript entitled *Hasht Bihisht*, purportedly by 'an eyewitness to events of early Babism', which was in reality 'a polemic against Bahaism' Ruhi had largely authored himself.[14]

This story has often been told and the point in briefly reviewing it here is that at the heart of it lies a paradox of Browne's orientalism. From a Baha'i point of view if he had 'got it right' and recognised the supremacy of Baha'ullah, his succession, and the direction in which he was taking the Babi movement, he would have been celebrated and showcased by them much more than he was. He did admit, however, quite freely the superiority of Baha'ullah's religion to the Bab's on several occasions.[15] More importantly, as a trained observer who laid claim to an orientalist's dispassionate objectivity, if he had simply recorded the facts in a balanced way Browne's esteem might have been better preserved, but even if he had done so he would still not have escaped the opprobrium cast on his topic of research by fellow orientalists. As it happened, there is a sense that what lowered Browne in their esteem was the personal identification he as a Westerner (and Christian) had with the claims of a mahdi sect in an Islamic country. In case of the *Hasht Bihisht* because he agreed with the Azali case too readily he had fallen prey to deception. Nonetheless, even if Browne seems to present it an obsessive manner there was truth in what he was trying to establish. Baha'is reconfigured Babism according to their own orientation; this began with *Traveller's Narrative* and would be continued in *Dawn-Breakers*. Both Shoghi Effendi and Ahmad Ruhi changed the narrative of Babism. The Guardian's performance of rewriting and interpolation may have been qualitatively different to Ruhi's with its forged claims, but the dispensing of blame depended on taste, so to speak. Both Azalis and Baha'is developed their own Babi narratives to justify the new directions each was moving in. Browne put his finger on the fact that the older narrative was being altered, but where exactly was this to be found? It was difficult to lay his hands on a document that would exemplify Babi ideas authentically. He misdirected charges against Baha'is for suppressing particular texts (the *Nuqtat al-Kaf* which he argued was the sole work of Haji Mirza Jani). Some argued a pure, unadulterated narrative of early Babism of the type he was searching for did not exist.[16] Leastways, there was something Quixotic about the whole affair.

While discerning impressive qualities in Baha'is early on, Browne opted to amplify Azal's character and claim to be the successor of the Bab. Here there was proof in the proposition that Azal had been nominated by the Bab, but it was eventually outstripped by Baha'ullah's amplification of himself in the 'most extreme expression of Shi'i and Babi theories of theophany'.[17] Using dubious anti-Baha'i 'information' given to him by Azalis, Browne entered into their schismatic quarrel with Baha'is instead of maintaining the kind of balanced neutrality anti-Saidians consider to be a vindication of the 'true' orientalism. There were definite elisions in the Baha'i version of Babi history which Denis MacEoin would later demonstrate conclusively. To choose a parallel: in order to placate Rome the evangelists smoothed out Jesus' 'disruptive prophetic action' against the Temple in Jerusalem which 'appears to be what provoked his arrest and crucifixion as a rebel leader'.[18] In the Baha'i narrative of Babism the attempted Babi revolution is exchanged for an unrealistic utopian vision of a peaceful messiah who understood religion in a completely non-political way. Even if the Bab had not represented a threat to the state personally, the Babi movement collectively definitely had done. Browne eventually published *Nuqtat al-Kaf*, a text that did not exclude extreme acts committed by some Babis similar to those found in *Nasikh-i Tavarikh*, and thus succeeded in showing Babis in a completely different light to *Travellers' Narrative*. Missionaries and Ahmadis would have a field-day quoting from this Babi text, seriously undermining the official Baha'i narrative.[19]

Although he could not give his imprimatur to *Traveller's Narrative*, the work Browne translated into English incorporated the first official Baha'i narrative of Babism, and in the introduction he wrote a moving pen-portrait of Baha'ullah that has been widely used in Baha'i literature as well as a reverential one of Subh-i Azal which has not. Also rarely mentioned, the structure and tone of Browne's narrative style had a formative influence upon Shoghi Effendi's writing and is something else Browne bequeathed to the Baha'i faith. Disillusioned eventually by the internecine struggles of a movement embedded within which he had once believed was the story of 'the birth of a faith which may not impossibly win a place amidst the great religions of the world',[20] Browne moved on to follow new paths, ones that attracted greater notice to his name. In addition to his work on Babism, on which he came to be recognised as a major authority, he achieved eminence in other areas of Persian studies. As Abbas Amanat has suggested, his support for the Persian revolution was a re-channelling of the hopes for Iran's renewal that he previously attached to Babism. Also, Browne's training of, and support for, Iranian orientalists impacted substantively on Iranian cultural production.²¹ In orchestrating a campaign for a 'Persian national awakening' in *The Persian Revolution, 1905–1909*, and outlining an Iranian national narrative in his four volume *Literary History of Persia* (1906–24), Browne influenced later Iranian nationalist thought in a manner that has been strongly aligned with a type of orientalism more sophisticated than the kind Said pilloried.²²

There is a consistency in Browne's practice of promoting religious and/or national causes while at the same time acting in a high-handed orientalist manner. As I have argued elsewhere, such a trait was shared by a small group of orientalist travellers to the Middle East, later dubbed 'trouble-makers'.²³ These developed a form of split-orientalism acting in the imperious manner of orientalist experts in support of eastern causes while messaging against the betrayal of their own government. Orientalism does not have to signify, as Said suggested, Europeans' total inability to place themselves on a par with easterners. The narratives orientalists produced did not always demonstrate an urge to dominate the East. Orientalism of the kind practised by David Urquhart, W. S. Blunt and E. G. Browne was applied to sponsorship of oriental causes such as passionate espousal of the Ottoman Empire, the desirability of returning the caliphate to the Arabs, or the promotion of an obscure Iranian mahdi movement. These orientalists took upon themselves the mantle of truth-tellers in proclaiming their preferred causes and we can see that in Browne's efforts on behalf of both the Babis and Iranian self-determination, in comparison with the oriental party under advocacy when it came to the power to sponsor, enunciate and narrate it was the Western orientalist who occupied the more privileged subject position.

Appropriating Orientalism: Browne and Curzon's Place in Baha'i Literature

Besides being co-opted for the experts' notes to *Dawn-Breakers* (though often without his author name being cited), Browne's influence on Shoghi Effendi was important for the style and even the lexical items he employed in his estimation of the significance of the Babi movement as a potentially new world religion. The sense of this is summed up by Browne, albeit in sober style in one of his last major publications on the subject of Babi-Baha'ism:

But the chief interest of the study of the Babi and Baha'i movements is, as it seems to me, neither political nor ethical, but historical, because of the light it throws on the genesis and evolution of other religions. Renan emphasised this in his work *Les Apôtres*, and it was he, I think, who said that to understand the genesis and growth of a new religion one must go to the East where religions still grow.[24]

The emergence of the Babis and Baha'is evidenced to the perennial spirit of the East, in particular to the fertile 'theological activity of the Persian mind'.[25] Missing here are eulogies on the heroism of the Babis of the kind that once enthused Browne's writing on the subject. Babism is no longer described as a faith 'worth suffering and dying for' (which as we saw had once been a paramount factor for both Gobineau and Renan).[26] Somewhat ironically, of the handful of introductions Browne wrote to his books on the subject of the Babis and Baha'is, the one in *New History* is closest in its prosody to Shoghi Effendi's. We can see from the passage below how it begins by celebrating the Bab and his faith in oratorical mode, before swerving toward diatribe, implicitly aimed against the Baha'i leadership:

> Half a century has not yet elapsed since Mirza 'Ali Muhammad, the young Seer of Shiraz, first began to preach the religion which now counts its martyrs by hundreds and its adherents by hundreds of thousands; which seemed at one time to menace the supremacy alike of the Kajar dynasty and the Muhammadan faith in Persia, and may still not improbably prove an important factor in the history of Western Asia; and which, within the memory of men not yet arrived at an age in any way unusual, has passed successively through the Prophetic and Apostolic periods, and entered on that phase of intestinal dissension and political opportunism whither, sooner or later, every religion . . . inevitably comes.[27]

Shoghi Effendi's *magnus opus* on the Babi and Baha'i faiths (incorporating both movements as a unitary 'Cause' over the first one hundred years of its history) is *God Passes By*. A reader well acquainted with the text might note how it remoulds Browne's phrase 'Prophetic and Apostolic periods' as 'the Heroic, the Primitive, the Apostolic Age of the Faith of Baha'u'llah', and later simply 'the Formative Age of the Faith of Baha'u'llah'. Browne's expression 'nascent faith', used a page further on from the passage quoted above reverberates in *God Passes By* in such phrases as 'momentum of God's nascent Faith', 'God's nascent Revelation', moving on to 'nascent institutions' and 'nascent community'.[28] Both writers excel at the construction of complex single sentences sometimes stretching over a whole page, employing myriad subordinate clauses and parallelism:

> That a young visionary should arise proclaiming a new religion designed to replace and supersede all existing creeds; that many persons of learning, virtue and position should eagerly embrace and boldly proclaim his doctrines; that gorgeous but unsubstantial visions of a New Creation wherein there should be neither injustice nor discord, of a Reign of God's Saints on Earth, and of a Universal Theocracy conformed in every detail to a mystical Theosophy . . . should exercise so powerful an influence, not only over philosophers and scholars, but over peasants and artisans, as to make them ready and eager to meet death in its most terrible forms not by scores, but by hundreds; that this new faith, set forth, for the most part, not in the language of the people, but in Arabic treatises of interminable length . . . should have power to inspire its votaries with a courage so stubborn as to threaten for several years the very existence of the established religion and the reigning dynasty, and should stir up an insurrection which all the armed forces of the Persian king . . . all the tortures which an Asian tyrant could devise . . . could . . . only check for a while, but not permanently subdue . . .[29]

> He Who communicated the original impulse to so incalculable a Movement was none other than the promised Qá'im (He who ariseth), the Sahibu'z-Zaman (the Lord of the Age), Who assumed the exclusive right of annulling the whole Qur'anic Dispensation, Who styled himself "*the Primal Point from which have been generated all created things* . . . The People among whom He appeared were the most decadent race in the civilized world, grossly ignorant, savage, cruel, steeped in prejudice, servile in their submission to an almost deified hierarchy, recalling in their abjectness the Israelites of Egypt in the days of Moses, in their fanaticism the Jews in the days of Jesus, and in their perversity the idolators of Arabia in the days of Muhammad. The arch-enemy who repudiated His claim, challenged His authority, persecuted His Cause, succeeded in almost quenching His light, and who eventually became disintegrated under the impact of His Revelation was the Shi'ah priesthood. Fierce, fanatic, unspeakably corrupt, enjoying unlimited ascendancy over the masses, jealous of their position, and irreconcilably opposed to all liberal ideas . . .[30]

Repetition of syntactical forms, elevated register and ornate lexical flourishes are evident in both passages and demonstrate Shoghi Effendi's choice of a Victorian prose-style similar to, though not solely imitative of, Browne's. A high incidence of Latinate lexis dispersed throughout his writings witnesses to the influence of his preferred author Edward Gibbon. (Why he employed what I consider to be a colonial style of writing will be discussed in connection with his orientalism in Chapter 7.)

Browne influenced not only the Guardian's style but the way in which, particularly in *Year Amongst the Persians*, he sets out Muslim–Azali–Baha'i emnities in the form of in-depth synchronic slices (see below). Not only is the book an invaluable historical source it lays out the ground plan of a dispute that still reverberates even today. But Browne's distinctly individual view of nineteenth-century Persia did not so much stress the malign activities of the Shi'i ulama as the weaknesses and cupidity of Shah Nasir al-Din. *Year Amongst the Persians* was not Shoghi Effendi's source for the belaboured condemnation of 'the Shi'ah priesthood' seen in the extract from *God Passes By*. In a Gobineauesque way Browne's work portrays a variegated society in which there is room for all types of manifestation of the spirit of the Orient. To find the ulama epitomised as moribund, corrupt and fanatic in the way they appear in *Dawn-Breakers* and *God Passes By* we must turn to the accounts of other Western travellers of the period, most notably *Persia and the Persian Question*, George Nathaniel, later Lord, Curzon's monumental description of a decaying oriental society. Curzon's expertise as a politician who 'knew' the East was growing around the time Browne was establishing himself as a young orientalist concentrating on his own pioneering study of Babism. Curzon and the school of Tory imperialism appear to have overemphasised the size and role of Baha'is in Iran proposing for them, at the expense of the Shi'i ulama, a role as agents in the revival of a weak Persia vulnerable to the penetration of Russia.

When Shoghi Effendi turned to his work Curzon had been dead some six or seven years. As we saw in Chapter 3, *Dawn-Breakers* is characterised by its incorporation of a large number of quotations from European orientalists in the form of footnotes. In the introduction it goes so far as to reproduce multiple chunks from Curzon's book, in the process valorising *Persia and the Persian Question* as Curzon intended it to be, an epitome of scholarship on Persia which subsequent writing could not avoid referencing and quoting from.[31]

Shoghi Effendi's extensive borrowing from *Persia* had the effect of syphoning off its authority for his own narrative, as well as providing a summative statement on Persia's social and religious arbitrariness and tyranny. In Saidian terms, Curzon's is a canonical orientalist text for the way in which it pronounced on the binary of East and West, the stasis of Persia as an oriental society, and the perfidy of Persians as orientals. In reusing such a quintessential piece of orientalist writing to help set the scene for his history, Shoghi Effendi was in effect signing up Baha'is as believers in Curzon's magisterial dismissal of Islam as a fixed, unchangeable entity. Under the flag of this vision of a decadent Persia, with its incontestable orientalist tropes and monolithic binaries, the emerging Baha'i discourse was enlisted into mainstream orientalism.

> Marvellously adapted alike to the climate, character, and occupations of those countries upon which it has laid its adamantine grip, Islam holds its votary in complete thrall from the cradle to the grave. To him, it is not only religion, it is government, philosophy, and science as well. The Muḥammadan conception is not so much that of a state church as, if the phrase may be permitted, of a church state. The undergirders with which society itself is warped round are not of civil, but of ecclesiastical, fabrication; and, wrapped in this superb, if paralysing, creed, the Musulman lives in contented surrender of all volition, deems it his highest duty to worship God and to compel, or, where impossible, to despise those who do not worship Him in the spirit, and then dies in sure and certain hope of Paradise.[32]

In addition to pronouncing on the decay of Islam, the borrowed passages project an essentialist view of Persians in a trans-historical rendition of the fiendish 'Persian character' trope:

> Nothing is more shocking to the European reader, in pursuing his way through the crime-stained and bloody pages of Persian history during the last and, in a happily less degree, during the present century, than the record of savage punishments and abominable tortures, testifying alternately to the callousness of the brute and the ingenuity of the fiend. The Persian character has ever been fertile in device and indifferent to suffering; and in the field of judicial executions it has found ample scope for the exercise of both attainments.[33]

By these means the voice of the soon-to-be viceroy of India, under the rule of one of whose predecessors, Lord Canning, rebels of the Great Rebellion of 1857 had been fired from the mouths of British canons, is written into the official Baha'i narrative of Babism. Muslims and Islamic achievement are confined to a finalised historical past, as superseded by the impetus of modern civilisation as the Quran was by Baha'ullah's *Kitab-i Aqdas*, and the Baha'i faith is located within the idiom of enlightened modernisation.

Perhaps the main difference between Curzon and Browne's view of Persia is that whereas the former stands outside his subject typically as an orientalist reporter, in *Year Amongst the Persians* 'Browne does not observe, he participates'. Quite correctly absolving Browne of orientalism, we should specify of the Curzonian type, MacEoin is right to situate his book within the pilgrimage genre of Middle East travel writing.[34] In an expanded register of orientalisms, Browne's therefore falls into the category of the orientalised-Westerner, or sympathiser with the orient, as I shall argue in Chapter 7. For Curzon, the East was not without its allure but he never for a moment felt tempted to go native on his journeys. *Year Amongst the Persians* sees Browne seeking to keep his interest in Babism hidden from his hosts and the others he meets along the way, almost all of whom are Muslims. The text can, however, be read in such a way as to uncover a Muslim–Babi (and Baha'i–Azali) animosity running through many of the dialogues. While pursuing his fascination for the Bab and his heroic followers, the first person narrator needs to retain a façade of being all things to all men. His sympathy for Azalis and Baha'is is apprehendable at the obvious level of their membership of a persecuted minority; their animosity toward Muslims comes across to the reader by means of their being granted a voice through the mediation of the narrator. We are especially made aware of how Baha'is perceive themselves as followers of a new modernising religion, and how in stark contrast they view the Shi'a population as oafish and trapped in backwardness. (It should, however, be borne in mind that independently of their oppression of Baha'is and Azalis, Shi'a moral turpitude is also pointed out in the mistreatment and marginalisation of Zoroastrians.) Browne goes so far as to portray an embryonic Baha'i triumphalism that derives from Babi-Baha'i scriptures and the sufferings of the believers at the hands of ulama and secular rulers alike. This consciousness would receive fuller articulation in Shoghi Effendi's writings, especially *God Passes By* which projects a triumphant 'destiny' for the new faith that is dualistically marked off against a drastic decline in Islam's worldly fortunes with a condign punishment waiting to be meted out to the persecutors of Babi-Baha'is. This providential narrative features in vignettes taken from the Babi equivalent of the 'Sufferings of the Saints' genre of writing. One example is the reported fate of the mullah who actively strove to accomplish the death of the Bab and who ends up on his death-bed:

> his face turned black, save that one side flecked with white spots; [. . .] loathsome alike to sight and smell, smearing his countenance with filth, and crying upon God to whiten his face on the Last Day, when the faces of others should be black. So he died.[35]

Set in juxtaposition is a passage from Baha'ullah's 'epistle to one of the Turkish ministers who had oppressed him [foretelling] the catastrophes impending over the Ottoman Empire'.[36]

From the period when their consuls lobbied for the alleviation of their persecution, to the moment when European power directly penetrated the Ottoman Middle East at the close of the Great War, the elite of the Western states (and it might be added, Russia in its earlier Tsarist phase) sometimes displayed sympathy toward Baha'is. Travellers consistently inflated their number: John Wishard in *Twenty Years in Persia* set them at five-hundred thousand; the Persian mimic-man turned American missionary Isaac Adams raised the number at the start of the 1890s to three million, that is, nearly one third of the population of Iran at the time. Curzon estimated it at one million and London *Times* Middle East editor Valentine Chirol at one and a half million.[37] Why this overestimation? It has been suggested to me by a Baha'i scholar that at this moment in time the reputation of the Baha'is was very widespread causing outsiders to misconstrue their numbers. In other words, the inflation of Baha'i numbers might well have been linked to wishful thinking about the possibility of their becoming agents of change who could bring about a more favourable orientation within Persia (as far as British interests were concerned). In the mind of the British governing class Baha'is were 'modern' and if they took over the country it would be friendly to Britain (Russians might have felt similarly). Beyond overestimating Baha'i numbers and their potential influence in Iran, parallels could be drawn between Baha'is and Muslims in Persia and the position of Muslims in British territories. In their native land Baha'is were not potentially rebellious like the Muslims of India; as a small quietist group in Palestine they represented no threat to the British occupation, while in Britain itself, the tiny number of indigenous Baha'is mostly went unnoticed and were not viewed as 'the enemy within' like converts Abdullah Quilliam, Marmaduke Pickthall, and other Muslims who supported Ottoman Turkey.[38]

Ahmadi Schism, Western Conversions and anti-Baha'i Polemic

The Baha'is saw off their Azali adversaries while carrying on their struggle with the mujtahids in Iran, the power centre of the world's Twelver Shi'a. The 1908 counter-coup against the Persian constitutional movement which led to the deaths of a number of Azali activists meant the eclipse of the Azal faction brooked no return.[39] In the same year the Ahmadiyya mahdi-messiah Ghulam Ahmad died, and though for a few years a veneer of unity was maintained in the community under his long time second-in-command, now first khalifa, Hakim Nuruddin, underneath two parties were forming. As Spencer Lavan noted, a new calibre of convert had begun to come to prominence, in particular two fluent English speakers, both educated in law at Forman Christian College, Punjab. Muhammad Ali assumed editorship of *Review of Religions*, and Khwaja Kamaluddin took strides in Ahmadi-led propagation of Islam centred at the Woking Mosque in England. Muhammad Ali used his position to soften adversarial elements in Ahmadism and to elide references to Ghulam Ahmad's claim to be a prophet with the aim of broadening the periodical's appeal. The leader of the other party, Bashiruddin Mahmud Ahmad, the surviving second son of Ghulam Ahmad, became khalifa on the death of Hakim Nuruddin in 1914, commanding the loyalty of the majority of Ahmadis. The party that included Muhammad Ali and Khwaja Kamaluddin split away. Beneath the petty disputes lay a rift between,

> those . . . prepared to commit themselves to more open relationships with fellow Muslims and for a more active concern for political issues [the Lahoris] as against those who closely identified with all the claims and position of Ghulam Ahmad as Promised Messiah [the Qadianis].[40]

Yohann Friedmann argued that 'Prophetology ... was one of the main reasons why the Ahmadi community split in two sections in 1914'.[41] Ghulam Ahmad's claims had been contradictory:

> In his early work he stopped short of claiming the title of prophet, but his reticence gradually faded away and was replaced by a bold and persistent claim to prophetic status ... the existence of this varied material allowed each of the two factions to argue that its interpretation was the correct one and that its adversaries were guilty of corrupting the original message of the founder.[42]

As in the case of the Babi schism, the smaller, more intellectually dynamic group would eventually lose out to the hugely more numerical one which would proclaim the founder's mahdi-messiah claims more shrilly and unreservedly. Nonetheless, for more than two decades after the split with the majority Qadianis the Anjuman Ahmadiyya Isha'at Islam in Lahore oversaw a notable campaign of recruitment in the name of Islam in Europe. Their success at gaining Western converts placed them in a strange position. Mainstream Muslims, including the leader of the Salafi movement and editor of the influential journal *al-Manar*, Muhammad Rashid Rida, were very hostile. However, Umar Ryad writes: 'we find that these Muslim reformists harshly attacked the Ahmadiyya doctrines, particularly their pacifistic view of jihad in Islam, but often praised their *da'wa* (missionary) activities in Europe on the other'. Another Salafi, Moroccan writer Taqi l-Din al-Hilali 'reached a conclusion that the Ahmadiyya mission in Europe was *useful* and *harmful* at the same time'. Rida accused Muhammad Ali's translation of the Quran into English of 'attempt[ing] to destroy Islam from within by disseminating the Ahmadiyya's "false" doctrines on revelation and by abrogating Qur'anic rulings, such as jihad' while the Ahmadiyya movement as a whole faced the familiar charge of 'collaboration with ... British colonial authorities'.[43] Here was a paradox indeed: Ahmadis were both aligned with British colonialism and at the same time converting Britons, upper-class ones such as Lord Headley who under the spiritual tutelage of Khawja Kamaluddin embraced Islam in 1913. In their proselytism the Ahmadis were designedly non-sectarian and most British converts identified as Muslim rather than Ahmadi. Clearly connected to the establishment, by merely becoming a Muslim Headley was engaging in an act which members of his class in church and government (albeit to varying degrees) would have considered subversive. He announced his reasons for converting in two articles in the Woking Mosque's house journal *Muslim India and Islamic Review* in which 'he welcomed Islam as a simple, monotheistic and, above all, classless faith without leaders and bodies bidding for temporal power'.[44] Ahmadi Islam might have been heretical and tarred with colonialism, but it was also modern, especially in its promulgation of a tolerant sectarian-free Islam, and without challenging the coloniser in a political way was spreading the religion of the Empire's despised Other in a far more direct and open way than Baha'ism was at the same time.[45]

So far, the main focus has been trained upon the Babi and Baha'i movements, in particular how Baha'ism developed out of its Babi millennialism from which its leaders sought to distance themselves as far as the Ottoman milieu in which they lived would permit. We have viewed how this past, especially its Iranian Babi stage, was scrutinised by orientalists like E. G. Browne and how this in turn impacted upon later official Baha'i narratives. As the pathfinder in this area of transcending *khatm al-nubuwwa* or moving beyond the fundamental Islamic tenet of Muhammad the final prophet, it is hardly surprising that Baha'ism should have engaged a new contender who might want to measure himself against his predecessors. In the late 1890s before he became the first Ahmadi khalifa, it is a curious fact that Hakim Nuruddin was in contact with distinguished Baha'i scholar Abul Fazl Gulpaygani. They seem to have had a cordial correspondence, with the future khalifa posing a number of questions on topics related to stories and ordinances common to Christianity and Islam.[46] An Ahmadi critique of both Babi and Baha'i movements did not begin until Ghulam Ahmad's pieces appeared in *Review of Religions* between 1907 and 1908. Ghulam Ahmad's articles and later ones by Muhammad Ali and some Qadiani scholars collectively suggest that, to employ an idiomatic phrase, Ahmadis had Baha'ism 'in their sights', but so far the favour has not been returned.[47] The Ahmadi polemic against Babism and Baha'ism falls outside the Irano-centric categories MacEoin had in mind when he referred to Muslim polemic against the Baha'is of Iran.[48] Ahmadi criticism demonstrates a preoccupation with their own mahdi narratives as they emerged from both sides of the Ahmadi schism, so it is not surprising that their anti-Baha'i writing is not congruent with the type constructed by other Muslims. Ahmadi texts focused on unpicking key aspects of Baha'i narratives, particularly those on Babism and the Azali–Baha'i split, as well as later factionalism among Baha'is themselves. Understandably, the messianic claims of both the Bab and Baha'ullah also receive treatment, most importantly in Ghulam Ahmad's writings. The *Review of Religions* articles all purport to be by Ghulam Ahmad himself but some, particular the last of February 1908 may have benefited from the assistance of an editor, namely, Muhammad Ali.[49] Outside of these the first extensive statement on the Baha'i narrative of Babism was set out by Muhammad Ali in his *History and Doctrines of the Babi Movement*, published in 1933 (at the start of the second decade of the guardianship and a year after the publication of *Dawn-Breakers*). In 1960 a compilation of articles previously published in Urdu by Qadiani Ahmadi scholars appeared under the title *The Babi and Baha'i Religion*.[50]

Ahmadi–Baha'i criticism has yet to be the subject of sustained academic study. The presumption must be that the former viewed the Baha'i faith as a competitor, and it would be interesting to isolate the theological issues under dispute and to scrutinise more closely how Ahmadis relate these to their own truth claims. The overall significance of their polemic could then be gauged relative to the space the respective Ahmadi groups saw their own missions as occupying. Analysis of these areas could, among other things, help to clarify the respective modernist pretensions of the Ahmadis and Baha'is in juxtaposition to their mahdi orientations, and both highlight and situate their responses to the issues surrounding the extension, modification, or superseding of Islam described in the Rippin quote at the beginning of the book. Although considerations of space preclude an extensive comparison on these lines, a preliminary sketch of the issues will be attempted below. It is clear from Ghulam Ahmad's articles that the Ahmadi response to the Babi-Baha'i development would be mainly limited to negative accounts of its history accompanied by close scriptural readings often though not always of a nit-picking kind. Discussion below will centre on contrastive analysis of Ahmadi positions vis-à-vis Baha'i narratives in which particular focus falls on factors such as mahdi claims and the doctrine of jihad, as well as upon how the work of orientalist E. G. Browne, as suggested by MacEoin, operates as an anti-Baha'i polemical aid. A further dimension to the Ahmadi critique of Baha'ism that will be discussed in the succeeding section will be the manner in which it links to concerns belonging to the larger debate between orientalism and Islam during the colonial period in which both Baha'i and Ahmadi narratives were composed.

The head of the Lahori branch of the Ahmadiyya did not limit his comments on the Iranian mahdi movements solely to his book *History and Doctrines*. Babi-Bahaism is also addressed in a chapter Muhammad Ali included in *The Ahmadiyya Movement*, first published in Urdu in 1931. It begins with the heading 'Ahmadiyyat is not a separate religion'.

> There are many misconceptions prevailing among people about the Ahmadiyya Movement. The greatest of all is that it is a religion quite separate from Islam like Babism or Bahaism . . . It is apparent that had Ahmadiyyat been a separate religion, like the Babi or Bahai faith, its activities obviously would not have been confined to the spread of Islam. Whatever work has been done in this age about the propagation of Islam, in Europe, America and other countries of the world, the greater part of it is due to the efforts of the followers of the Ahmadiyya Movement. In this connection the literature produced by Muslims is either the result of the activities of this Movement or has been done under its influence.[51]

From the beginning Muhammad Ali informs the reader of the Lahori emphasis on *da'wa*. Babism and Baha'ism provide a vehicle for criticising the Qadianis since both mahdi movements had set off on different routes which led them into treating *mahdawiyya* differently. Lahori Ahmadis for their part were wedded to their role as missionaries of Islam as clearly stated by Muhammad Ali. Implicit in the argument he is making is that Ahmadiyyat in its Lahori version was opposed to carrying Ghulam Ahmad's claims so far as to move outside of mainstream Islam, which was the path the Qadianis had taken. The anti-Baha'i critique taken up by the Ahmaddiyya of both parties concentrated on the two Iranian movements' heterodoxy, framing Babism as an extremist Shi'a sect that with the aid of *kitman* became increasingly more heterodox until it finally broke the bounds of Islam entirely.

The Bab had derived his title from 'either the Ismailis or earlier Shia literature'. Referring to the transfer of the rump Babi leadership to Baghdad in 1853 after the failed assassination attempt on the shah, Muhammad Ali notes: 'in its early stages an offshoot of the Shi'a sect [Shakhism], it was more suited for the Persian temperament, and the Sunni Turk has had little fascination for it'.⁵² The Babi episode as a whole was of a kind to seriously shock a mainstream Sunni audience. At the fort known as Shaykh Tabarsi in northwest Iran, government forces were besieging a group of Babis led by Mullah Husayn-i Bushrui who had initially raised the Black Standard of the Qaim in Khorasan. They are shown to have committed murders in a local village. This demonstrated the practice of violent jihad that was opposite to all that Ahmadism stood for: 'The Babis took up the sword to establish a Babi kingdom, as they sincerely believed that to fill the earth with justice, the Mahdi must in accordance with the traditions take up the sword'. In response to this militancy, 'the Government took action against [the Babis] very cautiously, and only when they began to commit atrocities against the civil population'.⁵³ Needless to say, this interpretation represents an exact reversal of the official Baha'i stance in *Traveller's Narrative* which Muhammad Ali actually quotes from. But it could be substantiated by reference to the *Nuqtat al-Kaf* from which he quotes more extensively. He also recounts incidents at the conference of Babis at Badasht which elicited the contempt of Muslims who read about them in *Nasikh-i Tavarikh*. The court history together with *Nuqtat al-Kaf* is the main source for emphasising the lawlessness of the Babis.⁵⁴ This episode is also highlighted in the Qadiani work, *The Babi and Baha'i Religion*, though not by citing *Nuqtat al-Kaf* which the authors seem not to have read. Here the Bab's abrogation of Islamic sharia is foregrounded along with a list of nine points in the new Babi programme including its exclusion of all non-Babis, except traders, from a future Babi state, and the insertion into a new Babi sharia of the ordinance 'any one who hurts the feelings of the Bab, or his successors after him, was to be killed; and for bringing about his death every possible means could be adopted'. The Qadiani account also manages to raise the matter of 'foreign powers', specifically the part played by the Russian embassy in saving Baha'ullah's life during the 1852 massacres.⁵⁵

As the Christian missionaries did in their polemical literature, Muhammad Ali uses Browne's collection of documents in *Materials for the Study of the Baha'i Religion* to highlight the Baha'i–Azali and the later intra-Baha'i schism (between the mainstream cohort who were obedient to Abdul Baha and the small party of defectors led by his brother Muhammad Ali). While Baha'ullah is blamed for the killings of Azalis and his behaviour displayed as duplicitous and immoral the aim, of course, is to discredit the movement in general.[56] All of this confirms MacEoin's point that Browne's conclusions 'were drawn on by opponents of the Baha'i movement', in this case by a competitor mahdi sect. Ahmadi works tend to dismiss Ali Muhammad Shirazi as a failed mahdi, instancing as proof his death and the erasure of so many of his followers. Muhammad Ali, as we might expect from someone whose forte was polemical debate, displays scholarly thoroughness of a sort in his analysis of the Babi-Baha'i concept of divine manifestation which he suggests is transferred barely altered from the Bab to Baha'ullah and traces to its Ismaili origin. In each instance he argues the doctrine that substantiated both figures' claims implied the claim to divinity, a blasphemy for which he finds evidence in earlier extremist Shi'i sects. Baha'is would argue that his readings of Baha'ullah's statements implying divinity are literal and that they should in fact be taken figuratively, but this is part of Muhammad Ali's project of assigning both Iranian mahdi movements to the *ghuluw*. The conclusion to *History and Doctrines* equates 'Babism, and its offshoot, Baha'ism, with a repetition not only of the doctrines of the Ismailiyya but also of the horrible deeds of murder in the attempt to bring about a revolution'.[57] The Lahori Ahmadis' attempt to mute the mahdi-prophet element in Ahmadism is evident in the emphases made by Khwaja Kamaluddin and Muhammad Ali in their *da'wa* work and scholarship, respectively. The latter took pains to establish the difference between the Lahori stance of loyalty to Islam and its opposite: that of the Babis and Baha'is who had eagerly sought separation from Islam. As can be seen in his attacks on all stages of Babi-Baha'ism, Muhammad Ali's criterion of heterodoxy was divergence from Hanifite-Sunni Islam and hence his position was essentially anti-Shi'a, although his condemnation of Babi violence was also intended to emphasise the Ahmadi position on jihad. (This was perhaps opportunistic since he must have been aware that it clearly undermined the position of official Baha'ism.)

To conclude this survey, we return to the beginning of the Ahmadi critique, to a performance of some singularity in which one would-be mahdi dismisses two other messengers. Ghulam Ahmad's characterisation of himself as the true Mahdi leads him to contrast his claim to those of the Bab and Baha'ullah. Responding to well-known prophesies of Baha'ullah's such as his prediction of the fall of the Emperor Louis Napoleon, Ahmad has in mind his own career of weaponising prophecy by announcing the likely times of death of his opponents and predicting pandemics and earthquakes:

> Accepting all these [Baha'i] interpretations to be true, they show nothing more than this that the signs of the advent of a messenger promised to appear in the latter days have all been fulfilled and therefore the present is the time of the appearance of that messenger. They do not show Bab or Bahaulla to be that messenger. To establish their claims it must be shown that signs were shown by them. Such proof, however, we do not meet with anywhere in the Babi literature, and in its absence a seeker after truth is compelled to reject their claims. The only sign of Bahaulla that is related . . . is the downfall or destruction of certain monarchs to whom Bahaulla addressed letters or tablets containing the 'Announcement of His perfect presence . . .' some of the imperial 'creatures' of Bahaulla are said to have heard his message respectfully and they were saved while others were said to have treated it contemptuously and they met with ruin. It needs hardly to be added that these assertions are as far off from being *proofs* of the truth of the revelation of Bahaulla as the fanciful explanations of the words of the Holy Quran and the Bible referred to above.[58]

The criterion of fulfilling and making prophecy in a manner that was verifiable and constituted proof of prophethood, on which basis he dispatched the claims of the Bab and Baha'ullah, was clearly a serious matter for Ghulam Ahmad. His chief and arguably most effective lieutenant, Muhammad Ali took a more sophisticated view: he attempted to smooth out claims of prophethood as part of a method of encouraging believers and reviving faith; prophecy therefore was not a sure sign of a new revelation. In contrast Bashiruddin Mahmud Ahmad continued to refer to his father's prophecies.[59] In these aspects the Qadianis and Baha'is share a common aspiration extending well beyond that of the reformer or *mujaddid* figure, playing prophetology large, and becoming the winners in the schisms that conflicted their respective movements. While the Azalis turned away from prophethood to political action, Muhammad Ali's distancing of the Lahoris from it brought him closer to the Islamic fold, as confirmed by Marmaduke Pickthall who worked amicably with him (and Khwaja Kamaluddin). Though he knew about Muhammad Ali's Ahmadi background, Pickthall believed 'his premises are sound . . . There are some, no doubt, who will disagree with his general findings, but they will not be from those from whom Al-Islam has anything to hope in the future'.[60]

More Ahmadi Positions: Orientalism, Modernism and In-betweenness

Integral to my analysis of the various discourses emerging from these mahdi movements is the aim of locating them within the colonial contexts in which they were written. Regarding the proposition that the Ahmadiyyat endorsed orientalists in a similar way to Baha'is, we have seen that a figure such as Muhammad Ali who, unlike the Qadiani scholars, could read sources in English as well as Arabic and Persian ones, used Browne's version of the Persian text of *Nuqtat al-Kaf* as well as the English texts in *Materials* to advantage his argument against Babism and Baha'ism. But using orientalist scholarship was not the same as indulging in orientalism. Besides, when it came to study of his own faith, with the exception of missionaries and Christian scholars (e.g., Walter and Addison), in Muhammad Ali's lifetime few orientalists studied the Ahmadiyyat. Later in the twentieth century, however, Western scholars of Urdu such as Lavan and Friedmann wrote solid historical studies on the movement and more recent scholarship (e.g., by Antonio Gualtieri) has tended to defend Ahmadism relative to mainstream Islam. Nicholas Evans has very recently emphasised the Qadiani Ahmadi movement's adversarial aspects and pointed out its sense of exceptionalism and strategy of condemning non-Ahmadi Muslim violence as heretical (*takfir*) and abuse of jihad.[61] Despite their anomalous situation, holding tenaciously to the position that they are Muslims, Ahmadis have remained on the Islamic side of arguments concerned with upholding and sustaining Islam per se. In relation to their relatively orthodox interpretation of sharia, and as upholders of the law of separation of the sexes, the Qadianis could hardly entertain orientalists' arguments about the degradation of Muslim women in purdah. Moreover, Lahori intellectual figures such as Khwaja Kamaluddin and Muhammad Ali were quite close in the positions they took to pro-British Indian modernists like Sayyid Ahmad Khan, Sayyid Amir Ali, and Khuda Bakhsh who upheld liberal, rational and tolerant positions.[62] Smith characterised Muhammad Ali as the 'intellectual, slightly nationalist' ('for his reaction to the Cawnpore mosque incident') leader of Ahmadiyyat who approached 'nearer to ordinary liberal Islam'. The Lahori, nonetheless, dismissed Ahmad Khan's efforts to solve the problems facing Muslims in the modern world as 'slavish imitation of European thought', but he did not seriously depart from the Ahmadi movement's sycophantic panegyric of the British government as its protector and saviour.[63] Under Muhammad Ali's editorship (up to 1914) *Review of Religions* ran a diet of articles, as Ron Geaves has pointed out, designed to fulfil,

> three goals: to inspire and reinvigorate new Muslim converts in the West . . . to offer a clearer understanding of Islam to non-Muslim intellectuals; and to disconcert Christians who were anti-Islam and keen to promote their own theology of divinity and salvation.[64]

Even allowing for its trade-mark mixture of Ahmadi doctrines on Ghulam Ahmad's prophethood, abolition of jihad and subversion of Christian and mainstream Muslim teaching on the death of Christ, the journal rarely strayed into orientalist territory. In fact in India it set the bar for a movement that shared with other Muslim modernists a desire for 'reform of the more obvious superstitions and corruptions; [together] with a little liberalism . . . an emotional security against Christianity . . . and the authoritarianism of an accepted dogmatic infallibility'.[65]

According to missionary H. A. Walter however, in his Urdu writings,

> [i]t would seem that Ahmad painted the picture of present-day Islam as black as possible largely in his own interest. If the decadence of Islam has been due to its falling away from the teaching and example of the living Muhammad of the seventh century, its rejuvenation in the twentieth can only come through the teaching and example of a living 'magnetizer' to use a favourite Ahmadi expression. This person is the promised Messiah.[66]

Ahmadi vitriol against non-Ahmadi Muslims and Christians compared not so well with Abdul Baha's patient endorsement of progressive doctrines that conduced to universalism (particularly of the type promoted by liberal pre-war Christian movements) and inter-communal understanding. Ahmadi writers attacked the *maulvis* for 'incendiary preachings of the doctrine of *Jehad* and inflammatory writings of the *Mullas* of the old ignorant school [which] serv[ed] [to] keep alive the combustion of fanaticism in the emotional hearts of the blind zealots'.[67] However, this did not operate in the mode of sustained anti-clericism to be found in Baha'i publications post-Abdul Baha which increasingly were empowered by the anti-Islam rhetoric of hardline Western orientalism. During Ahmad's lifetime his attacks against the '*ghazi jihadists*' among the Indian ulama had an imperial context and were generated out of his special linkage of his prophethood and the prerogative this gave him to cancel *dar al-harb* in the context of British rule. They did not feed on any binaries he might have picked up from orientalists. Later, under Khalifa al-Masih II Bashiruddin Mahmud Ahmad, the Ahmadi polarisation vis-à-vis mainstream Muslims developed in new ways, but even then, as Adil Hussain Khan demonstrates, Muslims were ready to work alongside Mahmud Ahmad in the All-India Kashmir Committee activities.[68]

Ironically Ahmadism shared with Baha'ism a congruent marginality in the colonial period. Ahmadis may have been anxious about distinguishing themselves from Baha'is, but both clung to the skirts of empire and did not align with Muslim fears over Western penetration of the Islamicate domains. In the cause of spiritual universalism each movement vehemently eschewed any trace of anti-colonial rancour and continually proclaimed their peaceful intentions. However, in defining itself as a new world faith with leave-taking from Islam embedded within it since its Babi stage, the Baha'i position did not lack clarity. In contrast, the Ahmadi claim not to be a new religion but to retain its anchorage within Islam, which was a feature of its declared mission more generally as well as of its anti-Baha'i polemic, meant holding to a more anomalous stance than that of the Baha'i faith's, one that Islamists as varied as Muhammad Iqbal and Abul Ala Maududi could clearly see.[69] The Lahori Ahmadis, who in India belonged to the strand of 'little liberalism', but who with Ahmadism in general also functioned within an Islamic conservatism observable in the retaining of veiling and purdah, wished to be more conciliatory toward their fellow Muslims than the Qadianis. But they were left in an even stranger condition of in-betweenness in the Interwar Period that stretched to the Ahmadi relationship with Christianity. In his Woking Mosque journal *Islamic Review* Khwaja Kamaluddin certainly softened the missionary baiting which had attracted Muslims in India, and Ghulam Ahmad's mahdi-messiah claim which particularly incensed Christians. Westerners alienated by Christian dogmas and intolerance were attracted to this modern form of Islam, yet once the stream of British converts dried up, their insistence on remaining 'good' Muslims did not help the Lahori Ahmadis from losing out to the Qadianis in the long run and from being unable to retain control over the Woking Mosque.[70]

Conclusion: Browne's Babi-Baha'i Legacy and the Scope of *Mahdawiyya*

In want of a comprehensive biography, perhaps no better outline of of E. G. Browne's career and achievement can be found than in Arthur Arberry's piece on him in *Oriental Essays: Portraits of Seven Scholars*. In addition to an extract from Browne's translation of a poem attributed to Babi poetess Quratul Ayn, Arberry gives ample space to his descriptions of his personal encounters with Baha'is and Azalis in *Year Amongst the Persians* including a sample dialogue in which Browne interacts with individuals from the contending groups in Kirman. The English orientalist's ear captures the extravagance and extremities of mystical discourse to which he 'listened in consternation, half-frightened . . . half-disgusted at their doctrines yet withal held spell-bound by their eloquence'.[71] Moving on to a later interest, Arberry quotes a section from Browne's *Press and Poetry of Modern Persia* in which Browne advocates Iran's accomplishment of its own potential 'material regeneration . . .[un]impeded by malignant external forces' at the same time denouncing the 'represent[ation] of such Asiatic peoples as the Persians as entirely decadent and degenerate'.[72] In his condemnation of the orientalist denigration of 'the Persian character' his idealism clashes with Shoghi Effendi's self-orientalising incorporation of this denigration into his scriptural statements.[73] Arberry's essay allows us to come to tentative conclusions on a number of significant issues raised in this chapter. His survey of his varied interests strongly confirms that Browne was a 'peculiar orientalist' where that expression encompasses the all round individual brilliance of his achievement as a Persianist.

Browne's own assessment of his work on the Babis (he still preferred this term to the current 'Behais' or 'Behaists') can be found in his introduction to Myron H. Phelps' *Life and Teachings* of *Abbas Effendi*. Published in 1903, at a moment when Baha'ism had emerged from obscurity and was comparatively well known, one could even say approaching the height of its fame among orientalists, the text poses three critical questions which come from the mouth of an unnamed 'English diplomatist freshly returned from Persia'. The first, regarding the wisdom of publishing 'the History of Haji Mirza Jani' (*Nuqtat al-Kaf*) in spite of the Baha'is' desire to destroy 'the one surviving copy of the book . . . to which [he had] gained access', elicits the unvoiced answer that Browne had been right to do so. He had translated a work that purported to present Babism 'warts and all', and he remained especially proud of his persistence in discovering and translating it. The second question also raises an implied criticism, this time over his role in the struggle between Azal and Baha'ullah, which the diplomat, evidently a Baha'i sympathiser, equates with a contest between 'an obscure Jewish sect' and a new version of Christianity. To this Browne offers no answer, but his silence seems to suggest the comparison of Baha'ism with Christianity might be an overstatement. Finally, questioning him about the doctrine of the immortality of the soul the 'diplomat' adverts to the phenomenon of Babi martyrdom, prompting Browne to recall a couplet recited by Sulayman Khan, one of the 'Seven Martyrs of Tehran' who had died for his Babi faith en route to his execution in 1852.[74] The quotation has the effect of reviving the sect's original fascination for Browne. Suddenly the interlocutor's question and his own response to it come to encapsulate the entire field first opened up by Gobineau. It was this which had proved so enticing for Browne, and before him Renan and Arnold, and later on for the Christian universalists. The Bab and Christianity joined by the martyr motif had exercised such a strong hold on the imaginations of these scholars, litterateurs and liberal clergymen. Now Browne is telling us, as an individual and orientalist, he had nothing to regret about the part he had played in all that.[75]

In searching out a trajectory for the mahdi movements emerging in Islamicate territories and then crossing over to the West, Babism is of primary importance not only because it came first but because in its Baha'i renovation the potentialities of a transformational 'beyond mahdism' project were much more fully explored. In the early 1900s as we have seen, Baha'ism had achieved a priority recognised by missionaries and orientalists alike, one to which Ahmadis saw it necessary to respond. In order to do so, Maulana Muhammad Ali in particular, deemed it advantageous to enter into the domain of Babi historiography set out by E. G. Browne, accessing his pioneer 'discovery' of the raw disorder of *Nuqtat al-Kaf*, and availing himself of his questionable assembly in *Materials* of documents so obviously marked by Baha'i intra-sectary strife. In recent years academic interest has reversed the order of the two mahdi movements in terms of their perceived significance. If Ahmadism is a more studied topic today it is partly because of its model engagement in overseas missionary activities on behalf of Islam in the early twentieth century, and partly because of present-day Ahmadi visibility as a distinctive Muslim community in London and Berlin, and a still embattled and persecuted one in Pakistan and Indonesia. After its earlier attraction to orientalists, the Baha'i faith has been unable to establish itself as a significant field of scholarly investigation and today excites interest mainly among its own followers.[76] Historically, however, both constitute a specialised, more intensive early form of engagement with the West than is the case with most other modern Muslim movements.

6

Empire and Orient: Baha'is in Russian Transcaspia and Palestine

The connection of Baha'is and Ahmadis to empire, in its British and Russian forms, may well be a topic obfuscated by modern Shi'i anti-Baha'i and Sunni anti-Ahmadi polemic, however, it remains a tantalising one. From the point of view of Baha'is, severely persecuted in their native land and hardly less welcome in Ottoman domains, the protection of European imperial power, albeit unsystematic, proffered them respite and as émigrés the possibility of finding sanctuary where it might be possible to flourish. While the appeals to colonial powers are not difficult to understand, the response they got is not so easily calibrated. It would be simplistic to follow the logic of their opponents' arguments and claim they were mere puppets – inventions even – of empire, or in more measured terms to state that Baha'is or Ahmadis were formally protected, as were the Maronites and Druze in Syria-Lebanon, or sponsored throughout the British Empire as were the Aga Khan's Ismailis.[1] Moojan Momen points out, apropos a letter from Abdul Baha to Lord Curzon appealing for protection of Baha'is following the murder of one of their number in Sultanabad in May 1920, that they were 'at no time under protection of any foreign power in the same way as . . . other minority groups were'. He notes that five years after the above incident the British declined to give support in the case of more killings in Jahrum and attributes this to a decline in their influence in Iran caused by 'the fiasco over the proposed Anglo–Persian Treaty' which draws from him an indictment of British 'diplomatic and political expediency' such as we rarely see from a Baha'i author.[2] However, the clearest instance of Baha'is coming under de facto protection of a European power was the case of a migrant Baha'i community in Transcaspia and the Caucasus. The context was recent expansion of the Russian Empire to the borders of Iran. Territory under Russian control proved an attractive place to establish Baha'i communities safe from the intrusion of the Persian government. For their part, as Soli Shahvar states, Russian diplomats 'must have been aware of the possibilities that their support to and protection of the Babis could hold for Russia's regional interests'. As an imperial power, Russia may have responded to representations for their protection from the persecuted Baha'i minority in Ashkhabad by seeing them as a further opportunity to exercise its power in 'the Middle East in general and Iran in particular'.[3] Documents released from the Russian archives show an interplay of Tsarist Russian government officials and orientalists within the military in which all cards appear to have been on the table ranging from full protection of the Baha'i community to the expulsion of its members back to Iran, a fate that eventually befell it early in the Soviet period. This chapter will also review British imperial protection in the form of the relationship between the Baha'i leadership and establishment figures in Palestine and Britain during the Mandate period, ending with a briefer look at how Ahmadis courted power in British India. In each situation the relationship between imperial officials and the two movements under focus will be probed and, in conclusion, an assessment will be made of the process whereby empire beneficiaries found themselves in due course victims in the post-colonial age.

Russian Orientalism and the Baha'is of Transcaspia and the Caucasus

Despite the scholarly effort brought to bear on elucidating the origins and early development of the Babi and Baha'i movements in the context of Iranian Shi'ism, up to now Edward Said's codification of orientalism has not been systematically applied to analysis of discourses produced both from within and from outside Baha'i circles. That is, in spite of the role European orientalists played in the uneven but not superficial documentation of their development from the mid-nineteenth to the early twentieth centuries. A major aim of the present work is to demonstrate the lack of serious interrogation of the two movements in terms both of orientalist reporting and classification, and of Baha'i engagement with orientalism more generally, an omission that continues up to the present. This state of affairs partly arises from the fact that study of the Baha'i faith within the former field of oriental studies remains under-problematised, while the Baha'i faith continues to be studied so rarely outside of departments of Islamic, Middle Eastern or Iranian studies – disciplines not usually noted for an interest in Said's work. On the other hand, the crudely stereotypical encodings of the Baha'i faith regurgitated mainly by its enemies in the Middle East can hardly be considered to raise a serious orientalist critique of Babi/Baha'ism.

So far in the present study only passing reference has been made to the relationship between Baha'is and modern Russia. Antagonists of the Baha'i faith, as we saw in an Ahmadi critique in the previous chapter, instanced the Russian consul's rescue and offer of asylum to Baha'ullah during the anti-Babi maelstrom of 1852 as though it contained some dark purpose. The Russian reaction to the Babi episode is, therefore, a good starting point to view one of the long-standing myths about imperialist connections between Russia and the Babi-Baha'i movements of Iran.[4] This began with a story derived from the fiction that Dimitri Ivanovich Dolgorukov (the Russian minister in Iran between 1845 and 1854) converted to Islam and was behind the manufacture of Babism, recruiting Husayn Ali Nuri, Baha'ullah as a spy. From its inception in the 1930s to its later reinvigoration during the Iranian revolution the myth, based around a text purporting to be Dologrukov's 'Memoirs', morphed into a prolonged conspiracy theory aimed at Baha'is, fuelled by what MacEoin called popular interest in 'the secret machinations of the imperial powers during the nineteenth and twentieth centuries, designed to weaken and control Iran from within and to destroy the influence of Islam among the people'.[5] The opening of the Russian archives more than a decade ago provided ample evidence to test out such theories, and two volumes were duly published by Israeli historians Soli Shahvar, Boris Morozov and Gad G. Gilbar, entitled *The Baha'is of Iran, Transcaspia and the Caucasus*. Another work, *The Development of Babi/Baha'i Communities: Exploring Baron Rosen's Archives*, was produced by senior researcher at the Institute of Oriental Manuscripts at the Russian Academy of Sciences, Youli Ioannesyan. As indicated per the title of the latter, both projects extensively mined the archive of Baron Viktor Rozen. If anything the letters and reports collected by these researchers, the first of which date from more than thirty years after the supposed intervention of Dologrukov, are quite anodyne and provide no evidence of a conspiracy, at least not between Baha'is and Russian orientalists of Rozen's school. The authors, however, are largely innocent of any desire to elucidate much more than the surface connection between the projects of Russian imperialism, Russian orientalism, and the Transcaspian Baha'i communities. Whether, and to what extent, Russian orientalism per se was an innocuous hobby of mainly military officers acting out of love for a craft which they practised merely as amateurs in their spare time, or whether there was another dimension to their interest in Baha'is linked to Russian imperial interests in Iran, these volumes do not tell us. As Stephanie Cronin's review of both books pointedly comments, 'on the central question of the extent to which Edward Said's critique of orientalism is applicable to the Russian (and Soviet) experience, these volumes are silent'.[6]

In the broader field of Russian studies, the opening of the archives following the collapse of the Soviet Union has generated a growing interest in study of 'Russia's Orient' and the part late Tsarist and Bolshevik orientologists played in the eastern territories captured by Russia in the 1860s.[7] It is within this context that we will view the volumes containing new archival material relating to Russian orientalists' study of the Baha'is. Before focusing on the orientalists' work on Baha'ism, however, a brief overview of the debate conducted over recent decades over the nature of Russian orientalism should put us in a position to gain, at the very least, a better understanding of the context in which orientalists were working during the period of late Tsarist rule in Transcaspia and the Caucasus. In her survey of this debate Stephanie Cronin commences with the argument that given that *Orientalism* mentions Germany only in passing and Russian orientalism, with its strong link to German orientalism, hardly at all, Said's theory is not applicable in the Russian context. A reason commonly adduced for Russia's case being different relates to 'an alleged uniqueness, or at least "distinctiveness" possessed by Russian history and geopolitics', which made Russians both of the West and of the East, European and Asiatic.[8] Professor Cronin, however, doubts that arguments about Russia's exceptionalism absolve Russians from orientalist ways of thinking and perceiving. Evidence for her scepticism is supplied by Elena Andreeva's *Russia and Iran in the Great Game: Travelogues and Orientalism*, a study built on more than two hundred travelogues written by Russians who had travelled through Persia, many of them military officers. Applying a Saidian analysis Andreeva asserts Russians' sense of in-betweenness led to the creation of split personalities; the contradiction between the West-oriented and the East-oriented sides of the split Russian national identity 'led to their overemphasizing their Europeanness and their equivalence to the Western Europeans. Most of the travelogue authors try to prove that being Russian means being European'.[9] Russians saw Iran through European eyes and accentuated European development and Iran's backwardness while forgetting Russia's own.

> In this sense, the Russian experience of deploying an imaginary East in order to clarify and bolster its own Western identity seems a perfect fit with Said's orientalist paradigm . . .[T]he Russian variety of Orientalism [comes across] as an exaggerated, even grotesque version of its western European prototype. The prejudices of the Russian travelers whom [Andreeva] discusses were inflated by their own insecurities and were both extreme and freely expressed, although they have a familiar ring to anyone acquainted with the writings of their British counterparts. These prejudices included a deep hostility towards Islam, a prurient obsession with the allegedly degraded position of women, an admiration for the ancient past, the better to denigrate the present, and a preference for religious and ethnic minorities, supposedly more receptive to the imperial embrace.[10]

Germane to the present focus, Andreeva notes:

> Like other European travelers, most of the Russian travelers favor non-Muslim Persians: Armenians, Babis (a Shi'i sect), Zoroastrians, and, occasionally, Jews . . . While in Iran, Russian travelers usually associate with non-Muslims, if with anyone at all among the local people. This preference . . . demonstrates the Russians' implementation of the old colonial principal: 'divide and rule'.[11]

Before turning to the specific role military officers like Alexandr Tumanskii played in collecting information on Baha'is, it is important to consider the overall role of Russian military officers in orientalism. Concerning the military context of Russian orientalism Stephanie Cronin states:

> [m]any tsarist officers and administrators became authorities in the field of oriental studies while orientalists found employment in the administrations

of Central Asia and the Caucasus and in the Russian foreign ministry. This interpenetration would, however, again seem to make the Saidian paradigm more rather than less relevant.[12]

Though he tends to privilege Foucault's methodological framework as more appropriate to the analysis of late Tsarist imperial structures, Denis Volkov concedes 'it is obvious that in Said's own terms and in the concrete colonial context of late Imperial Russia the power/knowledge nexus is most evident in the military domain'.[13] With respect to Russia's policy in Persia, this was put into practice at the turn of the century by means of

> massive ... penetration carried out by versatile means: economic, political and military. Russian economic weakness and non-competitiveness was supposed to be compensated by its political influence and military presence. This character of Russian involvement in Asia in the nineteenth and the early twentieth centuries predetermined the substantial role which the Russian military played in the development of Oriental studies.[14]

Andreeva confirms that during the 1890s and the ensuing decade Russia's colonial interests in Iran were at their height. 'Mostly Russian travelers were either in government or military service ... Their reports usually provided information that was used to further imperial goals'.[15] Of the material contained in such reports mapping not only Persia's borders but likely routes deep inside the country featured prominently.

Regarding individual orientalists, Volkov notes how the orientalism debate has shifted according to how the positions of seminal Russian orientologists are viewed.[16] Vera Tolz makes specific claims for the Rozen school and for Vasilii Bartol'd in particular of being well aware of the political and cultural construction of concepts such as 'East' and 'West', as in Bartol'd dismissing 'the East–West dichotomy as a figment of the European imagination'. Bartol'd, with his critique of the Western bias toward the historiography of the Orient, was a Saidian *avant la lettre*.[17] Volkov agrees and asserts 'Rozen's whole school anticipated Edward Said's postulations'.[18] A consensus, at least concerning Rozen's school, is therefore that these orientalists dismissed binaries of East and West and were more likely to be sympathetic to eastern peoples, but with the implication that inclining toward the E. G. Browne approach 'they insisted on their right to speak on behalf of the peoples of the "Orient", whose histories and cultures they often claimed they knew best'.[19] Andreeva affirms, however, that Russian academia was put to the service of the government. This was the case with university professors of oriental studies, of whom an earlier example was Aleksandr Kazem Bek, 'a distinguished orientalist professor who taught at Kazan University from 1827 to 1849'. According to Bartol'd: 'The period in the history of Russian orientalism when the needs of scholarly orientalism were totally sacrificed to the real or alleged interests of political life is closely connected with the name of Kazem Bek and his most talented students'.[20] Persian-born, Professor of Persian Literature at the University of St Petersburg from 1849 to 1860 after moving from Kazan, Kazem Bek was together with Gobineau, the earliest orientalist to publish on Babism.[21] To turn from Kazem Bek to Baron Rozen and his co-workers in the field of Babi-Bahaism is to delimit but not exhaust the scope of Russian interest in the subject of the Babis. Youli Ioannesyan considers Rozen and Tumanskii's contribution to the field, together with E. G. Browne's, 'exceptionally valuable', but there were also 'Russian diplomats and diplomatic staff in nineteenth-century Iran [who] were especially active in collecting materials relating to the emerging new religion'.[22]

According to Denis Volkov in 1894 Tumanskii was,

> sent on a reconnaissance mission from the southern Caspian coast through the whole of Persian territory, right down to the Persian Gulf. At the same time, he obtained a number of valuable documents and manuscripts on the Babi sect, which he made available to his teachers.[23]

Fortunately, Shahvar's commentary on some of Tumanskii's letters provides a context to his journey if not a clear assessment of the Russian government's interest in the Baha'i community. Before he set out, Turmanskii wrote to Rozen on March 1 about 'receiving certain instructions of a military character' from 'Headquarters'.[24] We might assume that, in addition to reporting on the Baha'is of Isfahan, Shiraz and Yazd, he would be performing reconnoitres of a less ethnographical nature. Tumanskii's letter moves on to the collection of Babi and Baha'i texts and the reader is entitled to assume, because this is the major feature of most of his letters, that this (and not military spying) is his main interest. From Tumanskii's own account in his letter to Rozen from Ashkhabad, dated 2 February, we learn that the secrecy did not relate to 'the collection of statistical-geographical data' but, on the contrary, he states he was 'was sent by the Ministry of Defence to Iran to conduct secret "*research into the religious-political sect* of Babis"'. However, 'General Kuropatkin ordered him to collect material for military and economic purposes as well, though from Tumanskii's letters it appears he went on this journey mainly to collect information about the Baha'is'. However, there is a suggestion of some incompetence over the travel orders.

> Originally it was to be a kind of secret mission. The Ministry of Defence planned to send him secretly as an expert to ascertain the actual status of the Baha'is in Persia, but later he was sent openly as a Russian officer collecting military-statistical data.[25]

A number of questions arise from this situation which Shahvar et al. do not consider. Why was Tumanskii's research journey visiting the Baha'i communities in Iran initially intended to be secret? And why was this arrangement later changed? Tumanskii writes about being sent as 'a secret agent' with attendant dangers, but on learning that he is to go as a '"Russian officer"' is relieved since in that case he would have diplomatic immunity and his wife would be able to accompany him on part of the journey.[26] Overall, the purpose of the journey is obscured but clearly it was not intended, at least by the government, as an academic research field-trip. Were the Baha'i leadership – and here one naturally thinks of the canny and astute mind of Abdul Baha who was in touch with affairs in Ashkhabad through his emissary Mirza Abul Fazl Gulpaygani – aware of the political considerations involved in the journey? Granted it might not have been advantageous for the Russians to openly show interest in the Baha'i communities in Iran itself, but in that case why was Tumanskii eventually instructed to travel openly as a Russian officer and still able to connect with Baha'is?

As regards their position in Transcaspia, Baha'is were of course following Baha'ullah/Abdul Baha's instructions and were sworn to non-involvement in political matters and to be devoted only to religious ones. This should have rendered them above suspicion which is precisely the response reported by Shahvar in the context of concern over possible Baha'i involvement in the 1892 assassination of the shah: 'satisfied that the Baha'is were of a peaceful, apolitical, and civically responsible character and therefore posed no threat to public order, Russia granted them the same status as that of other (non-Russian Orthodox) religions'.[27] However, this leaves unanswered the matter of Russia's own political interests. According to Shahvar,

> the Russian Government may . . . have *hoped to use the Baha'is, and their communities in Iran, as a source from which to gather intelligence* in a country where Russia had many interests . . . Seen through the prism of the Great Game, it could have, no doubt, provided the Russians with an excellent excuse to meddle in territories historically regarded as a British zone of influence.[28]

The case of the murder in 1889 of Haji Muhammad Riza Isfahani, a Baha'i in the city of Ashkhabad, something of 'a safe haven for the Iranian Baha'is', crystallised Russian interests. 'The Russians saw the possibility of using the presence of these émigrés as a bargaining card to pressure the generally anti-Baha'i Iranian government, and to extract concessions from it'.[29] The Russian authorities' decision to execute two of the Shi'i extremists involved in the murder and to exile the others to Siberia drew an angry response from the Iranian government: protection of the Baha'is was badly received in Tehran and another similar case endangered Russo–Iranian relations, leading some Russians to suggest evacuation of the Baha'i enclaves. As we would expect given its close proximity to Iran, Russia was the European power that knew most about the country, assigning, proportionally, the largest amount of resources to reconnoitre it (to use a polite expression), and its relations with the Baha'i community were at least in part bound up with that.

Ashkhabad's Baha'i Community: An Oasis of Modern Religion?

The concentration of Baha'is in the city of Ashkhabad from the mid-1880s focuses a number of the issues raised above and gives an insight into the self-image of Baha'is as followers of a modern religion that transcended the backwardness of their Shi'a compatriots. In 1881 the area in which the new city was located formally became part of the Russian territory of Transcaspia, and Baha'is began to settle there on the instigation of a merchant from the prestigious Afnan family who was supported by the leadership in Palestine. Russian orientalists stressed the constructive features of Baha'is, while Baha'i sources have continued to celebrate the establishment of a business-oriented, self-organising community, linked to the progressive flow of converts in Iran including substantial numbers from the Zoroastrian and Jewish minorities, and to a broader project of modernisation that encompassed the setting up of Baha'i schools and hospitals.[30] The presence in Ashkhabad of Baha'i rationalist scholar Mirza Abul Fazl Gulpaygani added to the mystique of modernity accruing round what Baha'is see as the first substantive attempt to implement their new faith's modern social principles. In the first decade of the twentieth century prominent Baha'is Hippolyte Dreyfus and Mason Remey went to Ashkhabad (in 1904 and 1908, respectively) to inspect and subsequently write about the foundations of a Baha'i temple (*mashriq al-adhkar*).[31] This discourse of reform and development is invariably set against the backward Shi'a Muslims who in receiving punishment for murdering the Baha'i Muhammad Riza Isfahani had seriously misjudged Russian intention to implement justice, a rare occurrence in the story of their persecution of Babis and Baha'is in Iran and Central Asia.

The same discourse that upholds the modern features of Baha'ism incorporates a confrontation with, in the context of the Russian-controlled Transcaspian territories of the time, a much greater foe than the Shi'a. After they had taken over from the Tsarist regime, the Bolsheviks, Baha'i sources affirm, recognising that Baha'ism was concerned with modern problems, considered it a threat to their Marxist view of religion as backward and fossilised. The story of the Baha'i–Bolshevik encounter as encapsulated by different Baha'i commentators will help us to better understand their image of the Baha'i faith, specifically the distance this modern movement in Iranian history had travelled since the inception of Babism in 1844; it entails looking back to the demolition of the community of Ashkhabad which was completed by the late 1930s, and views Baha'is have continued to hold on how their faith has developed in the broader world since then. To articulate this story I shall employ three Baha'i sources: an essay by Anthony Lee dating from 1979 that has the virtue of being built around oral interviews with Baha'is who had lived in Russia, or whose relatives had. Much of his material is reused in Moojan Momen's 1991 book chapter which accentuates the Ashkhabad episode as a high in the showcasing of a Baha'i modernity; the third source is an unpublished talk by Amin Banani dating from 1981.[32] Lee states that between the trial of Muhammad Riza's murderers and the completion of the Russian revolution, the Baha'is of Ashkhabad had built up their own society and institutions, such that by the end of the period they could 'boast that theirs was the most fully developed Baha'i community in the world'. The *mashriq al-adhkar* had been erected; it was surrounded by gardens and buildings, comprising two elementary schools, a pilgrim house and a medical clinic.[33] Momen amplifies the significance of the Ashkhabad experiment in a series of key points: it numbered 4,000 inhabitants by 1918; it had great importance as a centre of Baha'i scholarship; its growth fed on the pattern of persecutions in Iran; it was strategically located in terms of the new Transcaspian railway; by the time the Bolshevik revolution came the Baha'i community was possibly the wealthiest in the city. Baha'i institutions, monthly meetings and celebrations of holy days were also in place and functioning. Lee notes that owing to Russian law forbidding conversion of Christians, Baha'i proselytisation was curtailed and the community grew isolated socially and exclusively Persian; according to one reminiscence, Baha'is 'were generally prosperous and often distracted by material pursuits, especially the youth'.[34] However, for Momen the litmus test of the community's success was the challenge it proffered as a modern religion, and to substantiate the claim he quotes from Walter Kolarz, *Religion in the Soviet Union*:

> Islam, both in its Shiite and Sunnite form, is attacked by the communists because it is reactionary, encourages nationalist narrowmindedness and obstructs the education and emancipation of women. Baha'iism [*sic*] has incurred communist displeasure for exactly the opposite reasons. It is dangerous to Communism because of its broadmindedness, its tolerance, its international outlook, the attention it pays to women's education and its insistence on the equality of the sexes. All this contradicts the communist thesis about the backwardness of all religions. In the political sphere social reformers appear to the communists more harmful than 'reactionaries', and in the religious field an outlook which is mindful of modern social problems is thought more obnoxious than out-of-date obscurantism. This is perhaps why Baha'iism has attracted the attention of the Soviet communists to a much greater degree than might be warranted by the numerical strength of its supporters.[35]

As practical confirmation of the validity of this narrative, reverting to the Ashkhabad experience, Momen states:

> As early as 1922, an article appeared in the official Government press attacking the Baha'is for turning the thoughts of young people away from Bolshevism. But initially, the increased activities of the Baha'i community were not openly opposed. Evidently the authorities were confident that people could be won away from religion through debate and polemic. From about 1926 onwards, the pressure intensified.[36]

Kolarz's book seems to have been extensively reviewed around the time of its publication in 1961 attracting comment particularly in regard to its representation of the Jewish community in the Soviet Union. From a discourse analysis perspective, however, the way in which his remarks reflect what Baha'is say about themselves suggests they might originate from second hand sources rather than his own research (a condition that still obtains among non-Baha'i commentators today.) With respect to Momen's comment about polemic and debate between Baha'is and Bolsheviks, I now turn to my third Baha'i source which addresses this issue in greater detail.

An alternative version of the Baha'i 'challenge' to Bolshevism was delivered by Amin Banani in a presentation to the Canadian Association of Baha'i studies in October 1981 addressing the subject of Marxist analysis of the Baha'i faith. Banani gave a frank exposé of what, in effect, were the limitations of the Baha'i discourse of religious modernism (so frank, in fact, that it was never published). The kernel of his argument is that while the Baha'i faith had once constituted a modern movement in terms of its Shi'i background, its later development showed a failure to move on and address wider aspects of modern thought. This accounted for Baha'is' lack of power to attract the younger, more educated members of society in Latin America, India and many parts of Africa. Essentially, the problem was that while at one time in Iran Baha'is were well able to successfully address ideas around messianic Shi'ism, they had an imperfect understanding of modern thought, specifically Marxism, to which they reacted like fundamentalist Christians who viewed Marxism as 'a godless fallacy'. Banani gives two instances where Baha'is interfaced with Communists: in Ashkhabad during the Russian Civil

War where a number of debates took place; and in Iran in the early 1940s, when the Tudeh party drew converts from disaffected youthful leaders of the Baha'i administration. His argument is that in the former situation, it was correct to say the Bolsheviks looked at the environment of Ashkhabad 'as part of the backward, feudal world of traditional religion, Islam . . .[and] they viewed the Baha'is as essentially a stepping stone for reaching the rest of this oriental society [or] a place to attract adherents'. In the debates, which were of course slanted in favour of the Bolsheviks, Mihdi Gulpaygani, nephew of Mirza Abul Fazl, was the chief spokesman for the Baha'i side:

> [his] arguments were based on an enlightened explanation of the need for divine education and the argument for the inadequacy of materialism alone. But he spoke largely in traditional terms, without a command of the basis of Marxist thought, and with only what little ability did exist in the Ishqabad community at the time.[37]

Later, Baha'is emerged who were university-educated in Russia and had some knowledge of Marxism and 'sometimes participated' in debate. The troubled times prevented Baha'is from challenging Marxism, but as time moved on among their educated 'there seemed to be a remarkable lack of awareness' of Marx's contributions to knowledge about human society. In Iran, the position was that Baha'is, who were the only ones to have a heightened awareness of the need for social justice and who were alive to answering the imperatives of organisation by creating a bureaucratic structure, were recruited to the Tudeh party or lost out in argument because of their 'unawareness of what the communists were saying, and how to respond to them'.[38]

More could be said to contextualise these debates, especially by reviewing Soviet orientalism and the way in which Muslims and sects like Baha'is, Ismailis and so forth were viewed in the period concerned.[39] Better known is the work of two Soviet orientalists of a slightly later period, Vladimir Minorsky who contributed to discussion on the social status of the Bab and his followers, and M. S. Ivanov who brought an interpretation of the class dimension to Babi preaching.[40] However, these studies do not materially alter the main discussion points in this section, which can be briefly summarised as follows: a background has been sketched with regard to relations between the Tsarist authorities, Russian orientalists and the Baha'i communities of Iran and Transcaspia, with the focus on Alexandr Tumanskii, after Rozen the most important member of his school in the area of scholarship on the Baha'is. Although application of Said's *Orientalism* does not feature in the work recent researchers have produced on relations between Baha'is and Russian orientalists, the survey undertaken of the opinions of current experts on Russian orientology suggests Said's views should be taken seriously. The background assessed gives grounds for thinking that Russian interest in Babis and Baha'is was not merely an innocent pastime and leaves open the matter as to whether the orientalists were engaged in spying activities ('reconnoitring') and the extent to which Baha'is understood the political context to their visits.

Only a cursory review is needed of Baha'i literature on the history of the faith during the period under review to register the positive attitude in which Tsarist Russia is held. Unsurprisingly, toward the Soviets who effectively demolished the Baha'i community throughout Russia, it is highly negative. In the development of a narrative of the Baha'i faith as a modern religion, the Ashkhabad community continues to be used as an exemplar by Baha'i scholars. However, the putative challenge Bahaism held out to Bolshevism is a topic that needs revision. The Baha'is' own reports suggest interest and conversions were the accrual from debates with members of the local Muslim population who, if Banani is correct, were attracted by a level of discourse that would not have impressed the Bolsheviks. Moreover, Amin Banani's presentation raises an issue which remains implicit in Baha'i literature today: how much do Baha'is simply believe their own narratives, repeating them without question, and to what extent are they tone deaf to current thinking? For a self-styled progressive religion, Baha'i ideas about modernity, it could be argued, are in need of thorough updating. The intellectual apparatus sustaining their argumentation has not been renewed since the time of Banani, whose opinion then was that it had already been outdated for several generations before that.

The Baha'is, Palestine and Great Britain

From the start of the period of the guardianship under Shoghi Effendi, the relationship Abdul Baha had established with the British became paramount.

To quote historian of the early twentieth-century British Baha'i community, Lil Osborn:

> The importance of Palestine to the Baha'is is demonstrated by the attendees at the opening of the Baha'i Centenary Celebrations in London [in 1944]. A telegram dated 25th November 1943 [from Shoghi Effendi] instructs the British NSA: 'Advise contact Herbert Samuel Ronald Storrs Tudor-Pole and other sympathisers which National Assembly may suggest vigorous action necessary safeguard interests faith insure success celebration'.[41]

Dr Osborn's gloss on 'the three men named in the telegram' states that 'all were connected to Palestine'. Wellersley Tudor Pole, occultist and seer, had served in the military there during the First World War; Samuel was a Liberal MP and Zionist who became first High Commissioner for Palestine in 1920, and Storrs as Military Governor (1917–20) and Civil Governor (1920–6) of Jerusalem strove to ride both Zionist and Arab Palestinan horses. The presence of such men at the Baha'i celebration 'cannot have been incidental but rather an attempt to "safeguard interests faith" in Palestine'.[42] All three were friendly with Abdul Baha and it was through such figures, notably Pole and Lord Lamington, both of whom had met Abdul Baha in Egypt before the Great War and had secured his safety in Palestine in 1918 that his grandson and successor's path to education in Britain was smoothed. Lord Lamington and Tudor Pole were effectively Shoghi Effendi's guardians, and given their connections to his grandfather it was not surprising that he would identify with them. A British imperial stalwart closely connected with Abdul Baha and proxy guardian of Shoghi Effendi in his Oxford days, Lord Lamington would be pro-active in alerting British attention to the safety of Abdul Baha in 1918. In spite of Shoghi Effendi's sense of the uniqueness of his role as Guardian of the Baha'i faith, which he would assume so suddenly under difficult circumstances after the death of Abdul Baha in the year after his arrival in England, at this time and in the future an ongoing deference to senior British authority figures is embedded in his writings. The Guardian's wife Ruhiyyih (Rabbani) Khanum, author of the official biography of him, refracts this attitude especially in the extracts she quotes from his correspondence during the days of the British Mandate in Palestine.[43]

The precise moment when the British authorities became conscious of Abdul Baha in the Palestine context was months after British troops had entered Jerusalem in December of the previous year, in the spring of 1918, when the Turks were fast losing hold of the whole territory. Baha'i Lady Sara Blomfield, who had a line to Mount Carmel, was warned about the situation of Abdul Baha. She also had aristocratic contacts in London, notably Lord Lamington who alerted the foreign office. Secretary of state for foreign affairs Arthur Balfour cabled General Allenby instructing him when Haifa was taken to assure the safety of the Persian religious leader and his family. From that time onwards Abdul Baha was generally familiar to the senior British figures in the occupying force who frequently visited him, and on 27 April 1920, 'in the Garden of the Military Governor of Haifa, 'Abdul-Baha was invested with the insignia of Knighthood of the British Empire'.[44] A photograph of the event records the presence among others of the Mufti of Haifa and the Head of the Druze Community, but this has not deterred some opponents of the Baha'i faith from seeing in this evidence of a perfidious link between Baha'is and Great Britain. British documents relating to conferment of the honour, a round-robin between the war and foreign offices, include comments by Sir Percy Cox, the British Ambassador in Tehran, and Nusratul Dawleh, the Persian Minister for foreign affairs. The outstanding issue they raise is whether Abdul Baha would have any objection to receiving a decoration in the form of the cross. Moojan Momen, who published the documents in his extensive compendium of material on Babis and Baha'is in government archives, sees no reason to be coy about the fact that in comparison to the 'inefficient and corrupt workings of the Ottoman Empire' Abdul Baha was appreciative of the British authorities.[45]

When Shoghi Effendi succeeded Abdul Baha as Guardian of the Baha'i Faith, he took over Abdul Baha's personal relationships with the British, many of them now his own carried over from his short sojourn in Britain. Ruhiyyih Rabbani's narrative introduces senior figures from the British Mandate almost as though they were personal friends. Besides Herbert Samuel, we are told another High Commissioner Arthur Wauchope (1931–8), and Lieutenant-Colonel George Stewart Symes Governor of North Palestine (1920–5) and Chief Secretary to the Government of Palestine, 'had a personal liking for Shoghi Effendi'.[46] Chapter 12 of the biography reads like a who's who of minor royalty (some dethroned) together with a roll call of VIPs whose contact with Shoghi Effendi stretching well beyond the Middle East seems to validate at least in his wife's estimation, the importance of the religion he headed, as well as amplifying the refinement of his personality:

> The catholicity of spirit which so strongly characterized the Guardian, his complete lack of any breath of prejudice or fanaticism, the sympathy and courtesy that distinguished him so strongly, are all reflected in his letters and messages to such people. He carried on a lengthy correspondence, during the earliest years of his ministry, with Grand Duke Alexander of Russia . . .
> . . . [He] was in touch not only with Queen Marie of Rumania and a number of her relatives, but with other people of royal lineage, such as Princess Marina of Greece who later became Duchess of Kent, and Princess Kadria of Egypt. To many of these, as well as to men of such prominence as Lord Lamington, a number of former High Commissioners for Palestine, Orientalists, university professors, educators and others, Shoghi Effendi was wont to send copies of the latest *Bahá'í World* volumes or one of his own recently published translations, with his visiting card enclosed – practically the only occasion on which he ever used one, as their main function seemed to be for him to keep notes on![47]

Despite the lack of official recognition Shoghi Effendi felt the civil authorities afforded him as leader of a world religion throughout the period of the Mandate he not only maintained good relations with British officials, but seemed to court ones who, if Ruhiyyih Rabbani's selection is correct, were either open Zionists or friendly to Zionism. She writes:

> [He] was wont to receive in his home the visits of many distinguished people, such as Lord and Lady Samuel; Sir Ronald Storrs, another friend of 'Abdu'l-Baha; Moshe Sharett, later to become one of Israel's most loved and prominent officials; Norman Bentwich and many writers, journalists and notables.[48]

Apart from the chameleon Storrs who played both sides, Herbert Samuel and Norman Bentwich, an 'ardent Zionist' and the Attorney-General of the Mandate Administration, were figures who secured the transition of Palestine from mandated territory to the state of Israel.[49] Sharett became Israel's second prime minister. That Shoghi Effendi sent *The Dawn-Breakers*, his version of Nabil Zarandi's narrative of the Babi movement, his epitome of the history of the Baha'i faith *God Passes By*, and copies of *Baha'i World* to government officials like Wauchope and Israel's first Prime Minister David Ben-Gurion confirms one elite section of the intended audience of these texts.[50] Ben-Gurion would presumably have been less impressed by Lord Curzon's opinions on Persia assuming he was aware of the former foreign secretary's objections to the Balfour declaration and the British government's pro-Zionist policy.[51]

Contemporaneous with the the Egyptian government's annulment of the civil rights of the tiny Baha'i community of Egypt and the seizure of the house of Baha'ullah in Baghdad by the order of prominent Shi'i clerics, in Palestine the native Arab population was heightened to the fact that they had been given no share in the government of their country, no realistic, proportionate form of representative input into its likely destiny, and that indeed the land of Palestine was in process of being taken from them. Shoghi Effendi wrote to Colonel Symes:

> We are greatly heartened by the thought that at a time when we are faced with delicate and perplexing issues, Palestine is under an Administration which is actuated by the highest of motives of fairness and justice and for which we as Baha'is have every reason to be appreciative and thankful.[52]

Two years later, following the Buraq/Wailing Wall revolt in August 1929, in a letter to another High Commissioner Sir John Chancellor, Shoghi Effendi wrote:

> The Bahá'í Community of Palestine, who, by reason of the Faith, are deeply attached to its soil truly deplore these *violent outbursts of religious fanaticism*, and venture to hope that, as the influence of Baha'i ideals extends and deepens, they may be enabled in the days to come to lend increasing assistance to your Administration for the promotion of the spirit of good will and toleration among the religious communities in the Holy Land.[53]

However, there is another side to the involvement of Baha'is with the British administration and its policies in the wider Arab Middle East. Through Abdul Baha's good relations with the British and support for their governance a number of the small colony of Baha'is living in Palestine held appointments in the Mandate Administration. Several leading British figures of the administration mention Baha'is in their memoirs. Norman Bentwich states:

> One of my principal assistants was an Egyptian magistrate, formerly my pupil at the Cairo School of Law. He was an ardent Bahai, member of that Moslem reform movement which had spread from Persia westwards, and had visions of religious, racial and international peace. He and a few others at my department were genuinely keen for good understanding between the religious-national groups of Palestine.[54]

Edwin Samuel, District Commissioner of Galilee from 1933–4, had a similar story to report of one Baha'i subordinate in his department:

> In charge of the Tiberias sub-district, with the most progressive town in my division, was an unusual man named Tewfik Yazdi. He belonged to that strange sect – the Bahais – originally from Persia where they had broken away from Islam and were severely persecuted in consequence: a section had settled in Acre. Yazdi was intelligent, energetic and got on well with Moslems, Christians and Jews, all of whom regarded him as neutral. He helped me a great deal to carry out my plans for the development of his area.[55]

A third Baha'i who occupied various positions in Palestine, starting as Inspector of Education in Jerusalem in 1920, was Husayn Ruhi. His obituary in *Baha'i World* foregrounds his service to both Abdul Baha and Shoghi Effendi in Haifa and refers to his earlier career as an educationalist in Cairo, where he established a school admitting both Baha'i and non-Baha'i pupils, with girls and boys' sections. This coincided with a period when Abdul Baha was staying in Cairo, during which he made a visit to the school complimenting Ruhi on his success. Abdul Baha's secretary Ahmad Sohrab points out that Ruhi had 'years ago' accompanied a Persian Baha'i missionary to the United States and that he was 'a short man who knew English and Arabic very well'.[56] That is the extent of information on Ruhi available from published Baha'i sources, but these make a major omission: the matter of Ruhi's proficiency in the two languages referred to by Sohrab featured in a *cause célèbre*, for it was he who translated for the British side in the McMahon–Husayn correspondence which has exercised historians of the Middle East of the ilk of George Antonius, Elie Kedourie, A. L. Tibawi and many others. Ruhi invited passing mention in T. E. Lawrence's *Seven Pillars of Wisdom* but it is in *Orientations*, the memoir of Ronald Storrs, that Ruhi's escapades for the British were first recorded in some detail. Storrs, who had a penchant for employing Baha'is, gave Ruhi the appellation 'my little Persian Agent' and the man worked for him during the period he held the office of Oriental Secretary to the British Agency in Cairo (1909–17). In Storrs' words: 'Our Arabic correspondence with Mecca was prepared by Ruhi, a fair though not profound Arabist (and a better agent than scholar); and checked, often under high pressure, by myself'.[57] Academic Hilary Farb Kalisman, author of an article on Ruhi's World War One role in British intelligence, sums him up as 'a petite spy, translator, poet, and textbook author who spent decades working for British officials, diplomats, spies, and educationalists'. Her summary of his unusual career, perhaps not one typical of Baha'is in Palestine in general, nonetheless hints at another dimension to the Middle East community out of which he grew:

> The story of this extraordinary individual illustrates the tactics of British espionage, the afterlife of an informant, the strange trends of government service in the Middle East during the interwar period, and the striking problem of nationality exposed by the division of the Ottoman Empire . . . [Ruhi's] interactions with colleagues in the Mandate bureaucracy, as well as the British individuals who had hired him, point to the chameleon-character of the man himself . . . underscoring the incongruity between nationality, language, and citizenship in the region.[58]

Ruhi was the kind of figure we might expect the Mandate to have thrown up – 'an Egyptian "of Persian origin" and an "Arabic-speaking Persian"' like other people from varied backgrounds attracted to employment in Palestine during the Mandate he was hard to categorise in terms of nationality. 'By choosing Ruhi, a Baha'i of unclear nationality, the British presumed, to some degree correctly, that they could command a greater sway over Ruhi's loyalties than those of other Egyptians, Persians, or Palestinians'.[59] In relation to official Baha'i protocol with its lofty apolitical stance inculcating in mandated Palestine as anywhere else willing obedience to the governing power Ruhi was, we might say, its flip side or dark other. In him the (barely) repressed identification with imperial power returns in the form of shady acts born out of obsequiousness and deracination. His case, though an extreme one, demonstrates how Baha'is situated in a hostile sea of orthodoxy on the cusp of the post-colonial epoch, gravitated toward the orbit of the colonial power which in turn found a use for diasporic individuals from minority communities.

Zionism, Israel and the Baha'i Faith

Lil Osborn proposes,

> the relationship [of Baha'is] with Zionists deserves some attention because, whilst attacks on Baha'is in Muslim majority countries have traditionally been on the grounds of apostasy, this is increasingly hard to sustain as a diminishing proportion of Baha'is have a Muslim heritage ... consequently a new justification has been devised ... [relating to] the Baha'i presence [in Israel].[60]

Baha'is' 'obedience to the government of the place in which they reside' coupled with 'the international funding of the huge shrines and gardens in Haifa has led to accusations of support for Zionism, which is demonstrably not the case, as the Baha'is are merely quietist in their approach to any political movement'. The Baha'i presence 'predates the declaration of the state of Israel in 1948', and Baha'ullah and Abdul Baha, who had lived in Ottoman Palestine since the late 1860s, were buried in Akka in 1892 and in Haifa in 1921, respectively. Osborn contextualises the connection between Palestine and the Baha'i faith as of 'great significance' owing to the fact that,

> it was where Baha'u'llah had been imprisoned, where he had died and where he was buried. A small community around the Holy Family, comprising mainly of Persians had formed a "Baha'i colony" in Haifa, but most importantly Mount Carmel was ... [where] Baha'u'llah had prophesied he would "pitch his tent" ... to be the site of the Baha'i World Centre.[61]

In November 1917, Arthur Balfour had issued a declaration on behalf of the British government stating that Britain looked favourably on the establishment of a Jewish national home in Palestine. As a long term resident with his finger on the pulse of world affairs, Abdul Baha was qualified to comment on the increasing Zionist activity there from the first decade of the twentieth century onwards. Quizzed by an American journalist in the summer of 1919 on his view of the country's future he seemed upbeat, clearly appreciative of its new rulers but leaving open the likely impact of the Zionists: 'If [they] mingle with the other races and live in unity with them, they will succeed. If not, they will meet certain resistance. For the present I think a neutral government like the British administration would be best'.[62] It was an argument which an Ahmadi would enthusiastically have endorsed, but it might also have been considered typical of the pro-British sentiments of a significant number of Arab notables in Palestine at the time.[63] At the time of the interview, however, except for responsible ministers in London and a committed pro-Zionist group within the colonial and foreign offices, few knew what Britain's intentions were toward the different peoples in the mandated territories. Abdul Baha stated to the reporter that the Jews would fail if they were racially exclusive, but if they could 'elevate all the people . . . and develop the country for all its inhabitants', if they came 'in such a spirit . . . they [would] not fail'. A similar conciliatory way of thinking with regard to the competing parties had been Abdul Baha's position during the Constitutional Revolution in Persia. As for the Zionists, there was a lot of talk about what they intended to do, there was a role for them, but he also told the journalist – '[l]et them come and do more and say less'.[64] An equivocal remark, this might have been an oblique reference to the short period of military administration (1917–20) that preceded the civilian administration headed by the first High Commissioner of Palestine, during which the Zionist Commission arrived in Palestine in (early 1918) making a lot of noise. When addressing the need for the country to be developed in the newspaper interview, Abdul Baha invoked the millennial vision of the Old Testament 'prophets Isaiah, Jeremiah and Zachariah'. Such an amalgam of regard for ancient prophecy and for contemporary events also featured in a response Abdul Baha gave to an inquiring member of his flock a decade and a half earlier, later published in the book, *Some Answered Questions*. There Abdul Baha also had recourse to prophecy to support the Jews' return to their ancient 'homeland' which was already beginning to gather steam in 1906:

. . . Israel, scattered all over the world, was not reassembled in the Holy Land in the Christian cycle; but in the beginning of the cycle of Baha'u'llah this divine promise, as is clearly stated in all the Books of the Prophets, has begun to be manifest. You can see that from all parts of the world tribes of Jews are coming to the Holy Land; they live in villages and lands which they make their own, and day by day they are increasing to such an extent that all Palestine will become their home.[65]

Underlying both statements was a teleological reading of Zionism that made the reconstruction of ancient Israel part of God's plan for the world, and for Baha'ism in particular. Alongside Christian evangelical dispensationists, though perhaps not to the same degree, Baha'is had an investment in the success of Zionism. The Baha'i version of the return of Christ coincides with the return of the Jews to the Holy Land, but, needless to say, not in the same way as it does for the various millennialists, dispensationalists and Christian Zionists.[66] Baha'ullah was both the return of Christ and greater still, the Biblical Lord of Hosts whose appearance was going to bring about the glorious kingdom at the end of time foreseen in the Books of Isaiah and Daniel. The quandary here is how we are to reconcile Abdul Baha's two positions, the teleological Biblically-derived view of the return of the Jews to the Holy Land at the end of time, and the photoshot of events as they appeared in 1919. He seems to have envisaged the obvious dangers attending the influx of Zionist Jews, though it is unlikely he would have penetrated the motives of the 'just' British government, which to be fair was difficult in 1919 but which would in the course of time, during the early years of the guardianship of his grandson, become more evident. Suffice to say, the Baha'i leadership under Abdul Baha and even less Shoghi Effendi seems not to have had any qualms about the manner in which this momentous, divinely-ordained event was coming into effect.

> In sponsoring the Zionist project for its own ends, Lloyd George's British imperialist government adopted a unique, hybrid colonialism in Palestine: they 'administered' while Jewish immigrants 'settled'. They were thus responsible for creating, as prophesied, a problem in Palestine that in time long grew to be beyond their capacity to solve.[67]

There are a number of considerations which might be taken into account in assessing Abdul Baha's remarks. The intended audience for the journalist's piece which was published in the *New York Globe and Commercial Advertiser* was Christian and Jewish, as it had been for the talk in *Some Answered Questions*, but obviously not Muslim. On the other hand, the Quran was not as clear on the return of the Jews to Palestine as the Hebrew Bible was. Moreover, in the multi-ethnic, multi-religious society of Palestine in the earliest years of the British Mandate the likelihood of sectarian clashes was not difficult to foresee. One salient factor has strong grounds for inclusion in an overall assessment of Baha'i attitudes toward Zionism and Israel in the first half of the twentieth century. The international Baha'i community established in Haifa (in so far as we can speak of such an entity in 1919) had been a generation in the making as far as European and American believers were concerned, and it was preponderantly from a Christian background. The formative institutions in the Baha'i world in the decades to come (and still today) would be overseen in the main by male North Americans of Protestant extraction. These factors would weigh heavily on the attitude those in high positions in the Baha'i faith would take toward the state of Israel.[68] They decisively inflected the journey their religion had taken away from the Islamic milieu in which it had grown up where, for Quranic reasons the Jews were considered untrustworthy and deniers of revelation, a thought-world in which Ali Muhammad the Bab had fully participated, though orientalists might have reported otherwise.[69]

During the first two decades of the twentieth century as far as some British converts to Baha'ism were concerned, the mythical, the Biblical, even the occult, coalesced in such a way us to vindicate the prophecy of Abdul Baha. No one has penetrated that world better than Lil Osborn. She quotes the following lines from a British Baha'i poet, Edward Hall, entitled 'The Isles Unveiled':

> At length the hour, the darkest she had known –
> The harvest-hour of ill the world had sown –
> Heaped woe on woe; and facing thunderous hate,
> She warred her way towards her destined fate
> To be a servant of the Will Divine

In building up a prosperous Palestine.
Search through the world and nothing stands so clear
As this event foreseen by sage and seer.
Indeed, through war the Holy Land was freed
By British hand from negligence and greed,
And one who dwelt serene on Carmel's height
Proclaimed the day as of Prophetic Light,
The Persian sage and British general met
For one brief hour that none should e'er forget,
For he, the Servant of the Lord was sign
Of that great day that marked the Will Divine,
How strange! The Jews – those exiles of the world
Like loosened leaves the eddying winds have swirled
By these strong Isles are granted friendly aid
To now return where none need be afraid.
If Zion smiles, if Bethlehem gives praise,
Say 'tis of God – and great are all His ways:
These Western Isles from nothingness grew great
To serve the Lord in opening wide his gate.

The title, 'presumably . . . a pun on Blavatsky's *Isis Unveiled*', gestures toward an occult dimension which Hall shared with Tudor Pole, Alice Buckton and others on the fringe of the early British Baha'i community. The Persian sage was Abdul Baha, and Allenby the British General who led the Egyptian Expeditionary Force into Jerusalem in December 1917. As for its content, Osborn informs us:

> The poem is a peon of praise to the civilising mission of the British Isles in world history. However, it is in no way simply a tribute to British imperialism, it clearly connects Britain to Palestine and relates the roles of Abdu'l Baha and General Allenby to the return of Jews to Palestine and the spiritual significance of such an event.[70]

The context of the Baha'i community in Israel during the first decade of its existence between the foundation of the state in 1948 and the death of Shoghi Effendi in London in 1957, is defined in part by the process of its decoupling from the Muslim context out of which it had grown in Iran, and in whose orbit it had moved during its long gestation in Ottoman territories from 1853–1918. Abdul Baha, as we have seen on the occasion of his visit to the Woking Mosque, performed *salat* according to Sunni rite and was generally in the habit of attending Friday prayers in Akka. His final days show how his daily life was embedded within that world. 'On the last Friday morning of his stay on earth [25 November 1921] . . . 'Abdu'l-Baha attended the noonday prayer at the Mosque . . . After tea the Mufti of Haifa and the head of the Municipality . . . were received by him'. At his funeral, the Mufti of Haifa and other distinguished Muslims, together with a Christian Arab and a Jewish representative delivered orations.[71] Shoghi Effendi radically reoriented this milieu even as the scope of his daily life grew smaller and his public life greatly reduced since he rarely appeared in official gatherings and had minimal contact with individual Muslims. His important relationships, apart from those with his fellow Baha'is were, if we are to accept the emphasis of Ruhiyyih Rabbani's biography, largely with British officials and later with Israeli ones.

A recent article based on material drawn from various archives in Israel puts us in a position to see in practice how the relationship between the emergent Baha'i Word Centre and the Israeli government evolved. No clearer expression of this can be found than in the latter's endorsement of the expansion of land and property allowed to accrue to the former, partly on the understanding (which has proved to be a valid one) that the beautification of the Baha'i gardens and mausoleums would attract tourists.

> With Israeli government agreement, permission, and support, new lands – including contested lands claimed by absentee Arab landowners – were turned over to the Baha'is in post-independence Israel and vast and breathtaking new gardens were added on the slopes of Mount Carmel and in Bahji (on the outskirts of Acre), the Baha'i world's holiest place.[72]

The land where the Baha'i monuments are located in Haifa contiguous to Abbas Street named after Abdul Baha (Abbas Effendi) is popularly known as the 'Persian Gardens'. After the withdrawal of the British (21 April 1948) and the capture of Haifa by Haganah (23 April) in the city where 70,000

Arabs were estimated to have dwelled until 1948, their number had dwindled to around 6,000.[73] Over the following months these were 'evacuated' to a 'permitted area' of the city which included the Abbas quarter and contiguous ones (the Wadi Nisnas and Wadi Saib quarters). In other words, the physical residue of the Palestinian *nakba* in Haifa was living in the vicinity of the Baha'i holy places on Mount Carmel.[74] The remaining Arab population, the proportion of Arab Muslim families now somewhat smaller than Arab Christian, was concentrated in isolation away from the Jews and minorities including Armenians, Greeks and Baha'is who 'hitherto had been integrated in lifestyle and place of residence within the Arab population'. The minorities were not required to be transferred but 'mostly remained where they were'.[75] Geller notes: 'In fact, on the day before the relocation of Haifa's Muslim and Christian Arab population, Shoghi Rabbani wrote directly to Prime Minister Ben-Gurion praising the re-establishment of the Jewish state and the ingathering of the Jewish Exiles'. Not only did 'the Baha'i leadership successfully tr[y] to take advantage of Arab flight during the 1948 War to purchase land', within the Ministry of Religions the Baha'i community was at their request detached from the Department of Druze and Muslim Affairs. Geller notes the Baha'is' residence in Haifa and Acre can be adduced to explain the fact 'there is virtually no record of Baha'i complaints regarding the restrictions associated with Military Government rule'.[76] It is very difficult to imagine there ever could have been any security issues for Baha'is in the new state. Aside from religious reasons the whole *raison d'etre* of their existence in Israel was that they were everything that the indigenous Arab population were not.

It must have seemed that the seamless transfer of sovereignty from the British Mandate to the new state of Israel was a providential act (though it is fair to say Shoghi Effendi did not air this view in public) delivering the 'nascent faith of God' from its enemies. That the Babi-Baha'i narrative Shoghi Effendi had constructed in *God Passes By* to coincide with the centenary celebrations of 1944 should have been set into play by a racial thinker such as Gobineau is no less ironic than the fact that after 1948 the Baha'i World Centre should be incubated in the midst of a newly established state raised upon the foundation of an ethno-nationalist ideology such as Zionism, when Shoghi Effendi had already located nationalism and racism at the core of the modern malaise. For this reason it is very important to understand that he construed his relationship with the British Mandate authorities, and later with the state of Israel, as vital in safeguarding the interests of the Baha'i faith. While Israel might have registered as a point of identification for Baha'is from evangelical Protestant backgrounds, for Shoghi Effendi, whose primary concern was always the interests of the Baha'i faith as a discrete religion, with its spiritual and administrative headquarters established in Haifa and its vicinity, support for Israel was more a matter of exigency, abeit highly beneficial, than founded in any profound belief in the virtue of a Jewish state.[77] However, his wife, daughter of architect Sutherland Maxwell, was demonstrably more enthusiastic about the outcome of what 'became known in Israeli ideological pronouncements as the "War of Independence"', terminology she happily employs in *Priceless Pearl*.[78] Combined with the obedience to the government in which they were situated, and the international leadership's strategy for Israel (non-conversion of Israelis; maintenance of a limited regulated presence of Baha'is in the country) Western Baha'is were accumulating a strong identification with Zionism and Israel.

If under Abdul Baha, Baha'ism in the West was patronised by Christian universalists, under Shoghi Effendi converts from Christianity, most notably Canon George Townshend of the Church of Ireland, helped him take the Baha'i faith in a direction that absorbed key Zionist and orientalist elements. Townshend wrote in his introduction to *God Passes By*:

> The proclamation of His [Baha'ullah's] Faith was made in 1844, the year when the strict exclusion of the Jews from their own land enforced by the Muslims for some twelve centuries was at last relaxed by the Edict of Toleration and 'the times of the Gentiles' were 'fulfilled'.[79]

Besides the inaccuracy over 1844 which is the date of the start of the Babi movement (not Baha'ullah's faith), Townshend, relying on an earlier American Baha'i who got the date from Christian millennialist Edward Bickersteth, was repeating a nonsensical statement about Jewish presence in the holy land being barred by Muslims which was a typical feature of Christian orientalism.[80] Such activity as there was in the 1840s for 'restoration of the Jewish nation in Palestine' was inspired by British Christians and consisted of representations in high places. Lord Ashley was canvassing Jewish opinion about their return to the holy land: 'whether they would be willing to go and when would they be ready'.[81] According to Walter Laqueur's definitive *History of Zionism*, projects for the 'return of the Jews to their homeland' of this period,

> were all romantic and artificial constructions suspended in mid-air . . . The spate of projects at this time was a direct outcome of the acute crisis in the Near East, the beginning of the dissolution of the Ottoman empire. But they did not coincide with any marked rise in Jewish national awareness.[82]

At the time Jews in Europe were committed to the goal of emancipation. '*The idea of settling in an uncivilised, backward country, subject to the whims of arbitrary and cruel Turkish pashas, was unlikely to appeal to them*'.[83] Laqueur makes no mention of an 1844 'Edict of Toleration'.

By the late 1940s Baha'is had adopted a teleological Biblically-derived understanding of the holy land that drew heavily on texts very similar to those used in Christian millennialism, and came to see Israel's establishment as part of the divinely preordained plan in their own religion. The process was in the making from the time Western Baha'is who started to visit Abdul Baha in Akka from 1899 returned with interpretations of prophecy. These embedded Islamic dates within an otherwise typical Christian millenarian hotchpotch of Biblical quotations from the Hebrew prophets, notably the Book of Daniel, and from the New Testament Book of Revelations, according to which the appearance of the Bab and Baha'ullah was to be ascertained as the return of John the Baptist and Christ, respectively.[84] This type of mythologising can be seen in an extended form in a book by an American former TV presenter which is simultaneously a popular piece of Baha'i proselytic literature and the most forthright statement of what might be termed Christian-Baha'i Zionism. Categorised by MacEoin as a form of Baha'i writing 'in which a direct and sometimes detailed comparison is made between Christ and the Bab', William Sears' *Thief in the Night* attempts to link Christ's return with the brief mission and martyrdom of Ali Muhammad, pinning dates and events in Babi history on to erstwhile Christian millennialist prophecies concerning the Last Day/Return of Christ. In line with other American Baha'is, Sears anachronistically misapplies 'Israel' repeatedly when he means historical Palestine.[85]

Ahmadi Colonial and Post-Colonial Orientations

It would be naïve to have expected Shoghi Effendi not to have prayed for a Zionist victory in 1948. His wife comes close to confirming this: 'Many times Shoghi Effendi referred to the miraculous protection the World Centre received during the disturbed and dangerous period of the end of the British Mandate and the firm establishment of the Jewish State'.[86] The Palestinian Arabs and their allies in the 1947–8 war were preponderantly Muslims. Had they possessed the power and organisation to win control they most probably could not have been relied upon to have treated the Baha'i World Centre, stretching over split sites in Akka and Haifa, in as friendly a way as did the conquering Jewish militias. Writing in the *Daily Mail* in January 1923, a generation before imposition of political Zionism on the Arab population had caused their amicable relations with Britain to sour, journalist J. M. N. Jeffries opined: 'We *made* the Arabs during the [1914–18] war, and till we brought in and imposed Zionism, the Arabs of Palestine throbbed to have a British occupation'.[87] On this spot on the earth, being empire's beneficiary meant a smooth transition into the post-colonial period (although serious reservations need to be overcome before Israel can be termed a post-colonial state).

Ahmadis had not been subject to destabilising pressures in colonial India. Roles were therefore in some ways reversed, for though despised by other Muslims in their native land they were not continual objects of discrimination and at times victims to violent persecution as were Babis and Baha'is in Iran. In colonial times the Ahmadiyya community was not alone among Muslim groups in maintaining a conciliatory attitude toward the British. Sayyid Ahmad Khan and his followers had a very amicable relationship with them in the Anglo-Oriental College venture at Aligarh. Abrogation of jihad in the context of British rule in India was not limited to modernists, 'but also [expressed] by a number of tradition-oriented *'ulama'*.[88] The Ahl-i Hadith refused to countenance military action against British rule although Ghulam Ahmad insisted some of them were living a 'double life' under the British, in secret holding out hopes for a 'bloodthirsty Mahdi and Messiah'.[89] After the colonial protection of Britain was withdrawn Ahmadis found themselves situated within the new state of Pakistan and it was here that serious trouble began to brew. The contestation, opposition and eventual persecution to which Ahmadis were victim in the post-colonial period, mainly in Pakistan but also in other Muslim countries, comprised complexities that cannot be explained in simplistic terms.

Overall, the causes behind the adverse experience of Ahmadiyya in Pakistan have been well-accounted for. Spencer Lavan outlined anti-Ahmadi agitation at an early stage in the Punjabi riots of the 1920s, and the election of Ahmadi Zafrullah Khan to presidency of the Muslim League in 1931 which excited the beginning of anti-Ahmadi agitation spearheaded by the Majlis-i Ahrar-i Islam. His book stops in 1936 and is largely dictated by political issues relating to colonial rule and Ghulam Ahmad's pro-Britain stance. A. H. Khan's recent study concentrates its analysis in part on Khalifa al-Masih II Bashiruddin Mahmud Ahmad's intense engagement of the Ahmadiyya in the politics of Kashmir prior to and immediately after partition and brings out important considerations relating to the community's political involvement and temporary suspension in 1947 of Ghulam Ahmad's annulment of jihad. He also probes in detail the build up of opposition to Ahmadiyya in both colonial India and post-colonial Pakistan and is especially strong on the post-colonial period in which metropolis and periphery have largely disappeared and the South Asian actors occupy centre stage. Khan's particular insight into anti-Ahmadiyyat is that it builds over time. 'One must construct a more complete narrative of the development of the Ahmadi controversy in order to provide convincing explanations – taboo doctrine aside – for the rise of Ahmadi persecution and its role in contemporary South Asia'.[90] A significant factor is that,

> the instigators of anti-Ahmadi sentiment over the course of the past century shared common lineages with the original opponents of Mirza Ghulam Ahmad . . . Thus, it becomes clear that Ahmadi identity is not wholly based on [his] controversial claims, but is the outgrowth of multiple influences over time, including the particular South Asian context from which it emerged.[91]

The the twin organisations Majlis-i Ahrar-i Islam and Abu Ala Maududi's Jamaat-i Islami invoked Ahmadiyya complicity with the British in their cases against them. According to Sayyid Vali Reza Nasr, Maududi was alive to ramifications of this relationship when Britain condemned the Islamic law used to justify the death sentence on the Ahmadi missionaries in Afghanistan in 1924. By the time both organisations joined together to protest Zafrullah Khan's position as Pakistan's first foreign minister in 1953, the politics was entirely home-centred and involved both movements' jockeying for power as advocates of the role of Islam in the new state.[92] However, high among contributory causes to anti-Ahmadi persecution was Mahmud Ahmad's ruling, made within a short period after his assumption of leadership of the Qadianis that forbade Ahmadis from praying or marrying with non-Ahmadi Muslims or attending their funerals.[93] Khan states that in sociological terms this *takfir* (excommunication) of non-Ahmadis deepened the Qadianis' isolation.[94] The refusal of Zafrullah Khan to attend Muhammad Jinna's funeral (because it would mean his standing behind a non-Ahmadi imam), is often cited as further reason for the acceleration of the Ahmadiyya position toward exclusion from the umma as non-Muslims.[95]

Although the Ahmadi predicament today is far more complex than a case of peace-loving minority falls foul of Muslim intolerance, it is not unknown for the Ahmadi case to be stated in these terms. Anthea Lathan, for example, sums up the situation as one of 'accusations of apostasy and heresy as well as classification as a heterodox movement . . . motivated politically rather than religiously'. More pointedly she suggests: 'The Ahmadiyya understands itself as a reformist movement, and as interpreter of the "true" faith, whereas many Muslims accuse them of apostasy'.[96] However, postcolonial critic Terenjit Sevea sees the matter quite differently. She poses what she calls 'Islamist questions' which she takes to be related to 'Islamist critiques of the psyche' produced by Colonialism (with brackets around the capital *c*) rather than approaches (closer to those adopted here) that prioritise anti-colonial Islamist critique in terms of 'realism or the colonialism of late colonial India circa. 1857–1940s'.[97] The Islamist questions she focuses on are those of Muhammad Iqbal and Abu Ala Maududi, in particular the way in which the two Muslim thinkers are claimed to have 'challenged the psychological bases of colonial realities and/or policies'. Frequently invoking Frantz Fanon to elucidate her argument, Sevea proposes that a Nietzschean-like slavishness of the psyche is a condition of colonialism. She points out the other-worldliness which Iqbal saw as reprehensible in the kind of 'Sufism that had suppressed the action-oriented and self affirmation of "Islam"', and the '"Christianisation" of Islam'. A similar conditioning of the psyche was applicable to

Ahmadiyya: its product, Iqbal and Maududi argued, helped deliver a slavish morality 'to Colonial perpetuity . . . resonant of Nietzsche's attack on the slavish idea of redemption through Christ'. It was upon this 'slavish idea' that Muslims' condemnation of Ahmadiyya should focus, according to Iqbal, not on theological differences between mainstream Muslims and the Ahmadis, which was something he dismissed as belonging to medieval times.[98] Sevea envisages both Iqbal and Maududi entertaining a vision of some sort of ghost-like effect of colonialism in which Ahmadiyya participated, ceding power to the British government as a religious duty and thus dooming Muslims to slavery in perpetuity. Disrobed of its postcolonial theoretical circumlocutions the argument of Sevea's article builds on a strong footing in anti-colonialist discourse and reprises Iqbal's well-known objection to Ahmadiyya – a nationalist one that argued the pro-colonial stance of groups like the Ahmadis weakened Muslim unity. Needless to say, this is a position still widely held today among Muslims. In a long letter to Nehru, Iqbal set out his position on Ahmadiyya, pointing out that the political awakening of the Indian Muslims worried Congress and 'equally . . . [made] the Qadianis, too, feel nervous . . . because they feel that the rise in political prestige of the Indian Muslims is sure to defeat their designs to carve out from the Ummat of the Arabian Prophet a new Ummat for the Indian prophet'.[99] Ostensibly, Sevea's argument may function on the level of the 'psyche' but it nonetheless enables us to articulate a key faultline separating the mahdi movements and the position of prominent Muslim intellectuals who conceived of colonialism as a material and psycho-social danger to the umma, and who identified these movements as undermining its agency and the ability to effectively respond to outside threats. We will return to this topic in our final chapter.

7

Orientalism and Modernity in Baha'i and Ahmadi Writings

Drawing on Western orientalist tropes concerning the decadence of Islam, Baha'is in the first half of the twentieth century wrote histories of their community that cast the Muslim majority in a conspicuously degraded light. Not only the Baha'is but a tiny number of their adversaries from the much smaller Azali-Babi sect entertained a disdain for the role of Islam within Iranian society. To found a modern Iranian nationalism, quondam Azali-Babi Mirza Aqa Khan Kermani promoted a remodelled Aryanism borrowed from Western orientalists that figured Islam as an alien religion. Starting from a similar premise, specifically, that Shi'i Islam was archaic and moribund, Shoghi Effendi Rabbani projected a vision of a new world order spearheaded by the Baha'i community presided over by a Baha'i theocracy. Ambiguously condemning secularisation and the decline of religion in the world in general while welcoming it in Iran because it severely diminished the power and role of the Shi'i ulama in that society, Shoghi Effendi's perspective manifests clear similarities to the secularists of modern Turkey. The attitude might be epitomised by a comment made by an associate of Kemal Atatürk: 'We want to return to the Orient as Orientalists, but not as Orientals'.[1] Tracing this modernising outlook back to the 'Ottoman orientalism' of the *fin de siècle* Turkish reformers as well as considering it in relation to nationalism and race, this chapter will try to situate Baha'i and Azali positions within a taxonomy of reform programmes for eastern societies produced by nationalist, anti-Muslim (or post-Muslim) Middle Eastern intellectuals and religious thinkers of the first half of the twentieth century. We shall see how Shoghi Effendi's pen launched a codified Baha'i vision of modernity that combined modern and anti-modern aspects, together with hegemonic and triumphalist formulations that continue to hold the twenty-first century Baha'i community in a rigid vice. During the 1940s an Ahmadi version of a new order was constructed by Khalifa al-Masih II Bashiruddin Mahmud Ahmad that appeared to shadow, if not mimic, the Baha'i one. However, although the trajectories of both movements may be said to run in parallel in certain respects, most notably in clinging to the skirts of waning British colonial power, in positioning themselves within an emerging anti-umma world arc toward the close of the century, Baha'i orientalism was now entrenched while Ahmadi proselytism continued to face eastwards.

Revisionist Applications of Orientalism in the Context of Eastern Voices

Having probed Russian orientalism to find contemporary theorists have discerned parallels between Said and some in Rozen's school in their rejection of the othering of eastern societies, we will now reprise the theoretical issue of orientalism and its applicability to intra-Turkish and Iranian formations beyond the modes discussed in Said's *oeuvre*. This will involve reference to orientalism in elite Ottoman circles and later in Kemalist thought, as well as in the writings of Iranian intellectuals starting from the late Qajar period and well into the twentieth century. Analysis will focus on consideration of the various orientalisms on display in late nineteenth and early twentieth-century culture and politics, which was also the period in which Azali proponents of modernism and the first generation of Western Baha'i writers actively adopted orientalist tropes. A useful summative article written in the late 1990s resets the balance and brings into play the various orientalisms we will be discussing, starting with the classic Saidian form:

> [O]rientalists did place themselves in the service of European empires; the fortunes of the field were frequently linked to imperialism; and European assumptions of superiority to non-Europeans and of the progressive role of imperialism were widespread. On the other hand, it is important to note that some orientalists opposed imperialism or wrote favorably about Islamic culture and society; that some Middle Eastern nationalists were themselves inspired by Western orientalist writings; *and that nationalist and Muslim theological positions have their own biases and assumptions.*[2]

A space is opened here for the pro-eastern positions attributed to orientalists such as Browne, Bartol'd and others in the Rozen school; this leads on to opportunities of considering Middle-Easterners who, far from opposing orientalism, were actors espousing a variety of eastern nationalisms and actually appropriated orientalist texts and ways of thinking. From the moment *Orientalism* first appeared Said's approach was vigorously contested, and one of the more prominent criticisms concerned the rigid binary the work set up between orientalist discourse and its object. It was argued that this did not enable a space for the oriental to reply to the othering of the orientalist coloniser. Although orientalism enlisted both the coloniser and the colonised in a variety of ways, Said could not conceive of it moving beyond the state of being a Western style of dominating the East: 'Orientalism, in its post-eighteenth century form, could never revise itself'.[3] In this articulation of orientalist discourse the Western coloniser was producer of an image and the colonised the object, while the real 'Orient' (whatever that might be) was entirely absent. Homi Bhabha blurred this binary by demonstrating that far from being absolute, as implied by Said, on account of the seepage of the insidious voices of the colonised into orientalist discourse, it was in fact unstable and liable to slippage. Bhabha's work and that of others (such as Robert C. Young) focused on the British Empire in India and elsewhere exposing underling anxieties within colonial discourse.[4] A further important move was made by revisionist scholars who stretched the application of orientalism to easterners who were not officially incorporated into the British Empire or who belonged to nominally independent Islamic entities. Among these were Arab voices of the *mashriq* many of whom were, or had been, part of the Ottoman Empire; members of the Turkish elite who ruled that empire; and in the case of Iran, intellectuals who aspired to recreate a national entity that combined an imagined pre-Islamic past with a modern view of the world. Orientalism featured in different ways in all of their projects. As suggested by Burke, paradoxically it can be seen to have been an enabler of Arab, Turkish and Iranian nationalisms, as well as a stimulator of Islamist anti-colonial counter responses. In practice, therefore, objections to the monolithic orientalism Said had proposed were being addressed and new permutations engendered, though without undermining the importance of orientalism as a theoretic construct.

The Syrian intellectual Sadeq Al-Azm might be considered the first easterner to flag up the fallaciousness of insisting on the 'ineradicable distinction between East and West' that afforded Western orientalism a role so dominant that it effectively excluded any response. According to Al-Azm, Said had made the orientalist division between West and East an 'essentialist category' projecting 'radical ontological difference between the essential natures of Eastern and Western societies, culture and peoples'. Such 'reduction, representation and schematisation' only allowed for distinct cultures to speak to, or understand, one another as opposites.[5] Al-Azm coined the term 'Orientalism in reverse' with specific application to Arab nationalist and Islamist codifications that operated in a resistant mode. The term denotes a binary response on the part of Arabs who accept orientalist typology but in such a way as to reverse it, asserting instead Arab/Islamic superiority over Western decadence. Other eastern responses to orientalism developed simultaneous acculturative and resistant modes. 'Indeed, nationalists are inside-out orientalists, who revalorize what orientalists perceive as lacking. Thus, orientalism in effect summons nationalism into existence'.[6] Where they are encoded as forms of resistance these responses to orientalism invite incorporation into postcolonial frameworks, albeit that, according to Al-Azam, in their crude forms of denial they retained orientalist stereotypes and so allowed for, and even encouraged, their persistence.

Acculturative orientalism, on the other hand, while appearing outwardly to endorse the project of Western modernisation and cultural superiority, operated to shore up defences against Western penetration. Selim Deringil argues: 'the Ottoman elite adopted the mindset of their enemies, the archimperialists, and came to conceive of [the empire's] periphery as a colonial setting'. Copying the Russian model but also retaining features of British and French imperialism, their governing style operated as a kind of 'borrowed colonialism' intended to strengthen the empire against Western takeover. Adopting orientalist typology vis-à-vis the empire's 'backward Muslim' populations 'the Ottoman elite conflated the ideas of modernity and colonialism, and applied the latter as a means of survival against an increasingly hostile world'.[7] Labelling this mindset and its application as a method of governance 'Ottoman orientalism', Ussama Makdisi nonetheless considers it constituted a form of resistant modernity: 'It posited an empire in "decline" yet capable of an independent renaissance, westernized but not Western, leader of a reinvigorated Orient yet no longer of the "Orient" represented by the West, nor that embodied by its unreformed subjects'; it 'accommodated both strictly secularist and explicitly Islamist' modes.[8] With the collapse of the empire Ottoman orientalism morphed into 'Kemalist orientalism', an application of orientalism that was part of Mustapha Kemal's nationalist project of modernisation and Westernisation with its six-point programme of republicanism, statism (in economic policy), populism, laicism, nationalism, and reformism.[9] Kemalist orientalism dropped Ottoman orientalism's Islamist strand and branded 'oriental backwardness and Islamic civilization' equivalents. Between the wars Kemalist orientalism formed part of the 'anti-clerical rage' of Kemalists' whose project was founded on the 'imperative to destroy "tradition"'.[10]

In the Iranian context the debate around orientalism has largely centred upon scrutinising the part Western orientalists played in the construction of Iranian nationalism in what might be construed as a further application/intrusion of the Aryan myth into the history of eastern peoples. Where in India orientalism functioned in articulating an essentialist indigenous 'spirituality' in Iran its focus took the form of an imaginary excavation of a glorious pre-Islamic Persia. Stretching from the earlier phase which began in the last decades of the nineteenth century to the mid-twentieth century, Hamid Enayat noted:

> Iranian (or oriental) intellectuals tr[ied] to alleviate their present inferiority complex vis-à-vis the West through an uncritical glorification of their ancient past and culture. Ironically enough, however, orientalists have inadvertently boosted nativistic sentiment and have provided its proponents with ready-made arguments through their scholarly findings.[11]

Taking this forward Mehrzad Boroujerdi demonstrates how Iranian intellectuals dealt with double othering as Iran underwent rapid modernisation on the Western model. In the post-World War Two Pahlavi state they struggled under 'petrolic despotism', and the more distant othering of 'a larger entity called the West', and their 'tortured' debate included 'intense discussion about the merits and vices of orientalism and Orientalists'.[12] By the 1970s the Iranian intelligentsia were espousing an interweaving of complex and disparate narratives involving varied discourses, secular, nationalist, Marxist and Islamic. With respect to the problem of accommodating modernity and in particular the development of subjectivity Farzin Vahdat has shown how this invariably involved dialogue or altercation with a modern world often perceived of as at odds with Persian culture.[13] Latterly, Dabashi has urged a move beyond 'the colonial acts of representation' that concerned Said in *Orientalism*, and in a bid to uncover 'postcolonial agency' for 'Islam as a religion of protest' (a role historically taken up by Shi'ism in the Middle East), argues Shi'ism should now in a contemporary post-Islamist phase perform the role of 'resisting the Empire'.[14]

Hidden Intertextualities: Aqa Khan Kermani's Orientalism and Baha'i pre-Islamic Panegyric

Aqa Khan Kermani (1854/5–96) is one of the first modernisers in the Iranian context. An avowed proponent of ideas that would appear to set Iran on the trajectory of Western-style modernisation, he was also in touch with indigenous modernisers like Malkum Khan and associated with Jamal al-Din ('Afghani') Asadabadi in his pan-Islamic project. During the last ten years of his life, which were spent in Istanbul, Kermani acquired a fluent command of French and English in addition to Turkish. Pointing out that he was well aware of the positivist school of European thought, Vahdat presents him as a believer in the 'upholding of reason and modern science, both of which he viewed as directly and unavoidably opposed to religion'.[15] Another dimension to Kermani's thought, the part that particularly concerns his interaction with orientalism, was his racist nationalism. Developed out of 'the aristocratic pride of a well-born Persian who holds Arab culture in contempt', he shared this belief with the Caucasian reformer Fath Ali Akhundzadeh whose writings he imitated.[16] Among the cognate ideas they formulated were the designation of the pre-Islamic period as an Enlightened Age, condemnation of the Arabs for bringing Islam to Iran, and projection of the Islamic period 'as a time of misery, ruin'.[17] Whether these ideas were transmitted mainly through Western orientalism or indigenous sources is open to debate. The issue is argued from different ends by Mohamad Tavakoli-Targhi and Reza Zia-Ebrahimi. The former favours the view that, again like Akhundzadeh,

Kermani had his admiration for Iran's pre-Islamic past activated by Firdawsi's *Shahnamih* which he viewed as 'a foundation for preserving the "people/nation of Iran" (*millat-i Iran*)'.[18] Summing up Kermani's amplified hatred for 'the Arab lizard-eaters', Tavakoli-Targhi sees this as 'a double process of projection and introjection [in which] Iranian nationalists attributed their undesirable customs and conditions to Arabs and Islam. Obversely, desirable European manners and cultures were appropriated and depicted as originally Iranian'.[19] Reza Zia-Ebrahimi's portrayal of Aqa Khan Kermani and Akhundzadeh confirms this description but offers a counterpoint to the indigenous sources argument: 'Akhundzadeh's and Kermani's real muse – idealized beyond recognition, the model to emulate, the key to progress and prosperity – was very much Europe, more so than the times of Jamshid and Khosrow'.[20] For sure Kermani's nationalism was strongly influenced by European orientalists in the way Enayat suggested, the mystique of orientalism impacting on him in the same way as it did on twentieth-century Iranian intellectuals. Specifically, it was Gobineau, Renan, George Rawlinson, Noldeke, E. G. Browne and Percy Sykes who, Zia-Ebrahimi argues, through their 'racial-historicist view of Iranianness', fuelled nationalists' horror of any cultural or religious miscegenation, hence their aversion to the Arab component in Shi'ism.[21] Citing a number of passages from Browne's work, he demonstrates the 'parallels to be drawn between the founding texts of Iranian nationalism and orientalist views of Iranian history' in which Aryan Iranians are distinguished from Arabs.[22] The accent falls on the supposedly bloody conquest of Sassanian Iran by the wild, marauding Muslim Arab armies when the Arabs did their best to wipe out Zoroastrianism.[23]

As a literary-cultural figure, activist and nationalist thinker Kermani has long stood out for secular nationalist Iranians despite the part he played in the Azali–Baha'i episode. His Azali affiliation sits in his profile alongside other orientations: he 'claimed to be a Muslim, a Babi, an agnostic philosopher all at one and the same time'.[24] On account of his marriage to a daughter of Subh-i Azal, his anti-Baha'i co-activities with Shaykh Ahmad Ruhi, and the notoriety accruing from his execution for plotting against Shah Nasir al-Din, Baha'is would have no desire whatever to claim any association with Kermani.[25] Arguing the power of religion and standing in diametric opposition to racism of any kind, some Baha'i writings enthusiastically celebrate the Islamic heritage of Iran. J. R. I. Cole explored this orientation in a wide-ranging article on outstanding individuals from the Qajar period that places Abdul Baha's 1875 treatise *Mysterious Forces of Civilization* (Risalih-yi madaniyyih) in juxtaposition to Akhundzadeh's racist and nationalist views. On the latter's crude binarism Cole proffers a similar diagnosis to Tavakoli-Targhi and Zia-Ebrahimi:

> The Europeans are powerful, and therefore imitating them acts in a talismanic manner to transfer some of their power to Iranians, whereas the contemporary Arabic-speaking lands were from Akhundzadah's point of view weak and backward, so that continued mimesis of them doomed Iranians to enervation.[26]

In contrast to Akhundzadeh's nationalist chauvinism, *Mysterious Forces of Civilization*, written to apprise the Shah of the fallacies of those conservative forces in the country which opposed any type of reform, demonstrates Abdul Baha's catholicity. To support his argument, Abdul Baha appeals to a wide range of sources, from pre-Islamic to modern times. In addition to the usual sources of scripture, Persian literature, and traditions, he includes a story set in pre-Islamic Arabia, incidents from European history, and citations from several Western authorities. An extended section near the beginning of his work adverts to the greatness of the Persian Empire in the time of Cyrus both in terms of scope, government, and intellectual achievement, contrasting this with the decay into which contemporary Persia has fallen and charging Persians with lethargy and lack of resolution. Cole sums up Abdul Baha's position as one that 'celebrated the advent of Islam as an impetus to civilization that benefited the inhabitants of the Iranian plateau just as it did many others'. Abdul Baha did not 'accept an easy dichotomy between Zoroastrian Iran and Arab Islam. Even Arab Islam, he points out, borrowed military and other technology from non-Arab civilizations such as the Sasanian'. Iranians, therefore, 'do not have a single authentic self or culture, but rather have formed part of and benefited from a number of civilizations'. Cole is at great pains to establish that 'although 'Abd al-Baha, like Akhundzadah, appeals to the Zoroastrian and Indo-Iranian pasts in order to inspire nineteenth-century Qajar subjects with pride, and urges the adoption of European modernity, his underlying assumptions are anti-essentialist'.[27]

From a Baha'i perspective, however, there is another side to this: irrespective of his association with the despised Azali faction, Kermani's thought has connections with Baha'i positions that emerged after Abdul Baha when Baha'is began to produce writings which shared common features with Kermani's. The situation is not so surprising considering the fact that they had a common provenance in orientalism; it can be substantiated by viewing the establishment of an emergent early twentieth-century revisionist form of writing Baha'i history, which includes an underlying commentary on the condition of Iran that explicitly champions ideas about the superiority of pre-Islamic Iranian history and Iran's putative ancient Aryan origins. This writing was produced at a time when such ideas were ubiquitous in Iran and were a major component of Pahlavi nationalism. Baha'i writers even went so far as to express support for a political programme directed against Shi'i Islam. In comparison to the period of Abdul Baha's stewardship, the new position appearing in official Baha'i literature was moving either toward eulogies on Iran's pre-Islamic past or reformed Baha'i-delivered futures in which the defunct institutions of Islam were humbled. While the ongoing Baha'i discourse remained centred on Iranian or Near Eastern settings, it was produced mainly in Western locations, or from a Levantine outpost of the colonialising West. Before these points can be substantiated it is important to go back to the first few decades of the twentieth century and to trace how the strand of what we might term 'Baha'i orientalism' gained entry into the Baha'i consciousness. This will enable us to ascertain why and how with the aid of figures like Gobineau, Browne, Curzon and Chirol materials were assembled with which to denounce Qajar rule *in toto*, and to provide explicit validation of the policies of Reza Shah.

Orientalism in Writings of Early Western Baha'is

Orientalism entered the writings of early twentieth-century Western Baha'is via borrowings from orientalist writers such as Gobineau, Renan, Curzon, and E. G. Browne. Also influential were neo-orientalist ideas concerning 'world religions' connected to liberal Christianity and at the close of the nineteenth century orientalist ideas and tropes concerning 'East and West' that were 'in the air' at the time. Among the early North American converts to Baha'ism were wealthy and established society figures or professionals with lines to the social and political elite. Rich women like Phoebe Hearst and Laura Clifford-Barney played important roles, introduced to the new faith by others from solid middle-class backgrounds like Lua Getsinger and May Bolles who were in Paris when Baha'i activities got started in 1899.[28] Ethel Rosenberg was among a small Baha'i group established in London in the same year. At the 1908 Third International Congress for the History of Religion in Oxford, her paper constructed Baha'ism as a modern world religion built around a programme of progressive social teachings, its mahdi roots wholly neutralised:

> With Ali Mohammad . . . started that movement of living reform, elaborated and completed by the teachings of Baha'u'llah and his son Abdul Baha . . . Had the inspiration of this religious movement been confined to the teaching of the Bab, it is quite possible that it would have effected merely a reformation within the religion of Islam.[29]

Brendan McNamara notes how Rosenberg's presentation fitted into an agenda dating back to the first Parliament of World Religions held in Chicago in 1893, integral to its programme an 'affirmative orientalism' that overcame negative attitudes toward Islam, reflecting themes that would influence Abdul Baha's reception in the West, particularly at Westminster and in Oxford in 1912. As McNamara points out it was this background that ensured Abdul Baha as a savant from the Middle East who was not evidently Muslim would receive a positive reception under the sponsorship of liberal Christian clergymen, notably Estlin Carpenter and T. K. Cheyne.[30]

The thrust among the early Western Baha'is, especially in the United States, was supplied largely by males of Protestant ancestry. They had clearly imbibed attitudes to the East current in esoteric circles and through making journeys to the Far East visiting Akka, either on the way out or on the way back. Converts such as Sidney Sprague, Mason Remey, Stanwood Cobb and Horace Holley either brought with them, or quickly assembled, a portfolio of expertise that configured the scholar of oriental religions and Western traveller to the East in a way that was inflected by those special Baha'i roles, 'prominent believer' and 'travel teacher'. The Frenchman Hippolyte Dreyfus, however, was a scholar of another order with respect to his ability to produce analytic work on Baha'ism, especially its divergence from Muslim jurisprudence. Lil Abdo Osborn describes him as 'the first Occidental Jew to embrace Baha'ism' and 'the dominant European intellectual in Baha'i circles in this period' suggesting this prowess came from having been brought up in a religion 'with a strong tradition of jurisprudence, coupled with a mastery of the Code Napoleon'.[31] A lawyer in possession of a well-trained mind, he had a predilection for oriental languages and, with his wife Laura Clifford-Barney, was a regular visitor to Palestine where he was a valuable aid to Abdul Baha and later Shoghi Effendi. Among the first Western Baha'is to acquire the facility to read and translate Baha'i scripture from Persian and Arabic, he published *Essai sur le Béhaïsme* in 1906 and wrote learned pamphlets in which he weighed up his teacher, French orientalist Clément Huart's comparison of Babis to the Hurufis and concluded that in the East the 'Behais' had established fraternity among communities that were previously separated by insuperable (*infranchissable*) barriers. He provided an expert commentary on the Baha'i *mashriq al-adhkar* in Ashkhabad, distinguished from a mosque by its nine polygonal sides, eliminating the function of the *adhan* and interdicting the role of clergy by the prohibition of 'climbing *minbars*':

> En effet on n'y trouve ni le destiné aux ablutions, ni le *mihrâb* indiquant la direction de la *qiblah* et où se tient l'Imam pour la prière, ni le *minbar* où l'on monte pour exhorter les fidèles, et exciter leur ardeur au récit des martyrs. C'est qu'à vrai dire le Béhaïsme a apporté de radicale transformation dans l'Islam.[32]

In *Bahaism: The Universal Religion*, Dreyfus is close to Rosenberg in defining the Bab as notionally a universal Prophet whose revelation was, however, primarily limited in its horizon to Iranian Shi'ism – 'we cannot fail to notice in it a certain sectarian particularism which would have confined to Shiite Islam the benefits of . . . reform'.[33] This diminution of the Muslim element is emphasised more crudely by Mason Remey who writes of Christ and Baha'ullah as 'world prophets' and of Moses, Zoroaster, and Muhammad as 'local' prophets.[34]

Sorbonne-educated Sidney Sprague became a Baha'i in Paris at the turn of the twentieth century and spent more than a decade and a half in Europe and the Middle East. For Sprague to be a Western Baha'i traveller to the eastern societies inhabited by oriental Baha'is was to enact in one's person a unique privilege:

> Even some who had not become Baha'is had said to me: 'We have never opened our hearts to any Westerner as we have to you' so that if I, a worker in a great Cause, have succeeded in removing some of the prejudice and misunderstanding which separate the Oriental from the Occidental, and have helped to make East and West advance but one step nearer to each other, then I am well content.[35]

In these early Western Baha'i converts the dominant orientalist dicta of the epoch are to be found, beginning with the primary one: what amounted almost to a providential boundary separating East from West, with a subsidiary of the West fulfilling the masculine role and the East the feminine in human development. Both of these tropes were endorsed, qualified and ultimately transcended by the Baha'i message that,

> offers to the world a spiritual teaching which builds upon the teachings of the religions of the past and present, fulfilling their hopes and prophecies, and uniting all peoples, both East and West, in the spirit of God's Kingdom on earth.[36]

To Remey and other Western visitors to Akka, 'Abdul Baha spoke at some length regarding the uniting of the people of the West with those of the East – their spiritual unity – which is bringing about the regeneration of mankind.'[37] Remey also remarks that,

> Civilization is the outward expression of the inner or spiritual condition of a people. The Civilization of the West is in reality the fruit of the religion, which it has received from the East. The Orient is the mother, who has sent forth a man child, which is the Occident. Now that mother has grown old. She has been plundered and pillaged by her offspring of the West, and is helpless. The time is at hand for the Occident to go to her help, and in the spirit of love serve her and lift her from her present condition. By doing so the West will gain abundantly . . . through giving as well as receiving, for the Orient has much to give to the West.[38]

It was an idea of the time that attracted Westerners and Easterners and was most poetically phrased by an emigrant to Boston from the Middle East (see the English writings of Kahlil Gibran). In Abdul Baha's words, East and West were to come together to 'hold each other's hands and become as lovers'.[39] It was already happening 'through international relations, the increase of foreign commerce, and the travel and mingling of people'. But it could only be accomplished by spiritual affinity for 'the Oriental and Occidental are at variance in almost every way'. This was where the solution offered by Baha'ism came in through the mission of the Bab, Baha'ullah and Abdul Baha who were 'pre-eminent as lovers and servants of humanity'. 'With the fruition of this cause, the great Orient–Occident problem will be solved'.[40]

However, there was another side to this. Even a writer like Dreyfus, who was able to read A. L. M. Nicolas as well as E. G. Browne, could still write about Baha'ism emerging 'amongst the fanatical Muhammadans of Persia'. '[T]o-day [it] appears in the world as a lesson of liberalism'; 'the blood of [Babi] martyrs filtered into Persian soil; and, inspite of hostile fanaticism, produced an abundant harvest of generous ideas sustaining humanity!';

> [f]ar above Islam, in whose midst [Baha'ullah's] activity evolved, his higher thoughts flew towards the world of human sufferings, and already he conceived the remedy he would bring them: regeneration by work and love, these were the two pillars of his sociology.[41]

He employs qualifiers denoting backwardness and lowness such as 'fanatical' which is invariably prefixed to Muslim referents; 'fanaticism' set in opposition to the West's 'liberalism', 'higher thoughts', 'ideas sustaining humanity' (and so forth), with all of which Bahaism is associated. Other cognate words like 'scientific', 'rational', 'progress' are added to the semantic field without any qualification to offset the binary (e.g., the suggestion that innovative Muslim thinkers like Sayyid Ahmad Khan, Jamal al-Din 'Afghani', or Muhammad Abduh might also exist). This way of thinking confirms sedimentation of orientalism in Baha'i writing, a style which Baha'is henceforth make their own in adverting to the history of their movement. The precise inflection that emerges from the very beginning of Baha'ism's arrival in the West, with the incorporation of orientalist tropes into Baha'i literature, constructs a dual narrative: the Baha'i movement's mission to accomplish East–West unity and its embodiment of those principles of modernity (found in 'sociological' inquiry), that are blocked by the corrupt traditionalism of eastern/Iranian powers.

After the death of Dreyfus in 1928, Horace Holley could be considered the foremost *éminence grise* of the Western Baha'i community.[42] His early book, *Bahai: The Spirit of the Age* perfectly represents the confused amalgam of occultism, loose nineteenth-century organicism, social progressivism and belief in a 'New Age' – all of which were constituents of Baha'ism during this period. A decade or more before Shoghi Effendi's 'New World Order' conceptualisation started to appear, Holley's discourse was still woolly and pseudo-scientific but already featured a creeping magisterial note that becomes a distinguishing Baha'i feature. In the annunciation of the New Age the signs which designate the 'Rise of the Sun of Truth' may be of his own choice but they also bear heavily the imprint of Abdul Baha's talks delivered on his Western journeys a decade before. The failing religions of the past are in their present decay and corruption no longer capable of fructification in modern conditions.

> Innumerable are the 'rays' which even materialistic History must acknowledge have revealed their light and warmth in these past seventy or eighty years.
> The uniformity of cosmic law has been established by rational science and philosophy. Human slavery has been abolished. The long racial hope of the Jews approaches its magnificent realization. Christian Science has grown to powerful proportions. H. P. Blavatsky has transmitted from their secret hiding places the lost Esoteric Sciences. The movement for World Peace is irrevocably begun – an essential aspect of the rise of modern Industry. Kings and emperors have lost their ancient and supreme thrones. The Pope has lost his temporal authority. Women have rapidly arisen to the station of perfect equality with men. Psychic Research has become an authoritative science. Submerged economic groups press determinedly on for their right to education, responsibility and recreation. As many more 'rays' might be mentioned. Enough, surely, have been mentioned to show clearly enough that the earth of consciousness has been bathed in the Light of some spiritual Sun.[43]

Written in the following decade, an article in *Baha'i World* presents a more pronounced, embedded, condensed and tightly articulated view of organic progress:

> Civilization is the outworking of spiritual faith. That faith inspires fresh courage, removes the barriers of personality and groups, stimulates the mind to solve necessary problems from the point of view of the society as a whole, establishes a foundation of human reality raised above the bestial struggle for existence, and enables mankind to take one more forward step in its progress upon the eternal path.[44]

The Islamic notion of successive prophetic revelations in which the new absorbs and abrogates the previous one has been written over to create a theosophical effect where religions are seen to undergo a cycle of birth, infancy, adulthood and old age, linked to the efflorescence and decay of civilisations.

Baha'i World and the Civilising of Persia

It was not surprising given the hegemony of these thought-forms that Western Baha'is equated the civilising mission with the revelation of Baha'ullah and the norms of Western-led modernity. That is to say, early North American Baha'is invested wholesale in notions of their new-found faith working at the forefront of the dissemination of modernity and (Western) civilisation. In his talks in America, Abdul Baha encouraged (and indulged?) Americans and Europeans in their notions of civilisational superiority; he did not in the least wish to unsettle them by pointing out their imbrication in race theory, stating instead that God did not distinguish between black and white. The paternalist orientalism Abdul Baha exhorted Western converts to practise in the East was reversed in an address he gave to a black majority audience at Howard University, Washington, DC, and repeated in 'unity' gatherings of whites and blacks elsewhere on his travels in America. Blacks were exhorted to be 'grateful to the whites and the whites become loving toward the blacks'. Black Americans could see that Africans, 'semi-civilized and barbarous', had been deprived of education. They however, should look up to 'the civilization of Europe and America [as] an evidence and outcome of education'. The whites had emancipated the blacks and deserved gratitude in return for the, progress you [i.e., the Afro-Americans] have made . . . The first proclamation of emancipation for the blacks was made by the whites of America. How they fought and sacrificed until they freed the blacks. Then it spread to other places. The blacks of Africa were in complete bondage, but your emancipation led to their freedom also – that is the European states emulated the Americans, and the emancipation proclamation became universal. It was for your state that the whites of America made such an effort. Were it not for this effort, universal emancipation would not have been proclaimed.[45]

It is unfair to criticise Abdul Baha for not challenging formulations of race at a time when empire appeared to be at its zenith and his method was to address and bring out the best in his hearers with the aim of lifting them up to the heights of the Baha'i revelation. More than a generation after, Shoghi Effendi would bring racism to the fore in his letters to American Baha'is, especially its debilitating effect on future social coherence. However, it is correct to say that none of the Baha'i founders ever situated an evil such as racism – or the colonised's desire to resist it – in the context of the West's recent history of colonisation, which they also hardly ever mentioned, but left at the implied level of Abdul Baha's talks.

Looking at a range of modern European theorists, Bhikhu Parekh sees continuities in the way in which Western culture configured less powerful countries and their peoples.

> During the period of colonial expansion Europe had at least three influential traditions of thought that were committed to the ideals of human unity, equality, freedom and the inviolability of the human person, and which were in principle hostile to the violence and exploitation inherent in the colonial enterprise.[46]

In time, Christianity, liberalism and Marxism, which by and large approved the need for European colonialism opened up to the problem as to how Europeans might reconcile 'their basic moral commitments' from a position of power. Missionaries believed Christianity superior to the religions of the colonised; liberals entertained a view of enlightenment according to which in advanced human society human beings had, in J. S. Mill's words reached the 'maturity of their faculties [having] attained the capacity of being guided to their own improvement by conviction or by persuasion'. In Mill's view most European societies had 'long since reached' that stage. 'By contrast non-European societies were all "backward", and their members were in a state of nonage or infancy . . . Since backward societies lacked the capacity for self-regeneration, Mill argued that they needed to be civilised by outsiders'.[47] Even Karl Marx believed that for long-established social orders it was in their interests to be destroyed in order to achieve their historical goals. In course of time each of the three moderated its 'monistic vision' of the correct way, but this did not remove the central challenge with regard to 'the West and its others':

> All human beings were endowed with dignity. But precisely because of that, they were expected to lead a truly human way of life. Those who did not were misguided, ignorant, moral and political infants, and stood in need of guidance from those who did.[48]

Orientalism and the civilising mission were close of kin. Western Baha'i travel teachers carried with them a sense of their distinctiveness even before they were Baha'is. Remey and Sprague invariably identified eastern converts according to their previous religion. The lower status of women in oriental societies, and especially the custom of women wearing the veil, required tact and gradualism, but when it came to relating the history of persecutions against Babis and Baha'is, Remey and Dreyfus did not hesitate to point out the 'fanatic Muslims', products of the 'medieval' state of Islamicate territories like Persia, who had enacted them. Under the guardianship, orientalist discourse was openly employed in identifying opposition to Baha'is on the part of Muslim 'enemies of the faith'. Demarcating the new (Baha'i) movement from the old (Muslim) society invariably meant listing the pathological symptoms and vices diagnosed by Western orientalists as typical of the oriental condition. Great store was placed on the efforts being made – and these were certainly laudable – by North American pioneers to Iran who took a leading role in the newly established Baha'i schools and hospitals. Not surprisingly, some of these American believers' attitudes toward the Persian 'orientals' placed stress on the relationship.[49]

In spite of the new movement's ambiguous political neutrality under Abdul Baha, dedication to the Baha'i cause led, perhaps unavoidably, toward identification with particular stances within Iranian politics. On his narrative of his journey to Tehran in 1908, Mason Remey expressed open support for Shah Muhammad Ali's counter-revolution of that year; he states: 'we found the Baha'is in the utmost peace and happiness. As they had taken no part in the political troubles of the day they were in the good esteem and respect of the government, and now were enjoying unusual privileges'. At hearing the news of the outbreak of the Young Turk revolution he reports the rejoicings of Baha'is in Tehran who envisaged Abdul Baha being set free from his captivity in Akka. On his return journey home via Istanbul he reports approvingly the people 'singing songs of liberty and praising the constitution'. He was happy himself because he could now freely meet Baha'is there. Clearly Remey had no appreciation or understanding of the meaning of these political events: that is, the inconsistency in supporting the move against constitutionalism in Iran but applauding its apparent success in Turkey seemed not to strike or worry him: so long as the Baha'is were being well-treated he accepted the status quo. He even reported that 'several of the Baha'is had been appointed to high government positions' by the Shah.[50] Political neutrality aside, there was an implicit strain of support for the monarchy running through Baha'i alignments from the beginning and it lasted until the fall of the Pahlavis. Serious intentions were invested in the modernisation of Persia, in education, health, and economic and social progress and, as we shall see below, belief in progress was later translated into support for Reza Shah Pahlavi's reforms.

High-up American Baha'is of the 1920s and 1930s continued to look toward the East as an area of benighted backwardness crying out for the Baha'i message of light, civilisation and progressive modernity. This meant, in practice, that they judged oriental nations, pre-eminently Iran (or Persia as they continued to call it), according to the degree of progress their faith was making there and the opposition it was encountering. Holley's 'Surveys of Current Activities' appearing in *Baha'i World* volumes ostensibly serving as biennial records, fulfilled the purpose of self-articulation and self-definition as well as performing the public relations role of 'promulgation' (Baha'i parlance for announcing the Message), or more properly using them as a conduit for official representation to elite individuals and organisations. We come across statemental passages such as this extract from a letter to King Feisal of Iraq by the National Spiritual Assembly (NSA) of America regarding the seizure of Baha'ullah's House in Baghdad:

> The Cause of Baha'ullah transcends the limits of 'Iraq or Persia. It is no movement of heresy or reform contained within the boundaries of the Muslim Faith. The teachings of Baha'ullah and the Glorious influence of His Son, 'Abdul-Baha, have penetrated to the West as to the East . . .[51]

Or Horace Holley's juxtaposition of Persia's poor state of development which is said to be centuries behind modern civilisation, though it has aspirations to develop under Reza Shah's rule, and the Baha'i community of Iran holding a vision of the world in advance even of internationalists of the West:

> Consideration of the many facets of responsibility borne by the Persian believers gives one an inspiring picture of a community endeavoring on the one hand to raise itself above a well-nigh medieval plane of civilization – undergoing the throes experienced by European peoples over a period of hundreds of years – and at the same time that it is adjusting itself to modern science and industry, upholding an ideal of world community profounder than the internationalism now interesting advanced souls in the West.[52]

And preparing the ground for Keith Ransome-Kehler's reports of her mission to Reza Shah's Iran, a by now de rigueur juxtaposition of a backward clergy-ridden nation and the modern, advanced Baha'is, but with the suggestion that the secular nationalist medicine is beginning to work its way to the fore:

> With the interruption of a few cases of persecution which took place in smaller towns and villages, an era of increasing tolerance marked the history of the Faith in the land of its origin. The post-war rise of the secular attitude, particularly pronounced in the Near East, with its undermining of clerical privilege and influence, favored the development of a Cause possessing no professional clergy but identifying religion with ethical and moral values rather than with ritualistic ceremony and an artificial creed. Among a population still medieval in outlook and bereft of modern education, the Baha'is formed a nucleus from which a higher type of civilization could be developed.[53]

A letter to Reza Shah written in July 1926 by Horace Holley as secretary of the Baha'i NSA of the United States and Canada and published in *Baha'i World* produces a long rehearsal of the historic deprivation of Baha'is' rights resulting from their non-legal status in Iran. In it he invokes as evidence of the seriousness of the new faith the attention paid to it by orientalists of the calibre of Gobineau, Browne and Rozen before making specific reference to the torture and murder of eight Baha'is from Jahrum. This recent recrudescence of an old history of persecution causes Holley toward the end to issue the following challenge under the sub-heading 'Menace to Persia's Economic Development':

> We have felt keenly the need for cordial association and mutual spirit of cooperation between these two lands and peoples, in order to offset by an example of international justice and true morality the grievous effects of that previous contact of East and West so frequently founded on national or sectional greed. Is it not evident that Persia would benefit by direct financial cooperation from this country – enterprises of a non-political character intended to develop the natural resources of that economically undeveloped land? *But the consummation of any plan of financial cooperation between our people and Persia is impossible until real stability had been effected in Persia itself, and those processes of justice and security have been realized which are absolutely necessary as guarantees that large economic developments can succeed.* We have direct knowledge of one important enterprise recently abandoned by American interests for lack of these guarantees.[54]

Today, Western governments might write Human Rights clauses into treaties with states deemed to possess dubious records in these areas. Holley's letter, however, demonstrates a remarkable assumption of paternalistic superiority considering what an obscure body the NSA of the American Baha'is was in the 1920s (and may still be thought to be today). It is as though Holley is speaking for the US State Department to a recalcitrant nation on an issue of international importance. For those who are attuned, there are echoes of the position taken up later by US administrations in the 1980s in defence of the Baha'is of Iran. The statement is indicative of the sense of superiority a white Anglo-Saxon patrician like Holley felt toward Iran at a comparatively early stage in Reza Shah's reign. However, condescending as it is Holley's tone appears to look upon the new Pahlavi regime as one with which one might do business. Within a few years, as we shall see, the attitude was demonstrably upbeat, partly owing to the intervention of Shoghi Effendi but also due to the evident strides in modernisation the Pahlavi regime was seen to be undertaking.

From the Periphery

Edward Said famously prefaced *Orientalism* with Karl Marx's phrase from *The Eighteenth Brumaire of Louis Bonaparte*: 'They cannot represent themselves, they must be represented'. Denied the capacity or the space to articulate for themselves the meaning of their own lives, interests, or beliefs, let alone their aspirations, orientals needed to have this done for them by the linguistically empowered, all-knowing orientalist. Said has often been criticised for not allowing the 'subaltern to speak' owing to his assumption of the near unassailable, all-powerful and controlling edifice that was orientalism. We have argued that a number of orientalists so identified with an eastern party or cause that they took upon themselves the task of its advocacy. But advocacy achieves a transmutation when it is taken up against the odds by a prominent member of the disregarded party in the name of self-representation. The voice of the postcolonial writer is authentic and in demand because it contests and overcomes the obstacles the coloniser sets up against it. However, the message encoded in Shoghi Effendi's writings is not one of resistance to a colonising power, though it could be argued they retain embedded grievances directed against one or two powers in particular (but not Western ones!). Rather, as the Guardian he conceived and wrote narratives of the Baha'i faith as the appointed interpreter of God's Word. Even though these articulate the claims of an obscure religious sect originating in the East they are certainly not intended to be subaltern narratives. In postcolonial terms, however, we might feel they should not be dismissed *tout court* if for no other reason than that they were written from the colonial periphery addressing the western coloniser. For example, in his embrace of Western thinking, Abdul Baha had set the balance for his grandson when, in his sojourn in the United States, he delivered a speech about race that in the twenty-first century unavoidably appears skewed toward white apologetics. Shoghi Effendi's writings, as we saw, clearly bear the imprint of orientalist patterns, and these, together with his positioning as an easterner writing in a Western language are sufficient grounds for not excluding their author from a calibration on an identifiable spectrum of postcolonial enunciation.

So how is Shoghi Effendi's position of enunciation to be located? Rather than appropriating and abrogating the language of the coloniser he deploys this with the purpose of drawing down its cultural capital – which is not an unusual practice for writers situated outside the metropolis who desire to attract the attention of the metropolitan centre.[55] Some influential postcolonial theorists have expatiated on the role of a 'native informant/informer', a figure characterised in the work of Frantz Fanon as belonging to a colonised African or Afro-Caribbean people, in short a 'black' person who adopted a 'white mask' in order 'to tell the [coloniser] what they want to hear'. Hamid Dabashi has modified Fanon's terminology and applied the term native informer to 'brown' writers, intellectuals who he identifies as self-appointed experts who sided with the Bush administration and provided material support for the political and cultural wars it launched against Afghanistan, Iraq and, still pending, Iran.

> In all these pioneering cases [referring to studies by postcolonial authors], we see the colonized subjugated to the colonizers' assumption of cultural superiority . . . Native informers have immersed themselves in the white identified culture and now they serve it out of pure careerism.[56]

It would be untrue and grossly unfair to suggest that Shoghi Effendi worked out of the Baha'i World Centre on behalf of any organisation other than a Baha'i one, or promoted any cause other than that of the Baha'i faith. To imply otherwise would be to endorse charges made against himself, and these bodies and institutions by their enemies. The problem is that the ground that the Baha'i faith once occupied, materially and culturally incubated and protected by Great Britain, was later to be shifted in its significance in a later stage of international politics. Moreover, in the colonial world there were individuals from non-European backgrounds who identified with metropolitan culture; usually from colonised nations their predilections led them to adopt the culture of the coloniser. The Bengali writer Nirad Chaudhuri is an epitome: his *Autobiography of an Unknown Indian* (1951) caused him to become 'widely known for his unabashed admiration for Western, especially British, culture and his acerbic, contrarian views of Indian civilization'.⁵⁷ People like Chaudhuri might well be categorised as 'mimic men', those who having received privileged colonial educations swapped their native land and culture and went to live in the metropolitan heart of the European world. In fiction, figures from the colonised elite like Ralph Singh in Naipaul's novel *The Mimic Men*, and Mustapha Saeed in Tayeb Salih's *Season of Migration to the North*, characters from West Indies and Sudan respectively, allow themselves like Chaudhuri to become absorbed in the literature and cultural ideas of the power that ruled the territories they were born in. Educated on a Caribbean island before going to Oxford University, Singh had 'hoped to communicate . . . in a Gibbonesque history of Empire', the disorder of the processes of empire-building that brought into existence innumerable colonial 'half-made societies' such as his own, containing people, like himself, dislocated by 'the unnatural bringing together of peoples who could achieve fulfilment only within the security of their own societies'.⁵⁸ In Napaul's fiction other Indian characters are beset by a need to re-establish their origins as Brahmin Hindus. In Singh's case he imagines his 'Aryan ancestors' as horsemen in the process of becoming 'a settled people', looking back to a time 'when that wandering has seemed not futile but natural, not the mark of a "shipwreck" but a simple part of who one was'.⁵⁹ A marked feature of Naipaul's work is, rather like Gobineau's, the understanding that there is no refuge for the *déraciné* in the modern world; if he engaged like the Frenchman, but as a postcolonial writer, in spinning futile fantasies of origin it was clearly understood these were unrealisable. Portrayals of the homeland of his ethnic ancestors which appear in Naipaul's travel writing especially his earlier pieces are often brutal and dismissive. For Singh 'there is only one course: flight. Flight to the greater disorder, the final emptiness: London and the homecounties', an unreceiving place but one that affords a refuge of sorts from the disorder of the colonial margins.⁶⁰

Akka in Palestine was in 1897 an outpost of the Ottoman Empire. When he was a young man Shoghi Effendi's birthplace came under the control of another imperial power, Great Britain. Having spent several years as his grandfather's assistant and after obtaining a Bachelor's degree from the Syrian Protestant College (later American University) of Beirut he travelled to Britain. In the only full-length biography of the Guardian to date, his wife Ruhiyyih (Khanum) Rabbani presents a brief account of his education at Balliol College, Oxford, where starting in late 1920 he studied politics and economics. It is prefaced by a fascinating vignette in which 'a German woman physician, Dr J. Fallscheer, who lived in Haifa and attended the ladies of 'Abdu'l-Bahá's household' reports Abdul Baha's decision to send his grandson to Britain to further his education:

> At the present time [he says] the British Empire is the greatest and is still expanding and its language is a world language. My future Vazir [Shoghi Effendi] shall receive the preparation for his weighty office in England itself, after he has obtained here in Palestine a fundamental knowledge of the oriental languages and the wisdom of the East.[61]

In response to this information the German doctor queries whether the West's,

> rigid bonds of intellectualism, [might] stifle through dogma and convention his oriental irrationality and intuition so that he will no longer be a servant of the Almighty but rather a slave to the rationality of western opportunism and the shallowness of every day life?

Abdul Baha replies: 'I am not giving my Elisha to the British to educate. I dedicate and give him to the Almighty. God's eyes watch over my child in Oxford as well – Inshallah!'[62]

The intriguing prospect of the mind of Shoghi Effendi becoming a site for struggle between a spiritual but vulnerable East and a hegemonic godless West, a syndrome upon which Abdul Baha had dilated in much softer terms many times in his idealistic addresses in America and Europe, summed up in orientalist terms by the German doctor, is not followed up by the biographer.

That the power of the Baha'i Spirit would come out triumphant could not be doubted, and yet the passage leaves unanswered the possibility that the impact of Western education might have a different effect on the young future Guardian than the one proposed in the lady's question. Also left unaddressed is a possible reaction on Shoghi Effendi's part to the English upper-class racial snobbery he might encounter in Oxford. A letter he wrote to a friend in the early days of his stay there, discloses an impressionistic mind not unusual in a young man, but, given the writings we are about to review, a reception that is highly significant:

> I have through [Lord Lamington and Major Tudor Pole] come in close touch with eminent professors and Orientalists whether at Oxford or London University. Having secured introductions and recommendations from Sir Denison Ross, and Professor Ker, to Sir Walter Raleigh – professor of and lecturer on English literature at Oxford – and Prof. Margoliouth – the remarkable Arabic scholar and Orientalist of the same University, I hastened to Oxford after a busy week stay in London. In fact before leaving for Oxford, I had a letter from Margoliouth saying that he would do all in his power to be of help to a relative of 'Abdu'l-Baha. With this man and the Master of Balliol College – a College from which great men such as Lord Grey, Earl Curzon, Lord Milner, Mr. Asquith, Swinburne and Sir Herbert Samuel have graduated – I had the opportunity of speaking about the Cause and clearing up some points that to these busy scholars had hitherto been uncertain and confused.[63]

The fact that Baha'i accounts find the entire colonial resonance to Shoghi Effendi's Oxford education unremarkable might itself indicate a missing dimension in a Baha'i worldview. Little is said of the strangeness of the Guardian's position at Oxford as the heir apparent (at the time known to no one except his grandfather) to leadership of a tiny oriental sect from a small overseas area of land at the inception of its incorporation into the swathe of new territories coming under Britain's control in its very late 'moment in the Middle East'. On the import of Shoghi Effendi's letter R. Jackson Armstrong-Ingram offered a factual gloss as follows: 'the type of education developed by Jowett at Oxford was intended to produce the rulers of empire. We may note . . . in [the] letter . . . Shoghi Effendi lists "great men" who had been educated at Balliol . . .'[64]

Shoghi Effendi appears to share the stage with potentates of the British governing elite, firstly as a student in Great Britain, and later in his capacity as Guardian of the Baha'i faith in Palestine. His biography shows him residing at the Baha'i World Centre in Haifa, presiding over the spiritual destiny of the unfolding Baha'i community. He also has connections offstage with minor members of European royalty but rarely attends official ceremonial engagements in Haifa because his position as head of the Baha'i religion is not given sufficient recognition. For a few months before going to Oxford he had attended a sanatorium in Switzerland for his mental health and still clearly affected by the sudden death of his grandfather returned there again for a rest cure between April and December 1923. He was clearly a sensitive individual, surrounded largely by North American converts and erring Persian family members.[65] Cutting a solitary figure in estrangement from his family who he one-by-one excommunicated on grounds of disobedience to his authority as custodian of the Baha'i Cause, childless in his marriage, he will die of Asian influenza at the age of sixty in a London hotel in November 1957. The Guardian then, emerges overall as a lonely, perhaps even tragic individual, if the tragedy of a personal story is allowed a place in the teleological, triumphant metanarrative of a new world religion.

Shoghi Effendi belonged to a family looked up to in awe by the followers of an ostracised sect, the founders of which had been assigned to upwards of half a century and more of exile from their native land. He had seen the Ottoman milieu into which he had been born, and in which he had been brought up, crumble and disappear, to be replaced by a new imperial entity. He was introduced by his grandfather Abdul Baha to its leaders, men who brought order to the previously precarious situation of the Baha'is. However, British power was not long term either: the colonial world that appeared protecting was in the process of being withdrawn – it was in actuality disintegrating around him. No surprise then that Shoghi Effendi would have felt deterritorialised. Not seeing himself as belonging in the category of oriental but considering himself more as an outsider used to looking up to members of the British imperial elite – does this partly explain why he wrote about the land of his ethnic forebears in the way he did? It had driven his family into exile in the first place, and he writes of it as a place of disorder, decay, and corruption, in a style borrowed from his colonial protectors. According to his wife, Shoghi Effendi was an admirer of the prose of Edward Gibbon and Thomas Carlyle. (Baha'is consider that his lengthy sentences constructed in imitation of Gibbon's 'periods' blended with oriental prolixity constitute an authoritative and inimitable style of English.) From one perspective, his devising of this synthetic prose fulfils a similar function to Naipaul's Singh whose writing is also Gibbonesque, detaching or distancing the writer from a world he is linked to by ethnicity (in Singh's case the India of his Aryan ancestors) but estranged from by being born in a distant colony. Summarising Shoghi Effendi's extensive writings on Baha'i history, the Baha'i administrative order, and Baha'i doctrinal hermeneutics, perceptive as ever, MacEoin states:

> He writes as if himself a Westerner, viewing the Orient from outside and using racial and religious stereotypes that owe a great deal to nineteenth-century European concepts of Iran and Islam ... What distinguishes Shoghi Effendi's image of Iran and Islam from the condemnatory references of his predecessors, is that he draws so heavily, not on first-hand experience, but on secondary opinions drawn exclusively from the works of western writers ... Most importantly, these quotations together provide a consensus that is wholly Western in inspiration, through which Babism is interpreted and represented in a manner palatable to the modern Baha'i audience for whom Shoghi Effendi was writing.[66]

'Returning to the Orient as Orientalist, but not as an Oriental'

Having located the colonial background that helped form Shoghi Effendi as an individual we are in a better position to move on to appraise orientalism's impact upon the direction in which he took the Baha'i faith. This is also a good point at which to take store of orientalism and its effect on him as someone who, without positively electing to do so, had entered into what Mary Pratt terms the 'contact zone' where Western thinkers, travellers and orientalists encounter people from the non-West in general, and from colonised societies in particular. Our aim will be to establish where and how Shoghi Effendi's engagement with Western orientalists intersected with his own position of isolation on the periphery of empire. To help focus the theoretical issues involved I shall return to an important article by Arif Dirlik which has already been cited in the introduction to this study. In it Dirlik argues:

> Orientalism was an integral part ... of a Eurocentric conceptualization of the world that was fully articulated in the course of the nineteenth century, that placed Europe at the center and pinnacle of development, and ordered the globe spatially and temporarily in accordance with the criteria of European development. Non-European societies were characterized in this reordering of the world not by what they had but by what they lacked – in other words, the lack of one or more of the characteristics that accounted for European development ... Rather than provide commentary alternative to European

development, they were perceived predominantly as located at some rung or other of the ladder of European development that Europe already had left behind ... It is the burden of the past in one form or another that marks a society as traditional, which impedes its ascent to modernity.[67]

This passage, which begins as a rephrasing of Said's theory and then moves into the type of developmentalism that characterised Western thinking on the non-West up to the 1970s, can be applied to the orientalism of Shoghi Effendi's co-helpers, the Dreyfuses, Holleys and Townshends, who, as we have seen, built the kind of orientalist assumptions Dirlik outlines into their own writings about the Baha'i faith. However, Dirlik has refined Said's simple binaries to account for a number of aspects already seen in operation in this study. His argument runs as follows. He questions whether orientalism 'was just the autonomous creation of Europeans, or whether its emergence presupposed the complicity of "orientals"'. Like Edward Burke III, Dirlik adds a category of orientalists who opposed imperialism and wrote favourably about the East, in terms of this study, Islamic society and culture. Dirlik calls such people 'orientalized westerners'. In Chapters 3, 4 and 5 we saw them in the guise of travellers and orientalists entering the lists on the side of specific causes registering a split- or counter-orientalism. These are important for Dirlik because their 'sympathetic identification' with eastern societies brought them 'closer to the Other while distancing them from the society of the Self' and enabled them as orientalists 'to speak for the orient'. Such positioning could also lead orientalism to 'serve as a critique of European modernity, and a means of redirecting it'. Then, returning to the eastern voices scrutinised at the start of the present Chapter, Dirlik raises the issue already addressed above; he questions: 'Were the "orientals" ... as silent, or incapable of representing themselves, as Said's study suggests?'[68] 'Even more complex, is the question of the "orientalism of the orientals" ... [of] tendencies to self-orientalization which would become an integral part of the history of orientalism'. Here enter the so-called 'Asian traditions' (or 'invented traditions'), the assemblages of ancient mythological foundations put together by Western orientalists which eastern intellectuals were stimulated to take up and re-use in rethinking their nation pasts. While the examples Dirlik gives come from British India and China he might just as easily have been referring to the 'Aryan' myth and its offspring the modern nationalism Browne and other orientalists helped fuel among intellectuals in Iran. For Iran as for China, orientalists pointed out the possibilities of a new 'self-image', 'projecting . . . back in time to come to some mythic origin' to erase the indignities of the recent past.[69] Using Mary Pratt's term, Dirlik writes of a 'contact zone' where the 'orientalized westerners', who have 'entered "the Orient" intellectually and sentimentally' meet,

> 'the oriental', whose very contact with the orientalist culminates in a distancing from native society, where she or he becomes an object of suspicion, and who in the long run is better able to communicate with the orientalist than with the society of the Self.[70]

Dirlik's conceptualisation of this overlapping of the orientalist and self-orientalising oriental is applicable not only to an Iranian nationalist ideologue like Kermani, it also works in a similar way for Shoghi Effendi, who excoriates nineteenth-century Islamic Persia as much as Kermani except that he does not draw upon the myth of Iran's past as Kermani or, indeed, Abdul Baha had. Instead, orientalism informs his ideas in a different way by aiding his construction of a historicist challenge to the vestiges of eastern civilisation founded upon now defunct religious traditions, most notably those of the Islamic Near East.

If this is the time to confirm Shoghi Effendi as a 'self-orientaliser' we now need to consider how he performed this function alongside others who shared similar tendencies. Selim Deringil argues that 'the Ottoman elite conflated the ideas of modernity and colonialism, and applied the latter as a means of survival against an increasingly hostile world'. As we have seen, he proposes that Ottoman administrators applied a 'borrowed colonialism' in order to defend those parts of their realms where the people were still 'living in a state of nomadism and savagery':

> The novelty of the colonial idea meant that it had actually to be spelled out in books and pamphlets produced at the time. In a book entitled, 'The New Africa' (Yeni Afrika), obviously written on an official commission, Mehmed Izzed, 'one of the official interpreters for the Imperial Palace', felt that he had to clarify the mechanics of colonialism: 'The practice of "colonialism" is one in which a civilized state sends settlers out to lands where people still live in a

state of nomadism and savagery, developing these areas, and causing them to become a market for its goods'. Where Mehmed Izzed refers to peoples and tribes living to the south of Ottoman Libya, his attitude can pretty much be summed up as the White Man's Burden wearing a fez: '[these people] who are savages and heretics can only be saved by an invitation into the True Faith'.[71]

Shoghi Effendi could hardly be expected to activate self-orientalising in a self-defensive way, when the cause of a modernising eastern colonialism aimed to preserve an entity with an Islamic character. As has been clear so far throughout this study, the Baha'is were firmly staked on the opposite side to those whose project involved either the revival or the refurbishment of Islam in whatever shape. Baha'is were decidedly disinterested as far as any initiative to safeguard the umma was concerned. This is nowhere more obvious than in a section from *The Promised Day is Come* (1941) which implicitly valorises, as did other writings associated with the modernising and secularising programmes of Kemal Atatürk and Reza Shah, measures that reduced Islam in its traditional forms:

> The disuse of the veil which the mullas fought tooth and nail to prevent; the equality of the sexes which their law forbade . . . and . . . the efforts which are being made to disparage the Arabic tongue, sacred language of Islam and the Qur'an, and to divorce it from Persian [in Kemal's case Persian and Arabic would be excluded from Turkish] – all . . . have . . . lent their share to the acceleration of that impelling process which has subordinated to the civil authority the position and interests of Muslim clericals . . .[72]

The narrative then proceeds to create a mental picture of,

> the once lofty turbaned, long-bearded, grave looking aqa . . . as he sits, hatless, clean-shaven, in the seclusion of his home, and perhaps listening to western music, blared upon the ethers of his native land . . . Well might he muse upon the havoc which the rising tide of nationalism and scepticism has wrought in the adamantine traditions of his country. Well might he recollect the halcyon days . . . seated on a donkey, and parading through the bazaars and maydans of his native land . . .[73]

With the exception of Shoghi Effendi's hallmark, Gibbonesque prose-style the passage could be connected intertextually to any amount of twentieth-century anti-clerical passages in novels, short stories or essays by modern Arab, Persian or Turkish secular-minded authors. The image (almost cartoon-like in its conception) of the de-turbaned mullah shorn of all the accoutrements of his former power, now forced to listen to Western-style music over a loud speaker system is also an obvious orientalist one. Indeed, the manner in which the writer utilises the third person singular to qualify the Iranian mullah's country – 'the ethers of *his* native land', 'traditions of *his* country', 'maydans of *his* native land' – evinces a detachment that not only distances him from the backward practises of an oriental Muslim but inscribes his own distance from this concrete image of Iran – not *his* native land, only in an ideal sense the country of his forebears and 'the cradle of the (Baha'i) Faith'.

Shoghi Effendi's word-picture of the mullah might be compared with the cartoons to be found in an 'album of satirical cartoons by Salih Erimez, published in 1941 . . . based on a systematic ridiculing of the Ottoman world, depicted through the most blatant orientalist clichés'. For example, one

> . . . illustration from the album described 'the slumber of an elementary school teacher' that was evidently meant to give the reader an idea of what such schools looked like before the Republic. An ugly bearded and turbaned man half reclining in oriental fashion surrounded by his oriental props – a cigarette holder, prayer beads, and a whip – loses control of a classroom filled with fez-wearing children; the walls are decorated with simplistic educational material that reproduces the letters of the alphabet and a couple of religious inscriptions; and in a corner the symbolic spider web once again symbolizes the backwardness inherent to the entire scene located in a demonized ancien regime.[74]

Edhem Eldem characterises this as an example of 'Kemalist orientalism', itself a development on Ottoman orientalism and a form of writing intended to discredit the effete traditionalism, particularly the religious kind that stood in the path of the modernisation of Turkey.[75]

There is direct evidence of a sympathetic connection between a prominent Baha'i who was an international journalist and lecturer, and the leader of the new Turkish Republic. Indefatigable travel teacher of the Baha'i faith, Martha Root introduced the new religion during audiences with an array of European royalty and presidents including Queen Marie of Romania, who Baha'is have laid claim to as their first royal convert. The subject of Root's article published in the fall of 1933 is her searching out of links with Baha'ullah's period in Ottoman territory during the previous century. As a North American and hero-worshipper of Mustafa Kemal she was not alone (there were other female admirers like the British journalist Grace Ellison). On this occasion she describes hearing him on the radio delivering a speech to mark the tenth anniversary of the Turkish Republic:

> All heard the voice of the Ghazi Kemal Pasha the 'Father of the Republic of Turkey' speaking to his thousands of citizens here in such a way that each felt he was speaking personally, directly to him alone! The power of that voice, the tender sympathy, the good counsel: No one could hear that voice and not feel sure that the man who spoke had unbounded power to continue this Republic and evolve it educationally, socially, materially to a high place in the galaxy of nations.[76]

The article concludes with self-quotation from an article she wrote for *The Baha'i World*:

> Turkey, the new Republic under the powerful courage of Ghazi Kemal Pasha, has contributed a mighty forward impulse to world understanding, to the union of the East and the West. This great President . . . *has opened wide the mental dardenelles* so that the East and the West may come and go, so that there may be Arabic Latinised script, so there may be co-education, great freedom for women and progress in this eastern-western republic, and so there may be genuine free thinking, and freedom for all religions.[77]

Although Root's Kemalism is whole-heartedly expressed, earlier in her piece she writes of a romantic engagement with Islam in her visit to the Suleymaniyah mosque in Edirne (Adrianople) where Baha'ullah had called Subh-i Azal to a *mubahala* (which Baha'i sources say the latter was too afraid to attend). Here she is moved to pray, and not finding her way barred by the customary wall of Islamic fanaticism Western travellers invariably call out when visiting Muslim lands ('the caretakers did not treat me like a foreigner'), she did so. This calls forth a genuine feeling on her part of fellowship with Muhammad and the statement, 'I have learned to love and appreciate the Qur'an'. At the foot of her article stands a quotation in which Abdul Baha presents a modernist assessment of the Prophet with which Western Baha'is like Martha Root could feel comfortable.

Shoghi Effendi's version of a dehistoricised form of Islam, which, like Martha Root, he invokes in the context of the Baha'i doctrine of the equivalence of the divine prophets, or separates out as of fundamental importance for understanding the Baha'i revelation, tends to pale before his sustained assaults upon the incarnate Islam of the present and recent past to which no quarter is given. The larger part of his references to Islam are frozen at the orientalist stage, congealed by a combination of hardcore Curzonian invective, his own colonial education, and time spent either pleasing the coloniser or imbibing from him. Here indeed is a case of overlapping orientalist and self-orientalising oriental, but not 'overlapping' in the positive sense, where a Western orientalist like Browne might be valorised as fulfilling an 'orientalised' role owing to his affinity with eastern people(s). With the exception perhaps of A. L. M. Nicolas, Shoghi Effendi overwhelmingly prefers to quote hardline orientalist discourse of the kind codified by Said. Clearly, on his part there is a distancing from native society into which one doubts he had much occasion to stray while in Palestine, where as head of a breakaway quondam mahdist sect he could perhaps have become an object of suspicion, at least for some Muslims. It seems to be the case from the evidence of his education and interaction with Western dignitaries (some of whom like Margoliouth were orientalists who looked down upon orientals), that Shoghi Effendi was detached from Iran and its people and was better able to communicate with old-style orientalists than with the society of the Self.

Keith Ransom-Kehler and Reza Shah Pahlavi

The foundation of the Pahlavi dynasty in 1925 broadly coincides with a specific moment in the Baha'i construction of modernity in the Iranian context. Alternative versions of modernity entertained by Baha'is and Azalis had been tested by the Constitutional Revolution. The latter had taken a political route and for a short time were at the forefront of the constitutional parties, but they ran out of steam after the coup and civil war of 1908–9. Unable, or unwilling, to commit to public involvement in the watershed moment of modern Iran, Iran's Baha'i community proceeded with their investment in educational and health reform projects and, as émigrés in Russian Transcaspia, in mercantile activity. Depoliticised and quietist, they remained within their community, separate from the rest of their countrymen. In an article published in 1984 Patricia Higgins suggested that in spite of occasional outbursts of religiously-inspired persecution during the Pahlavi period Baha'is actually benefited from not being one of Iran's recognised religious minorities as defined in the constitution. This enabled them to gain access to employment at levels of the state from which Zoroastrians, Jews and Christians were barred.

> In the Pahlavi state, Baha'is could be seen as particularly good citizens. In addition to speaking Persian and implicitly supporting the government in power, they combined in their beliefs and traditions elements from both Islamic and pre-Islamic Iranian civilization and other progressive and Western-style ideas. Their beliefs in universal education, sexual equality, and service to humanity, for example, correspond to policies supported by the Pahlavis in their efforts to modernize Iran. The practice of these beliefs made Baha'is, on the whole, better educated than the average Iranian, and they probably have been over-represented among Iranian professionals. Thus, they could be seen as filling useful economic as well as political niches.[78]

For the Iranian Baha'i community disengagement from politics represented a passive acceptance of Pahlavi modernisation, comprised as it was of forced Westernisation and military dictatorship, in which they were entirely detached from affairs of state. Abbas Amanat has spoken of the later Pahlavi period, the 1960s and 1970s, as a time of 'petrified momentum' for Baha'is, when behaving as a minority they effectively ceded their version of modernity to the regime's, and the potential to impact upon change in society was lost.[79] Leila Chamankhah has pointed out the tension in the late Pahlavi period between economically and socially successful members among the Baha'i community of Iran and the Universal House of Justice in Haifa over their demonstrable closeness to Mohammed Reza's regime.[80]

To illustrate the semi-official ideological alignment of Baha'is to the Pahlavis in the remainder of this section I shall look at a case-study of an individual appointed as a representative of the American Baha'i community tasked with an important mission on behalf of the Baha'is of Iran. Keith Ransom-Kehler was sent by Shoghi Effendi in 1932 to try to obtain the lifting of the ban on Baha'i literature from entering Iran. A successful outcome would have represented tacit movement toward official recognition of the Baha'i faith in that country. The series of events, which draws in issues of modernity relating to human rights and religious tolerance and also identification with an increasingly authoritarian regime, was recorded in Ransom-Kehler's own words and published posthumously in the *Baha'i World*. Her report provides a picture of how Western Baha'is positioned themselves regarding the modernisation of Iran in general, and gives a strong impression of the extent to which Ransom-Kehler herself might have been articulating the American community's attitudes toward Pahlavi state ideology. On 11 August 1932 she had seen Court Minister Taymurtash 'and received from him the direct, unqualified assurance that Baha'i literature would be admitted freely into Persia and permitted to circulate'. When it became clear this promise had not been implemented she returned to Iran the following year on the same mission. In Tehran she addressed a letter dated 8 June 1933 to Reza Shah, restating the Baha'i position concerning the literature ban.

> A year ago this month I reached Persia as representative of the National Spiritual Assembly of the Baha'is of the United States and Canada, having traveled halfway around the world to present a petition on their behalf to your gracious Majesty requesting the removal of the ban on entry and circulation of Baha'i literature in Persia.
>
> This petition was framed because of the incalculable blessings which your Majesty's reign has bestowed upon Persia; because of the advancement, the liberation and the protection which, under the firm and spectacular power exhibited by your Majesty, have elevated this sacred land of ours to the forefront of progress and revival.
>
> Certainly it would have been folly to have sent such a communication in any period preceding your Majesty's accession, for at that time ears were deaf to every plea of justice, and Persia had become the tragic plaything of wilful, corrupt and ruthless lords.
>
> But mindful of the great blessings which have flowed from your Majesty's enlightened rule, the Baha'is of the United States and Canada felt that the time was now ripe, that the amazing accomplishments of your Majesty now favored the idea of consummating the complete emancipation of the Baha'is of Persia from the trammels and deprivations inherited from the dark past . . .[81]

The letter continues in the same vein, proffering fulsome praise of the Pahlavi ruler, endorsing his regime's dynastic nationalism and linking him with the celebrated monarchs of Iran's pre-Islamic age at the expense of illustrious ones of the Islamic period:

> We must look not to Shah Abbas nor to Nadir Shah but to the distant past – to the days of Cyrus, Darius and Jamshed – for anything comparable to the accomplishments which in twelve brief years have characterized your Majesty's achievements . . .
>
> These were the ideas we had in mind when petitioning your Majesty to remove this last barrier from the pathway of Baha'i freedom and progress in Persia by according us the privilege of the press, an ordinary civil right in all but the most backward of countries.[82]

In a cover letter from Tehran to the NSA of the Baha'is of US and Canada, dated 3 March 1933, Ransom-Kehler reported her interviews with Iranian ministers and civil servants, expressing her frustrations and personal assessment of the reasons for the failure of her petition. She was clearly confused as to why good intentions and talking up Iran (as the land of the Bab and Baha'ullah) in the outside world were insufficient to change minds about Baha'is in the country itself:

> Perhaps a reason for this resentment is because we of other lands have widely and easily succeeded in making friends for Persia where Persians themselves have been less successful; perhaps it is the mediaeval reflex that still grips the minds of those emerging from the dark night of Persia's ignorance and fanaticism into the Shining Era of Pahlavi.[83]

A more down to earth explanation for the continuance of the ban – but equally revealing of a Baha'i mindset – was alleged obstruction caused by the foreign minister, Mohammad Ali Foroughi, whose father was rumoured to have been an Azali. Here a note of resignation creeps in as the envoy considers the possibility that in spite of the shah's mission to sweep away the past, the old forms persisted and it would take time for the 'advanced dynasty' to dispel them.

When we recall the brilliant and spectacular manner in which His Majesty with astounding intrepidity, and no untoward results, changed many of the age-old customs of this country we are, of course, constrained to conclude that this regulation, supposedly devised by the present Foreign Minister and superimposed in the midst of the vicious and corrupt conditions of the past, now constitutes a law so powerful that even a new and advanced dynasty is forced to respect it . . .[84]

Ransom-Kehler continues her report with an account of her meeting with the Secretary for American Affairs, Mr. Shayastih, who informed her that despite the assurances she had been given the previous year by Taymurtash it was 'contrary to the law . . . to recognize any religion founded after Islam; since the Baha'i Movement cannot be recognized its literature can have no standing'. She responded by stating that she had searched the documents to see whether Baha'is were excluded under the Persian Constitution, and found this not to be the case.[85] A short three-way discussion then ensued which included the Persian translator. Ransom-Kehler turned to the dark forces eloquently described by Western orientalists that still seemed to stand in the way of the great destiny offered Persia by the present Shah.

'But the Persians have always been tolerant', [the secretary] said. I regret that I was sufficiently undisciplined to laugh out loud: the idea was so quaint. 'You must certainly have been informed of the 30,000 martyrs whom the Persian Baha'is have offered in the pathway of God?' I inquired.

Both men looked unaffectedly amazed.

'Certainly not so many', ventured Mr. Assadi [the interpreter].

[Ransom-Kehler:] 'On the authority of European historians, to whom the matter made no difference one way or the other, it is so estimated'. They then accepted the statement without further opposition . . .

. . . 'Woe betide the first Jew who crossed the path of a Persian on a holy day', I quoted Lord Curzon. 'What of the humiliating suppression of the Zoroastrians who could not even wear a new dress?'

'But they did not harm them', was the lame reply, as if such persecutions were harmless . . . A recollection of 'the fiendish ingenuity of the torture mongers of Tihran', as described by Count de Gobineau, Nicholas [sic], Lord Curzon, Captain von Goumoens and others flashed through my mind, however. I remembered my meeting a few days before with a young Baha'i, shockingly disfigured, because in infancy he had been thrust into an oven by these harmless people, and was thereby partially cooked . . .

Imagine my having to sit there and calmly listen while Persian officials discussed, without shame, the incapacity of their own monarch, certainly one of the most valiant, heroic, decisive and just rulers in the world, to handle this minor situation . . . Do they think that the press of the world has not been ringing with the stupendous accomplishments of the Shahanshah; of his intrepid onslaughts against the forces of ignorance, conservatism and decadence in this country; of his supreme determination to elevate Persia in spite of her own opposition and timidity above her mediaevalism to a position of advancement and modern culture?

Did they expect me to agree with them as to powerlessness of this superman who has securely established an enlightened dynasty; who has literally changed the physical face of his country in a few brief years; who has completely broken the paralyzing power of the clergy; who has set at naught the religious practices of centuries – the most difficult of all political accomplishments; who has taken trousers from women and skirts from men; who has inaugurated a new economic life for Persia; who is rapidly substituting patriotism for religious fanaticism; who has defied European powers; who has achieved for all religions, including the Baha'is, comparative protection and safety; the irresistible power of whose word is sufficient to accomplish the most far reaching and dramatic results?[86]

Shoghi Effendi's envoy (although some might question why he had chosen an American woman for such a task at such a time), Ransom-Kehler might also be considered de facto representative of the Baha'is worldwide, on what was evidently considered to be a vital, symbolic issue. We have quoted her commentary at some length for what it demonstrates about her apparently total faith in Reza Shah and his programme of modernisation, and her enthusiastic endorsement of his hitching the star of the Pahlavi regime to the glories of the rulers of pre-Islamic Persia. Her individual obsequiousness and unqualified celebration of the monarch's personal rule which has the effect of submerging all other perspectives seems idiosyncratic and naïve. It appears to fuel her belief *tout court* that his power and readiness to accede to her request must result in its implementation and would have done had he not been misinformed by those around him. However, there is ample evidence to suggest that other Baha'is shared her enthusiasm for the Shah and the list of policy successes she gives, beginning with Shoghi Effendi himself whose messages to American Baha'is echo, albeit less extravagantly, her statements. 'Writing in 1922 . . . he speaks of how the pace of reform in Iran "has been wisely regulated" and refers to the "salutary effects of the progressive regime established by [Iran's] enlightened ruler"'.[87] Seven years later he writes:

> Reforms of a revolutionary character are, without bloodshed and with negligible resistance, gradually transforming the very basis and structure of Persia's primitive society. The essentials of public security and order are being energetically provided throughout the length of and breadth of the Shah's dominion, and are hailed with particular gratification by that much harassed section of the population – our longsuffering brethren of the land. The rapidity, the incredible ease, with which the enlightened proposals of [Persia's] government, in matters of education, trade and finance, means of transportation and travel, and the development of the country's internal resources, are receiving the unqualified sanction of a hitherto reactionary Legislature, and are overcoming the resistance and apathy of the masses have undoubtedly tended to hasten the emancipation of our Persian brethren from the remaining fetters of a once-despotic and blood-stained regime.[88]

This passage is evidence enough to account for the sanguine view Ransom-Kehler held of Reza Shah's modernisation programme. As for her assertion of the predicament Baha'is had historically faced in Persia in her discussion with the officials she invokes the very same European orientalists Shoghi Effendi quotes in *Dawn-Breakers* and *God Passes By*, and she rivals her leader in the number of rhetorical questions she employs. When she widens Baha'i suffering to include the country's other minorities, specifically the Jews and Zoroastrians who she argues had suffered continuous persecution under Muslim rule we observe again the influence of Curzon and Browne. The interpreter (correctly) demurs at her inflation of Babi-Baha'i martyrs to 30,000, which adds a further fifty per cent to the figure of 20,000 usually quoted by Baha'i sources which has itself been contested. She states this to be the total figure of *Baha'i* martyrs though the greater number would have been Babis. The two Iranians' silence in response to her citation of European authorities on these matters might confirm a tendency to self-orientalising widely distributed among Iranians at the time, evidencing to what Reza Zia-Ebrahimi remarks is,

> the sacrosanct status in which European scholarship was, and still is, held . . . Citing a European work was almost tantamount, in methodological terms, to citing a primary source. The entire *corpus* of modernist and nationalist literature is a long panegyric of Europe, its science, its scholars, its discoveries and the wish to turn Iran into Europe, if possible overnight. There was an element of an inferiority complex . . .[89]

According to Zia-Ebrahimi, the Iranian desire to emulate Westerners in everything, to escape their Middle East locale or withdraw into an imagined great past, accompanied a belief in an Aryan racial identity shared with Europeans and which derived from nineteenth-century orientalists. The Aryan racial identity was certainly floated by both rulers of the Pahlavi dynasty along with eulogies on Persia's past greatness of the pre-Islamic period, and invocation of the mythically supreme names of Cyrus, Darius and Jamshid. Ransom-Kehler repeated all this except for referencing the Aryan race.

From a twenty-first century perspective, Ransom-Kehler's case for rights to be accorded the Baha'i faith is of course incontrovertible. But in Iran in the 1930s, even in the secular-oriented regime of Reza Shah, the situation was different. As pointed out above, across the *durée* of the Pahlavi period as a whole Baha'is could be advantaged by not belonging to one of the recognised minorities and not being subject to the limitations imposed on these even if they were as a consequence left exposed as a people set apart. Aside from the issue of the rights of religious communities however, it was worrying – although it did not seem to worry Ransome-Kehler – that Reza Shah's violent proclivities had started to manifest in relation to his ministers. Abdul Husayn Taymurtash, who Ransom-Kehler had seen in Tehran in 1932, and to whom she refers in her letter as 'the ex-Minister of Court', had been murdered in jail in the supervening period. Among a key group of early supporters of Reza Shah (at the time known as Reza Khan), Homa Katouzian points out:

> [t]he fall of [Nusrat-i Dawlih] Firuz was the first ominous sign that henceforth no one was immune from arbitrary arrest. The murder of Taymurtash in jail in 1933 made this fact clear and unexceptionable. Sardar As'ad III quickly followed him both in prison and in death.[90]

Ransom-Kehler, though she indicts him as the son of an Azali whose enmity toward Baha'is might have been the obstacle barring their enfranchisement, deserves credit for pointing out the former Iranian foreign minister (and prime minister) Mohammad Ali Foroughi as a figure who embodied some cultural éclat. However, he too would fall victim to the transition to violent arbitrary rule which was building steam in the early 1930s and which for him came to a head in 1935.[91] Nonetheless, it was true that 'despite the deep hostility engendered by this bloody reign of terror, in many ways Reza Shah was the key figure in the modernisation of Iran. Above all, he created the strongly centralised character of modern Iranian government'.[92] How critical should a Western emissary in the cause of human rights choose to be? If Ransom-Kehler eagerly consulted the Iranian constitution as to the legality of exclusion of the Baha'i community from enjoyment of legal recognition, what might she have said on the matter of Reza Shah's tearing up constitutional rule to replace it by bloody dictatorship? As a Baha'i loyal to the government – any government, though clearly this was one toward which the Baha'i leadership was well-disposed – in her mind the issue clearly did not surface. The American might be compared to those Westerners who visited the Soviet Union during the same decade. Their preconceived notions about the cause of modernisation brought them, determined to admire, to a foreign land over which the shadow of tyranny already loomed. It would be naïve to suggest in either of these situations that the orientation each of the visitors carried with them was not politically freighted.

A coda to the semi-official pro-Pahlavi position passed down from Shoghi Effendi to the American Baha'i community occurred very suddenly in the year following the failure of Ransom-Kehler's mission and her untimely death in Iran. It concerned the closure of the Baha'i Tarbiyat schools in 1934.

Although this measure was also applied to other independent non-Muslim schools, there can be no gainsaying that this was a specific setback for Shoghi Effendi's upbeat assessment of Reza Shah's regime. According to Jasamin Rostam-Kolayi, by exceeding the conciliatory stance toward government previously adopted by Baha'ullah and Abdul Baha, and instead encouraging the schools to be assertive by closing them in observance of Baha'i holy days, the Guardian miscalculated the direction of Pahlavi state policy: 'forces in the Baha'i community, pushing for a distinct religious and public identity for Iranian Baha'is, challenged the dictates of the state, which was pursuing its own centralizing, nationalizing, and secularizing reforms'.[93] Both the Ransom-Kehler and Tarbiyat schools episodes demonstrated the political inexperience of the still relatively youthful Shoghi Effendi. His optimism over Reza Shah in the 1920s is not difficult to understand. After suffering reverses from almost the start of its history, his minority Iranian community might have been forgiven for expecting better things in what on the surface looked to be the beginning of a modern era for Iran. On the other hand, his reading of events showed poor judgement: the reforms that he believed were proceeding without bloodshed by the 1930s were anything but. As we have just seen, the regime was turning out to be arbitrary and brutal in its treatment of its own political servants. And it can only appear ironic that the same secularisation policy Shoghi Effendi lauded for depleting the power of the Shi'i ulama should have blown up in the face of Baha'is over the matter of the Tarbiyat schools.[94] Together these incidents demonstrated the tunnel-vision that is often characteristic of a sectarian movement too focused on, and self-assured about, its own internal narratives to be effective in reading the direction of national let alone world politics. These features only seemed to grow with the dissemination of Shoghi Effendi's New World Order letters, dominated as they were by an eschatological reading of contemporary history with a seam running through that justified crude, Western-inspired, politically-stilted agendas of modernisation in the Islamicate world.

The End of Colonialism and a New World Order

In this section it is proposed that when Shoghi Effendi was writing about the world crisis of the period from the 1920s to the late 1940s he experienced it unconsciously as a dying colonialism. Although he makes a lot of the downfall of European empires and the conditions that were preparing the coming European chaos he has no conscious understanding of their colonial significance. Writing with the voice of prophecy he decries the entrenchment of materialism and decline in religious belief while seeing in both evidence of the need for a new spiritual order, projecting the prophetic idea of a 'theocentric world in which the contradictions of reality can be solved theologically'.[95] In interludes, however, a pact with secularism surfaces in the form of an approved Kemalism. The Guardian's education at Balliol College, Oxford; his cultivation of British academics and orientalists; his residence in Palestine during the Mandate and close association with pro-Zionist figures; all helped inform his apocalyptic visions of world conflagration. His 'world order' genre of writings operated as did his historical writings on the Baha'i faith under the aegis of Western orientalist discourse and in the process helped promote a Baha'i orientalist idiom.[96] In line with the Western orientalists and in a collaborative exercise with Christian converts Canon George Townshend and Horace Holley, Shoghi Effendi incorporated into his description of Qajar Iran a Christocentric perspective on religion, with priests, prophets and a Church state. His portrayal of contemporary Islam employed stereotypes reminiscent of much late nineteenth and early twentieth-century Western writing devoted to winnowing out the multiple deficiencies and the desperate need for reform of the Islamic world. The register of orientalist condemnation employed is derived both from the conceit and moral superiority of the missionaries and the imperial high-mindedness of figures like Curzon whose writings, as we have seen, structure the Guardian's image of the land of his forebears. The special orientalist inflection of this writing, infused into his articulation of the Baha'i revelation and the foundation and contours of the 'New World Order' he was proposing, fits the moulds previously filled by Christian certainties and an in-bred European sense of racial supremacy (that is recognisably British). The old world order in decline was, however, a site of great anxiety for Shoghi Effendi, writing as he was as a self-orientalising subject from a point on the imperial margins threatened with breakup in a colonial struggle between Zionist Jews and Arabs in revolt against the seizure of their land by outside occupiers. The product, one might argue, with its embedded colonialist assumptions is an unsuitable discourse to deploy on behalf of a new religion with a programme of world peace although it can clearly be accounted for by the colonial background sketched out above.

The concept of a New World Order arose from writings of Baha'ullah and Abdul Baha in which they progressively built up a global vision of world peace and world government. Their statements were extensively embedded throughout Shoghi Effendi's communications to the Baha'i communities in which in his role as infallible interpreter he delineated their faith's unique destiny set against an old world order that was falling apart.[97] The analytic features of these writings, such as they were, married theological argumentation to exposition of contemporary affairs in the main relating to Europe and North America but on a global scale. Their overriding purpose was the delivery of judgement on world leaders – secular and ecclesiastic – who had failed to recognise Baha'ullah as the world redeemer, and to make wide-ranging pronouncements on the decline of the present world order in contrast to the potency and developmental urgency of a new Baha'i order. Shoghi Effendi's version of the future of the world is constructed as the goal and final stage of a process which was bringing to fulfilment all previous human endeavour while breaking down superseded cultures and religions:

> Unification of the whole of mankind is the hall-mark of the stage which human society is now approaching. Unity of family, of tribe, of city-state, and nation have been successively attempted and fully established. World unity is the goal towards which a harassed humanity is striving. Nation-building has come to an end. The anarchy inherent in state sovereignty is moving towards a climax. A world, growing to maturity, must abandon this fetish, recognize the oneness and wholeness of human relationships, and establish once for all the machinery that can best incarnate this fundamental principle of its life.[98]

The designation 'New World Order' first figures in a series of long open letters beginning with 'The World Order of Baha'ullah' (1930), and 'The Goal of a New World Order' (1931), pieces that build on Baha'ullah's vision of the Oneness of Mankind and including sub-headings such as 'A World Super State', 'A Living Organism', instancing forerunner organisations such as the League of Nations (a miserable failure, but in feeble ways a shadow of the true, divinely-ordained world institutions of the future).

Checking the terminology in terms of its distribution in the 1920s and 1930s, its analogues and contemporary applications, we find H. G. Well's *A Short History of the World* (1922), *The Open Conspiracy and its Enemies* (1928), *The New World Order: Whether it is Attainable* . . . (1940); the early volumes of Arnold Toynbee's *A Study of History* (1934–), not to speak of totalitarian 'new orders' in Italy, the Soviet Union and Germany. 'New World Order' is a term implied in utopias scientific, social and political, founded on blueprints revealed by political and secular messiahs. In short, it formed part of the *Weltanschauung* of a wide variety of thinkers, groups and movements between the two world wars. In utopian/dystopian novels of the 1920s, 1930s and 1940s the desire for palingenesia only comes to pass after violent cataclysm or revolution effected in the recent past. Shoghi Effendi's eschatological view of the end times is set very much in a present, that is, the 1930s and 1940s and looks forward to the future.

The structure and style draws upon his two favourite British authors, one a magisterial historian whose *magnum opus* was a treatment of the decline and fall of an empire over a thousand year period; the other, a Victorian sage who wrote history as a revelation of the celestial-infernal taking a religio-historicist view of the previous two centuries, focusing on episodes of upheaval but generally charting the descent of the modern world via social revolution into disastrous upheaval. Of the two authors, Edward Gibbon provided the prose structure but was less likely to have supplied the inspiration for Shoghi Effendi's apocalyptic pictograph in words that encompassed a failed world undergoing providential punishment. Apocalyptic writing is generally speaking not the forte of humanists. It takes an anti-humanist dissident who despises the progressive enlightenment discourse discussed by Parekh to recklessly pronounce upon the impending collapse of metropolitan culture. Situated in the (absent) 'heart' of Empire, ensconced in Chelsea close to the Westminster Parliament, Thomas Carlyle delivered his diatribes against parliamentary orators and glib political administrators who couldn't govern the disorder of England, let alone command the suppression of a revolt of former Jamaican slaves. While we cannot be sure exactly what Carlyle works Shoghi Effendi read, we can assume as an admirer he most likely dipped into *The History of the French Revolution* in which feature hovering abstract forces, charlatans, fanatics, and human psychopaths bent on the downfall of the otiose *ancien régime*. These were sufficient to stimulate his own conjuring of the triumvirate of spectres that haunt his nightmare vision of the twentieth century: 'Nationalism, Racialism and Communism'.[99] If he had read Carlyle's *Latter-Day Pamphlets*, however, he would have come across 'Mahomet', figured as the threatening destroyer of the idols of the 'scrip age' (the stocks-and-shares-worshipping 1840s) and would surely have taken to heart Carlyle's radical prophecy of doom hanging over the entire edifice of modern transactions: 'The heart of the world is corrupt to the core; a detestable devil's poison circulates in the life-blood of mankind; taints with abominable deadly malady all that mankind do. Such a curse never fell on men before'.[100] Moving from the late 1840s to 1941, the revelation of Baha'ullah 'set a new direction to this vast process now operating in the world. The fires lit by this great ordeal are the consequences of mankind's failure to recognize it'.[101] Ignorant of this supreme fact, humanity was moving through the unstoppable fires of destruction toward its eventual, inalienable destiny.

A sweeping vision of mainly Western and Near Eastern nations and their institutions, the world order narrative can also be thought of as feeding off the procession of past colonial representations of groups of national traditions, cultures and religions. Seen in the work of Herder, Goethe, Carlyle and others, these narratives constitute in Aamir Mufti's words,

> what we call modern Orientalism [which] is merely the cultural system that for the first time articulated the concept of the world as an assemblage of 'nations' with expressive traditions. For 'Orientalism' consists of those Western knowledge practises in the modern era whose emergence made possible for the first time the notion of a single world as a space populated by distinct civilizational complexes, each in possession of its own tradition, the unique expression of its own forms of national 'genius'.[102]

We are able to view the route Shoghi Effendi took toward his conceptualisation of the 'old world order' as an arrangement of once great but now fallen European monarchies and religious institutions, together with the declined Islamicate empires, which we saw featuring in his Baha'i faith-history narratives. These polities and the individuals that headed them are now merely residuals waiting to be cleared away to be replaced by the new Baha'i order in which Baha'ullah performs the central role of judge and the power that erases. European empires reigned over by arrogant monarchs recklessly building up weaponry, and clerical pontifs too immersed in their own purposes to recognise their Lord. Figures from the secular heights – erring sovereigns and kings in whose roles one senses the author set greatest store – fallen victim to the general dissolution of the two orders of authority, secular and ecclesiastic, from which power has been seized. The defunct Near Eastern entities ruled by tyrants in partnership with rotten religious hierarchies, are dismissed in the litanies of contempt employed by colonial observers and administrators. Consisting of 'arrogant, fanatical, perfidious, and retrograde clericals', Islamic religious orders are vividly (or luridly) represented as victim to the recent disasters befalling the two branches of Islam, Sunni and Shi'a. 'The pomp and pageantry of these princes of the church of Islam have already died out. Their fanatical outcries, their clamorous invocations, their noisy demonstrations, are stilled'.[103] In short, the Islamic detritus here is of the same ilk as the disarray of oriental 'medieval' practises dilated on by Curzon and Chirol, and indeed in the writings of early Western Baha'is. If in Palestine the British struggled to compel order on fanatical Arabs, Shoghi Effendi can with the stroke of his pen write off the defunct Church structures (Greek Orthodox and Catholic) that failed to quell the disorder attendant on the wave of secularisation in France, Austria-Hungary, Spain, Mexico and Russia. Performing the celestial-infernal function in Carlyle's *French Revolution* were the Jacobins who swept away the cant and lies of the decadent Deism of the eighteenth century before being consumed in the Terror they had themselves set in train. In *Promised Day* the blasphemous Bolsheviks (who had freshly wiped out the young Baha'i communities of Transcaspia) haul down the Orthodox Church, and in Iran and Turkey the parties of secularism roll away the Islamic order, only here they are valorised as agents of modernity. In the midst of their infallibility prophets have their favourites.

Another World Order and an Ahmadi 'Gift' to Edward, Prince of Wales

Shoghi Effendi's formulation of the Baha'i New World Order has been scrutinised through the prism of orientalism, a discourse which he may not have created by himself but which he greatly amplified and which enabled him to write 'with undisguised approval of the decline in the authority and influence of Islam in the modern period'.[104] In addition, the *Baha'i World* series has been interrogated as a medium for presenting aspects of a modern Baha'i self-image in which the construction of modernity was seen to operate in Iranian contexts by means of strongly accented orientalist tropes. This chapter concludes by reviewing several cognate areas in Ahmadi writings, treating these also as inscriptions of that community's self-identity and modern credentials. It is hoped that a contrastive analysis will demonstrate the commonalities and divergencies of the two discourses and help situate both mahdi movements against the background of late colonialism and the Islamicate contexts out of which they both emerged.

The arena where religion meets globalisation has attracted interest in the early twenty-first century, but before the global was the universal. Evangelical Christians at the turn of the nineteenth century were urged to spread the gospel around the world not only by their reading of scripture but by the 'the providential opportunities brought into existence and made plain by God himself', namely the opening up of non-Christian lands by Western empires.[105] Those on the receiving end of this dynamic were also exercised by the concept of universality: colonial contexts pressured Indian modernist thinkers Sayyid Ahmad Khan and Muhammad Iqbal to rethink Islam's universality. Javid Majeed characterises Iqbal's *Reconstruction of Religious Thought in Islam* as a landmark work that 'emerges from the cosmopolitan thought zones and global conversations that underpinned Indian intellectual life as a style and way of thinking in the nineteenth and twentieth centuries'.[106] Indian Muslim thinkers were forced to the recognition that as followers of the last great world religion: 'if Muslims could be said to have discovered the unity of mankind by way of Islam, or even to have developed this unity to its fullest potential, they could not claim to possess it exclusively or indeed forever'.[107] At almost the same time as Abdul Baha wrote *Mysterious Forces of Civilization*, Altaf Husayn Hali published *Mussadas: the Flow and Ebb of Islam* (1879) which 'catalogues the decline of India's Muslims in particular and those of the world at large in practically every department of social life, attributing their decadence to the betrayal of Islamic virtues'.[108] In his *risalih* Abdul Baha wrote of the same situation from the vantage point of Iran but envisaged the renewal of civilisation on a world scale, crucially without situating his ideas within a new or revived Islamic order. He saw 'the emergence of the world as a single place as a quintessentially modern development, made possible by profound technological and social changes'.[109] Ghulam Ahmad's exposition of the meaning of the appearance of the Mahdi also pointed out material changes in the world as signs of the times, which like the Christian missionaries he argued were providentially arranged, in his case for expediting the dissemination of his message 'like lightning' around the globe.[110] Morten Warmind quite rightly connects Baha'i and Ahmadi visions of an international order to their international missionising efforts, however, their staking out of potential universal institutions owed a lot to the shaking of the foundations in the political and secular orders as well as the changes in material conditions.[111] In the Interwar period this situation acquired even greater urgency.

The respective Baha'i and Ahmadi new orders were not tied to pan-Islamic projects of the past, despite both having 'an Islamic background [and] both [coming] into being during the second half of the 19th century'. The reason for this was that both initiatives were 'legitimated through claims of prophetic inspiration'.[112] Having bid to establish for themselves the authority to announce a time of renewal and pronounce on its needs, either from within Islam or from without, the founders of both movements had positioned themselves in such a way as to offer free-standing models for future development, in which intersections of religion and secular politics would necessarily be of great importance, even if the theorisers of modernity had marginalised religion and did not think it any longer had a role in such matters. In the decade following Shoghi Effendi's composition *World Order of Baha'ullah*, when Abul Ala Maududi's writings on the Islamic state as a self-ordered exclusivity were starting to achieve prominence, Mahmud Ahmad also came up with a plan on behalf of the Ahmadiyya. Their new order, like the others, evidenced to the perceived need to respond to ideological issues thrown up in the arena of contemporary world politics. A challenge to Shoghi Effendi's Baha'i world order letters, Mahmud Ahmad's 'New System' (*nizam-i nau*) was according to Nicholas Evans 'part of a more general movement within late colonial South Asian Islam to engage with European ideologies of fascism and communism to transform Islam into an equivalent and mutually exclusive ideological unit'. As a blueprint for a future world order the Ahmadi *nizam-i nau* aligned with Mahmud Ahmad's creation of the worldwide Ahmadi community's own 'extensive bureaucratic system now seen as "divinely" inspired; holding all executive power'.¹¹³ It functioned in a comparable way to the future world order conceived of by Baha'ullah which dovetailed with the Baha'i administrative system reared and nurtured by Shoghi Effendi. Both Baha'i and Ahmadi plans were launched from within colonial environments on the run up to, or during, World War Two, when Palestine and India were pregnant with emergent Muslim nationalisms with which Baha'is and Ahmadis neither identified nor sympathised. The annulment of the Ottoman caliphate and failure of the Khilafat movement only strengthened the scope of their new orders' address. Key differences between them reflected the trajectory each had taken as a movement growing from mahdi origins.

Typically, the Baha'i order is emphasised as a unique product of Baha'ullah's revelation and presented statementally by Shoghi Effendi in keeping with the stance he adopts as infallible interpreter. The Baha'i administrative order was 'fundamentally different from anything any Prophet [had previously] established'. Baha'ullah had 'Himself revealed its principles, established its institutions [and] appointed the person to interpret His Word and conferred the necessary authority on the body designed to supplement and apply His legislative ordinances'.¹¹⁴ The Ahmadi order was explicated in keeping with Ghulam Ahmad's claim to be both the Mahdi and Promised Messiah who had come to unite all Muslims and a prophet who rather than produce a new sharia would confirm and fulfil Islam's teachings. It also empowered second Khalifa Bashiruddin Mahmud Ahmad with the authority to produce new ideas of his own. Ghulam Ahmad had devised a system which he called *al-Wasiyyat*. A form of inheritance tax that would go toward funding the Ahmadi community in Qadian, he claimed to have derived it from Islamic teachings. Still to be fully implemented, in 1934 Mahmud Ahmad presented a revision, *Tahrik-i Jadid* (new scheme) that was relaunched in a talk he delivered in 1942 to his Ahmadi constituency in Punjab. Published as an Urdu pamphlet entitled *Nizam-i Nau* the following year, it was then repackaged and expanded in an English translation under a new title, *The New World Order of Islam*.¹¹⁵ In terms of presentation, where the divinely-inspired Baha'i order comes straight from Baha'ullah's pen and is fleshed out by his successor Abdul Baha and implemented by infallible interpreter Shoghi Effendi, the Ahmadi order emanates from a formula of Ghulam Ahmad's which is later revised and reapplied by Mahmud Ahmad before being encased in a broader application by Zafrullah Khan in his edited translation of the khalifa's Urdu essay. Not only is their some difference here in terms of contingency with the Ahmadi plan having a more ad hoc feel; it is also obvious from cursory comparative readings of *The World Order of Baha'u'llah* and *The New World Order of Islam* that there is a huge difference in the intended audiences for the respective messages. In fact, nowhere more than in the canonised writings of each can the most basic of differences between the two movements be observed: four decades into the twentieth century the primary constituency for the Baha'i messages consisted of sophisticated Anglophone Westerners. The Ahmadi audience, though already quite widely distributed in the continents of Asia, Africa, Europe and North America, consumed the khalifa's message primarily in Urdu, with English translations produced later for a wider readership. The Baha'i audience was wholly modern, the Ahmadi, at least in South Asia, still rooted within a traditional Islamic background. These facts are reason enough to explain the strong orientalist strain in Baha'i and its absence in Ahmadi writing.

A commonality both orders shared was their partial explication in terms of political doctrines and systems of government operative at the moment of composition. Yet here again the manner in which such comparisons were made reflected different orientations with respect to how fresh directions could be brought into a new Islamic or post-Islamic discourse. According to Shoghi Effendi the '[t]win institutions of guardianship and universal house of justice' together constituted a system of governance that drew upon, but in its perfection excelled, each of the three recognised forms of secular government, democracy, autocracy, and aristocracy:

> without being in any sense a mere replica of any one . . . It blends and harmonizes, as no government fashioned by mortal hands has as yet accomplished, the salutary truths which each of these systems undoubtedly contains without vitiating the integrity of those God-given verities on which it is ultimately founded.[116]

The Ahmadi text *New World Order of Islam* continues in what Nicholas Evans describes as a register 'in which the prophet is equated with analysis and evaluation'.[117] This can be seen in Ghulam Ahmad's construction of a narrative for

Jesus in Kashmir, purporting to access other scholars' research as well as his own idiosyncratic method of exegesis which rationalised the events behind Jesus's crucifixion and resuscitation employing literal interpretation of texts Christians usually read symbolically. In *New World Order of Islam* Mahmud Ahmad teases out an Ahmadi engagement with democracy, socialism, communism, national socialism and fascism, with liberal use of quotation from the Quran, material from the history of the early Muslim community, and by reference to Islamic principles like *zakat* and more broadly to Islam's social teaching with respect to power, poverty, and slavery. The writing is both expository and descriptive, with the content of each political category and its embodiment in specific modern parties sketched out in separate chapters (information that the audience of peasant farmers would have required before they could understand the grounds of comparison with Ahmadism). Zafrullah Khan's English version edits out a lot of repetition in the form of stories and anecdotes, instead bringing to the argument further information needed to situate Mahmud Ahmad's text more discursively. The orientation overall is Islamic in so far as its provenance is concerned, and critical of the secular movements (though not rhetorically condemnatory). Understanding is shown of the social inequality and hegemonic power relations these movements aimed to address, to the extent of endorsing their criticism of class privilege and the European colonial system. Shoghi Effendi's writings, crudely binary as they are and preoccupied with leaders and ecclesiastics, display little attempt to understand the appeal of the political movements of the period. The doctrines of Marx are not situated, but simply lumped together with racism and nationalism, without colonialism receiving a mention. Even allowing for the fact that his readers could be expected to be for the most part North Americans, these are telling omissions.

The same factors relating to reception are applicable to the publications intended to promulgate the beliefs and activities of the two movements. Set alongside the bound and well illustrated *Baha'i World* biennial volumes, Ahmadi English publications were modest in comparison. As an example, I will scrutinise the document *A Present to His Royal Highness the Prince of Wales from the Ahmadiyya Community of Qadian* which was presented to Prince Edward by a delegation of the Ahmadiyya Muslim Community during his visit to Lahore on 27 February 1922. Though a one-off, this short book went through several later editions and excluding prefaces numbers one hundred and seven pages. In the preface Mahmud Ahmad expresses 'his gratitude to the Crown of Britain for the religious tolerance they had exercised in India and their just ways of governance in the highly diverse region of the world'. An outline of the doctrines of the Promised Messiah is followed by a brief history of the Ahmadiyya Community concluding with an invitation to the Prince 'to the one and only true Faith, Islam'.[118] *Present to His Royal Highness* offers an insightful means of comparison with official Baha'i publications such as *Baha'i World*, primarily because it fulfils a comparable function of *da'wa* or 'proclaiming the message' to VIPs. If this publication alone were evidence, we might think Ahmadis were seeking to gain the heir apparent to the throne of Great Britain as their patron. In *Baha'i World* volumes, letters, reports of communications or visits, and lists demonstrate connections to titled individuals, ministers, heads of governments, even the occasional royal convert.[119] *Present to His Royal Highness* performs a similar function, although in a characteristically Ahmadi way since in this case the Prince is the sole recipient, one of the document's main aims seems to be to reaffirm the community's unflinching loyalty to the British throne. To demonstrate that this is not an occasional exercise in flattery, past occasions on which their loyal behaviour stood out in contrast with others are described.[120] As with *Baha'i World* Ahmadi stories of persecution present a similar self-image to the world of a modern movement suffering persecutions at the hands of cruel rulers or unrestrained mobs (understood to be incited by *maulvis*/mullahs) in backward societies. An appropriate sense of outrage is conveyed for such undeserved treatment while at the same time testifying to the lofty character of the martyrs. A notable case was Amir Habibullah Khan who, at the instruction of the Amir of Afghanistan, was stoned to death for promoting Ghulam Ahmad's teaching of abrogation of jihad during Ahmad's lifetime.

Ghulam Ahmad's promises to heal the ills of the modern world and his self-proclaimed success in prophesying modern events inevitably make an appearance in *Present to His Royal Highness*. The arguments it employs to persuade the reader to accept the claims of Ghulam Ahmad and especially the tailoring of his message to Christian audiences, invites comparison with comparable Baha'i proselytising exercises. In the resumé of the Promised Messiah's claims which are set against the signs of the times, and the particular manner in which they are supported by references from the Bible, there are striking similarities to Baha'i texts. Gospel quotations concerning the second coming of Christ and their figurative interpretation function in a very similar manner to the writings of Baha'ullah and Abdul Baha. Two examples illustrate this point: (1) the proposition that Jesus will not descend physically from the heavens on his return but in the human form of a messenger displaying Christ-like features; and (2) the parable of the Lord of the Vineyard in which both Baha'i and Ahmadi interpretations have the Father (either Baha'ullah or Ahmad) return to seize back the vineyard from the thieves. Here it should be born in mind that Ghulam Ahmad had devoted many years to polemical exchanges with missionaries in lectures and in articles he and his close aide Muhammad Ali had published in *Review of Religions*. Ahmad's speciality, the Jesus who is buried in Kashmir, which exercises so much commentary space in books on Ahmadiyyat by Christians from H. A. Walter to Simon Ross Valentine, is not mentioned directly in *Present to His Royal Highness*. Presumably, the decision not to do so was Mahmud Ahmad's and we can only speculate as to why it was not included. Perhaps the writer considered that the heir to the throne of England and Head of the Anglican Communion, no run-of-the-mill Christian missionary and obviously not a Muslim, was a personage he did not want to disrespect.

However, the book pulls no punches when it comes to rewriting the crucifixion. In an extended narrative episode Ghulam Ahmad's appearance in the Juma'a Masjid of Delhi is featured as a scene cut straight out of the Messiah's copybook. However, in marked variation to Jesus's interrogation by the High Priests at Jerusalem and the Bab's before the mujtahids of Tabriz, the Prophet-Messiah is accosted by a mob, only in his case opposition leads neither to crucifixion nor to a firing squad but to nothing more serious than rescue by the police. For Ghulam Ahmad, as we saw earlier, the Bab's death signified he was a false prophet, while the story of the Christ of Kashmir denies the cross in a similar way:

> Ye say that Jesus died on the Cross and thus ye proclaim him who was innocent accursed, and bring him who suffered travail for your sakes into contempt. For it is written in the Scriptures that he who dies on the Cross is a false prophet and shall be accursed.[121]

In contrast, Ahmad the prophet is initially shielded from the angry mob by twelve disciples [*sic*] and by divine arrangement (it seems) effects his escape with the British as proxy: 'At this stage the Superintendent of Police arrived with a force of a hundred constables and opened a way for him through the crowd and with great difficulty escorted him home'.[122]

In spite of Ahmad's attempts to mimic the idiom of the Sermon on the Mount (as seen above), and in spite of the providential role it affords the British, the Juma'a Masjid story clearly misjudges a Christian audience whose reaction, one would suppose, must be that the incident has missed the point of the crucifixion entirely. Even for non-Christians the episode's banal close invites a sense of deflation and anti-climax. It could be contested though that the Quran also appears to deny Jesus' crucifixion and that on this point the Ahmadi hermeneutic is, therefore, in line with mainstream Islam. However, Muslims impugn Ahmadism's revivification and transportation of Jesus to Srinagar as heresy because they believe he was raised to heaven without crucifixion. The point of the present discussion concerns the framing of the discourse of Ahmadism within several idioms, one as a means of attracting Christians and another as a counter-message to Christianity. The second would seem to better fit the Indian context of Ahmad's preaching. However, it might also be compared to Khawja Kamaluddin and Muhammad Ali's decision to downplay Ghulam Ahmad's claims and instead to successfully promote a non-sectarian form of Islam in Europe. Another point that could be raised here would be to compare both Ahmadi approaches to Baha'i success in recruiting Christians to the Baha'i faith in the West.

Documents such as *Present to His Royal Highness* and *Baha'i World* might be considered to belong to a specific genre of promotional mahdi literature. Each contains material that is designed to present and elicit confirmation from the reader of the successes of the respective movement and the force of its claims. Not only verification of truth claims but also the plausibility of self-image is at stake, that is, the look of being reformed, modern, possessing appropriate gravitas and the desire to demonstrate good-breeding, or what Baha'is often refer to as 'preserving the dignity of the faith'. Allowing for the respective distances from conservative Islam each has travelled by the 1920s and 1930s, it will also be appreciated that each publication evidences to the mores of its own faith community. Presentationally, each piece of literature gives clues as to the language, culture, and to some degree social class, of the movement's constituents. As to who the implied reader is, this is not difficult to decode in the Ahmadi case given the personage to whom the publication is addressed; as we have already seen, the Baha'i biennial also aims as high as British and European royalty as well as the higher classes.

Theological issues are not the subject of the present study, and which publication the reader is more impressed by (*Present to His Royal Highness* is a shorter and less arduous read than a weighty tome of *Baha'i World*) depends on factors such as taste, affiliation and so on. They might perhaps trigger a variety of responses, for example:

a) the claims of both movements can not be true; the claims of this one ring truer so the other must be false;
b) for taking a forbidden turn *both* are false;
c) both make similar far-fetched claims about their founders, proclaiming them to be Christ, the fulfilment of Islam and previous religions, etc.;
d) Baha'ism came first and in its employment of arguments and tropes Ahmadism is derivative of Baha'ism;
e) both have roots in Islam which cannot be erased and these limit their appeal to non-Muslims.

One important matter that has concerned this chapter is style and idiom. At times Ahmadi discourse seems closer to that of a reform movement in Islam and in staying largely within a horizon of discourse that is recognisably Islamic, remains outside orientalism and eschews self-orientalising tendencies. In moving into the twin territories of mahdism and messianism while claiming to be Muslim, Ahmadism possesses a character integrally its own. Although the Baha'i faith has travelled the furthest, both movements have made significant alterations and accommodations to suit Christians. Baha'is or former Baha'is continue to point out the Baha'i faith's Islamic roots; a few wish to celebrate these while others believe the faith's present apparatus still bears a strong Persianate if not Islamic tincture which will remain an obstacle in progressing it beyond its present stage.[123]

8

Muslim Responses and a Future for Mahdi Movements

From my study of mahdi texts it has been possible to analyse how, and in what form, each movement equipped itself with foundational narratives that reflect its own specificity, its spiritual raison d'etre and future goals. The narratives also incorporated observations on, and justifications for, the movements' separation from the religious traditions out of which they grew and developed, frequently contrasting the traditional ways of the former against their own self-renovations and justifying these on grounds of reason, modern outlook and practical implementation. Amply documented histories of persecution and othering can be accessed and are still being written. Allowing for variation, these narratives provide evidence to support the view that each movement intentionally steered a course away from the conditions of subjugation within Islamicate and post-colonial territories and was urged into following this course by courting or identifying with imperial power and its centres in the West. Equally important is how the innovations proposed by the mahdi movements were received by the Muslim majority. So far little has been said here about mainstream Muslim responses, if indeed there is such a thing as 'a mainstream Muslim' position and one capable of staging a unified response. In fact, as we shall see below, measures adopted or proposed against the leave-takers and justifications for these have not been uniform. Of particular significance is the extent to which the responses were animated by religious doctrine, political calculation, and/or a general adherence to the status quo and fear of the weakening of existing conservative societies. Another outstanding consideration is the relations these societies had with a spreading Western imperial presence and the desire to resist the intrusion of colonial power. Overarching all these matters this study's two major thematic concerns require summary evaluation: whether and to what extent the concepts of 'orientalism' and 'modernity' have been shown to structure the mahdi narratives and their attitudes toward mainstream Muslims and, in wrapping these points up, whether the criteria adopted, a framework of postcolonial analysis, has been applicable and effective in negotiating and interpreting the issues set out above.

Muhammad Iqbal on Ahmadism and Babi-Baha'ism – and the Category of 'Non-Muslim'

Two notable interventions into the issue of mahdism that focused on Ahmadism but also stretched to encompass Babis and Baha'is were those of Muhammad Iqbal and Abul Ala Maududi. As we saw at the end of Chapter 6, Iqbal in his letter to Nehru took (for him) a particularly strong line on the Ahmadiyyat arguing that in aiming to establish 'a new Ummat for the Indian prophet' it had succeeded in dividing Muslims, specifically within the context of British controlled India. For Iqbal the threat raised by the Ahmadi position, as Teena Purohit puts it, was that,

> the solidarity of Islam consists of the belief in its two basic principles – the unity of God and the finality of prophethood – which . . . have existed since the days of the Prophet and only recently have been undermined by Qadianis of India'.[1]

Clarifying what at first sight appears to be an argument over religious doctrine, Iqbal wrote:

> It is obvious that Islam which claims to weld all the various communities of the world into one single community cannot reconcile itself to a movement which threatens its present solidarity and holds the promise of further rifts in human society.[2]

In the circumstances, where Ghulam Ahmad's claim to prophecy was a perceived threat to Muslim unity, Iqbal unequivocally spelt out the dangers British colonial power represented to Indian Islam. 'It is no exaggeration to say that the solidarity of the Muslim community in India under the

British is far less safe than the solidarity of the Jewish community was in the days of Jesus under the Romans'.[3] When he questioned the motivation behind Russia and Britain permitting 'Babis' (i.e., Baha'is) and Ahmadis to open missions in Ashkhabad and Woking, Iqbal placed both movements on the same colonial footing. 'Whether Russia and England showed this tolerance on the ground of imperial expediency or pure broadmindedness is difficult for us to decide'.[4] He also extended the comparison by including both Ahmadism and Baha'ism within the framework of Magianism, essentialised as a traditional mindset which the Persians had brought into Islam.[5] Iqbal did not, however, see the Ahmadi and Babi-Baha'i threats to Islam as cognate. While the Ahmadis had reinvigorated Magianism and were a danger to the umma, though they had performed what amounted to much the same thing he did not consider the Iranian mahdi groups to be a threat. 'Bahaism appears . . . to be far more honest than Qadianism; for the former openly departs from Islam'. In fact Iqbal's solution to the 'Qadiani problem' was for the Ahmadis to act likewise – 'the best course for the rulers of India' was to 'declare the Qadianis a separate community'.[6] In his pamphlet on the same 'problem' Maududi pointed out the political and social challenges raised by Ahmadism, similarly embedding their danger within the colonial context of British rule. Like his mentor he removed Baha'ism from the frame because it had departed from Islam. However, Maududi expands Iqbal's Magian argument by invoking the danger Shi'ism represented to the Prophet's finality by revering 'spiritual leaders coming after the Prophet', thereby establishing the habit of eroding the Prophet's authority by spawning sufis, imams and mahdis.[7] This trend of thought appears to lead to the proposition that in establishing and perpetuating Magianism the Shi'a are closer to Baha'ism than orthodox Sunni Islam, even though as Purohit points out, Iqbal exonerated another Shi'i offshoot, the Agha Khan Ismailis, of the same misdemeanour. In a type of reverse orientalism Shi'ism is blamed as the tendency that introduced into Islam the initial infecting germ to threaten *khatm al-nubuwwa*.[8]

The disjuncture in condemning Ahmadiyyat for the danger it represented to the community of Muslims in India, while categorising Baha'ism according to its own self-view as a non-Muslim entity might be straight-cut if this view were widely held, for instance if it extended to Iran. But this has not been the case. If Ahmadis were supposed to adopt the same status as Baha'is and leave the Muslim community, why had this act not helped the latter in Iran in their defence against the charge of *irtidad* (apostasy) levelled against them by the custodians of Shi'i Islam? The lack of consistency makes the respective judgements on the two mahdi movements seem arbitrary to say the least. It was not as though comparisons between the two were not being made. Maududi, for example, quotes a statement from Ghulam Ahmad in which he pointed out the precariousness of the positions of Babis and Baha'is in nineteenth-century Iran, and their leaders' exile in Edirne and Akka which he compared to the treatment of Ahmadis in Afghanistan. Ahmad's conclusion was that Ahmadis were 'blessed' by their link with the British government. This reaffirmed Maududi's argument that where bondage to an infidel government was a calamity for Muslims it was 'a blessing for this new prophet and his followers'.[9] Here, however, Ahmad's point appears the more realistic in its awareness of the fact that the treatment of Babi-Baha'is and Ahmadis under Muslim governments, Shi'i or Sunni, was likely to be very similar, and the heresy/apostasy charge was made to work against them both. It did not matter what the charge was when the effect – repression and sometimes violent persecution – was the same.

It will be useful to go on to consider two modern approaches of the twenty-first century to the perceived problem of mahdi movements in Muslim-majority states. Looking at the recrudescence of persecution against Ahmadis in Indonesia where, up until recently, they were relatively tolerated, Ahmad Najib Burhani discusses confusion over the terminology heretic, apostate and non-Muslim. According to Burhani, Indonesian Muslims were in the previous century largely able to 'dismiss and simply ignore the Ahmadiyya as "incorrect" in their beliefs', but he dates the rise of intolerance and persecution directed against them from the immediate aftermath of the fall of Suharto in 1998. Since then Ahmadis have been condemned as 'a cancer' (a term also used by Maududi for Ahmadis in Pakistan); forced to live like refugees after their houses have been burnt down; deprived of access to education (like Baha'is in Iran); and denied healthcare and the right to vote. Their case, writes Burhani, demonstrates that in Indonesia heretics are considered worse than apostates or non-Muslims. However, he comes close to defining the root cause of the problem when he states:

> today ... some Muslims do not feel that Islam is secure. They feel that everything they see in this world is a threat to the existence of Islam ... Only by perceiving the Ahmadiyya as located between Muslim and non-Muslim, where their religious rights, at least according to conservative Muslims, [are] suspended, can the discrimination of the Ahmadis be fully understood.[10]

Since the beginning the Baha'i faith has in contrast been on a journey to assert its status as a non-Muslim religion. Shoghi Effendi saw a ruling of an Egyptian sharia court in May 1925 in which Baha'is were classified as followers of a separate religion to Islam as a victory. In addition, the ruling condemned Baha'is for apostasy and promoting heretical doctrines, moving Shoghi Effendi to refer to it as 'the first Charter of the emancipation of the Cause of Baha'u'llah from the fetters of Islamic orthodoxy'.[11] However, as he also conceded, the situation for Egyptian Baha'is in belonging to none of the three religions allowed for by the Egyptian constitution (in addition to Islam, the Jewish religion and Christianity, the religions of the 'People of the Book' as stated in the Quran) would continue to place them in a limbo and lay them open to future suffering. As far as the recognised legality of their marriages and their status as citizens is concerned, Egyptian Baha'is have continued to exist in a no-man's-land. However, in the early 2000s individual Baha'is brought legal cases petitioning for the right to have their religion entered on their identity cards in effect contesting previous twentieth-century rulings which banned their religion and in effect prevented them from obtaining legal documents. Each litigant had experienced inconsistencies with respect to recording their religious classification on birth certificates and passports – some had been allowed to enter 'Baha'i', 'other', or to leave blank spaces or dashes.[12]

From the time of Reza Shah the non-recognition of the Baha'i faith has been an ongoing issue in Muslim-majority states which nevertheless claim to have secular constitutions, and this non-recognition demonstrates that for mahdi movements the option of being non-Muslim, *pace* the statements made by Iqbal and Maududi, has been no more beneficial to themselves than continuing to proclaim a Muslim identity while maintaining beliefs that are held by the majority to contravene the *khatm al-nubuwwa* doctrine. This, however, does not satisfy the political dimensions of the dispute, and it would be naïve to ignore these. The late Saba Mahmood's analysis of the legal position of Baha'is as a very small, but much-debated, community within contemporary Egypt raises broad arguments that concern secularisation and the position of religious minorities in Muslim-majority countries. In line with rights legislation and processes set into motion by European secularisation starting in the nineteenth century, Egypt had respect for freedom of belief written into its constitution. This pertains to a key conceptualisation of secularisation rubric in Europe in which a distinction is drawn between the private and the public realms. In practice, Egypt's 'courts grant Baha'is rights to hold their beliefs but use the concept of public order to deny them the right to manifest these beliefs in public'. A need, therefore, arises 'to understand how Egyptian courts have tried to square the religious *inequality* of Bahais with their civil and political *equality* in the eyes of the law'.[13] Mahmood's analysis is largely instrumental, as she hones in on the accepted praxis by which international legislation on religious rights, while allowing freedom of belief, leaves to states 'a legitimate right to regulate and limit' privacy of religious belief 'in order to "protect public order, health or morals, or for the protection of the rights or freedoms of others"'.[14] The concept of public order, originally 'a neutral mechanism introduced by the British', as interpreted by an Egyptian court ruling of 2008, gave the state 'the authority to limit the expression of belief that flouts the social and moral order of the given polity', ergo, 'the Egyptian state is within its rights to limit public manifestations of the Bahai religion'.[15]

Mahmood's research confirmed her understanding that the court's conception of public order is in line with 'global genealogy' meaning its provenance comes from nineteenth-century European secularisation brought to the Middle East as an accompaniment to the thrust of colonialism. Secularisation is integral to notions of human rights, but it operates differently in different places. By this we are to understand that rulings by an institution like the European Court of Human Rights (EctHR) also limit individual religious rights in the name of public order, for example, in upholding judgements against the public wearing of the veil by Muslim women. Mahmood observes that,

> public order has no necessary definition but changes from society to society . . . it is the state's prerogative to define its scope and meaning, depending on its legal system and national norms . . . [it] has the right to rescind specific terms of international covenants . . . if they contravene its legal and social norms.[16]

In the Egyptian context '[i]t is primarily because Islam is the religion of the majority of the population that the state freely practices and recognizes its rites and rituals'.[17] In filling in the nineteenth-century back story in which Western Christian states imposed 'religious freedom' and minority rights on the Ottoman Empire, she comes up with this important corollary: 'the modern roots of religious strife belong equally to the history of secularization as to the legacy of Islamic rule'.[18] In reality, secular states are not neutral on religious issues and all manifestations of the state are subject to state authority, as can be observed in the ruling allowing for the display of a crucifix in an Italian public school and the prohibition of a Muslim teacher from wearing a headscarf in a Swiss school, both on the grounds of public order.[19] In the situation in which Baha'is are placed in Egypt, Mahmood sees similarities with the situation referred to the EctHR of Turkish women desiring to wear veils in public buildings who are disallowed from so doing on grounds that such an act contravenes the secularism of the Turkish state. The core problem – if you see it as a problem – lies within the Egyptian constitution because it invokes the sharia which 'prohibits the *public practice* of "anything but the recognized religions"'. She has little to say about the Baha'i faith's mahdi foundations, beyond noting in passing that where Baha'is received a judgement in 2008 allowing them to leave a blank space in their identity cards, this still made them 'vulnerable to religious discrimination' as the only group 'to have this distinction', indicating their 'deviation from the Muslim norm . . . for some, *a sign of their apostasy from Islam.*'[20]

Mahmood argued that religious freedoms are not universally applied, but often withheld based on different underlying objections which reflect the majority view of a society (or what a court considers that to be). The broader scope of her argument, however, is a postcolonial one and sets out to rebalance 'the terms *global* and *local*', that is, at base she is arguing that where Muslim societies are deemed to implement secular values more imperfectly than American/European societies this 'mask[s] the inequality of power relations between Euro-America and the Middle East, wherein "the global" stands for the former (universally and theoretically consequential) and the "local" for the latter (particular and theoretically inconsequential)'.[21] Mahmood does not attempt to use her analysis to defray the charge that the Egyptian state has been practising persecution of a peaceful and tolerant minority merely because its existence is unacceptable to the proclaimed orthodox religious susceptibilities of the country, though broadly speaking she accepts that to be the case. Her underlying argument is that there are double standards in arguing that in the Egyptian case Baha'is' human rights are being denied by a Muslim state when Muslims' rights are contravened on the same principle in Western countries. If what she argued was not the case her analysis could easily be filed away as another non-Western state seeking to extricate itself from universal human rights norms based on its recidivistic particularism. However, the question of rights issues which both Baha'is and Ahmadis have been more than ready to litigate in international courts is beyond the postcolonial remit adopted here.

Muslims, Mahdi Movements and Postcolonial Critique

While it is not within the scope of this concluding chapter to analyse in detail historical patterns of indigenous response to mahdi movements or indeed to further probe historical anti-Baha'i or anti-Ahmadi manifestations, we have touched on varied measures, formal and informal, recently enacted as the result of non-acceptance of mahdi movements in South Asia, Indonesia, and Egypt, as well as visiting an earlier ban on recognition of Baha'is in Pahlavi Iran. So far it would be fair to say a uniform response to the existence of these movements within Muslim-majority states has not been observed at least in those discussed, where different definitions of their positions were seen to operate, although it is probably correct to observe that mahdi movements have for the most part not been welcome. I shall now move on to consider the valence of assigning to Muslims a collective singularity with respect to their belonging to one umma in modern times. The category 'mainstream Muslim' has so far been used as a tag of convenience but it sacrifices complexity on a variety of levels. As a proposition it was raised earlier in relation to the Baha'i leaders' putative membership of a 'Muslim world' in the 1860s and 1870s. Cemal Aydin refers to the emergence of an 'imagined global unity' during the period of the Ottoman sultanate of Abdul Hamid and states an 'illusion of Muslim unity persists' today albeit a tortuous one.[22] During Sultan Abdul Hamid's caliphate (1876–1909), 'promotion of Ottoman spiritual sovereignty over the *Ummah*, alongside British temporal sovereignty, solidified the imagination of a geopolitical Muslim world in the age of high imperialism', but '[a]bolition of the caliphate brought to an end a half century of global Muslim political thought tied to the model of Ottoman modernism'.[23] Across the world Muslims then entered a period in which dissolution of spiritual and political leadership came fully into view, and it may be viable to speak of Muslims landing in a post-colonial age in search of a collective identity.

In colonial times there can be said to have existed what was always an imagined, if not palpable, Islamic threat as far as European imperial governments were concerned. In terms of postcolonial thinking, however, is there a case for talking about Muslim resistance, and of what sort? Mahmood Mamdani has proposed more specifically that political Islam was born in the colonial period but did not give rise to a terrorist movement until the Cold War.[24] Could resistance then be said to have come fully of age in the post-colonial period? Some will argue that while discrete cases of colonised, preponderantly Muslim, peoples such as those living in Palestine and Algeria did engage in anti-colonial struggles, these are not usually construed as instances of *Islamic* resistance. From a postcolonial position, Stephen Howe has argued,

> there are strong grounds for scepticism over whether, historically, there ever have been distinctive or generic Islamicate forms or experiences of empire (either as empire builders or as colonized subjects) or a distinctive Islamic or Islamist form of anti-colonialism or anti-imperialism.[25]

If correct, this would mean that important issues need resolving before the mahdi movements and the campaigns raised against them in the post-colonial age can be accommodated as part of a postcolonial view in which Muslims have rejected seceders from Islam on grounds that their existence weakened the umma. Interpretation that proposes Muslim collectivities staging 'resistance' to the coloniser or former coloniser during the first part of the twentieth century may not amount to a great deal and might be considered as belonging to the vapours of postcolonial theory which are, however, further obfuscated by a general disinclination on the part of Western postcolonal theorists to include Muslims in their formulations of postcolonial resistance. It might be trite to argue that Muslims, or an imagined number of them, who did not embrace the beliefs of mahdi movements – which were enabled or thought to be by western empires – were corporately self-defining as resisters to imperialism by excluding those who did.

Where might examples of such 'Muslim' resistance be said to have taken place? In Iran, 'in the historical narratives that proliferated in the [. . .] 1940s, [Baha'i] leaders were successively declared to be agents of Russia, the Ottoman Empire, Great Britain and Israel – their ultimate goal: to infringe the "religious and national unity of Iran".'[26] In Pakistan in 1953 allied with the Majlis-i Ahrar, Abul Ala Maududi rallied Muslims around the *khatm-i nubuwwat* movement and succeeded in forcing the politicians to cede 'power to mullahs, who had largely been excluded from the political process until now', in order to make the country an authentic Islamic state.[27] In both situations Muslims might be said to be acquiring a badly needed post-colonial identity and solidarity, but were they acting *as Muslims* against a perceived colonial threat? Or to look at these agitations from another perspective, can Maududi's argument regarding 'the Qadiani Problem' (encapsulated in similar terms by some Shi'a in their charges against the Baha'is in Iran) be considered a valid postcolonial one? This study has argued, at least in the case of the Baha'is, that during the first half of the twentieth century there was effectively a transfer of what had up until that time been a messianic reform movement from the Islamicate domains of Iran and Ottoman Turkey to a colonial theatre of activity in Palestine, and also to the metropolises of western Europe and North America where it is stretching matters to say they were conniving against Iran. In the Iranian context where neither exerted direct coloniser status, the activity of Britain or Russia in seeking out protégés from indigenous religious minorities was as we have seen ambiguous. To contest that the Babi and Baha'i movements were the creation or agents of Western imperialism is a crude distortion of a complex alignment of positions. Nonetheless, what has been written with regard to the Christians in Ottoman domains in the nineteenth century could be considered applicable to Islam's seceders too: 'the status of oppression that had been associated with non-Muslims gained a new and more powerful political connotation which begged for greater solidarity and sympathy of the West'.[28] This was certainly the case as the twentieth century wore on and, as we shall see, the Baha'is of Iran became more isolated.

On the other hand, Muslims who did not join mahdi movements, and who were in the overwhelming majority in lands threatened by the incursion of outside power, might have had reason to feel they were on the receiving end of othering by Western imperial powers. Aydin states: 'European discourses of Muslim racial inferiority, and Muslims' theories of their own apparent decline nurtured the first arguments for pan-Islamic solidarity'. These took a blow at the close of World War One with the dissolution of the Ottoman Empire and caliphate, however, in the Interwar years there was a 'persistence of shallow imperial notions of Muslim unity but also subaltern appeals to Muslim internationalism'.[29] Aydin's argument can be taken further, as he states:

> The seeming importance of Islam in the contemporary politics of Muslim-majority societies derives not from theological requirements or a uniquely high level of Muslim piety but from the legacy of imperial racialization of Muslimness and from the particular intellectual and political strategies of Muslim resistance to this racialized identity.[30]

This position *would* constitute being involved in, and reacting to, a postcolonial predicament, what Aamir Mufti identifies as the 'historical experience of being colonized'. Whether direct or indirect in form, this experience is disruptive of 'a narrative of continuous historical development as is possible in metropolitan societies – hence the specific forms that the crisis of authenticity ... takes in postcolonial societies'.[31] In these circumstances an 'illusion of Muslim unity' can be said at least in part to have been fuelled by Western orientalism in a conditioning of otherness. In the context of empire and Christian Europeans' 'racial assumptions' which inscribed a Muslim exceptionalism, European Islamophobes such as Renan and Chirol indulged 'racialized concepts of Muslims' decline'.[32] This being the case, a Muslim response looks like a reaction to orientalists creating for Muslims an identity that subsequently becomes an accepted reality.

Where then does this leave us in our effort to understand the positioning of the mahdi movements? First of all, it is important to recognise both that they were strongly involved in the Islamicate predicament of 'colonial subjugation' but that the steps they took in response to it led them in the opposite direction to the Muslim majority. Baha'is and Ahmadis appear to belong to movements which acculturated themselves to the modern world so successfully that they by-passed the threat to which Islamic societies were in danger of succumbing. This is not to say that they were not at particular stages of their development unmoved by the threat of imperialist dominance. The Babi revolution against the Qajar-mujtahid state has been defined as an uprising against indigenous corruption while being alive to Iran's inability to respond to the growing danger of British penetration of the economy. Walter accounted for Ghulam Ahmad's movement by stating it was a belated Muslim awakening to the presence of the British government, the Protestant missionaries and the work of orientalists – belated because the Muslims of India had been the last to respond owing to their being educationally the most backward.[33] Ahmadism could be said to have demonstrated a resistant response to the Western coloniser with respect to its religious formulation which was pointed against his religion, Christianity, this at the same time as being ultra accommodating toward British rule. (Maududi however, quotes statements made by Ghulam Ahmad to the British which claim such outward resistance was only a ploy.)[34] The Ahmadiyyat began as a 'Muslims in danger' manifestation which, in view of the weak position Muslims were in after failure of the Great Rebellion in 1857, might be said to have meant steering a sensible course by carrying on the struggle in the domain of religion. Baha'ism was undoubtedly inflected by its leaders' long period of exile, which both enabled them to take a broad view of the Islamicate world but also led them to become increasingly cosmopolitan and detached toward it. Compared to Babism the Baha'i movement came to occupy a stance that was deterritorialised, Westward-leaning, and which remained largely indifferent to the plight of colonised Middle Eastern peoples, Baha'ullah having suggested they were being oppressed because they had failed to accept his teachings.[35]

Issues situating modern Islam within postcolonial theory remain to be coherently addressed but are important for the arguments that have been set out in this study. European thought about Iran's place in history has been accorded attention by postcolonial scholars like Mirsepassi and Dabashi who have discussed how Iran features in colonial discourse from the time of Hegel up to the present 'post-civilizational period in global conflict'.[36] However, the case under review is a very restricted one: at the bar is a proposition that superficially bears resemblance to the charge outlined above – couched in crude terms this asserts that Baha'ism was a movement aligned with, if not created by, colonialism. It is one that is not entirely without substance. There is enough circumstantial evidence to confirm contact was established: tangential contact of Baha'ullah with a Russian diplomat after the Babi assassination attempt on the Shah and the offer to succour him in Russia; the exchange of brief messages with Austrian and French diplomats Prokesch-Osten and Arthur Gobineau, and further diplomatic toing and froing that has all been recorded in Moojan Momen's book. It is unlikely that a smoking gun remains to be found in the archive that will prove complicity beyond reasonable doubt. Most of these contacts lasted only for fleeting moments, based as they were very largely on humanitarian concern, and were without product. Even if Russian and French consuls protected Baha'is during moments of social unrest in Iran, such as during the Constitutional Revolution, their aid should be construed as amounting to nothing more than an 'evening up' when one considers the not infrequent, indigenously orchestrated campaigns against them. Considering he was at that time under threat from the retreating Jamal Pasha, Abdul Baha can certainly be said to have welcomed the British when they arrived in Palestine.[37] Nobody contests that he worked with the Mandate Administration gaining employment for members of the tiny Baha'i community, generally embedding the Baha'i faith (which was very imperfectly understood by his British administrative and military visitors) in an established, relaxed way. (Whether he knew of the exploits of Husayn Ruhi is unsure but cannot be ruled out.)

There is a more restricted postcolonial argument to this study, however; it relates specifically to the employment and incorporation of orientalist discourse within important texts which form a key part of official Baha'i narrative. The evidence accumulates, starting with the Christianising tendencies of Baha'ullah and Abdul Baha and their recognition of the superior global force of Western civilisation, and the stretching of a protean preaching style that could mean all things to all men. The terrain was thereby cleared for Baha'ism to acquire an orientalist dimension. Orientalism entered the writings of Baha'is themselves after Western converts from Christian and Jewish backgrounds started to arrive in Akka around the turn of the twentieth century. Putting to one side the early writings of those converts which were influenced by statements made about Baha'ism by orientalists, the major body of writing displaying orientalist features was composed by a Palestine-born writer of Iranian ethnicity who headed the Baha'i community. First of all, his writings raise the matter of the author's identity. To those who believe Shoghi Effendi to have been the infallible interpreter of the revelation of the most recent Manifestation of God this will appear irrelevant; viewed in this way his writings stand above such concerns, in fact they claim a semi-canonical status on a slightly lower level to the writings of Baha'ullah and Abdul Baha. But if we consider the salient factors shaping their author a different formation can be assembled. From a family of mixed descendants of the Bab and Baha'ullah intended by his grandfather to head the tiny Iranian sect, as a young man he started from the colonial periphery, was briefly educated at Oxford University, made and maintained connections with members of the British governing elite and returned to British-administered Palestine. The product can be formulated in three statements: through his education he was connected to Britain and had close links with British colonial officials; writing on Islam during the colonial era displays overt orientalist characteristics; Islam features in much of Shoghi Effendi's writing in the language forms of classic orientalism. The three statements are related: the first is factual and links to the second and third, while all have been demonstrated above as holding validity. Given its origins as a mahdi movement in an Islamic country, it is important that through colonial contact the Baha'i faith came to be inflected by orientalist thinking; as a movement which is 'for the world' and packs universal aspirations this colonial trammelling should be judged as an inclusive part of what it now stands for.

Some Twentieth-century Shi'a and Baha'i Configurations

An embryonic configuration in the nineteenth century that set indigenous Shi'i Muslim religious and political elites against modern-oriented Baha'is and their American and European sympathisers hardened in the early twentieth century and developed to include those forces within Iran that, following in the footsteps of Jamal al-Din 'Afghani', began to oppose Western imperialism. In the early 1920s, an American vice-consul murdered in Iran was rumoured (wrongly) to have been a Baha'i, '[m]atters [having] reached such a state that an American in Iran was automatically assumed to be a Baha'i'.[38] An argument now beginning to be assembled by some Muslim clerics and their secular allies was that Baha'ism was a political grouping and a tool of the West. Meanwhile, in the world Baha'is inhabited, the one where scripture was being enhanced by speculative imaginings (in English), leaders were investing in depictions of Islam as a culturally-bound backward, stagnant element in eastern societies. Moreover, as we saw from Amin Banani's critique of communities in Ashkhabad and Iran, Baha'is seemed inured to the great wave of colonial and post-colonial struggle that encompassed the twentieth-century world, and to distinguishing the anti-Muslim orientalist stereotypes produced by certain voluble British establishment figures. There is substantial evidence to suggest this was encouraged by the religious exceptionalism and triumphalism generated by mystic, inspirational thinking which largely left an intellectual vacuum within the developing Baha'i mind. By mid-century the struggle for the decolonisation of the Middle East placed a religiously deviant, sectarian, pro-Western community such as the Baha'is in a position of opprobrium distinctly all its own. Alongside the other religious minorities, Zoroastrians, Christians and Jews, Baha'is were condemned as a conduit of Western interference in Iran, but what set them apart from the others was their engagement in a unique theological dispute with Shi'i Islam over a Babi millenarian narrative that claimed the promised return of the Imam Mahdi had been fulfilled. While the other religious minorities could be allotted a defined, if precarious, niche in a Shi'i state as 'People of the Book' the more than a third of a million Baha'is could claim no such status.

In addition, those wider currents in the region that since the close of the nineteenth century had begun to produce channels of resistance to the incursions of foreign power now began specifically to comprehend the Baha'is within the scope of their condemnation (as well as Christians and to a lesser extent Jews). The argument spilled over into socio-politics. Baha'is gravitated toward the meritocratic (if cliquish) dynastic-nationalist regime of Mohammad Reza Pahlavi. The continuing divergence between traditionally oriented Shi'ism and the technocratically modernising Pahlavis took on a further dimension with the turn to radical Islamism. More broadly, Amanat identifies a shared heritage of antagonism to Baha'is that was not limited to Islamists but also included 'intellectuals on the left, academics, and the public at large'. His explanation: the minority were 'an enemy within', a scapegoat 'on whose shoulder could be placed all the faults of the past and fears for the future'. However, what was Baha'i orientalism but a kind of inverse reflection of this? (We might point out the unfortunate position of Iran's Baha'is in being caught in the middle, having had no input into Baha'i orientalism which had been written in a foreign language.) Behind the cordon sanitaire of political neutrality the price Baha'is paid for relative prosperity under the Pahlavis was social isolation and an ever-looming vulnerability that could only be cured by emigration. At the outbreak of the Iranian revolution their days of arbitrary arrest and execution on baseless charges fuelled by 'vile anti-Baha'i campaigns in the press and media ... [and] paranoid fears and conspiracy theories' had returned.[39] Even Dabashi, by no means a sympathiser with the Baha'i faith (or Shi'i clerisy for that matter) is quite clear about on whom the weight of blame for this set of conditions should be placed:

> In the 1940s and early 1950s the Shi'i clerical establishment concentrated their attention on the Baha'is and the communists. The entirely misplaced clerical hostility against the Baha'is was a remnant of their active opposition to the Babi movement of the nineteenth century. The Baha'is at this point were an entirely pacifist sect with absolutely no revolutionary or even political agenda, and their persecution was (and remains) a hallmark of shame in the chronicle of the Shi'i clerical establishment.[40]

In the wider world Muslim responses to Western technological and political dominance had been initially mixed according to modernist and revivalist positionings, but in the twentieth century increasingly took on anti-imperialist, anti-Western stances. For Muslim thinkers the argument that orientalism was a factor in the colonial domination of eastern countries and that it encouraged the embattled situation of Islam became a norm. At the same time as Arab scholars Anwar Abdel Malek and A. L. Tibawi were laying the foundations for the idea that would later be comprehended in Edward Said's *Orientalism*, Iranian intellectuals such as Fahkruddin Shadman, Jalal Al-e

Ahmad, and Ahmad Fardid moved in a similar direction.[41] In contrast, Baha'i publications maintained a reformist-universalist positioning that allowed for alignment with formulations of Western modernity, even if the cultural decadence of the West was at times condemned in vocabulary redolent of the Soviet Union or Sayyid Qutb.[42] While condemning racism, nationalism and communism and the moral laxity of Western social and public practice Baha'i writings had nothing to say about imperialism and the dominion of the West, and expressed no antipathy toward the hegemony of Western capitalism as a system. Though officially non-political with a 'universalist and tolerant outlook',[43] strong support for Iranian nationalism as a modernising force existed among Iranian Baha'is in their own country and in diaspora. The Pahlavi national myth that marginalised Iran's Islamic culture and propounded instead a narrative of monarchy reviving imagined Iranic pre-Islamic glory found a welcoming ear among them.

It has been pointed out that the term postcolonial has 'rarely been applied to Iran, because the country was never formally colonised by Western powers' but 'was semi-colonised by the UK and then the US'. Nonetheless, the Iranian revolution of 1978–9 was promoted 'in the name of anti-colonialism and the official rhetoric of the Islamic government is against cultural imperialism (*tahajom-e farhangi*)'.[44] Twentieth-century Iranian intellectuals registered variant attitudes toward the West, from Hedayat's worship à la Aqa Khan Kermani of all that was European, to Ali Shariati's critique of its imperialistic or colonialist ambitions, his and Al-e Ahmad's rejection of *rushanfikri* (the westernised intellectual) and Al-e Ahmad's denunciation of the West's materialism and colonisation of the Iranian consciousness.[45] Post-colonial Iranian intellectuals (i.e., those living in post-colonial times but not necessarily aware of postcolonial theory which begins in the 1980s and is largely a creation of Third World émigrés in the West), including those who veered toward Marxist ideas, were in their thinking polar opposite to most twentieth-century Baha'is. What intellectuals there were in the Iranian Baha'i community during the reign of Mohammad Reza were more likely to embrace technological and socio-legal facets of international modernity led by the Western world, much of which were valorised by the Pahlavi state too.[46] The revolution brought the two completely divergent orientations to a head. Writing during the decade of heightened repressive measures taken against Baha'is by the Iranian revolutionary government, MacEoin goes so far as to speak of, the Western view of the Baha'is and the Baha'i view of themselves as representatives ... or defenders of Western values in a stereotypically backward and hostile oriental society ... almost an exact mirror image of the general, stereotyped Iranian view of Baha'ism.[47]

Latterly, in so far as Baha'is were drawn into the simple binaries pertaining to the so-called 'clash of civilizations' based on the notion of the 'West versus Islam' they moved even further in the opposite direction to 'Islam'. This trajectory would be confirmed by any cursory review of popular Baha'i identification with the state of Israel going back to the second half of the last century up to the present day, which would not in itself be reprehensible if it were not so unquestioning. This is not intended in an anti-Semitic sense but according to one that upholds scrutiny of the European colonial project which enabled the creation of Israel. Baha'is need to be aware that the orientalism they have borrowed from Europe – and which supports their view of themselves as civilised and as supporters of Western values and Muslims/Arabs as backward – is, as Gil Hochburg has argued, a way of thinking that is a product 'primarily [of] Christo-European ideologies, whether anti-Semitic, Orientalist, or Islamophobic'.[48]

Conclusion – Baha'i and Ahmadi Futures

For quite some time external appraisal of the Baha'i faith seems to have been frozen. For example, in a textbook that has run through many reprintings historian of religion Trevor Ling noted Baha'ullah had 'developed [Babism] into a sect whose doctrines were rather milder and vaguer, of a somewhat universalistic humanitarian nature, but no longer Islamic in any orthodox sense'.[49] Little seems to have changed in the knowledge and understanding the world of scholarship entertains about the Baha'i faith. Writing admittedly before the mini-revival in study of the Ahmaddiyat, Ling opined:

> Perhaps one of the most significant features of the history of the [Ahmadiyya] movement is the very slight measure of success it has had – almost negligible – in spite of its claim to present a form of Islam for the modern age.[50]

Without generalising these statements, they point to problems that have not gone away for either movement. The Baha'i faith's investment in world unity and peace, in spite of the continuing urgency of these issues today, seems to have dried up as a point of attraction to converts. Indeed, urgency over world peace has taken on a specific form for Baha'is: the need to continually postpone the founders' prophecies as to its arrival.[51] As one writer notes, existing believers may well have been put off by 'the disappointment that the promises by leaders that mass enrollments are imminent have not been fulfilled'.[52] Toward the end of the last century, the Baha'i organisation began attracting criticism from former acolytes who accused it of developing theocratic and dogmatic features, admittedly milder, but still, some argue, bearing the traces of Baha'is' parental Islam. If this is the case, then the belief in freedom of thought which Renan prized so highly in Unitarianism appears to have succumbed to a more straightened modern religion, gesturing toward rationality and scientific method in the reduced space afforded by the withdrawal of the miraculous, the irrational and the literal, but existing in a state of tension with retained traditional authoritarian elements. World trends do not seem to be moving the Ahmadis' way either. The third khalifa stated in 1972: 'our goal is, as you know, to make Islam prevail over the whole world'.[53] While visiting Indonesia in July 2000 the fourth khalifa, Mirza Tahir Ahmad 'prophesied that Indonesia would be an Ahmadiyya state before the end of this century', a statement that only intensified the othering of the Ahmadi community in that country.[54] In reality, estimates of numbers are also near to frozen. Qadianis make inflated claims, the most conservative being fifteen millions with Lahoris remaining stagnant at 30,000.[55] The Ahmadi numbers are within the same range as nineteenth-century millennial Christian sects in the West, such as the Church of Jesus Christ of Latter-Day Saints (Mormons) which has around thirteen million members.[56] For decades a figure of five to six million has been proffered for Baha'is when the real figure may stretch to two or three million at the most.[57]

The argument of this book has not been that Baha'is or Ahmadis were simply stooges of imperial powers, but that in operating from the locations in which they originated and others in which they gained a foothold, facing the trials thrown up by the prevailing conditions in both, and in staging missionising in the West, they came to adopt imitative modes that drew them closer to the orbit of imperial power and its discourses. My purpose has not been to discredit these movements but rather given the changes in the world and the diverse perspectives that have opened up in the post-colonial era, to demonstrate the problems that accompany the formulations of orientalism and modernity they project, and to show how these have now become outmoded. The major outcome of the study has been to separate out the functional discourse of Baha'i orientalism of which previous scholars and critics – with the important exception of Denis MacEoin – seemed unaware, by tracking its development back to its origin in the mahdi movement that was the Babi sect. The formation of Baha'i orientalism has been demonstrated by the application of postcolonial methodology and forms one of the major findings of my book which can properly be said to fall within the disciplinary field of postcolonial religious and literary studies.[58] In addition, from my research I am able to present the following findings.

(1) Babis and Baha'is at the respective times of their foundation engaged ideas of modernity and reform that were stimulated by the growing power of the West but were indigenous in their origination and articulation. These ways of thinking about modernity helped initiate the growth of the Baha'i community, stimulating its innovation and implementation of modern modes of commerce and educational practice in western Central Asia and Iran where an intersection occurred with early western, predominantly American, converts centred on Abdul Baha's promotion of a message of East–West unity.

(2) By the close of the second quarter of the twentieth century Baha'is in the West had increasingly become indoctrinated in an orientalist and Manichaean view of the contemporary world. At a time when the 'liberal age' was in decline and with it the new-age optimism that had once fuelled interest in the Baha'i movement, Baha'i thought was entombed in Shoghi Effendi's triumphalist, outdated, historicist linear-narrative that derided all worldly efforts of improvement besides its own spiritual ones as futile. Stereotyping the Other as decaying and set to be replaced, the Baha'i faith is presented as the sole custodian of humanity's future and poised at the apogee of progress. Secular narratives built on similar logocentric modes relinquished these several generations ago.

(3) The Baha'i faith from *Travellers Narrative* onward has been constructed in the form of a highly-managed discourse that has smoothed out and elided

difference and plurality, and later drawing from the dominant, authoritarian, monologic discourses of modernism, has appropriated some of its worst features. Baha'i discourse followed modernism in its stress on homogeneity, in its futurism and consignment of alternative ways of thinking to erasure, allowing, for example, the oriental to remain only in skeletal forms (e.g., the Shi'i background in *Dawn-Breakers* and *God Passes By*). This repertoire of thought and writing undermines its own premises: 'unity in diversity' comes out as sameness and disavowal of plural versions of faith, and while condemning in the abstract the negative forces of racism and nationalism and claiming to be non-political, it mimics monologic modern political movements such as Kemalism, Pahlavism and Zionism.

(4) Islam was written off in an orientalist manner. Framing Twelver Shi'ism as backward and otiose and allowing it no other fate than continued decline was perhaps not the only but definitely one of Shoghi Effendi's worst short-term prognostications. Speaking more broadly, the orientalist image of Islam as incapable of renovation ignored the possibility of development in Muslim thought such as that produced by Muhammad Iqbal whose formulation of an Islamic universalism is a coherent and authentically Islamic view of the modern world.

(5) Campaigning against the human rights deprivations of its followers (exclusively) and simultaneously advocating world peace, so long as orientalism and the formative features of modernism listed above are retained within Baha'i narratives, these actions should be considered problematic. If it is contended this is just a matter of scripture condemning the forces that denied and opposed the latest Manifestation, and that Baha'i discourse is not constituted as a mode of othering *Islam* per se, such an argument should be juxtaposed alongside New Testament characterisations of Jews or 'the Jews'. Othering your religious enemies entails travelling down a slippery road. The Baha'i faith is strongly patterned by its Islamicate religious foundations, but implicitly sees itself as divorced from contemporary Islamic trends on account of its millenarian theology, its self-image as modern and progressive, and its writing of a 'lachrymose' history of persecution.[59] It upholds tenets of religious toleration (which do not extend to its own dissidents and 'covenant-breakers'), but so long as aspects of its scripture and modern orientation are wedded to ideas about the Islamic world which align

in part with Western orientalism there remains a danger of these shading into the Islamophobic.

(6) In the last quarter of the twentieth century a suddenly exploding Islamic revival in Iran paved the way for a particular strain of Shi'ism to seize control of the state. This was no recrudescence of 'medievalism'. The Shi'i regime gravitated toward a form of modernity that was resistant to the West but its rise to power was proof of the impact of modernity producing 'a new discourse between the clerics and the educated Shi'i elite . . . exchange between Western thought, elements of the local cultures and a traditional religious world view'.[60] Religions have a need to tell stories about themselves. The modern Shi'i narrative about Babism and Baha'ism is centred around a conspiracy theory that has little relation to reality. Like the *Protocols of the Elders of Zion*, the *Confessions of Dolgoruki* began as a piece of fiction; an anticolonial narrative that gained traction as a result of Iran's partition by foreign forces in 1941. 'In its narrative, Baha'is are the tools of foreign imperialism bent on disrupting the national unity achieved by Islam'. As May Yazdani demonstrates, this became a master-narrative and in spite of being disproved by multiple authorities still carries 'a theme that has dominated anti-Baha'i polemics ever since'.[61] The main belief embedded in the myth might be considered a shadow of the proposition tested out in this present study, one which I have attempted to rationalise in terms of the post-colonial politics as set out in the present chapter. Whatever the grievance that underlaid its creation its translation into forms of oppression and violence deserves unreserved condemnation.

(7) Ghulam Ahmad cannot be faulted for determination. His organisation is larger than that of the Baha'is in terms of followers; however, the direction in which the Ahmadiyyat has been taken has grown narrow and straightened. Moreover, a quick trawl of anti-Ahmadi websites will show how often the Ahmadiyya are denounced as a copy of the Baha'i faith by its adversaries. Ahmadis still appear to entertain hopes of converting the umma to their beliefs but will be fortunate if even a small fraction end up doing so. The Baha'i faith as a separate, independent religious entity might have broader options if only its leadership were bold enough to break out of the orientalist/Manichaean straightjacket in which Shoghi Effendi placed it. But questions still remain concerning the futures of these 'new

old religions' born in the age of imperialism,[62] with no arms other than the proselytic, nor aims other than the conversion of the whole of mankind to the message of their founders.

* * *

Any conclusions that can be drawn from the mutually hostile bifurcation between Shi'ism and Babi-Baha'ism both in the Islamicate context and in the space created by Western orientalists, and from Ahmadi separation from mainstream Sunni Islam in the context of Islamically-focused governments in Pakistan and Southeast Asia, must be multifaceted. In the twentieth century the conflicts gained added significance by being incorporated into the much greater polarisation between the secular West with its imperialist past and once formally colonised or indirectly managed states within the domains of Islam. For the new religious movements with mahdi origins their search for recognition and exposure acquired new urgency, while under pressure of the erasure of their history and identity that accompanied colonisation of their lands and imperial penetration of their societies, Muslim communities had radically different priorities. When situations of persecution arose the innovators did as they often had in the past: they made appeals to non-Muslim parties reviving charges of neo-colonialism. For Islamic lands, already fractured along the Sunni–Shi'a faultline without even considering the introduction of salafis and jihadists into the lists, trying to reach accommodation with mahdi or former mahdi movements would most likely have minimal importance. Present exigencies like the ugliness of jihadi violence that less than a decade ago spilled over into attacks in the Middle East against minority groups like Yazidis and Copts, and Muslim-on-Muslim violence can only reinforce this view. That said, the supposed danger the mahdi movements are said to represent to the umma, rationally speaking, barely attain the significance of a side show. On the other hand, the worldwide rise of Islamophobia and state-led repression of Muslim Uyghurs in northwest China, the Rohingya in Burma, and the threats against Muslims in India tip the balance heavily in another direction.

Acknowledging the imbalance of state power vis-à-vis the minority Baha'is in Iran or the Ahmadis in Pakistan, and the role of anti-Baha'i and anti-Ahmadi groups in the deprivation of their rights is important.[63] However, this does not privilege them above other claimants, whether individuals fighting for rights or secular or religious groups merely holding to a separate existence. In some ways the mahdi movements' case is a touchstone for the future of Western modernity and the Islamicate world, since they stand on the cusp of both, but it is nor radically different to, say, the embattled position of Christians in Pakistan or of Copts in Egypt. Given the West's colonial history in the Middle East and South Asia and the continuing present-day polarisations, the open and often politically-oriented condemnation of Western states regarding the deprivation of the human rights of Baha'is in Iran and Ahmadis in Pakistan, has not always helped those within civil society and the religious communities who wish to flag up and mitigate the injustices. On the other hand, the requirement for different forms of Islamism to acknowledge and facilitate the civil rights of heterodox or seceder groups like Baha'is and Ahmadis, along with other religious minorities is irrefutable. Both sides need to make accommodations but it is difficult to see an existing mode or apparatus that could bring the respective parties together in dialogue. Any Western agency, including ones with a human rights brief, will still be looked upon with suspicion by some and, as we have already said, considered disqualified on account of the colonial past of Western states.

What these mahdi movements show us when viewed against fractured, self-conflictive existing Islam, is not the universalism claimed in their messianic rubrics, but small, sectarian worlds in need of serious updates after more than a century and a half of their existence. In spite of the prophecies of the mahdi movements Islam still persists with far greater numbers of followers and in more varied modern forms, some of them expanding, some imploding, some manifesting a fearfulness that can (but by no means in the majority of situations does) result in hostility and violence toward leave-takers. In a utopia, all of these movements, organisations and sects would lay to rest their disputes and address themselves to the larger issues encapsulated in Iqbal's thinking. According to Javed Majeed,

> [w]hile Iqbal's major preoccupation was with Islam, at times he sought to outline how other religions shared its predicament in the modern world. Islam becomes an acute manifestation of the problems religions as a whole face in relation to modernity's processes of secularization and disenchantment and its 'scientism'.[64]

If the various religions share commonalities, as they are often said to, this is even more the case for the different divisions and sects of Islam, present and of the recent past. Sunni, Shi'i, Ismaili, Babi, Baha'i, Ahmadi, all share a common heritage. The challenges Iqbal sets out above pertain equally to them all. As things stand today, however, in none of the above is an effective or convincing case for religion as peacemaker and unifier being made, if only because their records all tend to demonstrate sectarian tendencies and continuing divisiveness that first emerged and later developed with their appearance in the world.

Notes

Chapter 1

1. 'President Reagan has now asked world leaders to join him in appealing to Ayatollah Khomeini not to carry out death sentences against 22 Baha'is awaiting execution in Shiraz; the likelihood of his being listened to is tiny', *The Economist*, 28 May 1983. Although he conflates the Babis and Baha'is by not identifying the former at all, travelling through Iran in the early 1980s V. S. Naipaul saw a parallel between the movement of the Bab with its call for '"heads to be cut off, books and leaves burnt, places demolished and laid waste, and a general slaughter made" . . . [and] an attempt to kill the king. Politically, though not in doctrine, the movement was like Khomeini's against the Shah', *Among the Believers: An Islamic Journey* (London: Penguin, 1981), p. 22.
2. See Esposito, J. L. (ed.), *Voices of Resurgent Islam* (New York: Oxford University Press, 1983).
3. Voll, J., 'Renewal and Reform in Muslim Society', in Esposito, *Voices*, pp. 32–47; Mardin, Ş., *Religion and Social Change in Modern Turkey: The Case of Bediüzzaman Said Nursi* (Albany, NY: State University of New York Press, 1989).
4. In suggesting the Ahmadi movement might profitably be studied alongside the Babi and Baha'i movements Barbara Metcalf gave as one reason the advantage of offsetting the danger of Irano-centrism. See Metcalf, B., 'Review of J. R. I. Cole, *Modernity and Millennium: The Genesis of the Baha'i Faith in the Nineteenth-Century Middle East*', *The Journal of Interdisciplinary History*, 30, 3 (1999), pp. 566–8. On the broader comparison of nineteenth century millennial movements including Babis, Baha'is, Ahmadis and the mid-nineteenth century Taiping Rebellion in China, see Keddie, N., *Iran: Religion, Politics and Society, Collected Essays* (London: Frank Cass, 1980), Ch. 1.
5. Bayly, C., *The Birth of the Modern World 1780–1914: Global Connections and Comparisons* (Oxford: Blackwell, 2004), p. 3.

6. Voll, J. O., *Islam: Continuity and Change in the Modern World*, 2nd edn (Syracuse, NY: Syracuse University Press, 1994), pp. 4–5.
7. Rippin, A., *Muslims: Their Religious Beliefs and Practices*, 3rd edn (London: Routledge, 2005), pp. 301–3.
8. Gibb., H. A. R., and J. H. Kramers, *Shorter Encyclopaedia of Islam* (Leiden and London: E. J. Brill and Luzac & Co., 1961).
9. See Amanat, A., *Resurrection and Renewal: The Making of the Babi Movement in Iran, 1844–1850* (Ithaca: Cornell University Press, 1989), pp. 1–13, and see pp. 324–8 on the broadening of Shi'i messianic nomenclature at the Babi conference of Badasht. On the various claims of Ali Muhammad Shirazi, see D. MacEoin, 'Bab, Sayyed 'Ali Mohammad Shirazi', *Encyclopaedia Iranica*, repr. D. MacEoin, *The Messiah of Shiraz: Studies in Early and Middle Babism* (Leiden: Brill, 2009), pp. 559–71. For an extensive discussion of Ghulam Ahmad's claims in the context of an Islamic understanding of 'prophet', see Friedmann, Y., *Prophecy Continuous: Aspects of Ahmadi Religious Thought and its Medieval Background* (Berkeley: University of California Press, 1989).
10. On Shaykh Ahmad Ahsai and Sayyid Kazim Rashti, see Amanat, 'Orthodoxy and Heterodoxy', *Resurrection*.
11. On the late nineteenth and early twentieth century semantics of 'Muslim World' see Aydin, C., *The Idea of the Muslim World: A Global Intellectual History* (Cambridge, MA: Harvard University Press, 2017).
12. Smith, P., 'Peter Berger's Early Work on Baha'i Studies', *The Journal of Religious History*, 43, 1 (2019), pp. 45–69; for further details on the Baha'i content of Berger's thesis see Abdo, L., Religion and Relevance: The Baha'is in Britain 1899–1930, PhD thesis, School of African and Oriental Studies, University of London.
13. King, R., *Orientalism and Religion: Postcolonial Theory, India and 'The Mystic East'* (London: Routledge, 1999), p. 1; my italics. On the spelling of 'postcolonial' as applied in the present study see note 74 below.
14. Halm, H., *Shiism* (Edinburgh: Edinburgh University Press, 1991), pp. 109–10.
15. Robinson, F., 'Prophets without Honour? Ahmad and the Ahmadiyya', *History Today*, June 1990, pp. 42–7 (pp. 42–3); Lavan, S., *The Ahmadiyah Movement: A History and Perspective* (Delhi: Monahar, 1974), p. 93.
16. Jonker, G., *The Ahmadiyya Quest for Religious Progress: Missionizing Europe 1900–1965* (Leiden: Brill, 2016), p. 22.
17. Gobineau, A., *Les Religions et les philosophies dans l'Asie Centrale*, in A. Gobineau, *Oeuvres*, ed. J. Gaulmier and V. Monteuil (Paris: Gallimard ([1865] 1983–7),

vol. 2, pp. 403–809; Nash, G. (ed.), *Comte de Gobineau and Orientalism: Selected Eastern Writings*, trans. D. O'Donoghue (London: Routledge, 2009).

18. On Ghulam Ahmad's *mubahala* and prophecies against Muslim *maulvis*, see Lavan, *Ahmadiyah Movement*, pp. 50–57; Addison, T., 'The Ahmadiya Movement and its Western Propaganda', *Harvard Theological Review*, 22, 1 (1929), pp. 1–32 (pp. 8–12). Regarding the Bab's practice of revealing verses, one missionary pointed out: 'In many ways the claims made [by Ali Muhammad] for the "Beyan" [*Bayan*] resemble those made for the Qor'an. Unbelievers are challenged to produce a book like unto the Qor'an, which comprises all the secrets of heaven and earth. All creatures working together could not produce the like of the "Beyan", which is incomparable and inimitable and includes all things. As the Qor'an contains passages which none can understand but God, so, too, the Beyan "is incomprehensible save to such as are divinely aided". As the Qor'an is said to confirm the earlier Scriptures, so the "Beyan" is in essence identical with the Gospel and Qor'an', Richards, J. A., *The Religion of the Baha'is* (London: SPCK, 1939), pp. 46–7. Todd Lawson points out: 'many of his [the Bab's] writings were produced before witnesses . . . were written with astonishing speed and fluency, [and] combined to present . . . an evidentiary miracle comparable, in every way . . . to the Qur'an itself', Lawson, T., 'Interpretation as Revelation: The Qur'an Commentary of Sayyid 'Ali Muhammad Shirazi, the Bab', in A. Rippin (ed.), *Approaches to the History of the Interpretation of the Qur'an* (Oxford University Press, 1988), pp. 223–53 (p. 226). On Baha'ullah's prophecies, see Browne, E. G., 'Babis of Persia', *Journal of the Royal Asiatic Society*, 21 (1889), pp. 485–526 (pp. 491–5).

19. On the Baha'i leaders' engagement with the Middle-Eastern milieu see Cole, J. R. I., *Modernity and the Millennium: The Genesis of the Baha'i faith in the Nineteenth-Century Middle East* (New York: Columbia University Press, 1998). On Ahmadism's engagement with its South Asian locale see Lavan, *Ahmadiyah Movement*; Friedmann, *Prophecy Continuous*; Khan, A. H., *From Sufism to Ahmadiyya: A Muslim Minority Movement in South Asia* (Bloomington: Indiana University Press, 2015).

20. Sharon, M. (ed.), *Studies in Modern Religions, Religious Movements and the Babi-Baha'i Faiths* (Leiden: Brill, 2004), p. 8; italics in original.

21. Mottahedeh, N. (ed.), *'Abdul-Baha's Journey West: The Course of Human Solidarity* (New York: Palgrave Macmillan, 2013); Germain, E., 'The First Muslim Missions on a European Scale: Ahmadi-Lahori networks in the Inter-War Period', in N. Clayer and E. Germain (eds), *Islam in Inter-War Europe* (London: Hurst, 2008),

pp. 89–118; Ryad, U., 'Salafiyyah, Ahmadiyya, and European Converts to Islam in the Interwar Period', in B. Agai, U. Ryad and M. Sajid (eds), *Muslims in Interwar Europe: A Transcultural Historical Perspective* (Leiden: Brill, 2016), pp. 47–87; Jonker, *Ahmadiyya Quest*; Geaves, R., *Islam in Britain: Muslim Mission in an Age of Empire* (London: Bloomsbury, 2018). Different to all the above because it juxtaposes both Baha'i and Ahmadi missions, is B. McNamara, 'Establishing Islam in Britain: The Founding of Woking Mission', *Journal of Muslims in Europe*, 7, 3 (2018), pp. 309–30.
22. Browne, E. G., *A Traveller's Narrative written to illustrate the Episode of the Bab* (Cambridge: Cambridge University Press, 1889), vol. 2, Note A, 3, pp. 200–11; Momen, M., *The Babi and Baha'i Religions: Some Contemporary Western Accounts, 1844–1944* (Oxford: George Ronald, 1981).
23. MacEoin, 'Bab'.
24. Ioannesyan, Y., *The Development of the Babi/Baha'i Communities: Exploring Baron Rosen's archives* (London: Routledge, 2013).
25. Walter, H. A., *The Ahmadiya Movement* (London: Oxford University Press, 1918). Among early articles see Griswold, H. D., 'The Ahmadiya Movement', *Muslim World*, 2 (1912), pp. 373–9; Addison, 'Ahmadiya Movement'.
26. Abdo, Religion and Relevance, pp. 68–71; B. McNamara, Religious Reformers in Britain at the turn of the Twentieth Century: The Visits of Abdul Baha (PhD Thesis, University of Cork, 2017). McNamara, B., *The Reception of 'Abdu'l-Bahá in Britain: East Comes West* (Leiden: Brill, 2021), book form of the above, appeared while the present work was in press.
27. Bach, M. *They have found a Faith* (Indianapolis: Bobbs-Merrill Company, 1946), pp. 201–3. Moshe Sharon sees the break from Islam and movement Westward in a positive way: 'the Babi-Baha'i venture was one of the major developments in the field of religion in modern times, especially because it was born out of the heart of Shi'ite Islam in the East, and succeeded in crossing the ocean, treading new paths into the heart of western civilization and the bosom of Christianity', Sharon, *Studies in Modern Religions*, p. ix.
28. Ahmad, G., 'Babi/Bahaism', *Review of Religions*, 6, 1 (1907), pp. 171–7 (p. 171).
29. See Geaves, *Islam in Britain*, chs 7–8; Gilham, J., *Loyal Enemies: British Converts to Islam, 1850–1950* (London: Hurst, 2014), pp. 138–40, 200–6; Addison, 'Ahmadiya Movement', passim.
30. Germain, 'First Muslim', p. 104.
31. Garlington, W., *The Baha'i Faith in America* (Westport, CT: Praeger, 2005), pp. 82–4.

32. McNamara, 'Establishing Islam', p. 324.
33. Ahmadiyya Anjuman Lahore Foundation, Khwaja Kamal-ud-Din's report of his second visit to the Woking Mosque <http://www.wokingmuslim.org/history//kh-mosque-second.htm> (last accessed 20 October 2021).
34. McNamara, 'Establishing Islam', p. 325.
35. Baha'i and Ahmadi proselytisation overlapped in several areas: recruitment of aristocratic converts, e.g., Lady Sara Blomfield (Baha'i) and R. G. A. Allanson-Winn, Baron Headley, and Baron Rolf Freiherr von Ehrenfels (Ahmadi); addresses by both Abdul Baha and Khwaja Kamaluddin to Theosophists, Spiritualists, and leaders of New Thought. See Germain, 'First Muslim', pp. 97, 99, 105; Gilham, *Loyal Enemies*, pp. 127–9.
36. Jonker, *Ahmadiyya Quest*, p. 26.
37. Quoted in Germain, 'First Muslim', p. 96.
38. Ibid. pp. 94–7. Pickthall and several other pan-Islamists who spoke together on public platforms about Turkey and Muslim issues worldwide were known as the 'Woking Gang' but despite their attachment to the Woking Mosque their dissident stance did not compromise Kamaluddin's reputation. See Gilham, *Loyal Enemies*, pp. 217, 221.
39. Bennett, C., *Victorian Images of Islam* (London: Grey Seal, 1992).
40. Momen, M., 'Early Relations between Christian Missionaries and the Bábí and Baháʾí Communities', in M. Momen (ed.), *Studies in Babi and Baha'i History* (Los Angeles: Kalimat Press, 1982), vol. 1, pp. 49–82.
41. Linton, J. L., Foreward to Richards, *Religion of the Baha'is*, p. viii. See also Zwemer, S. M., *Islam: A Challenge to Faith* (New York: Student Volunteer Movement for Foreign Missions, 1901).
42. Addision, 'Ahmadiya Movement', pp. 18–19.
43. MacEoin, *Messiah of Shiraz*, p. 515.
44. Ibid.
45. Khan, *Sufism to Ahmadiyya*, pp. 132–3; italics in original.
46. Evans, N. W., *Far From the Caliph's Gaze: Being Ahmadi Muslim in the Holy City of Qadian* (Ithaca: Cornel University Press, 2020), p. 39.
47. Evans, *Caliph's Gaze*, p. 13. 'With its message of "Love for all, hatred for none", and its presentation of *Jihad* "through dialogue based on logical arguments" . . . the *Ahmadi* present a peaceful Islam, an Islam in sharp contrast to the stereotypes of war and militancy often generated by the Western media', Valentine, S. R., *Islam and the Ahmadiyya Jama'at: History, Belief, Practice* (London: Hurst, 2008), p. xv; italics in original.

48. Nijhawan, M., 'Today we are Ahmadis: Configurations of Heretic Otherness between Lahore and Berlin', *British Journal of Middle East Studies*, 37, 3 (2010), pp. 429–47.
49. Effendi, S., *God Passes By* (Wilmette, IL: Baha'i Publishing Trust, 1944).
50. See the next chapter for further discussion of the work of these academics.
51. Smith, P., *The Babi and the Baha'i Religions: From Messianic Shi'ism to a World Religion* (Cambridge: Cambridge University Press, 1987); D. MacEoin, From Shaykhism to Babism: A Study in Charismatic Renewal in Shí'i Islam, PhD thesis, University of Cambridge, 1979, repr. *Messiah of Shiraz*, pp. 3–246; D. MacEoin, 'Orthodoxy and Heterodoxy in Nineteenth Century Shi 'ism: The cases of Shaykhism and Babism', in *Messiah of Shiraz*, pp. 631–44.
52. Gualtieri, A. R., *The Ahmadis: Community, Gender, and Politics in a Muslim Society* (Montreal: McGill-Queen's University Press, 2004); Evans, *Caliph's Gaze*.
53. Smith, *Babi and Baha'i*, pp. 74–8; Cole, *Modernity and the Millennium*, p. 68. Smith flags up Baha'ism's endorsement of 'rationalized codes and practices of legislation', p. 78, and Cole argues Abdul Baha's writing demonstrates 'a thoroughgoing defense of and plea for the adoption of key elements of modernity, a sort of manifesto for Weberian rationalisation'. He does, however, note Abdul Baha was 'extremely critical of other aspects of the phenomenon' of Western modernity, ibid. p. 85. Smith also points out caveats too: Western civilization was 'greatly wanting and its materialism was severely condemned' by the Baha'i founders, *Babi and Baha'i*, p. 78. On the limitations of Baha'i modernism and the problems it faces today, see Nash, G., 'The Impact of Fear and Authority on Islamic and Baha'i Modernisms in the Late Modern Age: A Liberal Perspective', *Religions*, 6 (2015), pp. 1125–36.
54. Among other things, MacEoin pointed out: the conflation of Babism and Baha'ism by Baha'i authors; erasures and omissions in rewriting Babi history first mooted by Edward Browne; the creation of a teleological narrative of 'Baha'i history' that smoothed out difference. He also explored claims concerning distortions putatively enacted by chief authority figures of the Baha'i faith regarding the succession to the Bab.
55. Sharbrodt, O., *Islam and the Baha'i Faith: A Comparative Study of Muhammad 'Abduh and 'Abdul-Baha 'Abbas* (London: Routledge, 2008), pp. 65–6.
56. Critical studies on Ahmadism are largely free of the contention found in Baha'i scholarship. As an example, the Lahori–Qadiani split that exercised scholars and authority figures from both sides has subsequent lost its significance, and non-Ahmadi academics now view it in the context of the respective movements'

overseas missions (see above, note 21). However, given that recent works on Ahmadiyyat approach the movement employing ethnographic methods, a study that adopted a more schematic reappraisal of its claims to be a modern, reforming movement alongside its traditional features is overdue.

57. Chatterjee, P., *The Nation and its Fragments: Colonial and Postcolonial Histories* (Princeton, NJ: Princeton University Press, 1993), p. 6.
58. Jung, D., *Muslim History and Social Theory: A Global Sociology of Modernity* (London: Palgrave Macmillan, 2017), p. 16; Jung, D., *Orientalists, Islamists, and the Global Space: A Genealogy of the Modern Essentialist Image of Islam* (Sheffield, UK: Equinox Publishing, 2011), p. 62. However, some theorists, notably Timothy Mitchell, have argued that the vocabulary of 'multiple' and 'alternative' modernities 'continued to imply "an underlying and fundamentally singular modernity", adapted to different cultural contexts, leaving undisturbed the epistemological hegemony of European forms of life and historical teleology', Mahmood, S., *Religious Difference in a Secular Age: A Minority Report* (Princeton: Princeton University Press, 2016), p. 10.
59. Turner, R. B., *Islam in the African American Experience* (Bloomington: University of Indiana Press, 2003), pp. 110, 123. Baha'is also proselytised African Americans at a similar epoch, but the response of white American converts made it difficult to jell the two races and different meetings were held for each. Clearly, the Ahmadi community had a larger intake of Afro-Americans in proportion to white converts than the Baha'is and were prepared to contest racist attitudes more forthrightly. See Garlington, *Baha'i Faith*, pp. 117–21. See also Chapter 7 for further discussion of the issue of race in the context of Abdul Baha's statement about blacks and whites in the United States.
60. Amanat, A., *Iran: A Modern History* (New Haven: Yale University Press, 2017), p. 180. For a Baha'i historian's attack on Qajar Iran under Nasir al-Din Shah, incorporating a long extract from Valentine Chirol, see Balyuzi, H. M., *Baha'u'llah: The King of Glory* (Oxford: George Ronald, 1980), pp. 430–55.
61. A notable exception is Sen McGlinn's postmodern rereading of what is now the official theocratic 'monist' understanding of Baha'i institutions' relation to government in the future Baha'i world order. He argues: 'the social structure of the Kingdom of God is not incompatible with a decentralized postmodern society', S. McGlinn, 'A Theology of the State from the Baha'i Teachings', *Church and State*, 41, 4 (1999), pp. 697–724 (p. 717). For whatever reason (one has not yet been given) this stance earned for McGlinn disciplinary disenrolment from membership of the Baha'i faith.

62. Dirlik, A., 'Chinese History and the Question of Orientalism', *History and Theory*, 35, 4 (1996), pp. 96–118 (p. 98).
63. Mirsepassi, A., *Intellectual Discourse and the Politics of Modernization: Negotiating Modernity in Iran* (New York: Cambridge University Press, 2003), pp. 24–35; see also Dabashi, H., *Post-Orientalism Knowledge and Power in a Time of Terror* (New Brunswick, 2015), pp. 139–49.
64. Lockman, Z., *Contending Visions of the Middle East, The History and Politics of Orientalism*, 2nd edn (New York: Cambridge University Press, 2010), p. 76. In an interview Said stated: 'In *Orientalism* I do not talk about Islam, but rather the portrayal of Islam in the West, offering a critique of the foundations and the goals on which the coverage is based', Viswanathan, G., *Power, Politics, and Culture: Interviews with Edward Said* (New York: Vintage, 2001), pp. 437–8.
65. Yue, I., 'Missionaries (Mis-) Representing China: Orientalism, Religion, and the Conceptualization of Victorian Cultural Identity', *Victorian Literature and Culture*, 37, 1 (2009), pp. 1–10 (p. 1).
66. Wilcox, A., *Orientalism and Imperialism: From Nineteenth-Century Missionary Imagining to the Contemporary Middle East* (London: Bloomsbury, 2018), p. 41.
67. Wilcox, *Orientalism and Imperialism*, p. 74. The Baha'is also attracted the attention of Christian missionaries to Persia, notably American Presbyterian William Miller and J. R. Richards of the London Christian Missionary Society who both wrote hostile but researched accounts which form a significant part of the literature on this religion. See Miller, W., *Baha'ism: Its Origin, History and Teachings* (New York: Fleming H. Revell, 1931); Richards, *Religion of the Baha'is*. It is clear, however, that Baha'is filled a niche space in Persian missionaries' writings as a group that had moved outside the orbit of Islam.
68. See Chapters 6 and 7 of this study.
69. Yue, 'Missionaries', p. 4.
70. There were notable exceptions however, in specific readings made of Shi'i ritual theatre and of sufi practice. In the nineteenth century Alexander Chodzko, Lewis Pelly, and Matthew Arnold in their expressions of admiration for Persian *taziya* drew parallels between the sacrifice of Imam Hussain and Christ. In the twentieth century the Aryanising idea that had worked for South Asian religions was applied by Titus Burckhardt, René Guénon, and Frithjof Schuon in reconceptualising sufism as Traditionalism or Perennialist philosophy. See Lipton, G., 'De-Semitising Ibn 'Arabi, Aryanism and the Schuonian Discourse of Religious Authenticity', *Numen*, 64 (2017), pp. 258–93. The Aryan motif recurs in the context of Shi'ism and Ali Muhammad Shirazi, the Bab – see Chapters 3 and 4 of the present study.

71. King, *Orientalism and Religion*, p. 86.
72. In 'the hands of Vivekenanda and Gandhi Colonial stereotypes . . . became transformed and used in the fight against colonialism. Despite this, stereotypes they remain'. Nevertheless, the inference is well made 'that such discourses do not proceed in an orderly and straightforward fashion, being in fact adapted and applied in ways unforeseen by those who initiated them', ibid. pp. 96, 86.
73. Niranjana, T., 'Translation, Colonialism and Rise of English', *Economic and Political Weekly* 25, 15 (14 April 1990), pp. 773–9 (p. 778); quoted in King, *Orientalism and Religion*, p. 93.
74. As opposed to its traditional usage where it might be defined as 'a body of writing or speech coherently organised', Robinson, D., *Translation and Empire: Postcolonial Theories Explained* (Manchester: St Jerome, 1997), p. 116; Childs, P. and P. Williams, *An Introduction to Post-Colonial Theory* (London: Harvester Wheatsheaf, 1997), p. 229. To some readers the words 'post-colonial' and 'post-colonial' used in the two texts cited where they both mean the same thing, can be confusing. I have therefore taken the unorthodox decision to use both 'post-colonial' and 'postcolonial' which I understand as follows: the former is used in relation to *historical periodicity*, 'after the colonial'; the later is employed in the usual manner to denote *theory*, i.e., postcolonial theory, a body of thought applied throughout the humanities. Hence, I speak of the position of the mahdi movements in the *post-colonial period*, and of *postcolonial* ways of reading a text such as *The Dawn-Breakers* (see Chapter 3). 'Postmodern' is used in the same way as 'postcolonial'.
75. Said, E. W., *Orientalism* (London: Penguin, 2003), p. 94; italics in original.
76. Levefere, A., *Translation, Rewriting, and the Manipulation of Literary Fame* (London: Routledge, 1992); Bruner, J., 'The Narrative Construction of Reality', *Critical Inquiry*, 18 (1991), pp. 1–21 (p. 5). See Baker, M., *Translation and Conflict: A Narrative Account* (London: Routledge, 2006).
77. This will be discussed in more detail in Chapter 7, including MacEoin's statements relating to Shoghi Effendi's Baha'i orientalism.
78. Effendi, *God Passes By*, p. xii.
79. Similar to the orientalist background set up by Said in his analysis of British orientalist-cum-political agents in the Middle East of roughly the same period, a micro-picture is formed of Baha'is in Palestine.

Chapter 2

1. Dallmayr, F., *Beyond Orientalism: Essays on Cross-Cultural Encounter* (Albany, NY: State University of New York Press, 1996), p. xvii; Said, *Orientalism*, p. 24.

2. Dallmayr, *Beyond Orientalism*, p. xviii; Todorov, T., *The Conquest of America: The Question of the Other*, trans. R. Howard (New York: Harper and Row, 1984).
3. Dallmayr, *Beyond Orientalism*, pp. xi, xix.
4. Ibid. p. xiv.
5. Quoted in Buck, C., *Paradise and Paradigm: Key Symbols in Persian Christianity and the Baha'i Faith* (Albany, NY: State University of New York Press, 1999), p. 178.
6. Lambden, S., Some Aspects of Isra'iliyyat and the Emergence of the Babi-Baha'i Interpretation of the Bible (PhD Thesis, University of Newcastle, 2002), pp. 291–4. Dr Lambden's thesis is an immensely erudite treatment of the Babi-Baha'i encounter with the Bible and Israiliyyat. It is important to add that Baha'ullah overturned the 'post-qur'anic assertion of the total loss or falsification of the Jewish and Christian Bible', which Dr Lambden argues 'is without doubt the greatest barrier to dialogue and mutual appreciation among Abrahamic religionists or "peoples of the Book"', Lambden, S., 'Islam', in J. F. A. Sawyer (ed.), *The Blackwell Companion to the Bible and Culture* (Oxford: Blackwell, 2006), pp. 135–57 (p. 153). Walter's *Ahmadiya Movement* gives a detailed account of the Ahmadi-Christian encounter during Ghulam Ahmad's lifetime, but obviously from a Christian perspective.
7. Amanat, *Iran*, p. 179. 'Europe's territorial gains and diplomatic pressures came with interventions in Iran's domestic affairs and with a race to acquire commercial and other advantages, capitulatory rights, and, later, economic concessions. Europe's condescending attitude, gradually setting in as Iran's weaknesses on the battlefield became more apparent, served as a cultural backdrop', Ibid. p. 190.
8. See Amanat, *Resurrection and Renewal*, ch. 8. sect., 'The Changing Economy', pp. 333–9. According to Hamid Dabashi, Professor Amanat does not provide any detail on how British involvement in Iran's trade might have impacted on the Babis. Dabashi sees the Babi movement as having 'a deliberate and conscious awareness of the onslaught of European economic colonialism, particularly in southern Iran, in Bushehr, where the Bab in fact commenced his messianic movement'. He calls it 'the very first modern Shi'i revolution', Dabashi, H., *Shi'ism: A Religion of Protest Harvard* (Cambridge, MA: The Belknap Press of Harvard University Press, 2011), pp. 374 n. 36, 200, 183.
9. Cole, J. R. I., *Colonialism and Revolution in the Middle East: Social and Cultural Origins of Egypt's 'Urabi Movement* (Princeton, NJ: Princeton University Press 1993), p. 12.
10. Said, *Orientalism*, p. 191.
11. See Ahmad, G., *The British Government and Jihad* (Government Angreizi aur Jihad) (London and Farnham: Islamic International Publications, 2018); see also

the discussion of the document *A Present to His Royal Highness the Prince of Wales from the Ahmadiyya Community* in Chapter 7 below.

12. See Momen, *Babi and Baha'i Religions*.
13. On the issue as to where the Baha'i leaders, i.e., Baha'ullah and Abdul Baha, located themselves vis-à-vis their position in the world, and in particular, as exiles in Edirne and Akka and how they related to the Ottoman Middle East, see Cole, *Modernity and the Millennium*; Scharbrodt, *Islam and the Baha'i Faith*; Alkan, N., 'Ottoman Reform Movements and the Baha'i Faith, 1860s–1920s', in Sharon, *Studies in Modern Religions*, pp. 253–74.
14. On Ali Pasha and Fuat Pasha's attitudes to the Babi-Baha'i figures, see Cole, J. R. I., 'Iranian Millenarianism and Democratic Thought in the 19th Century', *International Journal of Middle East Studies*, 24 (1992), pp. 1–26 (p. 5). In Cole's opinion the leaders of the Ottoman Tanzimat and ostensible enemies of Babism saw the movement as a threat to their reforming achievements 'by seeking to put all authority, religious and secular, back in the hands of a charismatic leader ... [but] missed the mark regarding Bahaullah's own ideas which were more compatible with the Tanzimat'. Cole does not add, however, that like the Bab, Baha'ullah – whatever the concessions he was offering as regards separation of religion and state – was also seeking to replace Islam with his own religion and that, therefore, there was continuity in the challenge both represented as far as the Ottoman state was concerned.
15. Aydin, C., *Idea of the Muslim World*, p. 5. 'This increasing sympathy for the Ottoman Empire, always tied to the new notion of the Caliphate as the symbol for the Muslim world's demands for reform and justice, did not necessarily contradict with other imperial identities ... Indian Muslim intellectual Cheragh Ali ... combined his admiration for the Ottoman Empire with his loyalty to the British Empire ... For [him] the Ottoman caliph symbolized the compatibility between the modern civilization and the Muslim faith tradition, and proved that Muslims were not inferior to Christians in their capacity for progress', Aydın, C., 'The Ottoman Empire and the Global Muslim Identity in the Formation of Eurocentric World Order, 1815–1919', in F. Dallmayr, M. Akif Kayapınar, and İ Yaylacı (eds), *Civilizations and World Order: Geopolitics and Cultural Difference* (Lanham, MD: Rowman and Littlefield, 2014), pp. 117–44 (pp. 129–30).
16. It might be argued that this belied Baha'ullah's apocalyptic worldview, although broadly speaking this was mainly focused on those monarchs and religious leaders who ignored him. See discussion of Baha'i eschatological writing in Chapter 7. While in America, Abdul Baha promoted its importance as a conduit of universal

peace, as expressed in a speech he made in Washington, DC, on 21 April 1912: 'May this American democracy be the first nation to establish the foundation of international agreement. May it be the first to establish the universality of mankind. May it be the first to upraise the standard of the Most Great Peace', *The Promulgation of Universal Peace* (Wilmette, IL: Baha'i Publishing Trust, 1982), p. 36.

17. Warburg, M., *Citizens of the World: A History and Sociology of the Baha'is from a Globalisation Perspective* (Leiden: Brill, 2006), p. 185.
18. Noori, Y., *Finality of Prophethood and a Critical Analysis of Babism, Bahaism, Qadiyanism* (Tehran: Madrasih-yi Shuhada, 1981), p. iii.
19. Kara, I., 'Islam and Islamism in Turkey: A Conversation with İsmail Kara', *Maydan*, 24 October 2017; italics added.
20. Mufti, A., *Forget English: Orientalisms and World Literatures* (Cambridge, MA: Harvard University Press, 2016), p. 463.
21. MacEoin, *Messiah of Shiraz*, p. 255; Said, *Orientalism*, p. 191.
22. *Messiah of Shiraz*, p. 254.
23. Ali, M., *True Conception of the Ahmadiyya Movement* (Columbus, OH: Ahmadiyya Anjuman Isha'at Islam Lahore ([1966] 1996), p. 3.
24. On Ahmadis and the Kashmiri issue see Khan, *From Sufism*. Khan sees a tension between Ghulam Ahmad's abrogation of jihad and Mahmud Ahmad's involvement of an Ahmadi battalion in military action in Kashmir in 1946.
25. Friedmann, *Prophecy Continuous*, pp. 2–3.
26. Ibid.
27. Esslemont, J. *Baha'u'llah and the New Era* (Oakham: Baha'i Publishing Trust, 1974), p. 22.
28. Taherzadeh, A., *The Revelation of Baha'u'llah, volume 2: Adrianople 1863–68* (Oxford: George Ronald, 1974), p. 7.
29. Cole, *Modernity and the Millennium*, p. 63; Baha'u'llah, 'Tablet to Queen Victoria', *Proclamation of Baha'u'llah* (Haifa: Baha'i World Centre, 1967).
30. Friedmann, *Prophecy Continuous*, pp. 15–16 n. 73.
31. Hardy, P., *The Muslims of British India* (Cambridge: Cambridge University Press, 1972), ch. 7, pp. 168–97; Robinson, F., 'Islamic Reform and Modernities in South Asia', *Modern Asian Studies*, 42, 2–3 (2008), pp. 259–81.
32. Correspondence regarding recognition of Ahmadiyya in Nigeria, Government House Nigeria: 'If by "recognition" Mr Nayyar wishes some assurance that his sect will, as far as is possible for Government to do so be protected from religious persecution, and the educational efforts he has started will receive the encouragement and support of the Government, I see no possible objection to

affording recognition. The Ahmadiyya Mission is therefore on precisely the same footing . . . as the various Christian missions in Nigeria . . . [We] welcome the Ahmadiyya mission and throw no obstacles in their way'. India Office, Activities of the Ahmadiyya Movement, Islam and an application for recognition in the in the British Colonies, IOR/L/PJ/6/1845, File 1660: Feb 1923–Oct 1924. On Ahmadi missions on the Gold Coast in the 1920s and the response of British colonial officials, see Hanson, J. H., *The Ahmadiyya in the Gold Coast: Muslim Cosmopolitans in the British Empire* (Bloomington: University of Indiana Press, 2017).
33. Friedmann, *Prophecy Continuous*, p. 179.
34. Ibid.
35. Ahmad, *British Government*, p. 32; italics in original.
36. Ahmad, M. B. M., *The Life of Muhammad* (London: Islam International Publications, 2014), pp. 108–19. This section also discusses the conditions in which the Quran sanctioned warfare.
37. See Qutb, S., *Social Justice in Islam*, trans. J. B. Hardie (Washington, DC: American Council of Learned Society, 1953).
38. 'I have come to you with an order: *jihad* with the sword has ended from this time forward, but the *jihad* of purifying your souls must continue. I do not say this of my own accord. This is indeed the will of God. Recall the *hadith* from *Sahih al-Bukhari* which honours the Promised Messiah by saying *yada-'ul-harb* [war is in the prophet's hands]. That is to say, when the Messiah comes he will put an end to religious wars', Ahmad, *British Government*, p. 17; italics in original.
39. Baha'u'llah, *Epistle to the Son of Wolf* (Wilmette, IL: Baha'i Publishing Trust, 1971), pp. 89–91; Matthew 22: 21, Romans 13: 1–7.
40. Smith, *Babi and Baha'i Religions*, p. 79.
41. Amanat, A., *Pivot of the Universe: Nasir al-Din Shah Qajar and the Iranian Monarchy, 1831–1896* (London: I. B. Tauris, 1997), p. 412.
42. Smith, *Babi and Baha'i Religions*, p. 79.
43. McGlinn, S., *Principles of Progress: Essays on Religion and Modernity by Abdu'l-Baha* (Leiden, 2018), p. 79.
44. Momen, M., 'The Baha'is of Iran: The Constitutional Movement and the Creation of an "Enemy Within"', *British Journal of Middle East Studies*, 39, 3 (2012), pp. 328–46.
45. MacEoin, D., *A People Apart: The Baha'i Community of Iran in the Twentieth Century* (London: Centre of Near and Middle Eastern Studies, School of Oriental and African Studies, University of London, 1989), pp. 13–15.

46. Abdul Baha made the following statement in Boston, 25 July 1912: 'The Baha'is must not engage in political movements which lead to sedition. They must interest themselves in movements that condone law and order. In Persia at the present time the Bahais have no part in revolutionary upheavals which have terminated in lawlessness and rebellion. Nevertheless, a Baha'i may hold a political office and be interested in politics of the right type. Ministers, state officials and governor-generals in Persia are Baha'is, and there are many other Baha'is holding government positions', *Promulgation*, pp. 238–9.

47. The non-political teaching for Baha'is was formulated by Shoghi Effendi as follows: 'The attitude of the Baha'is must be two-fold, complete obedience to the government of the country they reside in, and no interference whatsoever in political matters or questions. What the Master's statement really means is obedience to a duly constituted government, whatever that government may be in form. We are not the ones, as individual Baha'is, to judge our government as just or unjust – for each believer would be sure to hold a different viewpoint, and within our own Baha'i fold a hotbed of dissension would spring up and destroy our unity. We must build up our own Baha'i system, and leave the faulty systems of the world to go their way. We cannot change them through becoming involved in them; on the contrary, they will destroy us', Effendi, S., *Directives from the Guardian* (Wilmette, IL: Baha'i Publishing Trust, 1973), p. 56.

48. 'The caliphs have . . . been traditionally vague on the question of whether the caliphate will one day evolve into a political power . . . Ahmadis tend not to speculate on what the fate of nation-states will be once Ahmadiyyat achieves its inevitable dominance in the world, although they did draw upon statements by caliphs to indicate that Qadian would be the center of a new global order', Evans, *Far from the Caliph*, p. 50.

49. The principle of hereditary succession embodied in the guardianship in association with an elected body, the Universal House of Justice was vital to the functioning of the Baha'i institutional order envisaged by Abdul Baha in his *Will and Testament*. This vision was abruptly disrupted when Shoghi Effendi died without issue in 1957, leaving the Universal House of Justice, first elected in 1963, to take over the reigns of jurisdiction on its own. Paradoxically, since the hereditary principle had been so strongly affirmed after its untoward elimination the revised Baha'i order was brought closer in function to the Lahori branch of Ahmadiyyat which departed from the line of Qadiani khalifas, retaining instead a governing council headed by an amir.

50. Ahmad, M. B. M., *The New World Order of Islam* (Nizam-i Nau) (Qadian: Islam International Publications, 2017).
51. Warmind, M., 'Baha'i and Ahmadiyya: Globalisation and Images of Modernity', in M. Warburg, A. Hvithamar, and M. Warmind (eds), *Baha'i and Globalisation* (Aarhus: University of Aarhus Press, 2005), pp. 141–52 (p. 144). In so far as such strategies were reappropriations of ideas of previous times, they might be considered to have been forged out of marginal Islamicate (and pre-Islamic) pasts: Magianism, the syncretism of Akbar, sufi ideas of the Perfect Man, and the mysticism of Gnostic Shi'ism and Ismailism, with an added emphasis on a universalising modernity.
52. MacEoin, *People Apart*; Cole, 'Iranian Millenarianism and Democratic Thought', pp. 1–26.
53. Momen, W., 'Globalization Decentralization: The Concept of Subsidiarity', in Warburg, *Baha'i and Globalisation*, pp. 175–94 (p. 188). J. R. I. Cole states: 'Many Baha'is believe that their ecclesiastical institutions will eventually supplant the U.S. government (and other governments), so that a Baha'i theocracy will abolish the separation of religion and state'. This tendency among some members of the Baha'i Universal House of Justice held that 'the world was destined to be ruled by houses of justice and there will eventually be no distinction between church and state', Cole, J. R. I., 'The Baha'i Faith in America as Panopticon, 1963–1997', *Journal for the Scientific Study of Religion*, 37 (1998), pp. 234–48 (p. 239); Cole, 'Fundamentalism in the Contemporary U.S. Baha'i Community', *Review of Religious Research*, 43, 3 (2002), pp. 195–217 (p. 200).
54. McGlinn, *Principles*, p. 77.
55. This point will become obvious in Chapter 7 with respect to Baha'is' courting of Reza Shah's regime in the early 1930s.
56. Gibb, H. A. R., *Modern Trends in Islam* (Illinois: University of Chicago Press, 1946), pp. 63, 69. Said detected in Gibb's critique an 'Islamic Orientalism' that featured Muslim response to modernity as one of '*resistance* to change, to mutual comprehension between East and West, to the development of men and women out of archaic, primitive classical institutions and into modernity', *Orientalism*, p. 263; italics in original.
57. Smith, W. C., *Modern Islam in India* (London: Victor Gollancz, 1946), pp. 11–12; italics in original.
58. Keddie, *Iran: Religion*, p. 20.
59. Amanat, *Iran*, pp. 239, 245.

60. Quoted in Keddie, *Iran: Religion*, p. 48 n. 8.
61. Brookshaw, D. and S. B. Fazel (eds), *The Baha'is of Iran: Socio-Historical Studies* (London: Routledge, 2008) is conceived around this idea of the Iranian Baha'i community as a showcase of religious modernism, with the added contrasting element its persecution at the hands of Iranian state and ulama. This is discussed in more detail in Chapter 6 of the present study.
62. Lapidus, I., 'Islamic Revival and Modernity: The Contemporary Movements and the Historical Paradigms', *Journal of the Economic and Social History of the Orient*, 40, 4 (1997), pp. 444–60 (p. 446).
63. Cole, *Modernity and the Millennium*; Alkan, 'Ottoman Reform Movements'; Scharbrodt, *Islam and the Baha'i Faith*; McGlinn, *Principles of Progress*.
64. Scharbrodt, *Islam and the Baha'i Faith*, pp. 75–83.
65. Cole, 'Iranian Millenarianism'; Cole, J. R. I., 'Muhammad 'Abduh and Rashid Rida: A Dialogue on the Baha'i Faith', *World Order*, 15, 3–4 (1981), pp. 7–16; McCants, W., '"I Never Understood Any of this From 'Abbas Effendi": Muhammad 'Abduh's Knowledge of the Baha'i Teachings and His Friendship with 'Abdu'l-Baha 'Abbas', in Sharon, *Studies in Modern Religions*, pp. 275–98.
66. Scharbrodt, *Islam and the Baha'i Faith*, pp. 60, 65–6.
67. Amanat, *Iran*, p. 246.
68. Dreyfus, H., *Bahaism: The Universal Religion* (London: Cope and Fenwick, 1909); Holley, H., *Bahai: Spirit of the Age* (New York: Brentanos, 1921); Rosenberg, E., 'Baha'ism: Its Ethical and Social Teachings', *Transactions of the Third International Congress for the History of Religions* (Oxford: Clarendon Press, 1908), vol. 1, pp. 321–5.
69. See Effendi, S., *Guidance for Today and Tomorrow: Compiled from Writings by Shoghi Effendi the Late Guardian of the Baha'i Faith* (London: Baha'i Publishing Trust, 1953), ch. 9, pp. 138–65.
70. Lee, R. D., *Religion and Politics in the Middle East: Identity, Ideology, Institutions, and Attitudes* (Boulder, CO: Westview Press, 2014), p. 27.

Chapter 3

1. Said, *Orientalism*, p. 8. Elsewhere I argue that Edward Said's knowledge of Gobineau is clearly limited to his *Essay*, but he would also have encountered him in Raymond Schwab, *La Renaissance orientale*. See Nash, G., 'New Orientalisms for Old: Articulations of the East in Raymond Schwab, Edward Said, and two nineteenth-century French orientalists', in I. Netton (ed.), *Orientalism Revisited: Art Land and Voyage* (London: Rouledge, 2013), pp. 87–97.

2. Gobineau, A., *Religions et philosophies: Essai sur l'inégalité des races humaines*, *Œuvres* (Paris: Gallimard, [1853–5] 1983–7), ed. J. Gaulmier and J. Boissel, vol. 1, pp. 1179; Gobineau, A., *The Inequality of Human Races*, trans. A. Collins (London: Heinneman, 1915).
3. Barzan, J., *Race: A Study in Modern Superstition* (New York: Harcourt, Brace, 1937), pp. 74, 77–8.
4. Nott, J. and H. Hotz, *The Moral and Intellectual Diversity of the Races* (Philadelphia: Lippincott, 1856).
5. Schwab, R., *The Oriental Renaissance: Europe's discovery of India and the East, 1680–1880* (New York: Columbia University Press, 1984), pp. 184, 432.
6. Biddiss, M., *Gobineau: Selected Political Writings* (London: Jonathan Cape, 1970), p. 13.
7. Young, R. C., *Colonial Desire: Hybridity in Theory, Culture and Race* (London: Routledge, 1995), p. 103.
8. Todorov, T., *On Human Diversity: Nationalism, Racism and Exoticism in French Thought*, trans. Catherine Porter (Cambridge, MA: Harvard University Press, 1993); Nash, G. (ed.), *Comte de Gobineau and Orientalism: Selected Eastern Writings*, trans. D. O'Donoghue (London: Routledge, 2009).
9. '[C]'était . . . surtout, une autre forme de l'*ailleurs*, la survivance encore visible d'une réalité abolie en Europe par la modernité!', Boissel, J., *Gobineau biographie: mythes et réalité* (Paris: Berg International, 1993), p. 132; see also Boissel, J., *Gobineau, l'Orient et l'Iran* (Paris: Editions Klincksieck, 1973). Both biographies emphasise a 'love story' between Gobineau and Persia that was inflamed by his diplomatic posting. Boissel worked with Jean Gaulmier, the moving force behind the *Œuvres* which were published in three volumes by Bibliothèque de la Pléiade between 1983 and 1987. Gaulmier also published in 1965 a groundbreaking biography, *Spectre de Gobineau* (The Spectre of Gobineau). Almost single-handedly the two men instigated a revival in French Gobineau studies in the latter half of the twentieth century. Although there is as yet no collected edition of his correspondence, separate editions of Gobineau's letters to Tocqueville, and to the Austrian diplomat and personal friend Count Prokesch-Osten, as well as letters and diplomatic dispatches from Persia were published in the last century.
10. Irwin, R., 'Gobineau, the Would-be Orientalist', *Journal of the Royal Asiatic Society*, 3, 26, 1–2 (2016), pp. 321–32 (p. 326). See Keddie, *Iran: Religion*, ch. 1 – 'Gobineau, despite his errors, shows the nature of Iranian intellectual life, largely because he sees, as one Iranian scholar said, that "in Iran, things are never what they seem"', ibid, p. 26; italics in original.

11. Barzun, *Race*, p. 79; [James, H.], 'Review of Arthur de Gobineau, *Nouvelles asiatiques*', *Nation*, 23 (7 December 1876), pp. 344–5.
12. Gobineau, A., *Trois Ans en Asie, Œuvres* (Paris: Gallimard, 1983), ed. J. Gaulmier and V. Monteuil, vol. 2, pp. 27–401.
13. Hourani, A., *Europe and the Middle East* (London: Routledge, 1981), p. 61.
14. Irwin, 'Gobineau', p. 325.
15. Gobineau, A., *Mémoire sur l'état social de la Perse actuelle, Œuvres* (Paris: Gallimard, 1983), ed. J. Gaulmier and V. Monteuil, vol. 2, pp. 3–25.
16. To Tocqueville he wrote in November 1855 that the Babis were 'a sect more political than religious', having in mind the attempted assassination of the Shah by two Babis in 1852, see Tocqueville, A. de, *Correspondance d' Alexis de Tocqueville et d' Arthur de Gobineau, Oeuvres complètes* (Paris: Gallimard, 1959), vol. 9, p. 238.
17. Gobineau, *Religions*, pp. 595–6; Nash, *Gobineau and Orientalism*, p. 193.
18. In addition to Amanat, *Resurrection and Renewal*, pp. 1–13, see M. Bayat's summary of the Bab's understanding of his mission. She emphasises the terms employed in Shi 'i doctrines of prophethood, specifically the Ismaili belief in a continuous progression of divine manifestations, Bayat, M., *Mysticism and Dissent: Socioreligious thought in Qajar Iran* (Syracuse, NY: Syracuse University Press, 1982), pp. 101–4. Dabashi confirms the Bab's embedding within a traditional Shi'i worldview: 'Much time has been wasted on anachronistically insisting that Babism was something entirely new and unprecedented in Islamic and Shi'i history. Much more attention needs to be paid to the similarities, continuities, disruptions, and the enduring rootedness of Babism in its previous social and intellectual movements (that of the Hurufiyyah and the School of Isfahan in particular)', *Shi'ism*, p. 196.
19. Gobineau, *Religions*, p. 662.
20. Masuzawa, T., *The Invention of World Religions, Or, How Universalism Was Preserved in the Language of Pluralism* (Chicago: University of Chicago Press, 2005), p. 187. Here Masuzawa is referring to Buddhism; interestingly, Gobineau considered Buddhism, along with other mystic sects like Sabians and Mazdakites, as a likelier origin of sufi/gnostic Persian groups than Semitic Islam. See *Gobineau and Orientalism*, pp. 36, 50. In a letter to his close friend Prokesch-Osten, who like him was concerned with the way Husayn Ali was being treated during his periods of exile in Edirne and Akka, and who made representations on his behalf, Gobineau confirmed his belief that Baha'ullah (who he continued to refer to as 'the Bab') 'and his followers . . . are not at all Muslims'. For English translations of

the Gobineau–Prokesch correspondence, see Momen, *Babi and Baha'i Religions*, pp. 186–7, 207–9. French original: *Correspondance entre le Comte de Gobineau et le Comte de Prokesch-Osten*.
21. *Gobineau and Orientalism*, p. 134.
22. Lambden, Some Aspects, p. 231.
23. Ibid. p. 225; Browne, E. G., *Materials for the study of the Babi Religion* (Cambridge: Cambridge University Press, 1918), pp. 260–2.
24. Lambden, Some Aspects, p. 239.
25. Momen, *Babi and Baha'i Religions*, pp. 22–6.
26. Momen accepts the irony that the origins of the Baha'i faith that 'promote(s) the concept of the brotherhood of all men . . . should have been proclaimed by one who has, by some, been hailed as the father of racism', ibid. p. 17. A Baha'i translator of extracts from A. L. M. Nicolas' biography of the Bab calls Gobineau an 'infamous racialist', Terry, P., *A Prophet in Modern Times*, 2008/2015 <http://bahai-library.com/terry_nicolas_prophet_modern> (last accessed 12 October 2021).
27. Effendi, *God Passes By*, pp. 76, 81, 203–4 n. 1.
28. Nicolas, A. L. M., *Le Livre de Sept Preuves de la Mission du Bab* (Paris: Librairie Orientale et Americaine), p. v.
29. Browne, *Traveller's Narrative*, vol. 2, p. 203.
30. On Nicolas's scholarship on Babism and relations with Baha'is see Momen, *Babi and Baha'i Religions*, pp. 36–40.
31. *The Tarikh-i-Jadid or New History of Mirza Muhammad Ali the Bab, by Mirza Huseyn of Hamadan*, trans. E. G. Browne (Cambridge: Cambridge University Press, 1893); Browne, 'The Babis of Persia, 1. Sketch of their History and Personal Experiences amongst them 2. Their Literature and Doctrines', *Journal of the Royal Asiatic Society*, 21 (1889), pp. 485–526, 881–1009; Gobineau, *Religions et les Philosophies*; Nicolas, A. L. M., *Essai sur le Shaykhisme*, 2 vols. (Paris: Librarie Paul Geuthner, 1910, 1914); Nicolas, A. L. M., *Seyyed Ali Mohammed dit Le Bab* (Paris: Dujarric & Cie, Editeurs, 1905); Nicolas, A. L. M., trans., *Le Beyan Arabe: Le Livre Sacre du Babysme de Seyyed Ali Mohamed dit Le Bab* (Paris: Ernest Leroux, 1905); Nicolas, A. L. M., trans., *Le Beyan Persan: Seyyed Ali Mohmmed dit le Bab* (Paris: Librairie Paul Geuthner, 1911, 1913, 1914); Nicolas, *Le Livre de Sept Preuves*.
32. Lamben, Some Aspects, p. 257.
33. MacEoin, *Messiah*, p. 516.
34. Curzon, G. N., *Persia and the Persian Question*, 2 vols. (London: Longmans, Green and Co., 1892); Chirol, V., *The Middle East Question or some political*

problems of Indian defence (London: John Murray, 1903); Cheyne, T. K., *The Reconciliation of Races and Religions* (London: Adam and Charles Black, 1914); Estlin, J. Carpenter, *Comparative Religion* (New York: Henry Holt, 1913).
35. Effendi, S., *The Dawn-Breakers: Nabil's Narrative of the Early Days of the Baha'i Revelation* (Wilmette: Baha'i Publishing Trust, 1932), p. 17. Italics added.
36. For a further analysis of Shoghi Effendi's prose and its connections with orientalism, see Chapter 5.
37. Effendi, *Dawn-Breakers*, p. 307.
38. Ibid. pp. 84–5.
39. Lamben, Some Aspects, pp. 258–69. The Bab's address has often been reprinted in Baha'i proselytic literature. 'As a piece of salvation history it was very effective though it can hardly be deemed historical or to be what the Bab himself might have uttered', p. 263.
40. Levefere, A., *Translation, Rewriting, and the Manipulation of Literary Fame* (London: Routledge, 1992), pp. 50–1.
41. Venuti, L., 'Translation, Community, Utopia', in L. Venuti (ed.), *The Translation Studies Reader* (New York: Routledge, 2000), pp. 484–5 (p. 485).
42. Bassnett, S., 'The Translation turn in Cultural Studies', in S. Bassnett and A. Lefevere (eds), *Constructing Cultures: Essays on Literary Translation* (Clevedon: Multilingual Matters, 1998), pp. 123–40 (p. 130). We should not criticise Ruhiyyih Khanum in the late 1960s, long before postcolonial theory, for immediately grasping the nettle in pronouncing FitzGerald's translation a 'world' one and superior to the oriental original, and drawing a comparison with *Dawn-Breakers*: 'Although ostensibly a translation from the original Persian Shoghi Effendi may be said to have re-created it in English, his translation being comparable to Fitzgerald's rendering of Omar Khayyam's Rubaiyat which gave to the world a poem in a foreign language that in many ways far exceeded the merits of the original', Khanum, R., *Priceless Pearl* (London: Baha'i Publishing Trust, 1969), p. 215.
43. FitzGerald, E., *Letters of Edward FitzGerald* (London: Macmillan, 1901), vol. 1, p. 320.
44. Bassnett, S., 'Introduction: Intricate Pathways: Observations on Translation and Literature', in S. Bassnett (ed.), *Translating Literature (Essays & Studies)* (Cambridge: D. S. Brewer, 1997), pp. 1–13 (pp. 3–9).
45. Lefevere, *Translation, Rewriting*, pp. 74–5.
46. MacEoin, D., 'Bahaism: Some Uncertainties about its Role as a Globalizing Religion', in M. Warburg, A. Hvithamar and M. Warmind (eds), *Baha'i*

and Globalisation (Aarhus: University of Aarhus Press, 2005), pp. 287–306 (pp. 294–5).

47. The present study is not concerned with separating out fact from fiction as far as Shoghi Effendi's presentation of the Baha'i master narrative goes. Among the multifarious avenues opened up in the study of Babism by the collection of essays that comprise Denis MacEoin's *The Messiah of Shiraz*, the matter of the Baha'i faith's relationship with Babism, the 'religion' that preceded it, stands at the centre. As already observed in my introduction, MacEoin's work amplifies the charge originally made by Browne that, in practical terms, Baha'is altered the Babi episode remoulding it to fit with a narrative centred on Baha'ullah and his revelation. Readers who wish to be apprised of the details of this process should read especially, 'The Babi Concept of Holy War' (ibid. pp. 451–94) and 'From Babism to Baha'ism: Problems of Militancy, Quietism, and Conflation in the Construction of a Religion' (ibid. pp. 495–536). MacEoin insists the study of religion can be conducted without relinquishing religious faith: 'Historical truth should not prove destructive of faith. Destruction comes when attempts are made to deny simple facts, to wrap events in a caul of mystery, to challenge what was through an appeal to what should have been' (ibid. p. xviii). On the Baha'is' side, much of the anguish caused by MacEoin's intervention into their understanding of their own religious narratives might have been avoided by dispensing with the idea – more properly belief or doctrine – that there is such a thing as a 'correct' interpretation of facts when it comes to religious narratives. Religions, especially in their earlier stages, are prone to development and change, and as Renan's study, *Origins of the History of Christianity*, frequently exemplifies, change in circumstance or doctrine invariably requires erasure of earlier forms. The bone of contention here exemplifies the truism that the faithful cannot be expected to entertain more than one version of faith history; the latest one, triumphant for the present, replaces all previous versions.
48. Oxford Biblical Studies Online, 'Form Criticism', in W. R. F. Browning (ed.), *A Dictionary of the Bible* <http://www.oxfordbiblicalstudies.com/article/opr/t94/e693> (last accessed 12 October 2021).
49. Davison, R. and A. R. C. Leaney, *Biblical Criticism* (Harmondsworth: Penguin, 1970), p. 251.
50. Ibid., p.251.
51. Balyuzi, H. M., *The Bab: The Herald of the Day of Days* (Oxford: George Ronald, 1973), p. xi. By 'these pages' Balyuzi was referring to his own book, but the meaning could equally be applied to *Dawn-Breakers*.

Chapter 4

1. MacEoin, 'Bahaism: Some Uncertainties', p. 289.
2. Hourani, A., *Islam in European Thought* (Cambridge: Cambridge University Press, 1991), pp. 28–9. According to Hourani, Renan was 'one of the seminal figures in the formation of European ideas about Islam'.
3. The Indo-Aryan and the Semitic division exercised Renan and philologists of the early nineteenth century; a third group of noninflecting languages which included Chinese was later added. This was known as the 'agglutinative' or 'Turanian'. See Masuzawa, *Invention*, p. 161.
4. Olendar, M. *The Languages of Paradise, Race, Religion and Philology in the Nineteenth Century* (Cambridge, MA: Harvard University Press, 1992), pp. 6–9 (p. 15).
5. Said, *Orientalism*, p. 139.
6. Conrad, L. I., 'Ignaz Goldziher on Ernest Renan: From Orientalist Philology to the Study of Islam', in Martin Kramer (ed.), *The Jewish Discovery of Islam* (Tel Aviv: Moshe Dayan Center for Middle Eastern and African Studies, 1999), p. 141.
7. Masuzawa, *Invention*, p. 160.
8. On Schegel's influential *Language and Wisdom of the Indians*, and his general influence in promoting the idea of India as the Aryan cradle with strong Germanic overtones, see Schwab, *Oriental Renaissance*, pp. 70–5.
9. Renan, E., *Histoire générale et système comparé des langues sèmitiques* (General History of the Semitic Languages), *Œuvres complètes* (Paris: Calmann-Levy, 1946–61), vol. 8; Conrad, 'Ignaz Goldziher', pp. 141–2.
10. Masuzawa, *Invention*, 166–7.
11. Ibid. p. 162.
12. Renan, E., *Averroës et L'Averoïsme*, *Œuvres Complètes* (Paris: Calmann-Levy, 1946–61), vol. 3; Renan, E., 'L'Islamisme et la Science' (Islam and Science), *Œuvres complètes*, vol. 1, pp. 945–65 (p. 952); Hourani, *Europe and the Middle East*, p. 61.
13. Schwab, *Oriental Renaissance*, pp. 184–5.
14. Renan employs the noun, *le sémitisme*, and less often, *les Sémites*, as well as the adjective, *sémitique(s)*, to qualify: *les langues*, *les peuples*, *la race*, *l'esprit*, all of which are found in the opening chapter of his *General History of the Semitic Languages*. On the term 'Aryan' see Olender, *Languages*, p. 11, who includes Renan's use of it alongside Herder, Friedrich Max Müller, Adolphe Pictet, and Ignaz Goldziher. For Müller, however, the term Aryan had a linguistic and not a racial connotation, though he sometimes was guilty of blurring the distinction. See van den Bosch, L. P., *Friedrich Max Müller* (Leiden: Brill, 2002), pp. 204–9.

15. Renan, E., '*De la part des peuples sémitiques dans l'histoire de la civilisation. Discours d'ouverture du cours de langues hébraïque, chaldaïque et syriaque au Collège de France prononcé le 21 février 1862*' ('The Share of the Semitic People in the History of Civilisation'), *Œuvres complètes* (Paris: Calmann-Levy, 1946–61), vol. 2, pp. 317–35 (p. 321); *Studies of Religious History and Criticism*, trans. O. B. Forthingham (New York: Carleton, 1864), p. 151.
16. Renan, *Averroës et L'Averoïsme*, p. 17.
17. Ibid. p. 13.
18. Renan, *General History*, pp. 134–40.
19. Ibid. p. 144.
20. Renan, E., *Religious History*, p. 41.
21. Ibid. p. 115.
22. Mott, L. F., *Ernest Renan* (New York: D. Appleton, 1921), p. 184.
23. Renan, *Religious History*, p. 117. Instancing the many evidences of polytheism among the Semitic races, Max Müller contested the idea that these were specifically 'endowed with a monotheistic instinct', 'Semitic Monotheism', *Chips from a German Workshop* (London: Longman, Green, and Co. 1867), vol. 1, p. 345. Renan's repeated assertion of the lack of mythology among Semitic peoples, specifically Jews and Arabs, was strongly contested by Goldziher. See Conrad, 'Goldziher on Renan', pp. 142–6.
24. Conrad, 'Ignaz Goldziher', p. 146.
25. Renan, *Religious History*, p. 121. The quintessential Semitic society is defined as 'that of the tent and the tribe', *General History*, p. 153; later, Renan proposes the life still lived by the Arabs of the desert enabled study of 'the patriarchal society of antiquity as if it were still in existence', *History of the People of Israel: Till the Time of David* (London: Chapman and Hall, 1888), vol. 1, p. 12.
26. Renan, *Religious History*, p. 124. In the same collection of essays, Muhammad is said to embody a continuity of the Semitic spirit, 'Mahomet and the Origins of Islam', pp. 226–84. The Prophet and the Arabs are presented in a perhaps more favourable light here than in the Judaism essay, 'The History of the People of Israel', pp. 107–48.
27. According to Olender, the Semites were represented in nineteenth-century scholarship as 'immobile in time as well as in space' playing very little part in the modern historical process in contrast to Aryan mastery over nature, science and the arts, *Languages*, pp. 12, 14.
28. This trend of thinking reached absurd depths in the wild racial theorising of Emile Burnouf whose *coup de grâce* was to produce an 'Aryan' Jesus. On Arnold's

satirisation of Burnouf, see apRoberts, R., *Arnold and God* (Berkeley: University of California Press, 1983), p. 203. Comparison of the two is found in Faverty, F. E., *Matthew Arnold: The Ethnologist* (Evanston: Northwestern University Press, 1951), pp. 170–2; Masuzawa, *Invention*, pp. 248–56. Renan's notion of Jesus as 'destroyer of Judaism' has been linked with German theological attempts during the Third Reich to dejudaise Christianity; see Heschel, S., *The Aryan Jesus: Christian Theologians and the Bible in Nazi Germany* (Princeton, NJ: Princeton University Press, 2008).

29. Renan, 'Share of Semitic People', pp. 323, 326.
30. Ibid. pp. 323, 333.
31. Renan, E., *Life of Jesus* (London: Watts, 1935), p. 88. In addition to pointing out the references Renan made to Islam in his reading of the Palestinian landscape during his 1860–1 visit, Halvor Moxnes is especially insightful in revealing association of Jesus's Galilee with a childlike Aryan religion of nature – clear overtones here of Renan's own Brittany childhood, Moxnes, H., *Jesus and the Rise of Nationalism: A New Quest for the Nineteenth Century Historical Jesus* (New York: I. B. Tauris, 2011), 132–4.
32. Renan, *Jesus*, p. 90.
33. Ibid. p. 121.
34. Ibid. p. 123.
35. Renan, E., *Saint Paul* (London: Mathieson, 1890), p. 89.
36. Renan, *People of Israel*, vol. 1, p. x.
37. Renan, E., *Marcus Aurelius* (London, Mathieson, 1890), p. 313; Renan, *Religious History*, p. 350.
38. Gunny, A., *Perceptions of Islam in European Writings* (Leicester: The Islamic Foundation, 2004), p. 279 n. 21.
39. See Irwin, 'Gobineau'.
40. Gobineau, A., *Œuvres* (Paris: Gallimard, 1983–7), vol. 2, p. xx.
41. Gobineau, *Mémoire sur l'état social*, p. 5.
42. Renan, E., 'L'Islamisme et la science', p. 946.
43. Gobineau, *Religions et philosophies*, p. 505; *Comte de Gobineau*, p. 133.
44. Renan, E., *The Apostles* (London: Mathieson, 1890), p. 204.
45. Renan, *Apostles*, p. 201. The text then continues with a quote of a page or more from Gobineau, *Religions and Philosophies*, describing the event of summer 1852 when many Babis were executed after two of their number had attempted to assassinate Shah Nasir al-Din. See Momen, *Babi and Baha'i Religions*, ch. 7, pp. 128–46.

46. Renan, *Apostles*, pp. 202–3.
47. Ibid, p. 202.
48. Christian martyrdoms under Nero and Domitian are graphically described by Renan in *The Anti-Christ* (London, Mathieson, 1890) and *The Gospels* (London: Mathieson, 1890); and his *Marcus Aurelius*, ch. 19, contains an account of the second century martyrs of Lyon. *The Gospels*, p. 45, cites Babism as 'a fact of our days, [that] offers, in its nascent legend, parts that seem drawn from the Life of Jesus; the type of disciple who denies; the details of the sufferings and the death of the Bab, appear to be imitated from the Gospel'. At the close of a discussion of martyrdom as a feature of the earliest years of Christianity in *The Christian Church* (London: Mathieson, 1890), p. 171, Renan quotes an anonymous 'Asiatic' who claimed the formation of religions was a common occurrence in the East and that he himself 'was there whilst people who were cut to pieces and burnt, suffered the most horrible torture for days, danced and jumped for joy because they were dying for a man whom they had never known (the Bab) and they were the greatest men of Persia'. The speaker, most likely the superb Armenian-Iranian egoist, Malkum Khan, who told much the same story to Wilfrid Scawen Blunt, went on to claim a similar following for himself, but said that '[I was] obliged to stop my legend … to prevent the people from getting killed for me'. See Browne, E. G., *The Persian Revolution, 1905–1909*, ed. A. Amanat (Washington, DC: Mage, 1995), p. 38.
49. Renan, E., *The Future of Science: Ideas of 1848* (London: Chapman and Hall, 1891), pp. 77, 80. Here we can clearly see evidence to support the claim that 'a certain Romantic individualism, far removed from the familiar cliché of scientism with which he has so frequently been associated … was at the heart of [Renan's] work', Pitt, A., 'The Cultural Impact of Science in France: Ernest Renan and The *Vie de Jésus*', *The Historical Journal*, 43 (2000), p. 80. Olender argues Renan, 'and many others joined romanticism with positivism in an effort to preserve a common allegiance to the doctrines of Providence', *Languages*, p. 20.
50. Wardman, H. W., *Ernest Renan: A Critical Biography* (London: Athlone Press, 1964), p. 36.
51. Renan, *Religious History*, p. 219.
52. Renan, *Christian Church*, p. 171.
53. Renan, *Religious History*, pp. 51, 55.
54. Renan, *Jesus*, p. 227.
55. Caufield, J. W., *Overcoming Matthew Arnold: Ethics in Culture and Criticism* (Farnham: Ashgate, 2012), pp. 133–4.

56. Willey, B., 'Arnold and Religion', in K. Allott (ed.), *Matthew Arnold* (London: G. Bell, 1975), p. 239.
57. Stone, D. D., *Communications with the Future: Matthew Arnold in Dialogue* (Ann Arbor: University of Michigan Press, 1997), p. 60.
58. Willey, 'Arnold', p. 257.
59. apRoberts, *Arnold and God*, p. 107.
60. Gobineau, *Religions et philosophies*, p. 665.
61. Arnold, M., 'A Persian Passion Play', in *Matthew Arnold's Essays in Criticism, First Series, a Critical Edition*, ed. T. M. Hoctor (Chicago: University of Chicago Press, 1968), pp. 153–4.
62. Arnold, 'Passion Play', p. 156; italics in original.
63. Ibid. p.156.
64. Ibid, p. 137. Here Arnold is referring to a passage in which Gobineau discloses a remark presumably by one of his oral sources which embellishes his telling of this part of the Bab's story. The Bab's visit to Kufa is mentioned by the court historian, Sipihr, but does not appear in standard Babi or Baha'i accounts. The discrepancy is noted by Browne, 'Babis of Persia', p. 903.
65. Arnold, M., *Dissent and Dogma, The Complete Prose Works of Matthew Arnold*, ed. R. H. Super (Ann Arbor: University of Michigan Press), vol. 6, p. 146. According to David DeLaura: 'the masses need emotional and imaginative support for the practice of morality'; for Arnold 'this can only come from the Bible', DeLaura, D., *Hebrew and Hellene in Victorian England: Newman, Arnold, and Pater* (Austin: University of Texas Press, 1969), p. 105.
66. Arnold, 'Passion Play', p. 137. On Gobineau's misinformation on this aspect of the Persian prophet, see Stephen Lambden's critique discussed in Chapter 3 of the present work.
67. In his article of 1878, 'Les téaziés de la Perse' (The Persian Taziya), Renan reaffirms the ideas that we have already seen in Gobineau and Arnold. In the first paragraph of the essay Renan states that the astonishing religious venture of the Babis has demonstrated the ancient mystical and pantheist leaven which the Arab conquest (of Persia) could not extinguish. Using a favourite image of his own, he characterises the patriotism and imagination behind the *taziya* as an escape from the limiting walls that willingly enclose the mind of the real Muslim. The mystical genius of the Persian supplied Islam with something it lacked: the tender ideal of suffering, the motifs of mourning, the tearful complaint of the Passion, all of which testified to the absolute need of all religion. In the person of Ali and his sons, without directly imitating the Christian Passion, but drawing from the same

sentiments, the Shiites had created patient virtue, Renan, 'Les téaziés de la Perse' *Œuvres*, vol. 7, pp. 831, 849.
68. Frederic, E., *Matthew Arnold: The Ethnologist* (Evanston: Northwestern University Press, 1951), p. 170.
69. apRoberts, *Arnold*, 269; italics in original. Bennett, *Victorian Images*, shows how Christian writers sympathetic toward Islam in some respects also adopted this unchronological perspective.
70. Arnold, 'Passion Play', pp. 156–7.
71. Renan's travels in the holy land also confirmed his opinions on the issue of rigid Semitic monotheism especially with respect to Islam, see Nash, G., 'Death and Resurrection: The Renans in Syria (1860–61)', in *Knowledge is Light: Travellers in the Near East* (Oxford: ASTENE and Oxbow Books, 2011), pp. 69–77. The proposition that this monotheism is supposedly incapable of admitting liberty of thought has been creatively probed by Schwarz, R., *The Curse of Cain: The Violent Legacy of Monotheism* (Chicago: University of Chicago Press, 1997); and Assmann, J., *The Price of Monotheism* (Stanford, CA: Stanford University Press, 2010).
72. Keddie, N. R., *Sayyid Jamal ad-Din 'al-Afghani': A Political Biography* (Berkeley, CA: University of California Press, 1972), p. 190.
73. '[His] inconsistency is most bewildering when in the same article ['Islam and Science'] he professes that Islam kills science and philosophy and admits that it was within the heart of Islam that complete rationalism developed', Lahoud, N., 'Islamic responses to Europe at the Dawn of Colonialism', in T. Shogimen and C. J. Nederman (eds), *Western Political Thought in Dialogue with Asia* (Lanham, MD: Lexington Books, 2009), p. 171.
74. Keddie, '*al-Afghani*', p. 193.
75. Ibid, 197. Renan's address opened the debate; it appeared in *Journal des Debates*, 30 March 1883. The remarks Renan makes on the superiority of Persians over the other oriental and African races have already been quoted above. His denigration of Islam in racial terms had a colonial impact that should not be overlooked; in effect it provided justification for France's continuing entrenchment in the Maghreb; see Lorcerie, F., 'L'islam comme contre-identification française: trois moments', *L'Année du Maghreb* 2 (2005–2006), pp. 509–36.
76. Keddie, '*al-Afghani*', p. 196.
77. See See Keddie, *Iran: Religion*, ch. 1; Bayat, *Mysticism and Dissent*.
78. See Smith, P., '*Reality* Magazine: Editorship and Ownership of an American Periodical', in J. R. I. Cole and M. Momen (eds), *From Iran East and West: Studies in*

Babi and Baha'i History (Los Angeles: Kalimat Press, 1984), pp. 135–55; Smith, *Babi and Baha'i Religions*, pp. 100–14.

79. Zwemer, S. M., *Islam: A Challenge*, p. 149. The encounter between Baha'is and Christian missionaries in Iran at the end of the nineteenth century might have fascinated Renan and Arnold as a confrontation between evangelical scriptural literalism and modernist religious relativism. From believing Baha'is to be ripe for conversion, the missionaries' attitude toward them turned to bitter disdain on discovering they were possibly even less likely to convert than their Muslim compatriots. See Momen, 'Early Relations'.

80. Powell, A., *Muslims and Missionaries* (London: Curzon Press, 1993), p. 3. In an earlier encounter (1811) in Shiraz between some Persian mujtahids and sufis and pioneer Anglican missionary to India, Henry Martyn, the boot seemed to have been partly on the other foot. The Persians were totally oblivious of the 'torrents of Western military, diplomatic and eventually cultural intrusions which were soon to arrive'. However their debating 'strategies were at times novel and were coupled with an agile rhetoric'. Indeed, Amanat sees in one of the Shirazis (a sufi) the tendency 'dangerously close to disregarding the finality of Muhammad', and speculates such argumentation might have been on the brink of urging 'Mahdistic [. . .] manifestation', Amanat, A., '*Mujtahids* and Missionaries: Shi'i response to Christian polemics in the early Qajar Period', in R. Gleave (ed.), *Religion and Society in Qajar Iran* (London: Routledge Curzon, 2005), pp. 247–69 (p. 261), p. 266.

81. Barbara Metcalf points out even the superior German missionary, K. G. Pfander, 'found himself at a serious intellectual disadvantage in debates; for his Muslim opponents challenged him with the work of recent English Biblical scholars, wholly unknown to him, in order to prove their contention about the variability of the Biblical text. The argument of textual corruption was an old one for Muslims, but took on new force in this period because of Western scholarship itself', Metcalf, B. D., *Islamic Revival in India: Deoband, 1860–1900* (Princeton, NJ: Princeton University Press, 1982), p. 220.

82. Moadell, M., 'Conditions for Ideological Production: The Origins of Islamic Modernism in India, Egypt, and Iran', *Theory and Society*, 30, 5 (2001) pp. 669–731 (p. 686).

83. Cole, 'Muhammad 'Abduh and Rashid Rida'; Sharbrodt, *Islam and the Baha'i Faith*.

84. Alkan, N., '"The Eternal Enemy of Islam": Abdullah Cevdet and the Baha'i Religion', *Bulletin of the School of Oriental and African Studies*, 68, 1 (2005),

pp. 1–20; Polat, A., 'A Conflict on Baha'ism and Islam in 1922: Abdullah Cevdet and State Religious Agencies', *Insan and Toplum*, 5, 10 (2016), pp. 29–42.
85. Renan, *Religious History*, 168–9.
86. John Marenbon argues that Renan began in the mode of demythologising religion favoured by David Strauss before graduating in *Life of Jesus* to the place where his subject 'the historical Jesus, though not divine, *really* incarnated the virtues attributed to him', Marenbon, J., 'Ernest Renan and Averroism: The Story of a Misinterpretation', in A. Akasoy and G. Giglioni (eds), *Renaissance Averroism and its Aftermath: Arabic Philosophy in Early Modern Europe* (Dordrecht: Springer, 2013), pp. 273–84 (pp. 278–9).
87. Smith, P., *A Concise Encyclopedia of the Baha'i Faith* (Oxford: Oneworld, 2002), pp. 22–3. Gulpaygani was a late example of a type of person who Baha'is celebrate as an outstanding Shi'i scholar who converted either to Babism or Baha'ism. Momen's entry on him in the *Encyclopaedia Iranica* says that in 1873 he became head of Madrasih-yi Hakim Hashim, also known as Madrasih-yi Madar-i Shah, in Tehran. He must therefore have been well versed in Shi'ism. He converted to the Baha'i faith in 1876. His mission as an Iranian scholar at the Sunni Azhar nearly two decades later was to spread Baha'i axioms surreptitiously by way of *taqiyya*. His debating prowess, which impacted on Shaykh Muhammad Abdu but much less on his disciple Rashid Rida, was founded upon Abul Fazl's brand of rationalist methodology which was to a great degree of Abdul Baha's origination. See Cole, 'Muhammad 'Abduh and Rashid Rida'.
88. Cole, J. R. I. (trans. and ed.), Mirza Abu'l-Fadl, *Miracles and Metaphors* (Los Angeles: Kalimat Press, 1981), p. 9.
89. See Schweitzer, A., *The Quest of the Historical Jesus: A Critical Study of its Progress from Reimarus to Wrede*, 2nd edn, trans. W. Montgomery (London: A. & C. Black, 1926).
90. Cole, *Miracles and Metaphors*, pp. xix, 10.
91. Cole, J. I. R. (ed.), Mirza Abu'l-Fadl Gulpaygani, *Letters and Essays, 1886–1913* (Los Angeles: Kalimat Press, 1985), p. 81.
92. 'Working with meticulous care, produce *a correct history* that this book may be brought to a successful fruition by the will of the One True God. Thus may it be worthy of seeing publication by the scholars of the world', Gulpaygani, *Letters and Essays*, pp. 77–8; italics added.
93. Smith, *Babi and Baha'i Religions*, p. 156.
94. It would be churlish to fault them for this when a contemporary Renan scholar adds an 'Afterword' to a recent article on Renan's first study *Averroès et l'averroïsme*,

in which he acknowledges 'a notorious aspect of Renan's thought: despite being a pioneer of the history of philosophy in Islam, he severely criticised the religion and culture of Islam *on several occasions*'. Marenbon, 'Ernest Renan and Averroism', p. 283. Italics added. 'The history of Averroism also allowed Renan to develop this theme of philosophy and its oppression by religious orthodoxy on a wider scale, in discussing the extinction within Islam of the Aristotelian tradition of philosophy represented by Averroes and the struggles of the Latin Averroistic tradition against the Church authorities', Ibid, p. 276.
95. Lockman, *Contending Visions*, p. 81.
96. Hourani, A., *Arabic Thought in the Liberal Age, 1798–1939* (Cambridge: Cambridge University Press, 1983); Said, E. W., *Culture and Imperialism* (London: Chatto and Windus, 1993); Said, E. W., *The World, the Text, and the Critic* (Cambridge, MA: Harvard University Press, 1983). Among other things, Said used the two concepts 'to describe the way the network of affiliation links colonised societies to imperial culture', Ashcroft, B., and P. Aluwahlia, *Edward Said*, 2nd edn (London: Routledge, 2009), p. 25.

Chapter 5

1. Denis MacEoin refers to the 'invaluable pioneering work . . . in assembling and classifying Babi materials' of Browne and Rozen, who in his view had no successors, MacEoin, D., *Sources for Early Babi Doctrine and History: A Survey* (Leiden: Brill, 1992), p. 1. On Kazem Bek, see below, Chapter 7. 'Jean-Albert-Bernard Dorn (1805–1881) of St. Petersburg travelled in northern Iran, and he was the first European scholar to collect manuscripts written by Babi scribes. Dorn's Babi manuscripts together with manuscripts acquired later by the orientalist Nicolai Vladimirovich Khanykov (1819–79) made up a considerable collection of Babi manuscripts in St. Petersburg', Warburg, *Citizens of the World*, p. 34.
2. Wickens, G., 'Edward Granville Browne, i. Browne's Life and Career', *Encyclopaedia Iranica* <https://iranicaonline.org/articles/browne-edward-granville> (last accessed 14 October 2021).
3. Said, *Orientalism*, p. 223; passim.
4. Ibid. p. 224; Irwin, R., *For Lust of Knowing: The Orientalists and their Enemies* (London: Penguin, 2007), pp. 162–3, 204–7.
5. Said, *Orientalism*, p. 224.
6. Margoliouth, D., 'Introduction', *The Koran, translated from the Arabic by the Rev. J. M. Rodwell* (London: Dent, 1909), p. x. He also wrote a history of Islam and the Prophet that displayed 'Gibbonian scepticism, oddly combined with

Christian fervour' to produce 'a thoroughly hostile portrait of Muhammad', Irwin, *Lust of Knowing*, p. 211.
7. Bonakdarian, M., 'Selected Correspondence of E. G. Browne and Contemporary Reviews of the Persian Revolution 1905–1909', in E. G. Browne, *The Persian Revolution*, ed. A. Amanat (Washington, DC: Mage, 1995), pp. xxix–lxiv.; Bonakdarian, M., 'Edward G. Browne and the Iranian Constitutional Struggle: From Academic Orientalism to Political Activism', *Iranian Studies*, 26 (1993), p. 7–31.
8. Browne, 'The Babis of Persia', p. 486.
9. Browne, E. G., *A Year Amongst the Persians: Impressions as to the Life, Character and Thought of the People of Persia* (Cambridge: Cambridge University Press, 1893), p, 324.
10. Browne, 'Introduction', *Travellers' Narrative*, vol. 2, p. xii.
11. Ibid. p. xi.
12. Ibid. p. xv.
13. Browne, 'Introduction', *Tarikh-i-Jadid*, p. xi.
14. Cole, J. R. I., 'Browne, Edward Granville: ii. Browne on Babism and Bahaism', *Encylopaedia Iranica* <https://iranicaonline.org/articles/browne-edward-granville> (last accessed 14 October 2021).
15. Browne, E. G., 'Introduction', in M. H. Phelps, *Life and Teachings of Abbas Effendi* (New York: G. P. Putnam, 1903).
16. However, MacEoin concluded 'the *Kitab-i nuqtat al-kaf* deserves to retain its reputation as the earliest comprehensive internal history of Babism', *Sources*, p. 151.
17. See MacEoin, 'Divisions and Authority Claims in Babism (1850–1866)', *Messiah of Shiraz*, pp. 369–407 (p. 404). This is a core article that sums up a period after the martyrdom of the Bab during which claims and counterclaims were made, culminating in those of Baha'ullah which marked 'the final phases of Babi theophanic speculation', p. 406.
18. Horsley, R., 'Review of Reza Aslan, *Zealot: The Life and Times of Jesus of Nazareth*', *Critical Research on Religion*, 2, 2 (2014), pp. 195–205.
19. MacEoin, *Sources*, p. 131.
20. Browne, *Traveller's Narrative*, p. vii.
21. Amanat, 'Introduction', *Persian Revolution*; Bayat, M. *Iran's First Revolution: Shi'ism and the Constitutional Revolution of 1905–1909* (New York: Oxford University Press, 1991); Amanat, *Iran*, pp. 479–80.
22. Vaziri, M., *Iran as Imagined Nation: The Construction of National Identity* (New York: Paragon House, 1993); Boroujerdi, M., *Iranian Intellectuals and the West:*

The Tormented Triumph of Nativism (Syracuse: University of Syracuse Press, 1996); Zia-Ebrahimi, R., *The Emergence of Iranian Nationalism: Race and the Politics of Dislocation* (New York: Columbia University Press, 2016).

23. Nash, G., *From Empire to Orient: Travellers to the Middle East, 1830–1926* (London: I. B. Tauris, 2004); Nash, G., 'Friends across the Waters: British Orientalism and Middle East Nationalism', in G. MacPhee and P. Poddar (eds), *Empire and After: Englishness in Postcolonial Perspective* (New York: Berghahn, 2007), pp. 87–100.
24. Browne, E. G., *Materials for the Study*, p. xxii–xxiii.
25. Ibid. p.xxiii.
26. Browne, *Traveller's Narrative*, vol. 2, p. ix.
27. Browne, 'Introduction', *Tarikh-i-Jadid*, p. vii.
28. Effendi, *God Passes By*, chs 1, 6, 9, 16.
29. Browne, 'Introduction', *Tarikh-i-Jadid*, pp. xii–xiii.
30. Effendi, *God Passes By*, p. 4; italics in original.
31. One of the key traits of orientalism according to Said was the way in which particular texts, for example Edward Lane's *Manners and Customs of the Modern Egyptians*, were appropriated by later writers to confirm their own work's veracity. In practice this had the effect of establishing a repertoire that repeated and reinforced similar tropes and clichés.
32. *Dawn-Breakers*, p. 30. Shoghi Effendi must have felt his subject matter of such importance that it had to be inscribed it in the grandiloquent tones that were the norm in much orientalist writing about Persia. Compare it to the following concluding passage from a 'historical' source adverted to in the introduction to *Dawn-Breakers*: '. . . we may dwell upon the past history of Iran; the age of Rustum and his heroes, the precepts of Zoroaster, the gorgeous line of Sassanian Kings, the age of poets, the restored magnificence of 'Abbas, and finally the stream of history brings us down to the naked deformity of the Kajar rule and the desolation of modern Persia', Markham, C. R., *A General Sketch of the History of Persia* (London: Longmans, Green and Co, 1874), p. 525. The appeal to the 'past history of Iran' and its 'gorgeous' pre-Islamic kings, alongside denigration of the 'deformity' and 'desolation' of present-day Muslim rulers assimilates Sir John Malcolm's *History of Persia: From the Most Early Period to the Present Time* (1815) and *Sketches of Persia* (1827).
33. Effendi, *Dawn-Breakers*, p. 31.
34. MacEoin, D., 'Introduction', in E. G. Browne, *A Year Amongst the Persians* (London: Century Publishing, 1984), pp. vii–xiv; p. viii, p. xi–xii. MacEoin

confirms Browne's work as part of the pilgrimage genre of travel writing in a more restricted sense than Said who applied the term to 'every major work' in the genre, Said, *Orientalism*, p. 168. Curzon and Browne, it is worth pointing out, though one was a Tory and the other a liberal, both shared a common political opposition to the British Government's pre-World War One policy over Persia, Nash, *Empire to Orient*, p. 161. Browne includes Curzon's estimate of the number of Babis as one million, *Tarikh-i-Jadid*, p. vii.

35. Browne, *A Year*, pp. 442–3.
36. Ibid.
37. Curzon, *Persia*, vol. 1, p. 499; Chirol, *Middle-Eastern Question*, p. 123; Wishard, J. G., *Twenty Years in Persia: A Narrative of Life under The Last Three Shahs* (New York: Fleming H. Revel), p. 165; Adams, I., *Persia by a Persian: Personal Experiences, Manners, Customs, Religious and Social Life in Persia* (n.p.: n.p., 1900), p. 460.
38. See Ansari, H. *'The Infidel Within': Muslims in Britain since 1800* (London: Hurst, 2004); Gilham, *Loyal Enemies*.
39. 'With the deaths of those Azalis who were active in the Constitutional period, Azali Babism entered a phase of stagnation from which it has never recovered', MacEoin, 'Azali-Babism', *Encyclopaedia Iranica*. On the significant role Azali-Babis played in Iran's Constitutional Revolution see Bayat, *Iran's First Revolution*, pp. 61–70, passim.
40. Lavan, *Ahmadiya Movement*, p. 103.
41. Friedmann, *Prophecy Continuous*, p. 119. A Qadiani Ahmadi statement on the term 'mahdi' runs: '(1) The Mahdi and the Messiah would appear in the latter days. (2) They will not be distinct and separate personalities but would be one person whose main function would be the renaissance of Islam. (3) Within this overall framework, the Promised Messiah would effectively refute the doctrine of the cross, and expose the falsity of the doctrines of the Church like the Trinity, Atonement and Salvation through the blood of Jesus. (4) He would be the champion of Islam against all comers, and would establish the superiority of Islam over all other faiths as is indicated in [Quran] 9:33.' Khan, M. Z., *Ahmadiyyat: The Renaissance of Islam* (London: Tabsir Publications, 1978), p. 43. From a Lahori perspective, while Muhammad Ali freely applied Ghulam Ahmad's favoured title 'Promised Messiah', as well as *mujaddid* or 'renewer', his importance rested in his inspirational value: 'The acceptance of the claims of the Founder has . . . changed the lethargic attitude of his followers. It has given them a new power of faith . . . This is the only object in accepting Ghulam Ahmad as the Promised Messiah, Mahdi and

Mujaddid', Ali, M., *True Conception of the Ahmadiyya Movement* (Columbus, Ohio: Ahmadiyya Anjuman Isha'at Islam Lahore, 1996), p. 10.
42. Ali, *True Conception*, p. 147.
43. Ryad, 'Salafiyya, Ahmadiyya', pp. 50, 63, 57, 50; italics in text.
44. Gilham, *Loyal Enemies*, p. 132. Reportage of Ahmadism (as opposed to mainstream Islam) was not necessarily negative. Valentine, quoting an Ahmadi source, notes that: 'The London *Times* . . . in an obituary, noted [Ghulam Ahmad's] piety, stating that he was "venerable in appearance, magnetic in personality and active in intellect"', Valentine, *Islam and the Ahmadiyya*, p. 52.
45. A Baha'i convert of comparable social status to Headley was Lady Sara Blomfield. Widow of the Gothic revival architect Arthur Blomfield (who was the fourth son of Bishop of London Charles James Blomfield), she joined a tiny community of Baha'is in London in 1907; maintaining her connections to the elite she was able to help alert a British military response to the safety of Abdul Baha in Palestine in 1918. See Chapter 6 below.
46. For Gulpaygani's responses see Cole, *Miracles and Metaphors*, part 1, pp. 7–48.
47. See, however, Fazel, S., and K. Fananapazir, 'A Bahá'í Approach to the Claim of Finality in Islam', <https://wilmetteinstitute.org/wp-content/uploads/2017/01/5.3-Fazel-Fananapazir.pdf> (last accessed 14 October 2021).
48. 'The fact that many of Browne's conclusions have been extensively (and often undiscriminatingly) drawn on by opponents of the Baha'i movement in both Iran and the West has not helped preserve a clear line of demarcation between fair academic comment (however pointed) and outright polemic. Nor has the situation been made clearer by the development of orientalist writing about Islam', MacEoin, *Sources*, p. 131. Edmund Burke III points out that in the 1980s orientalist tropes were rehabilitated and applied as a 'new orientalism' against Muslims, Burke III, E., 'Orientalism and World History: Representing Middle Eastern nationalism and Islamism in the twentieth century', *Theory and Society* 27, 4 (1998), pp. 489–507 (p. 501).
49. 'The Babi or the Bahai Religion' etc., *Review of Religions*, 6 (1907), Part 1, pp. 171–7; Part 2, pp. 315–25; Part 3, pp. 351–7; Part 4, pp. 387–404; Part 5, pp. 427–42; 'The Teachings of Abbas Effendi', *Review of Religions*, 7 (1908), pp. 66–84. These articles demonstrate close reading of Baha'i texts and discuss topics such as laws from Baha'ullah's *Kitab-i Aqdas* and his eschatology drawing upon a book of Baha'i proofs entitled *Bahr al-Irfan* by Haji Mirza Muhammad Afshar (Bombay, c. 1890). To explicate Abdul Baha's teaching on matters such as the forgiveness of sins and the state of the soul use is made of the English text, Phelps, *Life and Teachings of Abbas*

Effendi which conclusively establish's the authorship as Muhammad Ali's. The argument weighs Abdul Baha's doctrines against the Quran, attributing to them excessive liberality, then goes on to compare them against Baha'ullah's teaching in an attempt to demonstrate change and inconsistency.

50. Ali, M., *History and Doctrines of the Babi Movement* (Lahore: Ahmadiyya Anjuman Isha'at-i-Islam, 1933); Beg, M. M., *The Bahai Creed: A Brief History and Doctrines of the Babi Movement* (Lahore: Ahmadiyya Anjuman Isha'at-i-Islam, n.d.); Niyaz, S. A. Q. (ed.), *The Babi and Baha'i Religion* (Tilford, Surrey: Islam International Publications, 1960).
51. Ali, *True Conception*, p. 1. The passage continues: 'Babism was in existence fifty years before the inception of the Ahmadiyya Movement. Did it start an Islamic literature? If Ahmadis had a new religion from Islam, they would have directed their efforts to the advancement of that "new" faith, but as they are entirely engaged in the service of Islam, they cannot, and in fact do not, owe allegiance to any other religion except Islam', p. 2.
52. Ali, *History and Doctrines*, pp. 3–4, 33; brackets in original.
53. Ibid. pp. 20–1.
54. In his introduction to *Nuqtat al-Kaf*, Browne points out differences between this text and *Tarikh-i-Jadid*, noting revisions brought into the latter to bring it in line with the Baha'i turn. While admitting the improvements brought about by Baha'ullah's new teachings he emphasises, for the record, that the original Babis 'might consider themselves as "meek", but they fully intended to inherit the earth; they held those who rejected the Bab as unclean and worthy of death; and they held the Qajar Shahs in detestation'. He points out passages which describe 'the extraordinary proceedings at Badasht, which seem to have scandalized not only the Muhammadans but even a section of the Babis . . . the sermon preached by Janab-i-Quddus on that occasion certainly lends some colour to the accusation made by the Muslims against the Babis, viz. that they advocated communism and community of wives', Browne, E. G. (ed.), *Kitab-i Nuqtatu'l-Kaf: Being the Earliest History of the Babis compiled by Hajji Mirza Jani of Kashan* (Leiden: E. J. Brill and London: Luzac and Co., 1910), p. xxxvii; p. xlii.
55. Niyaz, *Babi and Baha'i Religion*, pp. 31–3 (p. 19).
56. Ali, *History and Doctrines*, p. 45. Christian polemicists who used Browne's *Materials* include: Miller, *Bahaism: Its Origin*; Richards, *The Religion of the Baha'is*; and Speer, R., *Missions and Modern History: A Study of the Missionary Aspect of Some Great Movements of the Nineteenth Century* (New York: Revell, 1904).

57. Ali, *History and Doctrines*, ch. 8, 'Sources of Babism: Ismailiyya'; p. 115. On *ghulat* or extremist Shi'a, see Halm, *Shiism*, pp. 156–7; Momen, M., *Introduction to Shi'i Islam: History and Doctrines of Twelver Shi'ism* (New Haven: Yale University Press, 1985), pp. 66–8; passim.
58. Ahmad, *Review of Religions*, 1907, p. 442.
59. 'He foretold the appearance of many of these signs, as, for instance, the approach of the plague, the World War, universal earthquakes, the influenza epidemic . . .', Ahmad, M. B. M., *Ahmadiyyat or the True Islam* (Tilford, Surrey, 2007), p. 19.
60. Nash, G. P. (ed.), *Marmaduke Pickthall, Islam and the Modern World* (Leiden: Brill, 2017), pp. 9–10.
61. Evans, *Far from the Caliph*; Gualtieri, *Ahmadis*.
62. However, Bakhsh later moved from a pro-British to a pro-nationalist position, Smith, *Modern Islam*, pp. 58–9.
63. Ibid. pp. 299–300, 331 n. 10. The object of Sayyid Ahmad Khan was to save Islam from the onslaughts of the West but to this aim Islam was subjected to modern trends. The Ahmadiyya Movement not only wanted to save Islam but also to see it 'a triumphant religion of the world', Ali, *Concept*, p. 45. On the Ahmadi position regarding the Indian independence movement of the 1920s and 1930s, see Friedmann, pp. 37–8. British officials noted a slight difference on the scale of loyalty to the British government between London Lahori Ahmadis and London Qadianis – see India office file 1660.
64. Geaves, *Islam and Britain*, p. 85. H. A. Walter commented regarding the *Review of Religions* in which the articles on Babi-Baha'ism appeared: 'This paper was well named, for it has given its attention to a remarkably wide range of religions and to a great variety of subjects. Orthodox Hinduism, the Arya Samaj, the Brahma Samaj and Theosophy; Sikhism, Buddhism, Jainism and Zoroastrianism; Baha'ism, Christian Science and Christianity have all received attention, as well as Islam in all its ramifications, both ancient and modern, such as the Shi'ites, Ahl-i-Hadis, Kharijites, Sufis and such representative exponents of modern tendencies as Sir Syed Ahmad Khan and Syed Amir 'Ali', Walter, *Ahmadiya*, p. 17.
65. Smith, *Modern Islam*, p. 299.
66. Walter, *Ahmadiya*, p. 76.
67. Ali, M. 'God Save the King!' *Review of Religions*, 10.11 (1911), pp. 441–6 (p. 444).
68. Khan, *From Sufism*, p. 109.
69. See Chapter 8 for discussion of Iqbal and Maududi's comparison of Ahmadiyyat and Baha'ism. Iqbal's father and brother joined the Ahmadiyya and 'Iqbal himself allegedly took Ghulam Ahmad's *bay'at* (allegiance) in the 1890s even though he

clearly distanced himself from Ahmadi theology towards the end of his life', Khan, *From Sufism*, p. 122. In spite of the religious charges stacked up by Maududi in his attack on the Ahmadis, or the 'Qadianis' as he called them, which led to his imprisonment in Pakistan on one occasion, his argument was essentially political in nature. See Maududi, S. A. A., 'The Qadiani Problem' (Lahore: Islamic Publications (PVT) Limited, 1953).

70. Stephen Jones notes that modernist Islam was favoured by indigenous converts like Quilliam in Liverpool, 'an Asian lawyer' (Khawja Kamaluddin) at the Woking Mosque, and in the London Pan-Islamic society'. However, the period after the Second World War saw the influx of migrants from South Asia and elsewhere, and 'by the sheer weight of numbers, these . . . migrants have come to define the character of British Islam, with the modernist revivalism of Quilliam and others pushed to the margins', Jones, S. H., *Islam and the Liberal State: National Identity and the Future of Muslim Britain* (London: I. B. Tauris, 2020), pp. 19–20.

71. Arberry, A., *Oriental Essays: Portraits of Seven Scholars* (London: Allen & Unwin, 1960), p. 171.

72. Arberry, *Oriental*, p. 183.

73. Nash, *Empire to Orient*, pp. 127–30; pp. 153–4.

74. Browne, 'Introduction', in Phelps, *Life and Teachings of Abbas Effendi*, pp. xi–xxx; p. xxvii–xxviii; pp. xxviii–xxix.

75. Later he may have regretted publishing the accounts that libelled Abdul Baha in *Materials*. See Balyuzi, H. M., *Edward Granville Browne and the Baha'i Faith* (London: George Ronald, 1970), pp. 118–22.

76. Velasco, I., 'Academic Irrelevance or Disciplinary Blind-Spot? Middle Eastern Studies and the Baha'i Faith Today', *Middle East Studies Association Bulletin*, 35, 2 (2001), pp. 188–98.

Chapter 6

1. See Van Grondelle, M., *The Ismailis in the Colonial Era: Modernity, Empire and Islam, 1839–1969* (London: Hurst, 2009).

2. Momen, *Babi and Baha'i Religions*, pp. 346, 472.

3. Shahvar, S., 'The Baha'i Faith and its communities in Iran, Transcaspia and the Caucasus' in S. Shahvar, B. Morozov and B. B. Gilbar (eds), *The Baha'is of Iran, Transcaspia and the Caucasus*, vol. 1, *Letters of Russian Officers and Officials* (London: I. B. Tauris, 2011), pp. 16, 21.

4. 'Russian diplomats continued to extend protection to Bahá'ís in later years, prior to the revolution. In Isfahan in 1903, for instance, Bahá'ís took refuge

from mobs in the Russian Consulate, and M. Baronowsky, the Russian acting consul, petitioned Persian authorities on their behalf', Hassall, G., 'Notes on the Babi and Baha'i Religions in Russia and its Territories', *Baha'i Studies*, 5, 3 (1992), pp. 41–80; Momen, *Babi and Baha'i Religions*, pp. 376, 378–85.
5. MacEoin, *Messiah of Shiraz*, p. 253. According to Mina Yazdani, 'The Confessions of Dolgoruki was a 1930s political-spy fiction that was taken as history to create the masternarrative of espionage for the Baha'is of Iran', Yazdani, M., 'The Confessions of Dolgoruki: Fiction and Masternarrative in Twentieth-Century Iran', *Iranian Studies*, 44, 1 (January 2011), pp. 25–47 (p. 25).
6. Cronin, S., 'Review of Soli Shahvar et al., *The Baha'is of Iran, Transcaspia and the Caucasus* and Youli Ioannesyan, *The Development of the Babi/Baha'i Communities*', *Asian Affairs*, 45, 1 (2014) pp. 144–6 (p. 145). On the background to the opening of the Russian archives, see Volkov, D. V., 'Fearing the Ghosts of State Officialdom Past? Russia's Archives as a Tool for Constructing Historical Memories of its Persia Policy Practices', *Middle Eastern Studies*, 51, 6 (2015), pp. 901–21.
7. Tolz, V., *Russia's own Orient: The Politics of Identity and Oriental Studies in the Late Imperial and Early Soviet Periods* (Oxford: Oxford University Press, 2011); Cronin, S., 'Introduction: Edward Said, Russian Orientalism and Soviet Iranology', *Iranian Studies*, 48, 5 (2015), pp. 647–62; Volkov, D., 'Persian Studies and the Military in Late Imperial Russia (1863–1917): State Power in the Service of Knowledge?' *Iranian Studies*, 47, 6 (2014), pp. 915–32.
8. Cronin, S., 'Said, Russian Orientalism', p. 649.
9. Andreeva, E., *Russia and Iran in the Great Game: Travelogues and Orientalism* (New York: Routledge, 2007), p. 77.
10. Cronin, 'Said, Russian Orientalism', p. 650–1.
11. Andreeva, *Russia and Iran*, p. 172.
12. Cronin, 'Said, Russian Orientalism', p. 650.
13. Volkov, 'Persian Studies and the Military', p. 917.
14. Ibid. p. 920.
15. Andreeva, *Russia and Iran*, p. 81.
16. Volkov, 'Persian Studies and the Military', p. 916.
17. Tolz, *Russia's Own Orient*, p. 21.
18. Volkov, 'Persian Studies and the Military', p. 916.
19. Tolz, *Russia's Own Orient*, p. 21.
20. Andreeva, *Russia and Iran*, p. 82.
21. '[A] colorful figure who awaits an English-language biography, [he] was born in Rasht, converted from Islam to Protestantism (not to Orthodoxy), and became

professor of Arabic and Islamic law at Kazan university. Kazem-Bek himself, although his academic status was undeniable, seems to have joyfully internalized some stock orientalist tropes, revelling in the attention he attracted while promenading in the streets of Kazan wearing a silk turban and colorful robes', Cronin, 'Said, Russian Orientalism', p. 650.
22. Ioannesyan, *Development*, p. 6.
23. Volkov, 'Persian Studies and the Military', pp. 923–4.
24. Shahvar, *Baha'is of Iran*, p. 152.
25. Ibid. p. 67; italics added.
26. Ibid. p. 147. Shahvar summarises the situation regarding the Russian orientalists' relationships with Baha'is and Iran overall as one in which 'the Russians were quite careful not to get too close to . . . the Baha'is to avoid arousing not only the suspicions of the Iranian government and population, but also their animosity toward Russia', Ibid. p. 16. This may be true, but leaves open the roles played by orientalists later in Russia's, to say the least, heavy-handed intrusion into Iranian affairs during the events of the Constitutional Revolution. A Baha'i eyewitness states he met Tumanskii who was present when the Russian occupation took place in Tabriz in 1909. See Uskui, H. M. H. A., *Extracts from 'Tarikh-i Azerbaijan'* <https://bahai-library.com/manuchehri_tarikh_azarbeyijan_nicolas> (last accessed 16 October 2021).
27. Shahvar, *Baha'is of Iran*, p. 26.
28. Ibid. p. 21; italics added.
29. Ibid. p. 21.
30. Ibid. p. 7. On Jewish and Zoroastrian conversions see chapters by Mehrdad Amanat and Fereydun Vahman, and on the Baha'i schools by Moojan Momen, in Brookshaw and Fazel, *The Baha'is of Iran*. The volume as a whole is constructed around the argument that the Baha'i faith was a force for development in Iran. Shahvar, S., *The Forgotten Schools: The Baha'is and Modern Education in Iran, 1899–1934* (London: I. B. Tauris, 2009) is a detailed, in-depth study that views the Baha'i schools in similar terms.
31. Remey, M., 'Mashrak-el-Azkar: Descriptive of the Baha'i Temple', *Star of the West*, 6, 18 (1916), pp. 153–55; Dreyfus, H., 'Une Institution béhaie: Le Machreqou'l-Azkar d'Achqabad' (Paris: Ernest Leroux, 1909).
32. Lee, A., 'The Rise of the Baha'i Community of 'Ishqabad', in 'The Baha'i Faith in Russia: Two Early Instances', *Baha'i Studies* 5 (1979), pp. 1–14; Momen, M., 'The Baháí Community of Ashkhabad: Its Social Basis and Importance in Baha'i History', in S. Akiner (ed.), *Cultural Change and Continuity in Central Asia* (London:

Kegan Paul International and Central Asia Research Forum), pp. 278–305; Banani, A., 'Marxist Analysis of the Baha'i Faith' (Paper presented at the [Canadian] Association for Baha'i Studies Conference, October 1981.

33. Lee, 'Rise of Baha'i Community', p. 9.
34. Ibid. p. 13.
35. Momen, 'Baha'i Community of Ashkhabad', p. 290, quoting from Kolarz, W., *Religion in the Soviet Union* (New York: St Martin's Press, 1961).
36. Momen, 'Baha'i Community', p. 290.
37. Banani, 'Marxist Analysis'.
38. An article quoting official Baha'i sources does not mention any debates with Bolsheviks but reports instead 'vigorous dialogue' with local 'Muslim opponents' in an upbeat way: 'A report in *Star of the West* early in 1923 suggested "a large number of Russians, Tartars and other tribes" had become Baha'is and that meetings of up to 3,000 people were being held. A Baha'i newspaper *The Sun of the Orient* was being distributed widely … A report in April praised the public performances of Agha Mohammed Sabst and Agha Seyid Mehdi Gulpayagani, and indicated that separate meetings were being held for Muslim and Tartar inquirers, among whom there were "a number of firm believers"'. Hassel, 'Babi and Baha'i Religions in Russia'.

On the eventual fate of the Ashkhabad community and the Baha'is generally in Transcaspia and Turkestan during the early Soviet period see Ackerman, N. and G. Hassall, 'Russia and the Baha'i Faith: A Historic Connection', *Baha'i World, 1998–99* (Haifa: Baha'i World Centre, 2000), vol. 27, pp. 157–92. On Amin Banani's illustrious career see Ehsan Yarshater's obituary: 'Professor Amin Banani, 1926–2013: A Prominent Scholar of Iranian Studies', *Iranian Studies*, 47, 2 (2014), pp. 347–51.
39. For an overview of the transition and continuities of Russian orientalist views of Islam during the early Soviet period, see Bobrovnikov, V., 'The Contribution of Oriental Scholarship to the Soviet Anti-Islamic Discourse: From the Militant Godless to the Knowledge Society', in M. Kemper and S. Conermann (eds), *The Heritage of Soviet Oriental Studies* (London: Routledge, 2011), pp. 66–85.
40. Keddie, *Iran: Religion*, p. 48 n. 8. A generally applauded appraisal of Ivanov's thesis was included in an early career article by Momen, 'The Social Basis of the Babi Upheavals in Iran (1848–53): A Preliminary Analysis', *The International Journal of Middle East Studies*, 15, 2 (1983), pp. 157–83.
41. Osborn, L. 'The Baha'i Faith and the Western Esoteric Tradition' <https://bahai-library.com/osborn_bahai_western_esoteric> (last accessed 16 October 2021).
42. Ibid.

43. Khanum, *The Priceless Pearl*.
44. Balyuzi, H. M., *'Abdu'l-Baha* (Oxford: George Ronald, 1971), pp. 425–6 (p. 443).
45. Momen, *Babi and Baha'i Religions*, p. 343. Nonetheless, it is understandable that some Muslims and Iranian political radicals would have demurred at the symbolism of Abdul Baha readily acceding to the British presence in Palestine as conquerors of the last Islamic empire. See Dabashi's remarks about Abdul Baha's relations with the British in Dabashi, H., *Islamic Liberation Theology: Resisting the Empire* (London: Routledge, 2008), p. 83; historian Mohammad Reza Fashahi found the event 'deeply troubling to his anti-colonial sentiments', *Shi'ism*, p. 202.
46. Khanum, *Priceless Pearl*, p. 284.
47. Ibid. p. 270–1. Lord Lamington was an exception in not being a Zionist or Zionist sympathiser having changed his mind about the Jewish National Home as proposed in the Balfour Declaration. In a parliamentary debate on 27 March 1923 'he observed how on a recent visit to Palestine he had been forced to acknowledge "the absolute impossibility" of its effective realization', Mathew, W. M., 'Introduction', in J. M. N. Jeffries, *The Palestine Deception, 1915–1932: The McMahon–Hussein Correspondence, the Balfour Declaration, and the Jewish National Home*, ed. W. A. Mathews (USA: Institute of Palestine Studies, 2014), p. 13.
48. Ibid. p. 273.
49. According to journalist J. M. N. Jeffries writing in the *Daily Mail* on 20 January 1923, in an article headed 'Mr Bentwich: Key-Man of the Government', Bentwich was 'the type of enthusiast who has made Zionism, made it from the top downwards . . . the real motive power in the Government', Jeffries, *Palestine Deception*, pp. 93–4.
50. Khanum, *Priceless Pearl*, pp. 285, 289. No mention is made in Ruhiyyih Rabbani's biography of any visits of dignitaries from the indigenous communities in Palestine.
51. Curzon's biographer David Gilmore writes: 'Until his death in 1925 he regarded the Balfour Declaration as "the worst" of Britain's Middle East commitments and a "striking contradiction of our publicly declared principles". Shortly before he died, Curzon observed that all the prophecies he had made at the time of the Balfour Declaration had come true. Had he lived until 1948, they would have come truer still', Gilmore, 'The Unregarded Prophet: Lord Curzon and the Palestine Question', *Journal of Palestine Studies*, 25, 3 (1966), pp. 60–8 (p. 67).
52. Khanum, *Priceless Pearl*, p. 277.

53. Ibid. p. 283; italics added. Symes, who had an unalloyed orientalist view of Arabs and Jews, wrote in his memoir: 'Arabs often and obviously *couldn't*, the Jews for the most part wanted to, could, and *did*, manage their own affairs satisfactorily', Symes, G. S., *Tour of Duty* (London: Collins, 1946), p. 44, italics in original, cited in Longland, M. J., A Sacred Trust? British administration of the mandate for Palestine, 1920–1936 (PhD thesis, University of Nottingham, 2013).
54. Bentwich, N., *Mandate Memories* (London: The Hogarth Press, 1965), p. 40.
55. Samuel, E., *A Lifetime in Jerusalem: The Memoirs of the Second Viscount Samuel* (London: Vallentine, Mitchel, 1970), p. 132.
56. Sohrab, M. A., *'Abdul Baha in Egypt* (New York: J. H. Sears & Co, 1929), p. 14. Hasan Balyuzi of all people, who worked for years in the BBC Persian Service, would have been aware of Ruhi's work for the British. He calls Ruhi 'the capable and devoted son of a Baha'i of Tabriz . . . who had perforce abandoned home and taken the road to exile', Balyuzi, *'Abdul-Baha*, pp. 87, 527 n. 63. His silence on Ruhi's British connections is symptomatic of the record of elision and erasure in Baha'i publications on matters linking Baha'is with imperial politics.
57. Storrs, R., *Orientations* (London: Readers Union/Ivor Nicholson & Watson, 1939), pp. 157, 161. According to Storrs, Ruhi's father-in-law, another of his Baha'i employees, acted as a courier and spy in the Hijaz.
58. Kalisman, H. F., 'The Little Persian Agent in Palestine: Husayn Ruhi, British Intelligence, and World War I', *Jerusalem Quarterly*, 66, 16 (2016), pp. 65–74 (pp. 65–6).
59. Kalisman, 'Little Agent', pp. 66, 72.
60. Osborn, 'The Baha'i Faith'.
61. Ibid.
62. Weinstein, M., '[Abdul Baha] Declares Zionists must work with Other Races', *Star of the West*, 10 (1919), pp. 195–6 (p. 196).
63. According to the Palin Report of April 1920 on the Nabi Musa riots in Jerusalem in which Arabs killed four Jews and injured 200 others, until 'a very recent date the three sects, Moslem, Christian and Jews, lived together in complete amity . . . the native population, disappointed of their hopes, panic-stricken as to their future, exasperated beyond endurance by the aggressive attitude of the Zionists, and despairing of redress at the hands of the Administration . . . lies a ready prey for any form of agitation hostile to the British Government and the Jews', quoted in Mathew, 'Introduction', pp. 20–1. At this early point, however, the British were successful in their appeal to the Arab notables to return their people to order.

64. Weinstein, 'Declares', p. 196.
65. 'Abdul-Baha, *Some Answered Questions* (Wilmette, IL: Baha'i Publishing Trust, 1985), pp. 65–6. 'Indeed, perhaps taking note of this considerable immigration, Baha'u'llah announced "the imminent return of the Jews to the land of Israel" in a letter to French Jewish leader Edmund de Rothschild in 1891', Geller, R. S., 'The Baha'i minority in the State of Israel, 1948–1957', *Middle Eastern Studies*, 55, 3 (2019), pp. 403–18 (p. 406).
66. See Cohn-Sherbok, D., *The Politics of Apocalypse: The History and Influence of Christian Zionism* (Oxford: Oneworld, 2006).
67. Thompson, G., *The Legacy of Empire: Britain, Zionism and the Creation of Israel* (London: I. B. Tauris, 2019), p. 5. Ronen Shamir considers the situation of 'dual' colonisation in Palestine which consisted of a relationship between the 'two colonizing forces of Palestine' an ambiguous one. The Jews who were too Europeanised to be thought of as colonised had created an alliance with the colonial power to dispossess the Arabs, see Shamir, R., *Colonies of Law: Colonialism, Zionism, and Law in Early Mandate Palestine* (Cambridge: Cambridge University Press, 2000), pp. 18–20.
68. 'The architects of [Baha'i buildings on Mount Carmel], William Sutherland Maxwell and Charles Mason Remey, respectively, hailed from North America. Among other mainly North Americans, they would assume the highest possible positions of leadership in the Baha'i faith in Israel's post-independence era, second only to Baha'i leader Shoghi Rabbani himself. Their ascension to such heights reflected the decisive influence that powerful North Americans would have on the administration of the Baha'i faith from within the land of Israel during the state's founding decade', Geller, 'Baha'i minority', p. 403.
69. See Lambden, Some Aspects.
70. Osborn, 'The Baha'i Faith'.
71. Balyuzi, *'Abdul-Baha*, pp. 458–9, 461, 466–73.
72. Geller, 'Baha'i minority', p. 404.
73. Goren, T., 'Changes in the Design of the Urban Space of the Arabs of Haifa during the Israeli War of Independence', *Middle Eastern Studies*, 35, 1 (1999), pp. 115–33 (p. 116).
74. The celebrated Palestinian-Israeli novelist Emile Habibi, author of *The Secret Life of Saeed the Pessoptimist*, whose family were among the Arab Christians living in Haifa (at the heart of the Baha'i presence in the city) wrote of his mother Umma Wadie bemoaning the post-1948 absence of his two brothers: 'Umm Wadie was unable to overcome the shock of those days. By then her life was behind her, and

most of her sons and grandchildren were scattered in the diaspora . . . it became her custom to go secretly to a corner of Abbas Garden near our house. She would lean against a stone shaded by an olive tree and bemoan her destiny – lonely and separated from children, especially her youngest son Naim. "Naim, where are you now? What has happened to you without me?" Little did I know of her newly acquired habit until one day I overheard my two daughters playing at being Granny Umm Wadie bemoaning "O Naim'", Habibi, E.,'Haifa: Wadi Al-Nisnass and Abbas Street by Emile Habibi', *Al-Ahram Weekly*, 16 November 2000.

75. Goren, 'Changes', p. 123.
76. Geller, 'Baha'i minority', pp. 407, 409, 404.
77. As Denis MacEoin has pointed out, although Shoghi Effendi does not relish the humiliation of Jewish (as he does Christian and Muslim) organisations in the twentieth century and is not anti-Semitic, in Baha'i literature there is barely a reference to the Shoah and its theological significance, MacEoin, 'Uncertainties', p. 205 n. 11.
78. Massad, J., *The Persistance of the Palestinian Question: Essays on Zionism and the Palesinians* (London: Routledge, 2006), p. 19. Massad argues that Zionists consciously and astutely dropped 'colonisation' to denote what they were doing on the land of Palestine in exchange for 'either Zionist "anti-colonial resistance" or the Zionist "struggle for independence"'. Ibid. p.19.
79. Effendi, *God Passes By*, p. iv.
80. The 'Edict of Toleration (1844)' is something of a Baha'i myth and has spawned its own Wikipedia entry: <https://en.wikipedia.org/wiki/Edict_of_Toleration_(1844)> (last accessed 16 October 2021). Townshend also influenced the Orientalist presentation of Qajar Persia and Shi'ism that appears in the introduction to *Dawn-Breakers* (see Chapter 5).
81. Cohn-Sherbok, *Politics*, pp. 27–8.
82. Laqueur, W., The *History of Zionism*, 3rd edn (London: TaurisParke: 2003), p. 46.
83. Ibid.; italics added.
84. The period encompassed by Daniel's phrase 'the abomination of desolation' is made to end in 1844 CE/1260 AH and is computed as parallel to the close of 'the dispensation of Muhammad'. This date punctuates the punishment of the Jews for their recalcitrance during the Christian and Islamic dispensations and allows for the beginning of the Jews' return. In chapter twelve of the Apocalypse of St John the Divine, 'the child . . . which was born of the woman, was Mohammed'. Ali Muhammad was transformed into John the Baptist on the analogy of, forerunner (Bab), messiah (Baha'ullah); 'he spoke of himself as merely a herald of

another who was to follow him, who was to be Baha Ullah', Brittingham, I. D., *The Revelation of Baha-ullah in a Sequence of Four Lessons* (Chicago: Bahai Publishing Society, 1902), pp. 28–9. See also Ford, M. H., *Oriental Rose or The Teachings of Abdul Baha Which Trace The Chart of 'The Shining Path'* (Chicago: Bahai Publishing Society: 1910), pp. 7, 137–40; Abdul Baha, *Some Answered Questions*, pp. 67–72.

85. MacEoin, *Messiah of Shiraz*, p. 516 n. 55. Sears, W., *Thief in the Night: The Strange Case of the Missing Millennium* (Oxford: George Ronald, 1961) contains 'the edict of toleration' shibboleth (pp. 119, 135) and uses the phrase 'Baha'u'llah came to Israel' (pp. 143, 147) anachronistically. It refers to an article in *The Reconstructionist* (Reconstructionist Rabbinical College, Wyncote, PA) which states: 'While still in his Turkish jail in Acre, more than 75 years ago, Baha'u'llah wrote: "The outcasts of Israel shall gather and create a state that will become the envy and admiration of both their friends and their enemies, and outwardly and spiritually they will attain to such glory that their 2,000 years of abasement will be forgotten"'. A resume of these ideas is found in the spoof videofilm *Bahais in My Backyard* in which Baha'i World Centre Deputy Secretary-General Murray Smith tells the interviewer that the Israeli community has been chosen for the 'special bounty' of 'defending us', i.e., Baha'is. The assumption here is that since Baha'is do not bear arms, ergo, the IDF has been chosen by God to defend them. Baquia Baquia, *Bahais in My Backyard* <https://vimeo.com/22467795> (last accessed 16 October 2021).
86. Khanum, *Priceless Pearl*, p. 189.
87. Jeffries, *Palestine Deception*, p. 26; original italics.
88. Friedmann, *Prophecy Continuous*, p. 170.
89. Ahmad, G., *Jesus in India: Jesus' Deliverance from the Cross and Journey to India* (Qadian: Islam International Publications, 2016), p. 7.
90. Khan, *From Sufism*, p. 16.
91. Ibid. pp. 19–20.
92. Nasr, S. V. R., *Mawdudi and the Making of Islamic Revivalism* (New York: Oxford University Press, 1996), pp. 21, 43–4; Maududi, *Qadiani Problem*.
93. '[I]t is the duty of every Ahmadi that he should pray under the leadership of Ahmadi imams only ... it has been prohibited that Ahmadis should give their daughters in marriage to non Ahmadis ... Ahmadis should not attend the funeral service of non-Ahmadis, for it would amount to interceding for a man who has proved himself an enemy by denying and opposing the Promised Messiah', Lavan, *Ahmadiya Movement*, p. 114.

94. Khan, *From Sufism*, p. 78.
95. Friedmann balances this with similar measures adopted by the Muslim majority in (at that time) India against Ahmadis, apportioning the blame to both sides: 'When the Ahmadiyya established its own organizational structure and responded to the *takfir* of the Sunni 'ulama with a *tafkir* of its own, the two sides reached on their collision course a point of no return. The Ahmadiyya was inexorably driven – by itself and by its rivals – into a position of total isolation. It is, indeed, a tragedy of Ahmadi history that this should have happened to a movement which has always defended Islam against its adversaries and which has done for the propagation of the faith all over the globe more than any other modern Muslim group. Despite all its services to Islam, the Ahmadiyya now stands alone against the rest of the Muslim world', Friedmann, *Prophecy Continuous*, p. 183.
96. Lathan, A., 'The Relativity of Categorizing in the Context of the Ahmadiyya', *Die Welt des Islams*, 48, 3 (2008), pp. 372–93 (pp. 386–7).
97. Sevea, T., 'Islamist Questioning and [C]olonialism: Towards an Understanding of the Islamist Oeuvre', *Third World Quarterly*, 28, 7 (2007), pp. 1375–1400 (pp. 1382, 1381).
98. Sevea, 'Islamist questioning', pp. 1383, 1388–9.
99. Iqbal, M., 'Letter to Nehru' <https://wiki.qern.org/mirza-ghulam-ahmad/contemporaries/allama-muhammad-iqbal/letter-to-nehru> (last accessed 16 October 2021).

Chapter 7

1. Landau, R., *Search for Tomorrow: The Things which are and the Things which shall be Hereafter* (London: Nicholson and Watson, 1938), p. 245.
2. Burke, 'Orientalism and World History', pp. 489–507 (p. 490); italics added.
3. Said, *Orientalism*, p. 96.
4. Bhabha, H., *The Location of Culture* (London: Routledge, 1994); Young, *Colonial Desire*; Young, R. C., *White Mythologies: Writing History and the West* (London: Routledge, 1990).
5. Al-'Azm, S. J., 'Orientalism and Orientalism in Reverse', *Khamsin*, 8 (191), pp. 5–26; repr. Macfie, A. L., *Orientalism: A Reader* (Edinburgh: Edinburgh University Press, 2000), pp. 218–38 (p. 230).
6. Burke, 'Orientalism and World History', p. 495.
7. Deringil, S., '"They Live in a State of Nomadism and Savagery": The Late Ottoman Empire and the Post Colonial Debate', *Comparative Studies in Society and History*, 45, 2 (2003), pp. 311–42 (pp. 312–3).

8. Makdisi, U., 'Ottoman Orientalism', *American Historical Review*, 107, 3 (2002), pp. 768–96 (p. 772).
9. Tuçay, M., 'Kemalism', *The Oxford Encyclopedia of the Islamic World* <http://www.oxfordislamicstudies.com/article/opr/t236/e0440> (last accessed 19 October 2021).
10. Szurek, E., '"Go West": Variations on Kemalist Orientalism', in F. Pouillion and J.-C. Vatin (eds), *After Orientalism: Critical Perspectives on Western Agency and Eastern Re-appropriations* (Leiden: Brill, 2015), pp. 103–21 (pp. 112–13).
11. Boroujerdi, M., *Iranian Intellectuals and the West: The Tormented Triumph of Nativism* (Syracuse: University of Syracuse Press, 1996), p. 27.
12. Ibid. pp. 52–3, 141, 143.
13. Vahdat, F., *God and the Juggernaut: Iran's Intellectual Encounter with Modernity* (New York: University of Syracuse Press, 2002).
14. Dabashi, H., *Post-Orientalism Knowledge & Power in a Time of Terror* (New York: New Brunswick, 2009/15), pp. viii–xix; Dabashi, H., *Islamic Liberation*, pp. 17–18.
15. Bayat, M., 'Aqa Khan Kermani', *Encylopaedia Iranica*; Vahdat, *God and the Juggernaut*, p. 40.
16. Bayat, M., 'Mirza Aqa Khan Kirmani: A Nineteenth Century Persian Nationalist, *Middle Eastern Studies*', 10, 1 (1974), pp. 36–59 (p. 36).
17. Tavakoli-Targhi, M., *Refashioning Iran: Orientalism, Occidentalism and Historiography* (Basingstoke: Palgrave, 2001), p. 102.
18. Tavakoli-Targhi, *Refashioning Iran*, p. 99.
19. Ibid. p. 102.
20. Zia-Ebrahimi, *Emergence of Iranian Nationalism*, p. 128.
21. Ibid. p. 115.
22. Ibid. p 92. Kermani writes in *Sa Maktub*: 'One could . . . detect from among a crowd of Persians, Greeks, English, Ethiopians, Sudanese and Arabs who is civilized and who is primitive by their physical features such as the shape of the nose, the colour of the skin, the blood', Bayat, 'Persian Nationalist', p. 45. Here Kermani implies that the first three nationalities are civilised whereas the last three are not. This might be compared with Gobineau's placing of eastern races into a hierarchy in *Trois Ans en Asie*, ch. 3.
23. This statement about the Arab conquest of Iran is precisely the same point made by Gobineau in *Mémoire* (see Chapter 3).
24. Bayat, 'Persian Nationalist', p. 39.
25. 'When Aqa Khan Kermani came to Acre in the late 1880s to investigate the claims of the Baha'is, Bahaullah had dismissed him as a schemer', Cole, 'Iranian Millenarianism', p. 20.

26. Cole, J. R. I., 'Marking Boundaries, Marking Time: The Iranian Past and the Construction of the Self by Qajar Thinkers', *Iranian Studies*, 29, 1–2 (1996), pp. 35–56 (p. 43); 'Abdul-Baha, *Mysterious Forces of Civilization*, trans. J. Dawud (Chicago: Bahai Publishing Society, 1918); 'Abdul-Baha, *Secret of Divine Civilization*, trans. M. Gail (Wilmette: Baha'i Publishing Trust, 1957).
27. Cole, 'Marking Boundaries', p. 44–5.
28. Millionaire widow of George Hearst, Phoebe became a Baha'i after meeting Edward and Lua Getsinger. From a well-known liberal artistic family established in Paris Laura Clifford Barney became a Baha'i there around 1900, introduced by May Bolles who later married architect W. Sutherland Maxwell. The latter were the parents of Mary, later Ruhiyyih Khanum – Smith, *Bahai Encyclopedia*, pp. 180, 126.
29. Rosenberg, E. J., 'Baha'ism: Its Ethical and Social Teachings', *Transactions of the Third International Congress for the History of Religions* (Oxford: Clarendon Press, 1908), vol. 1, pp. 321–5 (p. 321).
30. McNamara, Religious Reformers, pp. 62–5.
31. Abdo, Relevance, p. 90.
32. Dreyfus, H., 'Une Institution béhaie', p. 6.
33. Dreyfus, H., *The Universal Religion: Bahaism* (London: Cope and Fenwick, 1909), p. 43.
34. Remey, M., *The Bahai Movement: A Series of Nineteen Papers* (Washington, DC: J. D. Milans, 1912), p. 38.
35. Sprague, S., *A Year with the Bahais in India and Burma* (London: The Priory Press, 1908), p. 53.
36. Remey, M., *Observations of a Bahai Traveler* (Washington, DC: J. D. Milans, 1914), pp. 13–14.
37. Ibid. p. 27.
38. Ibid. p. 11.
39. 'Abdu'l-Baha, *Promulgation*, p. 51.
40. Remey, M., *The Bahai Movement*, pp. 76–7.
41. Dreyfus, *Universal Religion*, pp. 33–4, 39, 46.
42. 'Holley first encountered the Baha'i teachings in 1909 en route to Europe. He later established himself in New York, and in 1923 was elected to the American national spiritual Assembly, serving as its secretary almost continuously from 1924 to 1953', Smith, *Baha'i Encyclopedia*, p. 182.
43. Holley, H., *Bahai: The Spirit of the Age* (New York: Brentanos, 1921), pp. 37–8.
44. Holley, H., 'Religion and World Order', *The Baha'i World, 1934–1936* (Wilmette, IL: Baha'i Publishing Trust, 1937), vol. 5, pp. 571–9 (p. 575). Overall, Holley's

writing of this period is typical of Western Baha'i enhanced imbrication in nineteenth/early twentieth-century historicism, emphasising the notion that 'history develops according to predetermined laws towards a particular end', Berger, S., 'Stefan Berger responds to Ulrich Muhlack', *Bulletin of the German Historical Institute London*, 23, 1(2001), pp. 21–33 (28, note).
45. 'Abdul-Baha, *Promulgation*, pp. 45, 84.
46. Parekh, B. 'The West and Its Others', in K. Ansell-Pearson, B. Parry and J. Squires (eds), *Cultural Readings of Imperialism – Edward Said and the Gravity of History* (London: Lawrence Wishart), pp. 179–93 (p. 173).
47. Ibid. p. 191.
48. Ibid. pp. 184–5.
49. Armstrong-Ingram, R. J., 'American Baha'i Women and the Education of Girls in Tehran, 1909–1934', in P. Smith (ed.), *Studies in Babi and Baha'i History: In Iran* (Los Angeles: Kalimat Press, 1986), vol. 3, pp. 181–210. However, Rostam-Kolayi argues the schools were self-generated and led by Iranian Baha'is rather than Americans, Rostam-Kolayi, J., 'The Tarbiyat Girls school of Iran, Iranian and American Baha'i Contributions to Education', *Middle East Critique*, 22, 1 (2013), pp. 77–93.
50. Remey, *Observations*, pp. 96–7, 123–4.
51. Holley, H., 'Survey of Current Activities in the East and West', *Baha'i World, 1926–28* (Wilmette, IL: Baha'i Publishing Trust, 1928), vol. 2, pp. 19–45 (p. 34).
52. Holley, H., 'Survey of Current Baha'i Activities in the East and West', *Baha'i World, 1928–30* (Wilmette, IL: Baha'i Publish Trust, 1930), vol. 3, pp. 28–61 (p. 34).
53. Holley, H., 'Survey of Current Baha'i Activities in the East and West', *Baha'i World, 1932–34* (Wilmette, IL: Baha'i Publishing Trust, 1936), vol. 5, pp. 18–136 (p. 23).
54. Holley, H., Letter, *Baha'i World, 1926–1928*, vol. 2, pp. 287–94 (p. 293); italics added.
55. See Ashcroft, B., G. Griffiths, and H. Tiffin, *The Empire Writes Back: Theory and Practice in Post-Colonial Literatures* (London: Routledge, 1989), pp. 38–44.
56. Dabashi, H., *Brown Skin, White Masks* (London: Pluto, 2011), p. 20; Fanon, F., *Black Skin, White Masks* (London: Pluto, 1986).
57. Basu, D. K., 'Chaudhuri, Nirad C.' <https://www.encyclopedia.com/international/encyclopedias-almanacs-transcripts-and-maps/chaudhuri-nirad-c> (last accessed 19 October 2021).
58. Thieme, J., *A Critical view of V S Naipaul's* The Mimic Men (London: Collins/British Council, 1985), p. 9; Naipaul, V. S., *The Mimic Men* (Penguin, 1969), p. 32.
59. Gorra, M., *After Empire: Scott, Naipaul, Rushdie* (Chicago: University of Chicago Press, 1997), p. 70.

60. Naipaul, *Mimic Men*, p. 11. 'Although Naipaul has one of the clearest visions of the nexus of power operating in the imperial-colonial world, he is paradoxically drawn to that centre even though he sees it contructing the "periphery" as an area of nothingness. Yet he is simultaneously able to see that the "reality", the "truth", and "order" of the centre is an illusion', Ashcroft, *Empire*, p. 90.
61. Khanum, *Priceless Pearl*, pp. 12–13. See also Smith, *Bahai Encyclopedia*, pp. 315–18.
62. Khanum, *Priceless Pearl*, pp. 12–13.
63. Ibid. p. 32.
64. Armstrong-Ingram, R. J., 'The Use of Generative Imagery in *Shoghi Effendi's The Dispensation of Baha'u'llah*', *Occasional Papers in Shaykhi, Babi and Baha'i Studies*, 2, 3 (March 1998). In her review of a book about Shoghi Effendi's Oxford reading, Lil Osborn comments: 'In one of the few passages of analysis, Khadem speculates on the difficulties Shoghi Effendi would have faced fitting in with the English upper class ethos of Oxford. This indeed must have puzzled him as none of the British Baha'is were Oxonians and only [J. E.] Esslemont a university graduate. It is a pity that so few of these reminiscences are reproduced or discussed', Osborn, L., 'Review of R. Khadem, *Shoghi Effendi in Oxford* and D. Marcus, *Her Eternal Crown: Queen Marie of Romania and the Baha'i Faith*', *Baha'i Studies Review*, 10 (2001), pp. 163–5 <https://bahai-library.com/abdo_khadem_Marcus_reviews> (last accessed 19 October 2021).
65. The family and other excommunicated Persian Baha'is would many of them leave during the Arab–Israeli war pursuant to the declaration of the state of Israel. Afterwards, against fierce opposition from the Baha'i World Centre, they were successful in returning. Geller, 'Baha'i minority', p. 404.
66. MacEoin, *Messiah*, p. 531. The section, pp. 529–36, constitutes a definitive resume of Shoghi Effendi's orientalism, with the emphasis falling on his employment of second-hand orientalist sources.
67. Dirlik, 'Chinese History', p. 100.
68. Ibid. pp. 100–3.
69. Ibid. pp. 103–4, 106.
70. Ibid. pp. 112–13. Pratt, M. L., *Imperial Eyes: Travel Writing and Transculturation* (London: Routledge, 1994).
71. Deringil, 'They Live', p. 311.
72. Effendi, S., *Promised Day*, p. 97.
73. Ibid. p. 97.
74. Eldem, E., *Consuming the Orient* (Istanbul: Ottoman Bank Archives and Research Centre, 2007), pp. 221–2.

75. See Eldem, E., 'The Ottoman Empire and Orientalism: An Awkward Relationship', in F. Pouillion and J.-C. Vatin (eds), *After Orientalism: Critical Perspectives on Western Agency and Eastern Re-appropriations* (Leiden: Brill, 2015), pp. 89–102.
76. Root, M., 'Seeing Adrianople with New York Eyes', *The Baha'i Magazine*, 25, 3 (1934), pp. 74–7 (p. 76).
77. Ibid. p. 77; original italics; *Baha'i World* (1930–2), vol. 4, p. 438.
78. Higgins, P. J., 'Minority–State Relations in Contemporary Iran', *Iranian Studies*, 17, 1 (1984), pp. 33–71 (pp. 53–4).
79. Amanat, A., 'Babis and Baha'is as Agents of Iranian Modernity' (Paper presented at Baha'i Studies Symposium, Kellogg College, Oxford, 30 June 2018).
80. Chamankhah, L., 'A Minority within a Majority: The Baha'i Principle of Non-Interference in Politics is Revisited', *Journal of South Asian and Middle Eastern Studies*, 38, 1 (2014), pp. 22–40 (pp. 38–9). Not having legal recognition as a religious minority afforded opportunities to hold posts in the government otherwise unavailable to the other recognised minorities. According to Chamankhah this led in the 1960s and 1970s to prosperous Baha'is ignoring the injunctions of the Universal House of Justice, it is implied, against involvement with the regime ('the two principles of "non-interference in politics" and "strict obedience from government" seemed to be burdensome' to them).
81. [Ransom-Kehler, K.], 'In Memoriam I. The Unity of East and West American Baha'i Sacrifices Her Life in Service to Persian Believers. Mrs. Keith Ransom-Kehler's mission', *Baha'i World, 1934–36* (1937), vol. 6, pp. 389–431.
82. Ibid. p. 394.
83. Ibid. p. 401.
84. Ibid.
85. Ibid. p. 403. Leila Chamankhah notes 'the constitution [of 1906], had not used the term "religious minorities"'. The first article of the amendment of the constitution [1907] declared the official religion of Iran to be Jafari Shi'ism, though the constitution was not 'religion-oriented . . . but rather inclined to be indifferent toward religion'. However the 1909 New Electoral Law, and later the Civil Code of the Pahlavi state, recognised the Zoroastrian, Jewish and Christian communities and 'guaranteed limited autonomy and freedom with respect to personal status and family law', but excluded any member of the designated minorities from ministerial office, Chamankhah, p. 37 n. 59. See also Browne, E. G., 'The Bases of the Persian Constitution', Appendix A, *The Persian Revolution 1905–1909*, New Edition, ed. A. Amanat (Washington, DC: Mage, 1995), pp. 353–400.

86. In Memoriam', pp. 404–5.
87. MacEoin, D., 'The Baha'is of Iran: The Roots of Controversy', *British Society of Middle Eastern Studies*, 14, 1 (1988), pp. 75–83 (p. 79).
88. Effendi, S., *Baha'i News Letter*, Special Issue, January 1929, p. 1; quoted in Rostam-Kolayi, 'The Tarbiyat Girls school', p. 90.
89. Zia-Ibrahimi, R., 'Self-Orientalization and Dislocation: The Uses and Abuses of the "Aryan" Discourse in Iran', *Iranian Studies*, 44, 4 (2011), pp. 445–72 (p. 465).
90. Katouzian, H., 'Riza Shah's Political Legitimacy and Social Base, 1921–1941', in S. Cronin (ed.), *The Making of Modern Iran: State and Society under Riza Shah, 1921–1941* (London: Routledge, 2003), pp. 15–37 (pp. 27–8).
91. Although Forughi was a survivor from the *ancien regime* he was also trusted by Reza Shah, but his 'downfall and disgrace' came about on account of his relative's involvement in a religious protest which the Shah ordered to be 'ruthlessly suppressed' since it was against imposition of the 'European ["Pahlavi"] bowler hat', a measure Katouzian labels one of 'pseudo-modernism', Katouzian, H., *State and Society in Iran: The Eclipse of the Qajars and the Emergence of the Pahlavis* (London: I. B. Tauris, 2006), pp. 314–15. Nevertheless, Forughi would return as Reza Shah's last prime minister on the eve of his deposition in 1941. For a summary of Forughi's substantial cultural achievements, see Amanat, *Iran*, pp. 475–6.
92. Zirinsky, M., 'Riza Shah's Abrogation of Capitulations, 1927–1928', in Cronin, *Making of Modern Iran*, pp. 84–102 (p. 86).
93. Rostam-Kolayi, 'The Tarbiyat Girls School', pp. 90–1.
94. According to Amanat, however, 'the Baha'i schools were the first victims of the government's nationalization of education. Their closure . . . at least in part was tainted with growing anti-Baha'i propaganda', *Iran*, p. 468.
95. Fry, P., Introduction to the Theory of Literature, Lecture 18: The Political Unconscious, Yale University, 2020 <https://oyc.yale.edu/english/engl-300/lecture-18> (last accessed 19 October 2021). Robert Young sums up a postcolonial understanding of the period in question as follows: 'After the Great War, the two contiguous empires of Austria-Hungary and Turkey were broken up, and Germany was deprived of its overseas colonies. Germany subsequently tried to turn Europe into its colonial empire in an enormous act of migrationist colonialism . . . [I]t was the great Martiniquan writer . . . Aimé Césaire who first pointed out that fascism was a form of colonialism brought home to Europe', Young, R. J. C., *Postcolonialism: An Historical Introduction* (Oxford: Blackwell, 2001), p. 2. The phrase 'a dying colonialism' was chosen as the English title of Frantz Fanon's *L'An Cinq, de la Révolution Algérienne*; see Fanon, F., *A Dying Colonialism*, trans. H. Chevalier (New York: Grove Press, 1965).

96. Effendi, S., *The Promised Day is Come* (Wilmette, IL: Baha'i Publishing Trust, 1967); Effendi, S., *The World Order of Baha'u'llah* (Wilmette, IL: Baha'i Publishing Trust, 1938).
97. 'Shoghi Effendi defined his own infallibility as being confined to the interpretation and application of scripture and to the protection of the Baha'i Faith. It did not extend to economics, science or technical matters', Smith, *Baha'i Encyclopedia*, p. 197.
98. Effendi, *World Order*, p. 202.
99. Effendi, *Promised Day*, p. 117. Both Carlyle and Shoghi Effendi, it should be pointed out, considered humanity's core problem rested in its turning away from God. *Promised Day* is an eschatological text which explains political and social phenomena as symptoms of a failing world for which Baha'ullah as the promised one has provided the remedy. The apocalypse of destruction set in train is the consequence of secular and religious leaders failing to recognise him. Although it brings in secularisation and the 'three false gods' as manifestations of social evils, *Promised Day* makes no attempt, unlike (as we shall see) Ahmadi texts, to account for symptoms of modern conflict in terms of broader forces such as capitalism, imperialism and social movements that premote or contest them. In Carlyle's writings atheism and mammonism, manifesting as callous laissez-faire in social relations and economic greed, are part of a general denial of God's laws. 'Carlyle must inevitably appear [to proponents of atheistic modernity] as anti-modern . . . By modernism here I mean the spirit of substituting man for God . . .', Tennyson, G. B., *Carlyle and the Modern World*, Occasional Paper, 4 (Edinburgh: Carlyle Society, 1971), p. 26 (the published version of a lecture delivered to the Carlyle Society, Edinburgh, 6 March 1971). I think Shoghi Effendi's writings also contain a similar element of anti-modernism.
100. Carlyle, T., *Latter-Day Pamphlets* (London: Chapman and Hall, [1850] 1871), p. 265.
101. Effendi, *Promised Day*, p. 127.
102. Mufti, *Forget English*, p. 35.
103. *Promised Day*, pp. 95–6.
104. MacEoin, *Messiah of Shiraz*, p. 532.
105. Porter, A., *Religion versus Empire? British Protestant Missionaries and Overseas Expansion, 1700–1914* (Manchester: Manchester University Press, 2004), p. 43.
106. Majeed, J., 'Introduction' in Iqbal, M., *Reconstruction of Religious Thought in Islam* (Stanford, CA: Stanford University Press, 2013), p. xiii.
107. Devji, F., 'Muslim Universality', *Postcolonial Studies*, 14, 2 (2011), pp. 231–41 (p. 232).

108. Ibid. p. 232.
109. Cole, J. R. I., 'Globalization and Religion in the Thought of 'Abdu'l-Baha', in Warburg, *Bahai and Globalization*, pp. 55–76 (p. 58).
110. 'God has Himself provided the means for fulfilling His prophecy that the message of the Messiah will spread in the world like lightening [sic] and will encompass all four corners of the earth like the light from a tower. The railways, telegraph, steamships, excellent postal services, easy modes of travel and tourism and other such means have been established to fulfill the prophecy that the message of the Messiah will illuminate every corner like lightening [sic]', Ahmad, G., *British Government*, p. 18.
111. Warmind, 'Baha'i and Ahmadiyya', p. 142.
112. Ibid. p. 142.
113. Evans, *Caliph's Gaze*, pp. 52, 42. 'The final stage in the reification of Islam, but arguably also in its rationalisation, was its conceptualisation as a system. This was the particular achievement of Mawdudi, growing out of his concern to establish an Islamic vision of life to set against that of the West, and which was to be protected against the West. He describes Islam as a *nizam*, a system, which was comprehensive, complete and covered all aspects of human existence', Robinson, 'Islamic Reform', p. 276.
114. Effendi, S., *The Dispensation of Baha'u'llah* (London: Baha'i Publishing Trust, 1947), p. 55.
115. Ahmad, M. B. M., *The New World Order of Islam* (Qadian: International Publications, 2017), pp. ix, xiv. Not to be outdone in 1944 there issued from the pen of Lahori chief Maulana Muhammad Ali, *The New World Order* (Lahore: Ahmadi Anjuman Isha'at Islam), a document which rather than proffering new organisational forms revisits the established Islamic economic and social teachings which are considered the middle way between Bolshevism and capitalism, and 'the only stable World order', p. 42. Also included are essays on gender relations and the constitution of the state with recapitulations of the perfect government of Medina under the Prophet and the peaceful meaning of jihad.
116. Effendi, *Dispensation*, p. 64.
117. Evans, *Caliph's Gaze*, p. 38.
118. Ahmad, M. B. M., *A Present to His Royal Highness the Prince of Wales from the Ahmadiyya Community* (Tilford, Surrey: Islamic International Publications, [1922], 2015), p. ii.
119. For example, see on p. 322 of *Baha'i World*, vol. 5, the daunting list of V.I.P.s who had referred to the Baha'i faith, starting alphabetically with Archduchess

Anton of Austria and ending with Sir Francis Younghusband. A full page portrait of Queen Mary of Romania appears on the fifth page of the volume.
120. Reference is made to the disturbances in Punjab of the previous year (1921), 'the period when Martial Law was in force . . . and the situation was fraught with danger, so much so that in certain cases even Government officials were compelled to leave their posts and seek safety elsewhere, . . . [T]he members of this Community not only themselves continued loyal, but also induced a large number of other people to do the same. At some places the rioters inflicted loss and injuries on the members of the Community, but they could not shake them from their loyalty', *Present to His Royal Highness*, p. 9.
121. Ibid. p. 54.
122. Ibid. p. 63.
123. See MacEoin, 'Baha'ism: Some Uncertainties', p. 306. Todd Lawson considers Baha'is not to be Muslims yet still a community of the Quran and points out the extent to which the Bab and Baha'ullah addressed the Quran in their commentaries, Lawson, T., 'Baha'i Religious History', *Journal of Religious History*, 36, 4 (2012), pp. 463–70.

Chapter 8

1. Purohit, T., 'Muhammad Iqbal on Muslim Orthodoxy and Transgression: A Response to Nehru', *ReOrient*, 1, 1 (2015), pp. 78–92 (p. 80).
2. Iqbal, M., *Islam and Ahmadism* (Lahore: Ashraf Printing Press, 1980), p. 60.
3. Ibid. p. 63.
4. Ibid. p. 34.
5. Iqbal, *Reconstruction of Religious Thought in Islam*, ed. M. Saeed Sheikh (Lahore: Institute of Islamic Culture, 2003), pp. 114–15.
6. Iqbal, *Islam and Ahmadism*, p. 60 and Appendix 1 'Qadianis and Orthodox Muslims', p. 66.
7. Devji, 'Islamic Universalism', p. 241.
8. Purohit, 'Muhammad Iqbal', p. 87. It is significant that in *Reconstruction* Iqbal should have been contesting Oswald Spengler's application of the term 'Magian' to Islam, because although he admitted a 'Magian crust has grown over Islam' his aim was to emancipate the spirit of Islam from its 'Magian overlayings', in practice to revive Islam's Arab roots in India. Spengler's aim was orientalist in so far as he wished to separate from modern, anti-classical Europe a putative eastern culture of successive religions infiltrated by Zoroastrian eschatology and codification of primeval forms of good and evil. Embedded within the debate

was the older orientalist reading of Magianism fathered by Gobineau, to which Iqbal gravitates, in which Islam was alien but had been absorbed into a Magian form as Persian Shi'ism.

9. Maududi, *Qadiani Problem*, pp. 21–2.
10. Burhani, A. N., 'Hating the Ahmadiyya: The Place of "Heretics" in Contemporary Indonesian Muslim Society', *Contemporary Islam*, 8 (2014), pp. 133–52 (pp. 135, 138, 147).
11. Effendi, S., *Baha'i World*, vol. 2 (1928), pp. 31–2; Pink, J., 'Deriding Revealed Religions? Baha'is in Egypt', *ISIM Newsletter*, 10, 2 (2002), p. 30.
12. Human Rights Watch, *Prohibited Identities*, 11 November 2007 <https://www.hrw.org/node/255298> (last accessed 20 October 2021).
13. Mahmood, S., *Religious Difference in a Secular Age: A Minority Report* (Princeton, NJ: Princeton University Press, 2016), pp. 27, 155.
14. Mahmood, *Religious Difference*, p. 156.
15. Ibid. p. 165.
16. Ibid. p. 165.
17. Ibid. p. 166.
18. Ibid. p. 64.
19. Ibid. p. 169. Mahmood's discussion of the Baha'i case is set against the broader context of the Coptic Christians and to a much smaller degree, the Jewish community where '[d]espite the citizen's diverse [religious] allegiances, all Egyptians were expected to recognize Islam as essential to the formation of the nation in a way that other religions were not'. In the larger context, the dilemma for the Copts, though not for the Jews who left Egypt in the 1940s, was that the promise of equal citizenship was predicated upon [the European model of] the privatization and individualization of . . . religious life', Ibid. p. 12.
20. Ibid. p. 157, 163; italics added.
21. Ibid. p. 64.
22. Aydin, *Idea of the Muslim World*, p. 1, 97. He adds the caveat: 'Today the very people who claim to speak on behalf of all Muslims target other Muslims as their enemies; Muslim societies are more divided than ever, riven by civil wars and protracted conflicts across borders'.
23. Ibid, p. 130; original italics.
24. Mamdani, M., *Good Muslim – Bad Muslim: America, the Cold War, and the Roots of Terror* (New York: Three Leaves Press, Doubleday, 2004).
25. Howe, S., 'Imperial Histories, Postcolonial Theories', in G. Huggan (ed.), *The Oxford Handbook of Postcolonial Studies* (Oxford: Oxford University Press, 2011), pp. 162–8 (p. 166).

26. Tavakoli-Targhi, M., 'Anti-Bahaism and Islamism in Iran', in D. P. Brookshaw and S. B. Fazel (eds), *The Baha'is of Iran: Socio-Historical Studies* (London: Routledge, 2008), pp. 200–31 (p. 200).
27. Khan, *From Sufism*, p. 155.
28. Eldem, 'Ottoman Empire', p. 90.
29. Aydin, *Idea of the Muslim World*, pp. 3, 136.
30. Ibid. p. 6.
31. Mufti, *Forget English*, p. 47.
32. Aydin, *Idea of the Muslim World*, p. 136.
33. Walter, *Ahmadiya Movement*, p. 133. The three factors Walter mentions were first mooted by J. N. Farquhar in *Modern Religious Movements in India* (1915).
34. Maududi, *Qadiani Problem*, pp. 29–30.
35. Several brief passages in Baha'ullah's writings condemn the British bombardment and occupation of Alexandria in 1882 and Western conquest in the Middle East in general. J. R. I. Cole quotes from these to support his progressive interpretation of Baha'ullah as a Middle-Eastern proponent of internationalism. A careful reading of Baha'ullah's statements leads me to conclude that while there was condemnation of the Europeans' cunning, 'greed and avarice', this did not amount to a systematic 'strong denunciation of European imperialism' as Cole claims. On the contrary, as he says, the import of one remark was that Muslims 'were undergoing these tribulations . . . because they have rejected God's law as revealed by Baha'u'llah', Cole, *Modernity and the Millennium*, pp. 133–4. The same topic has recently (July 2020) been reactivated by Nader Saiedi, in recognition, it seems, of the need to show some sort of Baha'i awareness of the historical impact of Western imperialism upon the world. Like Cole, he interprets remarks of a general moral tenor criticising conquest, which he says demonstrate Baha'ullah's superiority to Muslims who oppressed Baha'is while he 'became encompassed with grief because the Muslims in Egypt were so wronged by a European colonial power', Saiedi, N., 'The Baha'i Critique of European Colonialism and Antisemitism', 29 July 2020 <https://bahaiteachings.org/bahai-critique-european-colonialism-antisemitism> (last accessed 20 October 2021).
36. Mirsepassi, *Intellectual Discourse*, pp. 31–2; Dabashi, *Islamic Liberation*, p. 34.
37. One enthusiastic Baha'i source goes so far as to credit him with an offer to supply the British army with cereal grown in some Baha'i villages: 'We learned that when the British marched into Haifa there was some difficulty about the commissariat. The officer in command went to consult the Master. | "I have corn", was the reply.| "But for the army?" said the astonished soldier. | "I have corn for

the British Army", said 'Abdu'l-Baha".' Blomfield, S. L., The *Chosen Highway* (Wilmette, IL: Baha'i Publishing Trust: 1967), p. 210.
38. Momen, *Babi and Baha'i Religions*, pp. 462–5.
39. Amanat, *Iran*, pp. 856–7.
40. Dabashi, *Shi'ism*, pp. 266–7.
41. Boroujerdi, *Triumph of Nativism*.
42. 'It can tolerate no compromise with the theories, the standards, the habits, and the excesses of a decadent age. Nay rather it seeks to demonstrate, through the dynamic force of its example, the pernicious character of such theories, the falsity of such standards, the hollowness of such claims, the perversity of such habits, and the sacrilegious character of such excesses', Effendi, S., *The Advent of Divine Justice* (Wilmette, IL., Baha'i Publishing Trust, 1969), p. 25. Shoghi Effendi's theoretical view of sexual licence in America (he never visited the USA) could usefully be compared to Sayyid Qutb's, who did. See Qutb, 'The America I Have Seen', in K. Abdel-Malik (ed.), *America in an Arab Mirror: Images of America in Arabic Travel Literature, An Anthology, 1895–1995* (New York: St Martin's Press, 2000), pp. 9–28.
43. Cole, J. R. I., 'The Genesis of the Baha'i Faith in Middle Eastern Modernity', *ISIM Newsletter*, 2 (1999), p. 9. Cole sees the Baha'i community in dualistic terms. One side is liberal, 'universalist and tolerant'; the other half is 'conservative . . . dreams of theocratic domination and insist[s] on scriptural literalism'.
44. Nanquette, L., 'Towards a Globalisation of Contemporary Iranian Literature? Iranian Literary Blogs and the Evolution of the Literary Field', in A. Ball and K. Mattar (eds), *The Postcolonial Middle East* (Edinburgh: Edinburgh University Press, 2019), pp. 383–406 (p. 384).
45. Boroujerdi, *Triumph of Nativism*, p. 127; Vahdat, *Juggernaut*, p. 139.
46. Mottahedeh, R., *The Mantle of the Prophet: Religion and Politics in Iran* (New York: Pantheon, 1985); Milani, A., *Eminent Persians: Men and Women Who Made Modern Iran, 1941–1979*, vol. 2, *From Rags to Riches to Revolution: The Iranian Economy 1941–1979* (Syracuse, NY: Syracuse University Press, 2008).
47. MacEoin, 'Roots', pp. 79–80.
48. 'This is evident when Zionist Jews defend Israel as a "Western nation" or "modern democracy" ("the only one in the Middle East"), which as such protects Western values from the barbarism of Arabs or Islam. It is similarly evident in the words of Muslim leaders who name Jews as the enemies of Christ, humanity, or Islam', Hochburg, G. Z., 'Remembering Semitism *or* on the Prospect of Re-membering the Semites', *ReOrient*, 1, 2 (2016), pp. 192–223 (p. 193).

49. Ling, T., *A History of Religion East and West* (Basingstoke: Macmillan, 1968), p. 389.
50. Ling, *History of Religion*, p. 390.
51. In the mid-1930s an entry in *Baha'i World*, vol. 5, stated: 'In the previous *Survey* reference was also made to the Baha'i teaching that by the year 1963 the foundations of universal peace will have been laid', p. 20.
52. Cole, J. R. I., 'Review of M. McMullen, *The Baha'i: The Religious Construction of a Global Identity*', *Journal for the Scientific Study of Religion*, 40, 3 (2001), pp. 555–6. Another factor that might hold back new entrants, according to the same author, was 'an open insistence on a fundamentalist orthodoxy and a clear condemnation of human rights principles', Cole, 'Baha'i Faith as Panopticon', p. 235.
53. Valentine, *Islam and the Ahmadiyya*, p. 33.
54. Burhani, 'Hating Ahmadiyya', p. 138.
55. Valentine, *Islam and the Ahmadiyya*, p. 37.
56. Bushman, R. L., *Mormonism – A Very Short Introduction* (Oxford: Oxford University Press, 2008), p. 1.
57. Garlington, *Baha'i Faith*, p. xxi; Warburg, *Citizens of the World*, p. 6.
58. Nash, G., 'What is Baha'i Orientalism?', *Humanities*, 10, 1 (2021).
59. Cohen, M. R., *Under Crescent and Cross: The Jews of the Middle Ages* (Princeton, NJ: Princeton University Press, 1994).
60. Machlis, E., *Shi'i Sectarianism in the Middle East: Modernisation and the Quest for Islamic Universalism* (London: I. B. Tauris, 2014), p. 5.
61. Yazdani, 'Confessions of Dolgoruki', pp. 41, 47.
62. Warburg, *Citizens of the World*, p. 68.
63. See Cohen, R. A., *The Hojjatiyeh Society in Iran: Ideology and Practice from the 1950s to the Present* (New York: Palgrave Macmillan, 2013), chs 3 and 4.
64. Majeed, Introduction *Reconstruction*, p. 7.

Bibliography

Abdo, L., Religion and Relevance: The Baha'is in Britain 1899–1930 (PhD thesis, School of African and Oriental Studies, University of London, 2003). *See also* Osborn, L.

Abdul Baha, *Some Answered Questions* (Wilmette, IL: Baha'i Publishing Trust, 1985).

Abdul Baha, *The Promulgation of Universal Peace* (Wilmette, IL: Baha'i Publishing Trust, 1982).

Abdul Baha, *Mysterious Forces of Civilization* (Risalih-yi madaniyyih), trans. J. Dawud (Chicago: Bahai Publishing Society, [1882] 1918).

Abdul Baha, *Secret of Divine Civilization*, trans. M. Gail (Wilmette, IL: Baha'i Publishing Trust, 1957).

Ackerman, N. and G. Hassal, 'Russia and the Baha'i Faith, A Historic Connection', *Baha'i World, 1998–99* (Haifa: Baha'i World Centre, 2000), vol. 27, pp. 157–92.

Adams, I., *Persia by a Persian: Personal Experiences, Manners, Customs, Habits, Religious and Social Life* (n.p.: n.p., 1900).

Addison, J., 'The Ahmadiya Movement and its Western Propaganda', *Harvard Theological Review*, 22.1 (1929), pp. 1–32.

Ahmad, G., *The British Government and Jihad* (Government Angreizi aur Jihad) (Farnham: Islamic International Publications, 2018).

Ahmad, G., *Jesus in India: Jesus' Deliverance from the Cross and Journey to India* (Qadian: Islam International Publications, [1908] 2016).

Ahmad, G., 'The Babi Religion', *Review of Religions*, 6 (1907), 1, pp. 171–7; 2, pp. 315–25; 3, pp. 351–7; 4, pp. 387–404; 5, pp. 427–42.

Ahmad, M. B. M., *The New World Order of Islam* (Nizam-i Nau) (Qadian: Islam International Publications, 2017).

Ahmad, M. B. M., *A Present to His Royal Highness the Prince of Wales from the Ahmadiyya Community* (Tilford, Surrey: Islamic International Publications, [1922] 2015).

Ahmad, M. B. M., *The Life of Muhammad* (Tilford, Surrey: Islamic International Publications, 2014).

Ahmad, M. B. M., *Ahmadiyyat or the True Islam* (Tilford, Surrey: Islamic International Publications, 2007).

Ahmad, S., A New Dispensation in Islam: The Ahmadiyya and the law in Colonial India, 1872 to 1939 (PhD Thesis, SOAS, University of London, 2015).

Ahmadiyya Anjuman Lahore Foundation, Khwaja Kamal-ud-Din's report of his second visit to the Woking Mosque <http://www.wokingmuslim.org/history//kh-mosque-second.htm> (last accessed 20 October 2021).

Ali, M., *True Conception of the Ahmadiyya Movement* (Columbus, OH: Ahmadiyya Anjuman Isha'at Islam Lahore, [1966] 1996) <https://alahmadiyya.org/wp-content/uploads/books/english/muhammad-ali/true-conception-of-the-ahmadiyya-movement/true-conception-of-the-ahmadiyya-movement.pdf> (last accessed 20 October 2021).

Ali, M., *The New World Order* (Lahore: Ahmadi Anjuman Isha'at Islam, 1944).

Ali, M., *History and Doctrines of the Babi Movement* (Lahore: Ahmadiyya Anjuman Isha'at Islam, 1933).

Ali, M., 'God Save the King!' *Review of Religions*, 10.11 (1911), pp. 441–6.

Alkan, N., '"The Eternal Enemy of Islam": Abdullah Cevdet and the Baha'i Religion', *Bulletin of the School of Oriental and African Studies, University of London*, 68.1 (2005), pp. 1–20.

Alkan, N., 'Ottoman Reform Movements and the Baha'i Faith, 1860s–1920s', in M. Sharon (ed.), *Studies in Modern Religions, Religious Movements, and the Babi-Baha'i Faiths* (Leiden: Brill, 2004), pp. 253–74.

Amanat, A., Babis and Baha'is as agents of Iranian modernity (Paper presented at Baha'i Studies Symposium, Kellogg College, Oxford, 30 June 2018).

Amanat, A. *Iran: A Modern History* (New Haven: Yale University Press, 2017).

Amanat, A., '*Mujtahids* and Missionaries: Shi 'i response to Christian polemics in the early Qajar Period', in R. Gleave (ed.), *Religion and Society in Qajar Iran* (London: Routledge Curzon, 2005), pp. 247–69.

Amanat, A., *Pivot of the Universe: Nasir al-Din Shah Qajar and the Iranian Monarchy, 1831–1896* (London: I. B. Tauris, 1997).

Amanat, A. (ed.), 'Introduction', E. G. Browne, *The Persian Revolution, 1905–1909* (Washington, DC: Mage, 1995).

Amanat, A., *Resurrection and Renewal: The Making of the Babi Movement in Iran, 1844–1850* (Ithaca: Cornell University Press, 1989).

Andreeva, E., *Russia and Iran in the Great Game: Travelogues and Orientalism* (New York: Routledge, 2007).

Ansari, H., *'The Infidel Within': Muslims in Britain Since 1800* (London: Hurst, 2004).

apRoberts, R., *Arnold and God* (Berkeley: University of California Press, 1983).

Arberry, A., *Oriental Essays: Portraits of Seven Scholars* (London: Allen and Unwin, 1960).

Armstrong-Ingram, R. J., 'The Use of Generative Imagery in Shoghi Effendi's *The Dispensation of Baha'u'llah*', *Occasional Papers in Shaykhi, Babi and Baha'i Studies*, 2.3 (1998) <https://www.h-net.org/~bahai/bhpapers/vol2/generate.htm> (last accessed 20 October 2021).

Armstrong-Ingram, R. J., 'American Baha'i Women and the Education of Girls in Tehran, 1909–1934', in P. Smith (ed.), *Studies in Babi and Baha'i History: In Iran* (Los Angeles: Kalimat Press, 1986), vol. 3, pp. 181–210.

Arnold, M., 'A Persian Passion Play', in *Matthew Arnold's Essays in Criticism First Series: A Critical Edition*, ed. T. M. Hoctor (Chicago: University of Chicago Press, [1871] 1968), pp. 135–58.

Arnold, M., *Dissent and Dogma: Complete Prose of Matthew Arnold*, ed. R. H. Super (Ann Arbor: University of Michigan Press, 1968), vol. 6.

Arnold, M., 'On the Study of Celtic Literature', *Lectures and Essays in Criticism, First Series: Complete Prose of Matthew Arnold*, ed. R. H. Super (Ann Arbor: University of Michigan Press, 1962), vol. 2, pp. 291–386.

Ashcroft, B., G. Griffiths, and H. Tiffin, *The Empire Writes Back: Theory and Practice in Post-Colonial Literatures* (London: Routledge, 1989).

Ashcroft, B. and P. Aluwahlia, *Edward Said*, 2nd edn (London: Routledge, 2009).

Aslan, R., *Zealot: The Life and Times of Jesus of Nazareth* (New York: Random House, 2013).

Assmann, J., *The Price of Monotheism* (Stanford, CA: Stanford University Press, 2010).

Aydin, C., *The Idea of the Muslim World: A Global Intellectual History* (Cambridge, MA: Harvard University Press, 2017).

Aydın, C., 'The Ottoman Empire and the Global Muslim Identity in the Formation of Eurocentric World Order, 1815–1919', in F. Dallmayr, M. Akif Kayapınar and İ Yaylacı (eds), *Civilizations and World Order: Geopolitics and Cultural Difference* (Lanham, MD: Rowman and Littlefield, 2014), pp. 117–44.

Bach, M., *They have Found a Faith* (Indianapolis: Bobbs-Merrill Company, 1945).

Baha'u'llah, *Epistle to the Son of the Wolf* (Wilmette, IL: Baha'i publishing Trust, 1971).

Baha'u'llah, *Proclamation of Baha'u'llah* (Haifa: Baha'i World Centre, 1967).
Baha'u'llah, *Book of Certitude* (Kitab-i Iqan) (London: Baha'i Publishing Trust, 1961).
Balyuzi, H. M., *Baha'u'llah: The King of Glory* (Oxford: George Ronald, 1980).
Balyuzi, H. M., *Edward Granville Browne and the Baha'i Faith* (London: George Ronald, 1970), pp. 118–22.
Balyuzi, H. M., *The Bab: The Herald of the Day of Days* (Oxford: George Ronald, 1973).
Balyuzi, H. M., *'Abdu'l-Baha* (Oxford: George Ronald, 1971).
Banani, A., *Modernity and [The] Millennium*, by Juan Cole: Some Reflections, *Baha'i Studies Review*, 9 (1999) <http://bahai-library.com/banani_reflections_modernity_millennium> (last accessed 20 October 2021).
Banani, A., 'Marxist Analysis of the Baha'i Faith' (Paper presented at [Canadian] Association for Baha'i Studies Conference, October 1981).
Baquia Baquia, *Bahais in My Backyard* <https://vimeo.com/22467795> (last accessed 16 October 2021).
Barzan, J., *Race: A Study in Modern Superstition* (New York: Harcourt, Brace, 1937).
Bassnett, S., 'The Translation Turn in Cultural Studies', in S. Bassnett and A. Lefevere (eds), *Constructing Cultures: Essays on Literary Translation* (Clevedon: Multilingual Matters, 1998), pp. 123–40.
Bassnett, S., 'Introduction: Intricate Pathways: Observations on Translation and Literature', in S. Bassnett (ed.), *Translating Literature (Essays & Studies)* (Cambridge: D. S. Brewer, 1997), pp. 1–13.
Basu, D. K., 'Chaudhuri (Nirad C.' <https://www.encyclopedia.com/international/encyclopedias-almanacs-transcripts-and-maps/chaudhuri-nirad-c> (last accessed 19 October 2021), 2021).
Bayat, M., 'Aqa Khan Kermani', *Encyclopaedia Iranica* <https://iranicaonline.org/articles/aqa-khan-kermani> (last accessed 20 October 2021).
Bayat, M., *Iran's First Revolution: Shi'ism and the Constitutional Revolution of 1905–1909* (New York: Oxford University Press, 1991).
Bayat, M., *Mysticism and Dissent: Socioreligious thought in Qajar Iran* (Syracuse, N Y: Syracuse University Press, 1982).
Bayat, M., 'Mirza Aqa Khan Kirmani: A Nineteenth Century Persian Nationalist', *Middle Eastern Studies*, 10.1 (1974), pp. 36–59.
Bayly, C. A., *The Birth of the Modern World 1780–1914: Global Connections and Comparisons* (Oxford: Blackwell, 2004).
Beg, M. M., *The Bahai Creed: A Brief History and Doctrines of the Babi Movement* (Lahore: Ahmadiyya Anjuman Isha'At-I-Islam, n.d.).

Bennett, C., *Victorian Images of Islam* (London: Grey Seal, 1992).
Bentwich, N., *Mandate Memories* (London: The Hogarth Press, 1965).
Berger, S., 'Stefan Berger responds to Ulrich Muhlack', *Bulletin of the German Historical Institute London*, 23.1 (2001), pp. 21–33.
Bhabha, H., *The Location of Culture* (London: Routledge, 1994).
Biddiss, M., *Gobineau: Selected Political Writings* (London: Jonathan Cape, 1970).
Blomfield, S. L., *The Chosen Highway* (Wilmette, IL: Baha'i Publishing Trust, 1967).
Bobrovnikov V., 'The Contribution of Oriental Scholarship to the Soviet Anti-Islamic Discourse: From the Militant Godless to the Knowledge Society', in M. Kemper and S. Conermann (eds), *The Heritage of Soviet Oriental Studies* (London: Routledge, 2011), pp. 66–85.
Boissel, J., *Gobineau biographie: mythes et réalité* (Paris: Berg International, 1993).
Boissel, J., *Gobineau, l'Orient et l'Iran* (Paris: Editions Klincksieck, 1973).
Bonakdarian, M., 'Selected Correspondence of E. G. Browne and Contemporary Reviews of the Persian Revolution 1905–1909', in E. G. Browne, *The Persian Revolution, 1905–1909*, ed. A. Amanat (Washington, DC: Mage, 1995), pp. xxix–lxiv.
Bonakdarian, M., 'Edward G. Browne and the Iranian Constitutional Struggle: From Academic Orientalism to Political Activism', *Iranian Studies*, 26 (1993), pp. 7–31.
Boroujerdi, M., *Iranian Intellectuals and the West: The Tormented Triumph of Nativism* (Syracuse: University of Syracuse Press, 1996).
Brittingham, I. D., *The Revelation of Baha-ullah in a Sequence of Four Lessons* (Chicago: Baha'i Publishing Society, 1902).
Brookshaw, D. P. and S. B. Fazel (eds), *The Baha'is of Iran: Socio-Historical Studies* (London: Routledge, 2008).
Browne, E. G., *Materials for the Study of the Babi Religion* (Cambridge: Cambridge University Press, 1918).
Browne, E. G., *The Persian Revolution, 1905–1909* (Cambridge: Cambridge University Press, 1910).
Browne, E. G. (ed.), *Kitab-i Nuqtatu'l-Kaf Being the Earliest History of the Babis compiled by Hajji Mirza Jani of Kashan* (Leyden: E. J. Brill/London: Luzac and Co, 1910).
Browne, E. G., 'Introduction', M. H. Phelps, *Life and Teachings of Abbas Effendi* (New York: G. P. Putnam, 1903), pp. xi–xxx.
Browne, E. G., *A Year Amongst the Persians: Impressions as to the Life, Character and Thought of the People of Persia* (Cambridge: Cambridge University Press, 1893).

Browne, E. G. (ed.), *The Tarikh-i-Jadid or New History of Mirza Muhammad Ali the Bab, by Mirza Huseyn of Hamadan* (Cambridge: Cambridge University Press, 1893).

Browne, E. G. (ed.), *A Traveller's Narrative written to illustrate the Episode of the Bab* (Cambridge: Cambridge University Press, 1891), vol. 2, English Translation and Notes.

Browne, E. G., 'The Babis of Persia, 1. Sketch of their History and Personal Experiences among them, 2. Their Literature and Doctrines', *Journal of the Royal Asiatic Society*, 21 (1889), pp. 485–526, pp. 881–1009.

Bruner, J., 'The Narrative Construction of Reality', *Critical Inquiry*, 18 (1991), pp. 1–21.

Buck, C., *Paradise and Paradigm: Key Symbols in Persian Christianity and the Baha'i Faith* (Albany, NY: State University of New York Press, 1999).

Burhani, A. N., 'Hating the Ahmadiyya: The Place of "Heretics" in Contemporary Indonesian Muslim Society', *Contemporary Islam*, 8 (2014), pp. 133–52.

Burke III, E., 'Orientalism and World History: Representing Middle Eastern nationalism and Islamism in the twentieth century', *Theory and Society* 27.4 (1998), pp. 489–507.

Carlyle, T., *Latter-Day Pamphlets* (London: Chapman and Hall, [1850] 1871).

Carpenter, J. E., *Comparative Religion* (New York: Henry Holt, 1913).

Caufield, J. W., *Overcoming Matthew Arnold: Ethics in Culture and Criticism* (Farnham: Ashgate, 2012).

Chamankhah, L., 'A Minority Within a Majority: The Baha'i Principle of Non-Interference in Politics is Revisited', *Journal of South Asian and Middle Eastern Studies*, 38.1 (2014), pp. 22–40.

Chatterjee, P., *The Nation and its Fragments: Colonial and Postcolonial Histories* (Princeton, NJ: Princeton University Press, 1993).

Chaudhuri, N. C., *Autobiography of an Unknown Indian* (London: Macmillan, 1951).

Cheyne, T. K., *The Reconciliation of Races and Religions* (London: Adam and Charles Black, 1914).

Childs, P. and P. Williams, *An Introduction to Post-Colonial Theory* (London: Harvester Wheatsheaf, 1997).

Chirol, V., *The Middle East Question or some political problems of Indian defence* (London: John Murray, 1903).

Cobb, S., *Islamic Contributions to Civilization* (Washington, DC: Avalon Press, 1963).

Cohen, M. R., *Under Crescent and Cross: The Jews of the Middle Ages* (Princeton, NJ: Princeton University Press, 1994).

Cohen, R. A., *The Hojjatiyeh Society in Iran: Ideology and Practice from the 1950s to the Present* (New York: Palgrave Macmillan, 2013).

Cohn-Sherbok, D., *The Politics of Apocalypse: The History and Influence of Christian Zionism* (Oxford: Oneworld, 2006).

Cole, J. R. I., 'Globalization and Religion in the Thought of 'Abdu'l-Baha', in M. Warburg, A. Hvithamar, and M. Warmind (eds), *Baha'i and Globalisation* (Aarhus: University of Aarhus Press, 2005), pp. 55–76.

Cole, J. R. I., 'Fundamentalism in the Contemporary U. S. Baha'i Community', *Review of Religious Research*, 43.3 (2002), pp. 195–217.

Cole, J. R. I., 'Review of M. McMullen, *The Baha'i: The Religious Construction of a Global Identity*', *Journal for the Scientific Study of Religion*, 40.3 (2001), pp. 555–6.

Cole, J. R. I., *Modernity and the Millennium*, a response by Amin Banani: Response to review, 1999 <https://bahai-library.com/cole_banani_modernity_millunnium> (last accessed 20 October 2021).

Cole, J. R. I., 'The Genesis of the Baha'i Faith in Middle Eastern Modernity', *ISIM Newsletter*, 2 (1999), p. 9.

Cole, J. R. I., *Modernity and the Millennium: The Genesis of the Baha'i Faith in the Nineteenth-century Middle East* (New York: Columbia University Press, 1998).

Cole, J. R. I., 'The Baha'i Faith in America as Panopticon, 1963–1997', *Journal for the Scientific Study of Religion*, 37 (1998), pp. 234–48.

Cole, J. R. I., 'Marking Boundaries, Marking Time: The Iranian Past and the Construction of the Self by Qajar Thinkers', *Iranian Studies*, 29.1–2 (1996), pp. 35–56.

Cole, J. R. I., *Colonialism and Revolution in the Middle East: Social and Cultural Origins of Egypt's 'Urabi Movement* (Princeton, NJ: Princeton University Press, 1993).

Cole, J. R. I., 'Iranian Millenarianism and Democratic Thought in the 19th Century', *International Journal of Middle East Studies*, 24 (1992), pp. 1–26.

Cole, J. R. I., 'Browne (Edward Granville: ii. Browne on Babism and Bahaism', *Encyclopaedia Iranica*, vol. 4 <https://iranicaonline.org/articles/browne-edward-granville> (last accessed 20 October 2021), 1990).

Cole, J. R. I. (ed.), *Mirza Abu'l-Fadl Gulpaygani, Letters and Essays, 1886–1913* (Los Angeles: Kalimat Press, 1985).

Cole, J. R. I. (ed.), *Mirza Abu'l-Fadl Gulpaygani, Miracles and Metaphors* (Los Angeles: Kalimat Press, 1981).

Cole, J. R. I., 'Muhammad 'Abduh and Rashid Rida: A Dialogue on the Baha'i Faith', *World Order*, 15.3–4 (1981), pp. 7–16.

Conrad, L. I., 'Ignaz Goldziher on Ernest Renan: from Orientalist Philology to the Study of Islam', in M. Kramer (ed.), *The Jewish Discovery of Islam* (Tel Aviv: Moshe Dayan Center for Middle Eastern and African Studies, 1999), pp. 137–80.

Cronin, S., 'Introduction: Edward Said, Russian Orientalism and Soviet Iranology', *Iranian Studies*, 48.5 (2015), pp. 647–62.

Cronin, S., 'Review of Soli Shahvar et al., *The Baha'is of Iran, Transcaspia and the Caucasus* and Youli Ioannesyan, *The Development of the Babi/Baha'i Communities*', *Asian Affairs*, 45.1 (2014), pp. 144–6.

Cronin, S., 'Review of E. Andreeva, *Russia and Iran in the Great Game: Travelogues and Orientalism*', *Middle Eastern Studies*, 46.3 (2010), pp. 460–1.

Cronin, S. (ed.), *The Making of Modern Iran: State and Society Under Reza Shah* (London: Routledge, 2003).

Curzon, G. H., *Persia and the Persian Question* (London: Longmans Green and Co, 1892).

Dabashi, H., *Post-Orientalism Knowledge and Power in a Time of Terror* (New York: New Brunswick, 2015).

Dabashi, H., *Brown Skin, White Masks* (London: Pluto, 2011).

Dabashi, H., *Shi'ism: A Religion of Protest Harvard* (Cambridge, MA: The Belknap Press of Harvard University Press, 2011).

Dabashi, H., *Islamic Liberation Theology: Resisting the Empire* (London: Routledge, 2008).

Dallmayr, F., *Beyond Orientalism: Essays on Cross-Cultural Encounter* (Albany, NY: State University of New York Press, 1996).

Davison, R. and A. R. C. Leaney, *Biblical Criticism* (Harmondsworth: Penguin, 1970).

DeLaura, D., *Hebrew and Hellene in Victorian England: Newman, Arnold, and Pater* (Austin: University of Texas Press, 1969).

Deringil, S., '"They Live in a State of Nomadism and Savagery": The Late Ottoman Empire and the Post-Colonial Debate', *Comparative Studies in Society and History*, 45.2 (2003), pp. 311–42.

Devji, F., 'Muslim Universality', *Postcolonial Studies*, 14.2 (2011), pp. 231–41.

Dirlik, A., 'Culture against History? The Politics of East Asian Identity', *Development and Society*, 28.2 (1999), pp. 167–90.

Dirlik, A., 'Chinese History and the Question of Orientalism', *History and Theory*, 35.4 (1996), pp. 96–118.

Dreyfus, H., *The Universal Religion: Bahaism* (London: Cope and Fenwick, 1909).

Dreyfus, H., 'Une Institution béhaie: Le Machreqou'l-Azkar d'Achqabad' (Paris: Ernest Leroux, 1909).

Dreyfus, H., *Les Préceptes Du Béhaisme* (Paris: Ernest Leroux, 1906).

Effendi, S., *Directives from the Guardian* (Wilmette, IL: Baha'i Publishing Trust, 1973).

Effendi, S., *The Advent of Divine Justice* (Wilmette, IL., Baha'i Publishing Trust, 1969).

Effendi, S., *The Promised Day is Come* (Wilmette, IL: Baha'i Publishing Trust, 1967).

Effendi, S., *Guidance for Today and Tomorrow: A Selection from the Writings of Shoghi Effendi, The Late Guardian of the Baha'i Faith* (London: Baha'i Publishing Trust, 1953).

Effendi, S., *The Dispensation of Baha'u'llah* (London: Baha'i Publishing Trust, 1947).

Effendi, S., *God Passes By* (Wilmette, IL: Baha'i Publishing Trust, 1944).

Effendi, S., *The World Order of Baha'u'llah* (Wilmette, IL. Baha'i Publishing Trust, 1938).

Effendi, S., *The Dawn-Breakers: Nabil's Narrative of the Early Days of the Baha'i Revelation* (Wilmette, IL: Baha'i Publishing Trust, 1932).

Eldem, E., 'The Ottoman Empire and Orientalism: An Awkward Relationship', in F. Pouillion and J-C Vatin (eds), *After Orientalism: Critical Perspectives on Western Agency and Eastern Re-appropriations* (Leiden: Brill, 2015), pp. 89–102.

Eldem, E., *Consuming the Orient* (Istanbul: Ottoman Bank Archives and Research Centre, 2007).

Esposito, J. L. (ed.), *Voices of Resurgent Islam* (New York: Oxford University Press, 1983).

Esslemont, J., *Baha'u'llah and the New Era* (Oakham: Baha'i Publishing Trust, 1974).

Evans, N. W., *Far From the Caliph's Gaze: Being Ahmadi Muslim in the Holy City of Qadian* (Ithaca: Cornell University Press, 2020).

Fanon, F., *Black Skin, White Masks* (London: Pluto, 1986).

Fanon, F., *A Dying Colonialism*, trans. H. Chevalier (New York: Grove Press, 1965).

Faverty, F. E., *Matthew Arnold: The Ethnologist* (Evanston: Northwestern University Press, 1951).

FitzGerald, E., *Letters of Edward FitzGerald*, vol. 1 (London: Macmillan, 1901).

Friedmann, Y., *Prophecy Continuous: Aspects of Ahmadi Religious Thought and its Medieval Background* (Berkeley, CA: University of California Press, 1989).

Fry, P., Introduction to the Theory of Literature (Lecture 18: The Political Unconscious, Yale University <https://oyc.yale.edu/english/engl-300/lecture-18> (last accessed 19 October 2021).

Garlington, W., *The Baha'i Faith in America* (Westport, CT: Praeger, 2005).

Geaves, R., *Islam in Britain: Muslim Mission in an Age of Empire* (London: Bloomsbury, 2018).

Geller, R. S., 'The Baha'i Minority in the State of Israel, 1948–1957', *Middle Eastern Studies*, 55.3 (2019), pp. 403–18.

Germain, E., 'The First Muslim Missions on a European Scale: Ahmadi-Lahori networks in the Inter-War Period', in N. Clayer and E. Germain (eds), *Islam in Inter-War Europe* (London: Hurst, 2008), pp. 89–118.

Gibb, H. A. R., *Modern Trends in Islam* (Illinois: University of Chicago Press, 1946).

Gibb, H. A. R. and J. H. Kramers (eds) *Shorter Encyclopaedia of Islam* (Leiden and London: E. J. Brill and Luzac and Co, 1961).

Gilham, J., *Loyal Enemies: British Converts to Islam, 1850–1950* (London: Hurst, 2014).

Gilmour, D., 'The Unregarded Prophet: Lord Curzon and the Palestine Question', *Journal of Palestine Studies*, 25.3 (1996), pp. 60–8.

Gobineau, A., *Les Religions et les philosophies dans l'Asie Centrale*, Oeuvres, ed. J. Gaulmier and V. Monteuil (Paris: Gallimard, [1865] 1983–7), vol. 2, pp. 403–809.

Gobineau, A., *Trois Ans en Asie (de 1855 à 1858)*, Œuvres, ed. J. Gaulmier and V. Monteuil (Paris: Gallimard, [1859] 1983–7), vol. 2, pp. 27–401.

Gobineau, A., *Mémoire sur l'état social de la Perse actuelle*, Œuvres, ed. J. Gaulmier and V. Monteuil (Paris: Gallimard, [1856] 1983–7), vol. 2, pp. 3–25.

Gobineau, A., *Essai sur l'inégalité des races humaines*, Œuvres, ed. J. Gaulmier and J. Boissel (Paris: Gallimard, [1853–5] 1983–7), vol. 1, p. 1179.

Gobineau, A., *Correspondance entre le Comte de Gobineau et le Comte de Prokesch-Osten (1854–1876)*, ed. C. S. de Gobineau (Paris: Librairie Plon, 1933).

Gobineau, A., *The Inequality of Human Races*, trans. A. Collins (London: Heinneman, 1915).

Goren, T., 'Changes in the Design of the Urban Space of the Arabs of Haifa during the Israeli War of Independence', *Middle Eastern Studies*, 35.1(1999), pp. 115–33.

Gorra, M., *After Empire: Scott, Naipaul, Rushdie* (Chicago: University of Chicago Press, 1997).

Griswold, H. D., 'The Ahmadiya Movement', *Muslim World*, 2 (1912), pp. 373–9.

Gualtieri, A. R., *The Ahmadis: Community, Gender, and Politics in a Muslim Society* (Montreal: McGill-Queen's University Press, 2004).

Gulpaygani, M. A., *Letters and Essays*, trans. J. I. R. Cole (Los Angeles: Kalimat Press, 1985).

Gulpaygani, M. A., *Miracles and Metaphors*, trans. J. I. R. Cole (Los Angeles: Kalimat Press, 1981).

Gunny, A., *Perceptions of Islam in European Writings* (Leicester: The Islamic Foundation, 2004).

Habibi, E., 'Haifa: Wadi Al-Nisnass and Abbas Street by Emile Habibi' (*Al-Ahram Weekly*, 16 November <https://www.palestineremembered.com/Haifa/Haifa/Story187.html> (Last accessed 12 August 2020), 2000).

Halm, H., *Shiism* (Edinburgh: Edinburgh University Press, 1991).

Hanson, J. H., *The Ahmadiyya in the Gold Coast: Muslim Cosmopolitans in the British Empire* (Bloomington: University of Indiana Press, 2017).

Hardy, P., *The Muslims of British India* (Cambridge: Cambridge University Press, 1972, 1972).

Hassall, G., 'Notes on the Babi and Baha'i Religions in Russia and its territories', *Baha'i Studies*, 5.3 (1992), pp. 41–80.

Heschel, S., *The Aryan Jesus: Christian Theologians and the Bible in Nazi Germany* (Princeton, NJ: Princeton University Press, 2008).

Higgins, P. J., 'Minority-State Relations in Contemporary Iran', *Iranian Studies* 17.1 (1984), pp. 37–71.

Hochburg, G. Z., 'Remembering Semitism *or* on the Prospect of Re-membering the Semites', *ReOrient*, 1.2 (2016), pp. 192–223.

Holley, H., 'Religion and World Order', *The Baha'i World, 1934–1936* (Wilmette, IL: Baha'i Publishing Trust, 1937), vol. 6, pp. 571–9.

Holley, H., *Bahai: The Spirit of the Age* (New York: Brentanos, 1921).

Horsley, R., 'Review of Reza Aslan, *Zealot: The Life and Times of Jesus of Nazareth*', *Critical Research on Religion*, 2.2 (2014), pp. 195–205.

Hourani, A., *Islam in European Thought* (Cambridge: Cambridge University Press. Hourani, A., *Arabic Thought in the Liberal Age, 1798–1939*, 2nd edn (Cambridge: Cambridge University Press, 1991).

Hourani, A., *Europe and the Middle East* (London: Routledge, 1981).

Howe, S., 'Imperial Histories, Postcolonial Theories', in G. Huggan (ed.), *The Oxford Handbook of Postcolonial Studies* (Oxford: Oxford University Press, 2011), pp. 162–8.

Huart, C., *La Religion de Báb* (Paris: Ernat Leroue, Rue Bonaparte, 1889).

Ioannesyan, Y., *The Development of the Babi/Baha'i Communities: Exploring Baron Rosen's Archives* (London: Routledge, 2013).

Iqbal, M., *Islam and Ahmadism: With a Reply to Questions Raised by Pandit Jawahar Lal Nehru* (Lahore: Ashraf, 1980).

Iqbal, A. M., *Reconstruction of Religious Thought in Islam*, ed. M. Saeed Sheikh (Lahore: Institute of Islamic Culture, [1934] 2003).
Iqbal, M., *Islam and Ahmadism* (Lahore: Ashraf, 1980).
Iqbal, M., 'Letter to Nehru', 1936 <https://wiki.qern.org/mirza-ghulam-ahmad/contemporaries/allama-muhammad-iqbal/letter-to-nehru> (last accessed 16 October 2021).
Irwin, R., 'Gobineau, the Would-be Orientalist', *Journal of the Royal Asiatic Society*, 26.1–2 (2016), pp. 321–32.
Irwin, R., *For Lust of Knowing: The Orientalists and Their Enemies* (London: Penguin, 2007).
[James, H.], 'Review of Arthur de Gobineau, *Nouvelles asiatiques*', *Nation*, 23.7 (December 1876), pp. 344–5.
Jeffries, J. M. N., *The Palestine Deception, 1915–1932: The McMahon–Hussein Correspondence, the Balfour Declaration, and the Jewish National Home*, ed. W. M. Mathew (USA: Institute of Palestine Studies, 2014).
Jones, S. H., *Islam and the Liberal State: National Identity and the Future of Muslim Britain* (London: I. B. Tauris, 2020).
Jonker, G., *The Ahmadiyya Quest for Religious Progress: Missionizing Europe 1900–1965* (Leiden: Brill, 2016).
Jung, D., *Muslim History and Social Theory: A Global Sociology of Modernity* (London: Palgrave Macmillan, 2017).
Jung, D., *Orientalists, Islamists, and the Global Space: A Genealogy of the Modern Essentialist Image of Islam* (Sheffield: Equinox Publishing, 2011).
Kalisman, H. F., 'The Little Persian Agent in Palestine: Husayn Ruhi, British Intelligence, and World War I', *Jerusalem Quarterly*, 66.16 (2016), pp. 65–74.
Kara, I., 'Islam and Islamism in Turkey: A Conversation with İsmail Kara' (*Maydan*, 24 October <https://themaydan.com/2017/10/islam-islamism-turkey-conversation-ismail-kara> (last accessed 20 October 2021).
Katouzian, H., *State and Society in Iran: The Eclipse of the Qajars and the Emergence of the Pahlavis* (London: I. B. Tauris, 2006).
Katouzian, H., 'Riza Shah's Political Legitimacy and Social Base, 1921–1941', in S. Cronin (ed.), *The Making of Modern Iran: State and Society under Riza Shah, 1921–1941* (London: Routledge, 2003), pp. 15–37.
Keddie, N. R., *Iran: Religion, Politics and Society, Collected Essays* (London: Frank Cass, 1980).
Keddie, N. R., *Sayyid Jamal ad-Din 'al-Afghani': A Political Biography* (Berkeley, CA: University of California Press, 1972).

Khan, A. H., *From Sufism to Ahmadiyya: A Muslim Minority Movement in South Asia* (Bloomington: Indiana University Press, 2015).
Khan, M. Z., *Ahmadiyyat: The Renaissance of Islam* (London: Tabsir Publications, 1978).
Khanum, R., *The Priceless Pearl* (London: Baha'i Publishing Trust, 1969).
King, R., *Orientalism and Religion* (London: Routledge, 1999).
Kolarz, W., *Religion in the Soviet Union* (New York: St Martin's Press, 1961).
Lahoud, N., 'Islamic responses to Europe at the Dawn of Colonialism', in T. Shogimen and C. J. Nederman (eds), *Western Political Thought in Dialogue with Asia* (Lanham, M D: Lexington Books, 2009), pp. 163–86.
Lambden, S., 'Islam', in J. F. A. Sawyer (ed.), *The Blackwell Companion to the Bible and Culture* (Oxford: Blackwell, 2006), pp. 135–57.
Lambden, S., Some Aspects of Isra'iliyyat and the Emergence of the Bab-Baha'i Interpretation of the Bible (PhD Thesis, University of Newcastle, 2002).
Lapidus, I., 'Islamic Revival and Modernity: The Contemporary Movements and the Historical Paradigms', *Journal of the Economic and Social History of the Orient*, 40.4 (1997), pp. 444–60.
Laqueur, W., The *History of Zionism*, 3rd edn (London: TaurisParke, 2003).
Lathan, A., 'The Relativity of Categorizing in the Context of the Ahmadiyya', *Die Welt des Islams*, 48.3 (2008), pp. 372–93.
Lavan, S., *The Ahmadiyah Movement: A History and Perspective* (Delhi: Monahar, 1974).
Lawrence, B., *The Qur'an: A Biography* (Vancouver: Douglas and McIntyre, 2006).
Lawson, T., 'Baha'i Religious History', *Journal of Religious History*, 36.4 (2012), pp. 463–70.
Lawson, T., 'Interpretation as Revelation: The Qur'an Commentary of Sayyid 'Ali Muhammad Shirazi, the Bab', in A. Rippin (ed.), *Approaches to the History of the Interpretation of the Qur'an* (Oxford University Press, 1988), pp. 223–53.
Lee, A., 'Half the Household was African: Recovering the Histories of two Enslaved Africans in Iran: Haji Mubarak and Fezzeh Khanum', *UCL Historical Journal*, 26.1 (2015), pp. 17–38.
Lee, A., 'The Rise of the Baha'i Community of "Ishqabad", in "The Baha'i Faith in Russia: Two Early Instances"', *The Canadian Association for Studies on the Baha'i Faith*, 5 (1979), pp. 1–14.
Lee, R. D., *Religion and Politics in the Middle East: Identity, Ideology, Institutions, and Attitudes* (Boulder, CO: Westview Press, 2014).
Levefere, A., *Translation, Rewriting, and the Manipulation of Literary Fame* (London: Routledge, 1992).

Ling, T., *A History of Religion East and West* (Basingstoke: Macmillan, 1968).
Lipton, G. A., 'De-Semitizing Ibn 'Arabi: Aryanism and the Schuonian Discourse of Religious Authenticity', *Numan*, 64 (2017), pp. 258–93.
Lockman, Z., *Contending Visions of the Middle East: The History and Politics of Orientalism*, 2nd edn (New York: Cambridge University Press, 2010).
Lorcerie, F., 'L'islam comme contre-identification française: trois moments', *L'Année du Maghreb*, 2 (2005–6), pp. 509–36.
MacEoin, D., 'Making the Invisible Visible: Introductory Books on The Baha'i Religion (The Baha'i Faith)', *Religion*, 43.2 (2013), pp. 160–77.
MacEoin, D., *The Messiah of Shiraz: Studies in Early and Middle Babism* (Leiden: Brill, 2009).
MacEoin, D., 'Baha'ism: Some Uncertainties about its Role as a Globalizing Religion', in M. Warburg, A. Hvithamar, and M. Warmind (eds), *Baha'i and Globalisation* (Aarhus: University of Aarhus Press, 2005), pp. 287–306.
MacEoin, D., *The Sources for Early Babi Doctrine and History – A Survey* (Leiden: Brill, 1992).
MacEoin, D., *A People Apart: The Baha'i Community of Iran in the Twentieth Century* (London: Centre of Near and Middle Eastern Studies, School of Oriental and African Studies, University of London, 1989).
MacEoin, D., 'Azali Babism', *Encyclopaedia Iranica*, vol. 3 <https://www.iranicaonline.org/articles/azali-babism> (last accessed 20 October 2021).
MacEoin, D., 'The Bab, Ali Mohammad Shirazi', *Encyclopaedia Iranica*, vol. 3 <https://iranicaonline.org/articles/bab-ali-mohammad-sirazi> (last accessed 20 October 2021).
MacEoin, D., 'Babism ii. The Babi Movement', *Encyclopaedia Iranica*, vol. 3 <https://iranicaonline.org/articles/babism-index> (last accessed 20 October 2021).
MacEoin, D., 'The Baha'is of Iran: The Roots of Controversy', *British Journal of Middle Eastern Studies*, 14.1 (1988), pp. 75–83.
MacEoin, D., 'Introduction', E. G. Browne, *A Year Amongst the Persians* (London: Century Publishing, 1984), pp. vii–xiv.
Macfie, A. L., *Orientalism: A Reader* (Edinburgh: Edinburgh University Press, 2000).
Machlis, E., *Shi'i Sectarianism in the Middle East: Modernisation and the Quest for Islamic Universalism* (London: I. B. Tauris, 2014).
Mahmood, S., *Religious Difference in a Secular Age: A Minority Report* (Princeton: Princeton University Press, 2016).
Majeed, J., Introduction to M. Iqbal, *Reconstruction of Religious Thought in Islam* (Stanford, CA: Stanford University Press, 2013).

Makdisi, U., 'Ottoman Orientalism', *The American Historical Review*, 107.3 (2002), pp. 768–96.

Mamdani, M., *Good Muslim – Bad Muslim: America, the Cold War, and the Roots of Terror* (New York: Three Leaves Press, Doubleday, 2004).

Mardin, Ş., *Religion and Social Change in Modern Turkey: The Case of Bediüzzaman Said Nursi* (Albany, NY: State University of New York Press, 1989).

Marenbon, J., 'Ernest Renan and Averroism: The Story of a Misinterpretation', in A. Akasoy and G. Giglioni (eds), *Renaissance Averroism and its Aftermath: Arabic philosophy in early modern Europe* (Dordrecht: Springer, 2013), pp. 273–84.

Margoliouth, D., 'Introduction', *The Koran, translated from the Arabic by the Rev. J. M. Rodwell* (London: Dent, 1909).

Markham, C. R., *A General Sketch of the History of Persia* (London: Longmans, Green and Co, 1874).

Massad, J. A., *The Persistence of the Palestine Question: Essays on Zionism and the Palestinians* (London: Routledge, 2006).

Masuzawa, T., *The Invention of World Religions: Or How Universalism was Preserved in the Language of Pluralism* (Chicago, University of Chicago Press, 2005).

Maududi, S. A. A., *The Qadiani Problem* (Lahore: Islamic Publications (PVT) Limited, 1953).

McCants, W., '"I Never Understood Any of this From 'Abbas Effendi": Muhammad 'Abduh's Knowledge of the Baha'i Teachings and His Friendship with 'Abdu'l-Baha 'Abbas', in M. Sharon (ed.), *Studies in Modern Religions, Religious Movements, and the Babi-Baha'i Faiths* (Leiden: Brill, 2004), pp. 275–98.

McGlinn, S., *Principles for Progress: Essays on Religion and Modernity by Abdu'l-Baha* (Leiden: Leiden University Press, 2018).

McGlinn, S., 'A Theology of the State from the Baha'i Teachings', *Church and State*, 41.4 (1999), pp. 697–724.

McNamara, B., *The Reception of 'Abdu'l-Bahá in Britain: East Comes West* (Leiden: Brill, 2021).

McNamara, B., 'Establishing Islam in Britain: The Founding of Woking Mission', *Journal of Muslims in Europe*, 7.3 (2018), pp. 309–30.

McNamara, B., Religious Reformers in Britain at the turn of the Twentieth Century: The Visits of Abdul Baha (PhD Thesis, University of Cork, 2017).

Metcalf, B. D., 'Review of J. R. I. Cole, *Modernity and Millennium: The Genesis of the Baha'i Faith in the Nineteenth-Century Middle East*', *The Journal of Interdisciplinary History*, 30.3 (1999), pp. 566–8.

Metcalf, B. D., *Islamic Revival in India: Deoband, 1860–1900* (Princeton, NJ: Princeton University Press, 1982).

Milani, A., *Eminent Persians: Men and Women Who Made Modern Iran, 1941–1979*, vol. 2, *From Rags to Riches to Revolution: The Iranian Economy 1941–1979* (Syracuse, NY: Syracuse University Press, 2008).

Miller, W., *Baha'ism: Its Origin, History and Teachings* (New York: Fleming H. Revell, 1931).

Mirsepassi, A., *Intellectual Discourse and the Politics of Modernization: Negotiating Modernity in Iran* (Cambridge: Cambridge University Press, 2003).

Moadell, M., 'Conditions for Ideological Production: The Origins of Islamic Modernism in India, Egypt, and Iran', *Theory and Society*, 30.5 (2001), pp. 669–731.

Momen, M., 'The Baha'is of Iran: The Constitutional Movement and the Creation of an "Enemy Within"', *British Journal of Middle East Studies*, 39.3 (2012), pp. 328–46.

Momen, W., 'Globalization Decentralization: The Concept of Subsidiarity', in M. Warburg, A. Hvithamar, and M. Warmind (eds), *Baha'i and Globalisation* (Aarhus: University of Aarhus Press, 2005), pp. 175–94.

Momen, M., 'The Baha'i Community of Ashkhabad: Its Social Basis and Importance in Bahá'í History', in S. Akiner (ed.), *Cultural Change and Continuity in Central Asia* (London: Kegan Paul International and Central Asia Research Forum, 1991), pp. 278–305.

Momen, M., *Introduction to Shi'i Islam: History and Doctrines of Twelver Shi'ism* (New Haven: Yale University Press, 1985).

Momen, M., 'The Social Basis of the Babi Upheavals in Iran (1848–53): A Preliminary Analysis', *International Journal of Middle East Studies*, 15.2 (1983), pp. 157–83.

Momen, M., 'Early Relations Between Christian Missionaries and the Babi and Baha'i Communities', in M. Momen (ed.), *Studies in Babi and Baha'i History* (Los Angeles: Kalimat Press, 1982), vol. 1, pp. 49–82.

Momen, M., *The Babi and Baha'i Religions: Some Contemporary Western Accounts, 1844–1944* (Oxford: George Ronald, 1981).

Mott, L. F., *Ernest Renan* (New York: D. Appleton, 1921).

Mottahedeh, N. (ed.), *'Abdul-Baha's Journey West: The Course of Human Solidarity* (New York: Palgrave Macmillan, 2013).

Mottahedeh, R., *The Mantle of the Prophet: Religion and Politics in Iran* (New York: Pantheon, 1985).

Moxnes, H., *Jesus and the Rise of Nationalism: A New Quest for the Nineteenth Century Historical Jesus* (New York, I. B. Tauris, 2011).

Mufti, A. R., *Forget English! Orientalisms and World Literatures* (Cambridge, MA: Harvard University Press, 2016).

Muhammad, S., *Sir Syed Ahmed Khan: A Political Biography* (Delhi: Meenakshi Prakashan, 1969).

Müller, [F.] M., 'Semitic Monotheism', *Chips from a German Workshop* (London: Longman, Green, and Co., 1867), vol. 1, pp. 341–79.

Naipaul, V. S., *Among the Believers: An Islamic Journey* (London: Penguin, 1981).

Naipaul, V. S., *The Mimic Men* (London: Penguin, 1969).

Nanquette, L., 'Towards a Globalisation of Contemporary Iranian Literature? Iranian Literary Blogs and the Evolution of the Literary Field', in A. Ball and K. Mattar (eds), *The Postcolonial Middle East* (Edinburgh: Edinburgh University Press, 2019), pp. 383–406.

Nash, G., 'What is Bahai Orientalism?' *Humanities*, 10.1 (2021).

Nash, G. (ed.), *Orientalism and Literature* (New York: Cambridge University Press, 2019).

Nash, G. (ed.), *Marmaduke Pickthall, Islam and the Modern World* (Leiden: Brill, 2017).

Nash, G., 'The Impact of Fear and Authority on Islamic and Baha'i Modernisms in the Late Modern Age: A Liberal Perspective', *Religions*, 6 (2015), pp. 1125–36.

Nash, G., 'New Orientalisms for old: articulations of the East in Raymond Schwab, Edward Said, and Two Nineteenth-century French Orientalists', in I. Netton (ed.), *Orientalism Revisited: Art Land and Voyage* (London: Routledge, 2013), pp. 87–97.

Nash, G., 'Death and Resurrection: The Renans in Syria (1860–61)', in *Knowledge is Light: Travellers in the Near East* (Oxford: ASTENE and Oxbow Books, 2011), pp. 69–77.

Nash, G. (ed.), *Comte de Gobineau and Orientalism: Selected Eastern Writings*, trans. D. O'Donoghue (London: Routledge, 2009).

Nash, G., 'Friends Across the Waters: British Orientalists and Middle East Nationalisms', in G. MacPhee and P. Poddar (eds), *Empire and After: Englishness in Postcolonial Perspective* (New York: Berghahn, 2007), pp. 87–100.

Nash, G., *From Empire to Orient: Travellers to the Middle East, 1830–1926* (London: I. B. Tauris, 2004).

Nasr, S. V. R., *Mawdudi and the Making of Islamic Revivalism* (New York: Oxford University Press, 1996).

Nicolas, A. L. M., *Le Livre de Sept Preuves de la Mission du Bab* (Paris: Librairie Orientale et Americaine, 1902).

Nijhawan, M., 'Today We are Ahmadis: Configurations of Heretic Otherness Between Lahore and Berlin', *British Journal of Middle East Studies*, 37.3 (2010), pp. 429–47.

Niyaz, S. A. Q., *The Babi and Baha'i Religion* (Tilford, Surrey: Islam International Publications, 1960).

Noori, Y., *Finality of Prophethood and a Critical Analysis of Babism, Bahaism, Qadiyanism* (Tehran: Madrasih-yi Shuhada, 1981).

Nott, J. and H. Hotz, *The Moral and Intellectual Diversity of the Races* (Philadelphia: Lippincott, 1856).

Olender, M., *The Languages of Paradise: Race, Religion, and Philology in the Nineteenth Century*, trans. Arthur Goldhammer (Cambridge, MA: Harvard University Press, 1992).

Osborn, L., The Baha'i Faith and the Western Esoteric Tradition <https://bahai-library.com/osborn_bahai_western_esoteric> (last accessed 20 October 2021).

Osborn, L., 'Review of R. Khadem, *Shoghi Effendi in Oxford* and D. Marcus, *Her Eternal Crown: Queen Marie of Romania and the Baha'i Faith*', *Baha'i Studies Review*, 10 (2001), pp. 163–5 <https://bahai-library.com/abdo_khadem_marcus_reviews> (last accessed 20 October 2021).

Oxford Biblical Studies Online, 'Form Criticism', in W. R. F. Browning (ed.), *A Dictionary of the Bible* <http://www.oxfordbiblicalstudies.com/article/opr/t94/e693> (last accessed 12 October 2021).

Parekh, B., 'The West and Its Others', in K. Ansell-Pearson, B. Parry and J. Squires (eds), *Cultural Readings of Imperialism – Edward Said and the Gravity of History* (London: Lawrence Wishart, 1997), pp. 179–93.

Pink, J., 'Deriding Revealed Religions? Baha'is in Egypt', *ISIM Newsletter*, 10.2 (2002), p. 30.

Pitt, A., 'The Cultural Impact of Science in France: Ernest Renan and the *Vie de Jésus*', *The Historical Journal*, 43 (2000), pp. 79–101.

Polat, A., 'A Conflict on Baha'ism and Islam in 1922: Abdullah Cevdet and State Religious Agencies', *Insan & Toplum*, 5.10 (2016), pp. 29–42.

Porter, A., *Religion versus Empire? British Protestant Missionaries and Overseas Expansion, 1700–1914* (Manchester: Manchester University Press, 2004).

Powell, A., *Muslims and Missionaries* (London: Curzon Press, 1993).

Pratt, M. L., *Imperial Eyes: Travel Writing and Transculturation* (London: Routledge, 1994).

Purohit, T., 'Muhammad Iqbal on Muslim Orthodoxy and Transgression: A Response to Nehru', *ReOrient*, 1.1 (2015), pp. 78–92.

Qutb, S., 'The America I Have Seen', in K. Abdel-Malik (ed.), *America in an Arab Mirror: Images of America in Arabic Travel Literature An Anthology, 1895–1995* (New York: St Martin's Press, [1951] 2000), pp. 9–28.

Qutb, S., *Social Justice in Islam*, trans. J. B. Hardie (Washington, DC: American Council of Learned Society, 1953).

[Ransom-Keller, K.], 'In Memoriam I. The Unity of East and West, American Baha'i Sacrifices Her Life in Service to Persian Believers. Mrs. Keith Ransom-Kehler's mission', *Baha'i World* (Willmette, IL: Baha'i Publishing Trust, 1932–4), vol. 5, pp. 389–407.

Remey, M., 'Mashrak-el-Azkar: Descriptive of the Baha'i Temple', *Star of the West*, 6.18 (1916), pp. 153–5.

Remey, M., *Observations of a Bahai Traveler*, 2nd edn (Washington, DC: J. D. Milans, 1914).

Remey, M., *The Bahai Movement: A Series of Nineteen Papers* (Washington, DC: J. D. Milans, 1914).

Renan, E., *The Future of Science: Ideas of 1848* (London, Chapman and Hall, 1890).

Renan, E., *History of the People of Israel: Till the Time of David* (London: Chapman and Hall, [1888] 1891), vol. 1.

Renan, E., 'L'Islamisme et la Science', *Œuvres complètes*, ed. H. Psichari (Paris: Calmann-Levy, [1883] 1952), vol. 1, pp. 945–65.

Renan, E., 'Les téaziés de la Perse', *Œuvres Complètes*, ed. H. Psichari (Paris: Calmann-Levy, [1878] 1955), vol. 7, pp. 830–52.

Renan, E., *Studies of Religious History and Criticism*, trans. O. B. Forthingham (New York: Carleton, 1864).

Renan, E., 'De la part des peuples sémitiques dans l'histoire de la civilisation. Discours d'ouverture du cours de langues hébraïque, chaldaïque et syriaque au Collège de France prononcé le 21 février 1862', *Œuvres Complètes*, ed. H. Psichari (Paris: Calmann-Levy, [1863] 1952), vol. 2. pp. 317–35.

Renan, E., *Etudes d'histoire religieuse. Œuvres Complètes*, ed. H. Psichari (Paris: Calmann-Levy, [1857] 1955), vol. 7.

Renan, E., 'Histoire générale et système comparé des langues sémitiques' (Introduction and bk. 1, ch. 1., *Œuvres Complètes*, ed. H. Psichari (Paris: Calmann-Levy, [1855] 1955), vol. 8, pp. 129–63.

Renan, E., *Averroës et L'Averoïsme, Œuvres Complètes*, ed. H. Psichari (Paris: Calmann-Levy, [1852] 1952), vol. 3, pp. 11–365.

Renan, E., *The History of the Origins of Christianity*, vol. 7, *Marcus Aurelius* (London: Mathieson, [1882] 1890).

Renan, E., *The History of the Origins of Christianity*, vol. 6, *The Christian Church* (London: Mathieson, [1879] 1890).
Renan, E., *The History of the Origins of Christianity*, vol. 5, *The Gospels* (London: Mathieson, [1877] 1890).
Renan, E., *The History of the Origins of Christianity*, vol. 4, *The Anti-Christ* (London: Mathieson, [1873] 1890).
Renan, E., *The History of the Origins of Christianity*, vol. 3, *Saint Paul* (London: Mathieson, [1869] 1890).
Renan, E., *The History of the Origins of Christianity*, vol. 2, *The Apostles* (London: Mathieson, [1866] 1890).
Renan, E., *The History of the Origins of Christianity*, vol. 1, *The Life of Jesus* (London: Watts, [1863] 1935).
Richards, J. R., *The Religion of the Baha'is* (New York: SCPK, 1932).
Rippin, A., *Muslims: Their Religious Beliefs and Practices*, 3rd edn (London: Routledge, 2005).
Robinson, D., *Translation and Empire: Postcolonial Theories Explained* (Manchester: St Jerome, 1997).
Robinson, F., 'Islamic Reform and Modernities in South Asia', *Modern Asian Studies* 42.2–3 (2008), pp. 259–81.
Robinson, F., 'Prophets Without Honour? Ahmad and the Ahmadiyya', *History Today*, June 1990, pp. 42–7.
Root, M., 'Seeing Adrianople with New York Eyes', *The Baha'i Magazine*, 25.3 (1934), pp. 74–7.
Rosenberg, E., 'Baha'ism: Its Ethical and Social Teachings', *Transactions of the Third International Congress for the History of Religions* (Oxford: Clarendon Press, 1908), vol. 1, pp. 321–5.
Rostam-Kolayi, J., 'The Tarbiyat Girls School of Iran: Iranian and American Baha'i Contributions to Education', *Middle East Critique*, 22.1 (2013), pp. 77–93.
Ryad, U., 'Salafiyyah, Ahmadiyya, and European Converts to Islam in the Interwar Period', in B. Agai, U. Ryad, and M. Sajid (eds), *Muslims in Interwar Europe: A Transcultural Historical Perspective* (Leiden: Brill, 2016), pp. 47–87.
Said, E. W., *Culture and Imperialism* (London: Chatto and Windus, 1993).
Said, E. W., *The World, the Text, and the Critic* (Cambridge, MA: Harvard University Press, 1981).
Said, E. W., *Orientalism* (London: Penguin, [1978] 2003).
Saiedi, N., 'The Baha'i Critique of European Colonialism and Antisemitism' (29 July <https://bahaiteachings.org/bahai-critique-european-colonialism-antisemitism> (last accessed 20 October 2021).

Samuel, E., *A Lifetime in Jerusalem: The Memoirs of the Second Viscount Samuel* (London: Vallentine, Mitchell, 1970).

Schwab, R., *The Oriental Renaissance: Europe's discovery of India and the East, 1680–1880* (New York: Columbia University Press, [1950] 1984).

Schwarz, R., *The Curse of Cain: The Violent Legacy of Monotheism* (Chicago: University of Chicago Press, 1997).

Schweitzer, A., *The Quest of the Historical Jesus: A Critical Study of its Progress from Reimarus to Wrede*, trans. W. Montgomery, 2nd edn (London: A. and C. Black, 1926).

Sears, W., *Thief in the Night: The Strange Case of the Missing Millennium* (Oxford: George Ronald, 1961).

Sevea, T., 'Islamist questioning and [C]olonialism: Towards an Understanding of the Islamist Oeuvre', *Third World Quarterly*, 28.7 (2007), pp. 1375–1400.

Shahvar, S., *The Forgotten Schools: The Baha'is and Modern Education in Iran, 1899–1934* (London: I. B. Tauris, 2009).

Shahvar, S., B. Morozov, and B. B. Gilbar (eds), *The Baha'is of Iran: Transcaspia and the Caucasus*, vol. 1, *Letters of Russian Officers and Officials* (London: I. B. Tauris, 2011).

Shamir, R., *Colonies of Law: Colonialism, Zionism, and Law in Early Mandate Palestine* (Cambridge: Cambridge University Press, 2000).

Sharbrodt, O., *Islam and the Baha'i Faith: A Comparative Study of Muhammad 'Abduh and 'Abdul-Baha 'Abbas* (London: Routledge, 2008).

Sharon, M. (ed.), *Studies in Modern Religions, Religious Movements, and the Babi-Baha'i Faiths* (Leiden: Brill, 2004).

Smith, P., 'Peter Berger's Early Work on Baha'i Studies', *The Journal of Religious History*, 43.1 (2019), 45–69.

Smith, P., *Concise Encyclopedia of the Baha'i Faith* (Oxford: Oneworld, 2002).

Smith, P., *The Babi and the Baha'i Religions: From Messianic Shi'ism to a World Religion* (Cambridge: Cambridge University Press, 1987).

Smith, P., '*Reality* Magazine: Editorship and Ownership of an American Periodical', in J. R. I., Cole and M. Momen (eds), *From Iran East and West: Studies in Babi and Baha'i History* (Los Angeles: Kalimat Press, 1984), vol. 2, pp. 135–55.

Smith, W. C., *Modern Islam in India* (London: Victor Gollancz, 1946).

Sohrab, M. A., *'Abdul Baha in Egypt* (New York: J. H. Sears and Co. Inc. for New History Foundation, 1929).

Speer, R., *Missions and Modern History: A Study of the Missionary Aspect of Some Great Movements of the Nineteenth Century* (New York: Revell., 1904).

Sprague, S., *A Year With the Bahais in India and Burma* (London: The Priory Press, 1908).
Stone, D. D., *Communications with the Future: Matthew Arnold in Dialogue* (Ann Arbor: University of Michigan Press, 1997).
Storrs, R., *Orientations* (London: Readers Union/Ivor Nicholson & Watson, 1939).
Szurek, E., '"Go West": Variations on Kemalist Orientalism', in F. Pouillion and J.-C. Vatin (eds), *After Orientalism: Critical Perspectives on Western Agency and Eastern Re-appropriations* (Leiden: Brill, 2015), pp. 103–21.
Taherzadeh, A., *The Revelation of Baha'u'llah, volume 2: Adrianople 1863–68* (Oxford: George Ronald, 1974).
Tavakoli-Targhi, M., 'Anti-Bahaism and Islamism in Iran', in D. P. Brookshaw and S. B. Fazel (eds), *The Baha'is of Iran: Socio-Historical Studies* (London: Routledge, 2008), pp. 200–31.
Tavakoli-Targhi, M., *Refashioning Iran: Orientalism, Occidentalism and Historiography* (Basingstoke: Palgrave, 2001).
Tennyson, G. B., *Carlyle and the Modern World*, Occasional Paper, 4 (Edinburgh: Carlyle Society, 1971).
Terry, P., *A Prophet in Modern Times* <http://bahai-library.com/terry_nicolas_prophet_modern> (last accessed 12 October 2021).
Thieme, J., *V. S. Naipaul, 'The Mimic Men': A Critical View* (London: Collins and The British Council, 1985).
Thompson, G., *The Legacy of Empire: Britain, Zionism and the Creation of Israel* (London: I. B. Tauris, 2019).
Todorov, T., *On Human Diversity: Nationalism, Racism and Exoticism in French Thought*, trans. C. Porter (Cambridge, MA: Harvard University Press, 1993).
Tolz, V., *Russia's own Orient: The Politics of Identity and Oriental Studies in the Late Imperial and Early Soviet Periods* (Oxford: Oxford University Press, 2011).
Tocqueville, A. de, *Correspondance d' Alexis de Tocqueville et d' Arthur de Gobineau, Oeuvres complètes* (Paris: Gallimard, 1959), vol. 9.
Tuçay, M., 'Kemalism', *The Oxford Encyclopedia of the Islamic World* <http://www.oxfordislamicstudies.com/article/opr/t236/e0440> (last accessed 19 October 2021).
Turner, R. B., *Islam in the African American Experience* (Bloomington: University of Indiana Press, 2003).
Uskui, H. M. H. A., *Extracts from 'Tarikh-i Azerbaijan'*, trans. S. Manuchehri <https://bahai-library.com/manuchehri_tarikh_azarbeyijan_nicolas> (last accessed 16 October 2021).

Vahdat, F., *God and the Juggernaut: Iran's Intellectual Encounter with Modernity* (New York: University of Syracuse Press, 2002).
Valentine, S. R., *Islam and the Ahmadiyya Jama'at: History, Belief, Practice* (London: Hurst, 2008).
Van den Bosch, L. P., *Friedrich Max Müller* (Leiden: Brill, 2002).
Van Grondelle, M., *The Ismailis in the Colonial Era: Modernity, Empire and Islam, 1839–1969* (London: Hurst, 2009).
Vaziri, M., *Iran as Imagined Nation: The Construction of National Identity* (New York: Paragon House, 1993).
Velasco, I., 'Academic Irrelevance or Disciplinary Blind-Spot? Middle Eastern Studies and the Baha'i Faith Today', *Middle East Studies Association Bulletin*, 35.2 (2001), pp. 188–98.
Venuti, L., 'Translation, Community, Utopia', in L. Venuti (ed.), *The Translation Studies Reader* (New York: Routledge, 2000), pp. 484–5.
Viswanathan, G., *Power, Politics, and Culture: Interviews with Edward Said* (New York: Vintage, 2001).
Volkov, D. V., 'Fearing the Ghosts of State Officialdom Past? Russia's Archives as a Tool for Constructing Historical Memories of Its Persia Policy Practices', *Middle Eastern Studies*, 51.6 (2015), pp. 901–21.
Volkov, D. V., 'Persian Studies and the Military in Late Imperial Russia (1863–1917): State Power in the Service of Knowledge?' *Iranian Studies* 47.6 (2014), pp. 915–32.
Voll, J. O., *Islam: Continuity and Change in the Modern World*, 2nd edn (Syracuse, NY: Syracuse University Press, 1994).
Voll, J. O., 'Renewal and Reform in Muslim Society', in J. L. Esposito (ed.), *Voices of Resurgent Islam* (New York: Oxford University Press, 1983), pp. 32–47.
Walter, H. A., *The Ahmadiya Movement* (London: Oxford University Press, 1918).
Warburg, M., *Citizens of the World: A History and Sociology of the Baha'is from a Globalisation Perspective* (Leiden: Brill, 2006).
Wardman, H. W., *Ernest Renan: A Critical Biography* (London: Athlone Press, 1964).
Warmind, M., 'Baha'i and Ahmadiyya: Globalisation and Images of Modernity', in M. Warburg, A. Hvithamar and M. Warmind (eds), *Baha'i and Globalisation* (Aarhus: University of Aarhus Press, 2005), pp. 141–52.
Weinstein, M., '[Abdul Baha] Declares Zionists must work with Other Races', *Star of the West*, 10 (1919), pp. 195–6.
Wickens, G. M. 'Browne, Edward Granville: i. Browne's Life and Academic Career', *Encyclopaedia Iranica*, vol. 4 <https://iranicaonline.org/articles/browne-edward-granville> (last accessed 14 October 2021).

Wilcox, A., *Orientalism and Imperialism: from Nineteenth-Century Missionary Imagining to the Contemporary Middle East* (London: Bloomsbury, 2018).

Willey, B., 'Arnold and Religion', in Kenneth Allott (ed.), *Matthew Arnold* (London: G. Bell, 1975), pp. 236–58.

Wishard, J., *Twenty Years in Persia: A Narrative of Life under the Last Three Shahs* (New York: Fleming H. Revell, 1908).

Yarshater, E., 'Professor Amin Banani, 1926–2013: A Prominent Scholar of Iranian Studies', *Iranian Studies*, 47.2 (2014), pp. 347–51.

Yazdani, M., 'The Confessions of Dolgoruki: Fiction and Masternarrative in Twentieth-Century Iran', *Iranian Studies*, 44.1 (2011), pp. 25–47.

Yue, I., 'Missionaries (Mis-) Representing China: Orientalism, Religion, and the conceptualization of Victorian Cultural Identity', *Victorian Literature and Culture*, 37.1 (2009), pp. 1–10.

Young, R. J. C., *Postcolonialism: An Historical Introduction* (Oxford: Blackwell, 2001).

Young, R. J. C., *Colonial Desire: Hybridity in Theory, Culture and Race* (London: Routledge, 1995).

Zia-Ebrahimi, R., *The Emergence of Iranian Nationalism: Race and the Politics of Dislocation* (New York: Columbia University Press, 2016).

Zia-Ebrahimi, R., 'Self-Orientalization and Dislocation: The Uses and Abuses of the "Aryan" Discourse in Iran', *Iranian Studies*, 44.4 (2011), pp. 445–72.

Zirinsky, M., 'Riza Shah's Abrogation of Capitulations, 1927–1928', in S. Cronin (ed.), *The Making of Modern Iran: State and Society under Riza Shah, 1921–1941* (London: Routledge, 2003), pp. 84–102.

Zwemer, S. M., *Islam: A Challenge to Faith* (New York: Student Volunteer Movement for Foreign Missions, 1901).

Index

Abbas I, Shah, 191
Abbasids, 74
Abbas Street, Haifa, 148
Abduh, Muhammad, 42–3, 92, 168
Abdul Baha (Abbas Effendi), 9, 11, 23, 59, 66, 92, 114, 123, 130, 148, 151, 163, 164, 165, 166, 173, 181, 188, 197
   and Muhammad Abduh, 43, 92
   and General Allenby, 138, 147; receives knighthood from, 29, 138
   on America, 247n16
   Anglophilia, 31
   and British, 136–8, 140, 145, 179, 224, 277n45
   in Cairo, 141
   and Christianity, Christianising, 37, 66, 118, 145, 209, 224; Christian universalism, 27, 91, 150
   and Constitutional Revolution, 38, 144, 188
   on East–West unity, 168, 231
   Howard University address, 170–1, 176
   and modernity, 242n53
   and New World Order, 199, 205
   on politics, 37–8, 172, 250n46
   prophecy, 17
   and race, 170–1
   on Shoghi Effendi's education, 179
   in the West, 10, 165, 169
   and Western Baha'is, 167
   and Woking Mosque, 11, 148
   and Young Ottomans, 39; Young Turks, 30
   on Zionism, 143–6
   writing: *The Mysterious Forces of Civilization*, 42, 163, 203; *A Traveller's Narrative*, 37, 58, 94, 100, 101, 114, 231; *Some Answered Questions*, 144, 146; *Treatise on Government* (Risalih-yi Siyasiyyih), 37, 39, 40
Abdul Hamid, Ottoman Sultan and Caliph, 220; *see also* Ottomans
Adams, Isaac, 108
Addison, James Thayer, 117
'Afghani', Jamal al-Din Asadabadi, 42, 89–90, 161, 168
Afghanistan, 177, 208, 215
Africa, 3, 134, 184, 206
Africans, 51, 81, 170–1, 177
African Americans, 171–2
Afro-Caribbean people, 177
Agra, Christian–Muslim debates, 91
Ahl-i Hadith, 152
Ahmad, Bashiruddin Mahmud, 17, 24, 35, 36, 109, 116, 209
   and Ahmadi new order, 39, 157, 204, 205, 207
   on non-Ahmadi Muslims, 33, 119, 154
   and Kashmir Committee, 119
   suspension of jihad ruling, 153
   writing: *New World Order of Islam*, 206, 207; *A Present to His Royal Highness the Prince of Wales*, 207–10, 211
Ahmad, Ghulam, 6, 8, 24, 109, 111, 204, 205, 233

abrogation of jihad, 27, 36, 110, 118; on *ghazi* jihadists, 119
ancestry, 34
on Babis, Baha'is, 10, 111–12, 115–16, 233
on British government, 34, 35
on Christianity, Christianising, 12, 13, 37; and Christian missionaries, 7, 223
Jesus in Kashmir, 7, 13, 118, 207, 209, 210
at Juma'a Masjid, Delhi, 209
on *maulvis*, 14; *see also* Ali, M.; Muslim ulama
and Christian audiences, 208–10
on Islam, Muslims, 24, 117, 118, 152
mubahala, 6
religious claims, 6, 27, 33, 36, 41, 109, 110, 118, 119, 208, 213; *Barahin-i Ahmadiyya*, 8
Ahmadiyyat, Ahmadism, Ahmadis, 2, 3, 4, 6, 9, 29, 38, 101, 206, 207, 211, 215, 216, 229, 236
African American converts, 18
anti-Ahmadi politics, 31, 123, 153
anti-Baha'i narratives, 101, 111–15, 125; *see also* Ali, M.
and (British) colonialism, 12, 21, 28, 29, 35, 110, 111, 119, 124, 152, 154–5, 157, 208, 213, 223
categorised non-Muslims, 15, 34
in London and Berlin, 122
inauguration of, 6
and Islam, 2, 8, 11, 12, 14–15, 33, 111, 117, 118–19, 152, 211
and Kashmir war 1946, 33
Lahori–Qadiani split, 109–10
London headquarters, 34
mahdi movement, 24
martyrs in Afghanistan, 14, 153, 208
as minority, 123
missionising in West, 8, 10–12, 16, 91, 110, 118, 122; Woking mosque, 91
and modernity, 17, 18, 40, 91, 111, 118, 203, 212, 223
narratives, 21, 24

nizam-i nau (new world order) *see* Ahmad, B. M.
and orientalism, 14–15, 24, 117, 118
and Pakistan, 153; riots 1953, 34
persecution of, 208
'religion of peace', 15
study of, 16–17, 122, 242n56
and Western governments, 32
Ahmad, Jalal Al-e, 227, 228
Ahmad, Mirza Tahir, 4th Qadiani khalifa, 230
Ahmad, Muhammad, 'the Mahdi', 28
Ahsai, Shaykh Ahmad, 3
Akhundzadeh, Fath Ali, 161, 163
Akka, 5, 10, 143, 165, 178, 215
Al-Azm, Sadeq, 159
Algeria, 220
Ali, Chiragh, 91
Ali ibn Abi Talib, 86
Ali Ilahis, 53 119
Ali, Maulana Muhammad, leader of Lahori Ahmadis, 24, 33, 109, 110, 116, 117, 118, 121, 209
and Ghulam Ahmad's claims, 113, 116, 210
anti-Baha'i polemic, 113–15; *see also* Qadiani scholars
on Lahori Ahmadi mission, 113
on *maulvis*, 118–19
writing: *The Ahmadiyya Movement*, 113; *History and Doctrines of the Babi Movement*, 112, 113
Ali, Muhammad, half-brother of Abdul Baha, 11, 114
Ali, Muhammad Shah, 38, 173
Ali Pasha, 30
Ali, Sayyid Amir (Syed Ameer), 91, 117
Alkan, Necati, 15, 38
Allenby, General Edmund, 138, 147
Amanat, Abbas, 15, 28, 41, 43, 62, 101, 189, 227
Resurrection and Renewal: The Making of the Babi Movement in Iran, 28
Amerindians, 25
Ammergau Passion play, 85

Ancient Greece, Greeks, 77, 78, 79, 85
  Greek thought, 61, 74, 75
Ancient Persia, 86; *see also* Iran
Andreeva, Elena, 126–7, 128
  Russia and Iran in the Great Game: Travelogues and Orientalism, 126–7
Anglican Communion, 209
Anglo-Oriental College, Aligarh, 152
Anglo-Persian Treaty 1919, 123
Anquetil du Perron, Abraham-Hyacinthe, 99
Anti-Baha'i groups, 234
Antonius, George, 142
apRoberts, Ruth, 84, 87
Arabic language, culture, 9, 15, 27, 50, 56, 59, 74, 78, 79, 89, 94, 97, 104, 117, 141, 142, 161, 162, 163, 166, 180, 185, 187
Arabs, 52, 74, 152, 161, 162, 198
  intellectuals, scholars, 158 227
  nationalism, 158, 159
  philosophy and thought, 74, 95
  voices, 158
  see also Palestine
Arberry, Arthur J., 120
Armenians, 32, 127
Armstrong-Ingram, R. Jackson, 180
Arnold, Matthew, 22, 67, 71, 83, 84
  'Aryan' in Babism, Shi'ism, 70, 87, 88
  and Babi-Baha'ism, 90, 121
  Hellene and Hebrew, 87, 89
  Husayn and Jesus, 86
  on Persians, 87, 88; *Culture and Anarchy*, 88; 'A Persian Passion Play', 85, 87, 88; *On the Study of Celtic Literature*, 87, 88
Arya Samaj, 6
Aryan, Aryanism, 20, 48, 72–3, 74, 89, 156, 160, 183; *see also* Gobineau, A.; Renan
Asai, Shaykh Ahmad, 3
Ashkhabad, 130, 131; *see also* Baha'i faith
Ashley[-Cooper], Lord Anthony, 150
Asquith, Herbert Henry, 180
Atatürk, Mustafa Kemal, 156, 160, 185, 187
Aurelius, Marcus, 89

Austria-Hungary, 202
Averroës, Ibn Rushd, 69, 93
Aydin, Cemal, 30, 220, 222, 247n15
Azal, Subh-i, 5, 6, 58, 99, 100, 101, 121, 162, 187
  sent to Famagusta, 5
Azalis, Azali-Babis, 6, 23, 30, 38, 50, 58, 66, 90, 96, 100, 101, 109, 114, 116, 156, 162, 188
  involvement with Constitutional Revolution, 188
Azali-Baha'i split, 112; *see also* Browne
al-Azhar, Cairo, 92, 93
al-Azm, Sadeq, 159

the Bab, 3, 5, 6, 7, 8, 9, 11, 23, 28, 41, 42, 46, 50, 53, 54, 55–6, 57, 59, 61, 68, 69, 82, 86, 89, 98, 100, 101, 102, 103, 104, 105, 106, 107, 115, 125, 146, 155, 156,165, 166, 191
  Aryan messiah, 23, 65, 70, 72
  Christianising of, 61–3, 66, 82, 151, 209
  and Christian Scriptures, 16, 55, 151
  in *Dawnbreakers*
  and European audience, 83
  as mahdi figure, 2, 3, 6; Imam Mahdi, 1, 5, 226, 254n18
  as martyr, 70, 82, 86, 121
  and Shi'ism, 254n20
  succession to, 58, 99, 100
  spiritual struggle at Kufa; *Bayan*, 7, 56, 239n18
Babism, Babis, 1, 2, 3, 5, 10, 24, 37, 46, 50, 53, 65, 83, 90, 103, 111, 112, 121, 124, 127, 132,146, 152, 214
  Ahmadi rewriting of, 112–15
  anti-Qajar writings, 13
  and colonialism, 12, 33
  and British penetration of Iran, 28
  Baha'i revision of, 41, 42, 59, 90, 100–1, 107, 182
  Gobineau's account of, 53, 56, 82
  mahdi movement, 6, 121
  martyrs, 195; 'Seven Martyrs of Tehran', 69, 92, 94, 121

Marxist interpretation of, 4, 42
and modernity and reform, 13, 41, 231
and orientalists, 22, 58, 67, 98, 105, 121, 129, 166
persecution of, 152, 172, 215
and religious renewal, 87, 96, 103
as revolutionaries, militants, 29, 38, 41, 53, 96, 223
and Russia, 124, 125, 127, 136
Badasht, Babi conference at, 114
Badger, George Percy, 19
Baha'i faith, Baha'ism, Baha'is, 1, 32, 67, 90, 94, 95, 100, 103, 108, 109, 111, 112, 122, 129, 162, 164, 186, 206, 211, 215, 221, 229, 230, 236
  administrative order, 39, 182, 205, 206, 251n53
  American converts, 10, 11, 13, 23, 146, 164, 165, 170, 172, 173, 181, 207, 231; Afro-Americans, 243n59
  Ashkhabad community, 42, 124, 130, 131–3, 226; Afnan family, 132; *mashriq al-adhkar*, 132; murder of Muhammad Riza Isfahani, 131; and Bolsheviks, 132, 134–5, 136; in Transcaspia and the Caucasus, 124, 126, 130, 189, 202
  and Britain, 12, 31, 37, 108–9, 136, 146, 157, 165, 177, 213
  centenary celebration, 1944, 137, 149
  and colonialism, 119, 224
  Egyptian Baha'is, 140, 217–18
  and Egyptian sharia court judgment, 216; see also Egyptian court
  holy places, Israel, 149
  in Iran, 40, 129, 132, 148, 152, 189, 221–2, 226, 234; and constitution, 189, 192, 196, 287n85; holding government positions, 173; persecution in Iran and the East, 1, 68, 132, 227, 232; unrecognised minority, 189,195, 287n80
  and Islam, 2, 8, 168, 211, 232
  Jewish and Zoroastrian converts, 9, 132, 225
  and missionaries, 9, 13, 37, 91, 244n67
  missionising in West, 8, 9, 10–11
  on modernity/modernisation, 16, 22, 40, 42, 90, 91, 132, 165, 169, 173, 174, 203, 206, 212, 223, 228, 231, 242n53
  narratives, 15, 16, 18, 107, 112, 224, 232
  National Spiritual Assembly of USA and Canada, 175, 190, 191
  number of, 108, 230
  and orientalism ('Baha'i orientalism'), 14, 119, 121, 124, 157, 164, 168, 182, 203, 206, 224, 225, 226, 227, 231, 233; see also Orientalism
  and Palestine, 137, 141, 142, 149
  and politics/political neutrality, 38–40, 173, 250ns46,47
  and Qajars, 164
  and Renan, 90, 92, 95
  and Reza Shah, Pahlavi dynasty, 173, 174, 175–6, 188–9, 190, 228
  and Russia (Tsarist and Soviet), 12, 33, 123, 125, 131, 136
  scholars, scholarship on Baha'i faith, 4, 15–18, 231
  and Shi'ism, 124; see also Shi'ism
  sociology of, 4
  Tarbiyat schools in Persia, 42, 172, 196–7; and *wilaya* (guardianship), 39, 206; and Zionism, 143–50, 151, 229
Baha'i Universal House of Justice, 189, 230
Baha'i World, 44, 140, 170, 190, 207, 208, 211; see also Holley, H.; Ransome-Keller, K.
Baha'i World Centre Haifa, 143, 146, 151, 180
  relations with Israel,148
Baha'ullah, 5, 8, 23, 27, 30, 68, 94, 99, 100, 101, 103, 105, 106, 114, 115–16, 121, 130, 143, 165, 166, 199, 201, 205, 229
  abrogation of jihad, 27

Baha'ullah (*cont.*)
  and Akka, 5, 8, 37
  aristocratic birth, 35, 40
  Baghdad House, 140, 174
  and Christianity, 37, 66, 151, 224
  declaration of 1863, 7
  and Edirne, 5, 187
  contacts with European representatives, 224
  letter to Queen Victoria
  mazhar-i ilahi (Manifestation of God), 5, 7
  and Middle East colonisation, 223
  mubahala with Subh-i Azal, 187
  on politics, 37
  and Ottoman Empire, 7; and Tanzimat, 247n14; and Young Ottomans, 39, 43
  prophecy, 17
  and Russian consul, 1852, 114, 125, 224
  in Suleymaniya, 7
  world peace and government, 30, 43, 199, 229–30
  writing: *Kitab-i Aqdas*, 39, 107; *Kitab-i Iqan* (Book of Certitude), 41
Bakhsh, Khuda, 117
Balfour, Arthur, 138
  Declaration 1919, 140, 143
Balyuzi, Hasan, 68
Banani, Amin, 93, 134–5, 136, 226
Bartol'd, Vasili, 128, 129, 158
Bayly, Christopher, 2
Bayreuth Circle, 48
Beirut, 178
Bell, Gertrude, 97
Ben-Gurion, David, 140
Bennett, Clinton, 13
Bentwich, Norman, 139, 141
Berger, Peter, 4
Besant, Annie, 20
Bhabha, Homi, 158
Bible, 27, 61, 145, 146, 151, 209, 232
  Biblical criticism, 84, 91, 92
Biddiss, Michael, 49
Blavatsky, Helena, 147, 169
Blomfield, Lady Sara, 138

Blunt, Wilfrid Scawen, 102
Bolles, May, 165
Bolshevism, Bolsheviks, 133, 202; *see also* Russia; Baha'i faith
Bopp, Franz, 73–4, 75
Boroujerdi, Mehrzad, 160
Britain, 10
  Government of India, 183, 215
  see also Baha'is; Ahmadis; India
British imperialism, 12, 22, 33, 123, 158, 159, 213, 214; *see also* Palestine
Browne, Edward Granville, 9, 16, 22, 56, 58, 65, 67, 68, 83, 112, 121, 162, 168, 175
  and Azalis, 58, 99, 101, 164
  and Bab, Babis, 99, 100, 102–3, 107, 108, 111, 120
  and Baha'ullah, Baha'is, 98, 99, 100, 101, 103, 107, 120
  and Baha'i/Azali schism, 96, 99–101, 107, 114, 121; and anti-Baha'i polemic, 112, 114–15, 117
  and Cambridge University, 97
  and Constitutional Revolution, 101
  and Gobineau, 50, 57, 97, 98
  and orientalism, 97–8, 100, 102, 107, 120, 129, 157, 158
  Nuqtat al-Kaf, 100, 101
  travels in Persia, 96, 98, 120
  Persian nationalism, 96, 102
  visit to Akka, Famagusta, 8
  writing: *A Year Amongst the Persians*, 99, 105, 107, 120; 'Babis of Persia' (*JRAS*), 59, 98; *Literary History of Persia*, 102; *Materials for the Study of the Babi Religion*, 103, 114, 117, 122; *The Persian Revolution, 1905–09*, 102; *Press and Poetry of Modern Persia*, 120
Buck, Christopher, 16
Buckton, Alice, 147
Buddhism, 20, 21, 84, 93
Buraq revolt 1929
Burhani, Ahmad Najib, 215
Burke, Edmund III, 158, 183
Burton, Richard, 64

Bush administration, 177
Bushehr (Persian Gulf), 51
Bushrui, Mulla Husayn-i, 114

Caliphate *see* Ottoman caliphate
Canadian Association of Baha'i Studies, 134
Canning, Lord Charles, 107
Carlyle, Thomas, 181, 200, 201, 211, 289n99
  History of the French Revolution, 200, 202
Carpenter, J. Estlin, 59, 91, 165
Catholic Church, 25, 92, 202
Caufield, James Walter, 84
Celts, Celtic, 78
Central Asia, 9
Cevdet, Abdullah, 92
Chamankhah, Leila, 189, 287n85
Chamberlain, Houston Stewart, 48, 74
Chancellor, John, 140
Chatterjee, Partha, 17
Chaudhuri, Nirad, 177–8
  Autobiography of an Unknown Indian, 177
Cheyne, T. K., 59, 91, 165
China, 19, 20, 183, 184
Chirol, Valentine, 68, 108, 164, 202, 222
  The Middle Eastern Question, 59
Christ *see* Jesus
Christianity, Christian-Church, 27, 31, 32, 76, 80, 83, 85, 87, 95, 119, 121, 146, 203, 216
  and colonialism, 171
  Evangelicals, 91, 203
  evangelical dispensationism, 145
  millennialism, millennial sects, 150, 151, 230
  missionaries in Asia, 2, 6, 7, 9, 12, 13, 14, 19, 20, 27, 32, 33, 55, 56, 91, 101, 114, 117, 121, 171, 198, 204, 209, 223
Christians
  in Iran, 189, 226
  in Ottoman Empire, 221
  n Pakistan, 235
Christian Science, 169
Christian universalism, 27; *see also* Abdul Baha

Christian Zionists, 145, 150
'clash of civilisations', 30, 229
Clifford-Barney, Laura, 165, 166
Clifford, James, 20
Cobb, Stanwood, 165
Cole, Juan R. I., 15, 16, 29, 38, 39, 42–3, 91, 162–3, 247n14, 251n53, 293n35
  Modernity and the Millennium, 16
Collège de France, 46, 78
colonialism, 17, 21, 25, 28, 95, 110, 145, 154, 155, 159, 171, 184, 185, 97, 203, 206, 217, 224; *see also* Ahmadiyyat; Babism; Baha'i faith
Columbus, Christopher, 25
Communism, 133, 201, 204, 207, 228; *see also* Marxism
Confucius, Confucianism, 20, 84
Conrad, Lawrence, 73
Copts, Egyptian Coptic Church, 234, 235
Cortes, Hernan, 25
Cowell, Edward, 63
Cox, Percy, 138
Cronin, Stephanie, 126, 127, 274n21
Crusades, 79
Curzon, Lord George Nathaniel, 22, 50, 68, 105, 107, 123, 140, 192, 198, 202
  and orientalism, 106
  Persia and the Persian Question, 59, 105–6
Cyrus II, the Great, 163, 191, 195

Dabashi, Hamid, 28, 161, 177, 224, 227, 246n8, 254n18
Dallmayr, Fred, 25–6
Damascus, 69
Darius I, 191, 195
Deringil, Selim, 159, 184
Dirlik, Arif, 18, 182–4
Dolgorukov, Dimitri Ivanovitch, 125
  Dolgorukov 'Memoirs'/*Confessions of Dolgoruki*, 33, 125, 233
Dorn, Bernhard, 96
Dreyfus, Hippolyte, 43, 165–6, 168, 169, 172, 183
  visits Ashkhabad, 132, 166
Druze, 32, 123

Edhem, Eldem, 186
'Edict of Toleration, 1844', 150–1
Edirne, 5, 187, 215
  Suleymaniyah mosque, 187
Edward, Prince of Wales, 208
Egypt, 11, 97, 137
Egyptian Expeditionary Force, 147
Egyptian (Urabi) revolution 1882, 29, 42
Egyptian court rulings on Baha'is, 216–19
Egyptian state and human rights, 217–19
Enayat, Hamid, 160, 162
Erimez, Salih, 186
Europe, European, 26, 27, 163, 182–3
  and eastern minorities, 30
  'discourses of Muslim inferiority', 222
  languages, 23
European orientalists, 124, 160
  'racialization of Muslimness', 222
  statements about Babi-Baha'ism, 225
  see also Orientalism; Baha'i faith
European Court of Human Rights, 217–18
Evans, Nicholas, 16, 117, 206

Famagusta, 99
Fanon, Frantz, 154, 177
Fardid, Ahmad, 228
Feisal, King of Iraq, 173–4
Firdawsi, Abul-Qasim, 162
FitzGerald, Edward, 63
  Rubaiyyat of Omar Khayyam, 63
Flaubert, Gustav, 45
Forman Christian College, Punjab, 109
Foroughi, Mohammad Ali, 191, 192, 196
Foucault, Michel, 22, 128
Fox, Richard, 20
France, 10, 46, 48, 50, 78, 202
  imperialism, 22, 31, 159
  orientalism, 80, 166
French language, literature, 4, 45, 161
French Legations in Persia, 50, 57
Friedmann, Yohanan, 34, 110, 117
Fuat Pasha, 30

Gandhi, Mohandas K., 20
Geaves, Ron, 118
Geller, Randall S.
Germany, Germanic, 78
German Orientalism, 80, 126
Getsinger, Lua, 165
Al-Ghazali, Abu Hamid Muhammad, 95
Gibb, H. A. R., 40
Gibbon, Edward, 105, 178, 181, 185, 200
Gibran, Kahlil, 168
Gilbar, Gad G., 125; see also Shahvar, S.
Gobineau, Joseph-Arthur Comte de, 22, 45, 61, 66–8, 69, 162, 164, 175, 178, 192, 224
  on 'Asia', 51
  and Aryans, 46, 48, 49, 51, 52, 55, 70, 72, 80, 81, 87
  brings Bab's story to Europe, 7, 53, 54, 67
  chef de cabinet, 47
  and Countess Mathilde de Tour, 47
  and cuneiforms, 50, 80
  diplomat, 47, 51, 57, 224
  and orientalism, 50, 55, 57, 66, 67
  and Persia, 47, 50, 55, 67, 80–1, 87
  and racial theory, racism, 45, 47–9, 51, 57, 67
  scholars of, 253n9
  on Shi'ism, 46, 52, 53, 70, 81
  and *taziya* (religious theatre), 46, 67, 85, 86
  writing: *Essai sur L'Inégalité des Races Humaines*, 46, 48, 49, 51, 55, 69, 80; *Mémoire sur l'état de la Perse actuelle*, 52; *Les Religions et Les Philosophies dans L'Asie Central*, 9, 46, 47, 50, 52, 53, 58, 59, 66, 69, 80, 81–2, 85; *Treatise on Cuneiform Texts*, 80; *Trois Ans en Asie*, 47, 49, 51
Goethe, Johann Wolfgang von, 201
Goldziher, Ignaz, 77
Greco-Sassanian civilisation, 74, 89
Greek Orthodox Church, 202
Gobineau, Thibault-Joseph de, 46
Gospels, 61, 65
Greece *see* Ancient Greece
Gualtieri, Antonio, 16, 117

Gulpaygani, Abdul Fazl, 43, 92, 93, 94, 111, 130, 132, 265n87
Gulpaygani, Mihdi, 135
Gunny, Ahmad, 80

Haifa, 148
  Arab population, 149
  Baha'i colony/community in, 143
Haganah, 148
Hali, Altaf Husayn, 203
  Mussadas: The Flow and Ebb of Islam, 203
Hall, Edward, 146
  'The Isles Unveiled', 146–7
Hedayat, Sadeq, 228
Hamadani, M. M. Huseyn (author, *Tarikh-i Jadid*), 58, 94
Hamid, Sultan Abdul, 220
Headley, Baron, R. G. A. Allanson-Winn, 12, 110
Hearst, Phoebe, 165
Hegel, Georg Wilhelm Friedrich, 19, 224
Heidegger, Martin, 26
Herder, Johann Gottfried, 201
'hermeneutics of difference', 25
Higgins, Patricia, 189
al-Hilali, Taqi l-Din, 110
Hinduism, Hindus, 20, 21, 29, 178
Hochburg, Gil, 229
Holley, Horace, 43, 44, 165, 169, 183, 198
  writing in *Baha'i World*, 173–6
Hotz, Henry, 49
Hourani, Albert, 52, 72, 73, 95
Howe, Stephen, 220
Huart, Clément, 68, 166
Humboldt, Wilhelm von, 73, 74
Human Rights of religious minorities, 190, 217–19, 232, 235
Husayn ibn Ali, 3rd Imam, 86

India, 2, 7, 19, 29, 31, 35, 205
  Rebellion, 1857, 35, 223
Indian Muslims, 7, 119, 203, 213, 223, 234; *see also* Muslims
Indian ulama, 119, 152
Indo-Europeans *see* Aryanism

Indonesia, 122, 215, 219, 230
Ioannesyan, Youli, 125, 129
  The Development of Babi/Baha'i Communities, 125
Iqbal, Muhammad, 119, 154, 203, 232, 235
  on Ahmadiyyat, 155, 213–14
  on Babi-Baha'ism, 214
  letter to Nehru, 115
  Reconstruction of Religious Thought in Islam, 203
Iran (Persia), 2, 22, 23, 27, 28, 29, 30, 31, 34, 40, 51, 52, 53, 57, 59, 60, 67, 68, 70, 81, 85, 87, 88, 103, 105, 106, 107, 108, 124, 127, 128, 161, 162, 175, 177, 182, 184, 185–6, 190, 202, 214, 219, 221
  Aryanism and racial conceit, 23, 160, 162, 164, 195
  in European colonial discourse, 224
  intellectuals, 158, 160–1, 228; and orientalism, 157, 160
  missionaries in, 91
  nationalism, 28, 156, 160
  religious minorities, 226
  trade, British penetration of, 246n8
Iranian Constitutional Revolution, 6, 38, 90, 96, 98, 101, 144, 188, 224
Iranian revolution, 1978–9, 29, 33, 38, 90, 125, 227, 228
Iranian studies, 125
Iraq, 177
Irwin, Robert, 50, 97
Isfahani, Muhammad Riza *see* Baha'is, Ashkhabad
Islam, 9, 10, 12, 53, 72, 76, 77, 85, 95, 106, 117, 154, 161, 165, 182, 187, 202, 213, 214, 216, 235
  modernism, 40, 118
  Orientalist view of, 19, 98
  and postcolonialism, 220–1, 223
  Revival, 2, 233
  Western conceptions of, 113, 156, 157, 244n70
Islamic Republic (of Iran), 33

Islamic studies, 125
Islamic/Islamicate world, 4, 5, 26, 29, 30, 184, 212, 220, 235
   and threat of imperialism, 223, 234
Islamism, Islamists, 31–2, 119, 154, 158, 159, 160, 220, 227, 235
   Islamic state, 204, 221
   'Pan-Islamic solidarity', 222
Islamophobia, 234
Ismailis, 123, 214, 236
Israel, 31, 139, 145, 146, 147, 149, 151, 152, 221, 229
isra'iliyyat, 56, 246n6
Ivanov, M. S., 4, 135
Izzed, Mehmed, 184–5

Jahrum, persecution of Baha'is 1926, 123, 171, 175
Jamaat-i Islami, 153
Jamal Pasha, 30, 224
James, Henry, 51
Jani, Haji Mirza, 100, 121; *see also* Browne, E. G.
Jeffries, J. M. N., 152
Jesus, 54, 55, 61, 65–6, 79, 86, 91, 93, 101, 155, 166, 214
Jews, Judaism, 32, 71–2, 76, 77, 85, 87, 88, 127, 151, 214, 216, 232
   in Iran, 189, 228
   Jewish return to Palestine, 17, 143, 144–5, 146, 147, 150
   see also Baha'i, Jewish converts; Zionism
jihad *see* Ahmad, G; Baha'ullah
jihadist movement, 1, 234
Jinna, Muhammad, 154
John the Baptist, 151
Jones, Sir William, 73
Juma'a Masjid, Delhi, 209
Jung, Dietrich, 17

Kalisman, Hilary Farb, 142
Kamaluddin, Khwaja, 11, 12, 24, 109, 110, 116, 117, 119
   non-sectarian form of Islam, 12, 110, 210

Kara, Ismail, 31
Kashmir *see* Ahmad, B. M.; Ahmad, G.
Katouzian, Homa, 196
Kazem Bek (Kazem-Beg), Aleksandr, 9, 96, 129
Keddie, Nikki, 41, 50, 89, 90
Kedourie, Elie, 142
Kemalism, 43, 157, 187, 198, 232
   Kemalist Orientalism, 160, 186
   see also Atatürk
Kermani, Aqa Khan, 23, 156, 161–2, 164, 184, 228
Khan, Adil Hussain, 153
Khan, Aga *see* Ismailis
Khan, Ami Habibullah, 1st Ahmadi martyr, 208
Khan, Chaudry Muhammad Zafrullah, 33, 153, 154, 206, 207
Khan, Malkum, 161
Khan, Sayyid Ahmad (Syed Ahmad), 41, 117, 118, 152, 168, 203
Khan, Sulayman (Babi martyr), 121
khatim al-nubuwwa, 7, 111, 214
Khatm-i nubawwat movement, 221
Kheiralla, Ibrahim, 11
Khilafat movement, 205
Khomeini, Ayatollah Ruhollah, 1, 38
Khorasan, 114
King David, 77
King, Richard, 4, 20
   Orientalism and Religion, 4
Klaproth, Heinrich Julius, 74
Kolarz, Walter, 133–4
   Religion in the Soviet Union, 133–4
Kufa, 86
Kuropatkin, General Aleksei Nikolaevitch, 130

Lahori Ahmadis, 11,12, 24, 33, 110, 113, 119–20; *see also* Ahmadiyyat
Lamartine, Alphonse de, 83
Lambden, Stephen, 16, 56, 59, 62, 244n6
Lamington, Lord, 137, 138, 180
Lane, Edward, 97
Lapidus, Ira, 42

Laqueur, Walter, 151
 History of Zionism, 151
Lathan, Anthea, 154
Latin America, 134
La Tour, Mathilde de, 47
Lawrence, T. E., 97, 142
Lawson, Todd, 15
Lavan, Spencer, 109, 117, 153
Layard, Austin, 80
Lebanon, 69
Lee, Anthony, 132, 133
Lefevere, André, 22, 63
Leroux, Pierre, 83
Levant, 9
liberalism, 171
Liberal Government 1906–14, 97
Libya, 28, 185
Ling, Trevor, 229
Lloyd George, David, 145
Lockman, Zachary, 19
London, 144, 157, 165, 178, 180
Lorient (France), 46

McCants, William, 43
MacEoin, Denis, 9, 15–16, 31, 33, 38, 39, 59, 64–5, 101, 111, 112, 115, 125, 182, 228, 231, 257n.47
McGlinn, Sen, 16, 38, 243n61
McMahon-Sharif Husayn correspondence, 142
McNamara, Brendan, 11, 165
Magianism, 53, 55, 214, 291n8
Mahdi, Mahdi movements, 2–5, 13, 17, 24, 26, 27, 36, 66, 100, 102, 111, 114, 115, 117, 121–2, 152, 154, 203, 204, 205, 212, 213, 214, 215, 216, 219, 220, 222, 223, 225, 231, 234, 235
 and colonial power, 28
 Imam Mahdi, 5, 55
 literature, 210–11
Mahmood, Saba, 217–19
Majeed, Javid, 203, 235
Majlis-i Ahrar-i Islam, 153, 221
Makdisi, Ussama, 159–60
Malek, Anwar Abdel, 227

Mamdani, Mahmood, 220
al-Manar, 110
Margoliouth, D. S., 98, 180, 188
Marie, Queen of Romania, 139, 186
Maronites, 32, 123
Marx, Marxism, 4, 132, 134, 135, 161, 172, 207; *see also* Baha'is, Ashkhabad
mashriq al-adhkar see Baha'is, Ashkhabad
mashrutih see Iranian Constitutional Revolution
Masuzawa, Tomoko, 73
Mathew, W. M., 277n47, 278n63
Maududi Abul Ala, 119, 153, 154, 155, 204, 213, 214, 215, 217, 221, 223
maulvis (Indian ulama), 14, 36, 118
Maxwell, William Sutherland
Mexico, 202
Middle East, 31, 32, 39, 42, 217, 218, 234
 and (de)colonisation, 226, 235
Middle Eastern intellectuals, 156
Mill, John Stuart, 171–2
Milner, Lord Alfred, 180
Minorsky, Vladimir, 42, 135
Mirsepassi, Ali, 19, 224
missionaries *see* Christian missionaries
Moaddel, Mansur, 91
modernity, 12, 17
 in Muslim societies, 5, 18
 varieties of, 17
Momen, Moojan, 15, 38, 123, 133–4, 138, 224
 The Babi and Baha'i Religions, 1844–1944, 15, 138, 224
Momen, Wendy, 39
Monnerot, Clémence (Madame de Gobineau), 47
Morier, James, 51
Mormons, Mormonism, 8, 230
Morozov, Boris, 125; *see also* Shahvar, S.
Moses, 166
Mufti, Aamir, 201, 222
Mufti of Akka, 148
Mughals, Mughal dynasty, 6, 26
mubahala, 264ns80, 81; *see also* Ahmad, G.; Baha'ullah

Muhammad ibn al-Hanifiya, 3
Muhammad, the Prophet, 10, 77, 98, 104, 118, 166, 187–8, 201, 213
Muir, William, 19, 97, 98
mujaddid, 1, 116
Muslim India and Islamic Review, 111, 119
Muslims, 4, 109, 118, 150, 151, 188, 212, 216, 219, 220, 229, 234
  anti-Ahmadi, 153
  thought, 156, 227, 232
  response to imperialism, 29, 220, 221, 222, 227
Muslim League, 153
Muslim nationalism, 205
Muslim reformists, 110
Muslim ulama, 6, 7, 31, 91; see also Shi'ism; Indian ulama
Muslim world, 247n15; see also Islamic world
Muzzafar al-Din Shah, 38

Nadir Shah, 191
Naipaul, V. S., 178, 181
  Among the Believers: An Islamic Journey, 237n1
  The Mimic Men, 178
Napoleon, Louis, 47
Nasir al-Din Shah, 35, 105, 162
Nasikh-i Tavarikh, 57, 101, 114; see also Sipihr
Nasr, Sayyid Vali Reza, 153
Nehru, Jawaharlal, 155
Nerval, Gèrard de, 45
New Age, 169
New History of Mirza Ali Muhammad the Bab see *Tarikh-i Jadid*
New Thought, 10
New World Order, 200; see also Ahmad, M. B.; Rabbani, S. E.
New York Globe and Commercial Advertiser, 146
Nicholson, Reynold A., 67
Nicolas, A. L. M., 57, 58, 59, 61–2, 68, 168, 188, 192
Nietzsche, Friedrich, 48, 74, 154, 155

Nöldeke, Theodor, 162
North Africa, 28
Nott, Josiah, 49
Nuqtat al-Kaf, 100, 101, 114, 117, 121; see also E. G. Browne
Nuri, Husayn Ali see Baha'ullah
Nuruddin, Hakim, 1st Ahmadiyya khalifa, 6, 109, 111
Nusratul Dawleh, 138

Olender, Maurice, 73, 88
Orientalism, 5, 12, 18–24, 158, 161, 201, 213
  affirmative, 20, 165
  and Babi/Baha'i narratives, 13–14, 21–2, 106, 125, 224–5
  and 'civilising mission', 172
  and India, 20; Anglicists v. Orientalists, 20
  and modernity,1, 5, 18, 22
  Romantic, 21, 46
  see also European Orientalism; Kemalism; Ottoman; Russia; Said, E.
Osborn (Abdo), Lil, 137, 143, 146, 147, 166
Ottoman caliphate, 102, 205, 220, 222
Ottomans, Ottoman Empire, 5, 12, 29, 30, 43, 102, 108, 109, 148, 151, 158, 178, 186, 220, 221, 222
  Young Ottomans, 42–3
Ottoman Orientalism, 156, 157, 159, 184, 186
Oxford University, 178, 179

Pahlavi, dynasty and state in Iran, 19, 160, 188, 189, 193, 195, 226
  nationalism, 23, 164, 232
  see also Aryanism
Pahlavi, Mohammad Reza, 40,189, 226
Pahlavi, Reza, 175, 185, 190–2, 193, 194, 196, 216
Pakistan, 15, 29, 31, 122, 152–3, 215, 221; see also Kashmir
Palestine, 27, 29, 31, 139, 140, 144, 147, 149, 188, 205, 220

Arabs of, 140, 144, 148, 149, 152
British Mandate, 124, 137, 138, 139, 141, 142, 146, 149, 150, 152, 198, 224
nakba, 149
Palmer, Edward Henry, 97
Parekh, Bhikhu, 171, 200
Paris, 46, 165, 166
Parliament of World Religions, Chicago 1893, 165
Parsees, 51; *see also* Zoroastrians
Persia *see* Iran
Persian Empire, 51
Persian language, literature, 3, 21, 46, 50, 56, 64, 163, 166
Persian studies, 101
Pharisaism (Fr. le Pharisaisme), 79
Phelps, Myron H.
Life and Teachings of Abbas Effendi, 120
Philby, Harry St John, 97
Pickthall, Marmaduke, 12–13, 109, 116
Pole, Wellesley Tudor, 137, 147, 180
political Islam *see* Islamism
postcolonialism, postcolonial theory, 198n95, 213, 224, 228, 231, 245n74
Pratt, Mary Louise, 182, 184
progressive/successive prophetic/revelation, 170
Prokesch-Osten, Baron von, 224
Protestantism, 71
Punjabi riots 1921, 153
Purohit, Teena, 213, 214

Qadiani Ahmadis, 11, 24, 33, 113, 117, 119, 120, 154, 213
number of, 230
see also Ahmadis, Ahmadiyya
'Qadiani problem' 214; *see also* Maududi, A.
Qadiani scholars, 112, 117
The Babi and Baha'i Religion, 112, 114
Qajars, dynasty in Iran, 13, 18, 20, 54, 103, 163, 198, 222
Quilliam, Abdullah, 109
Quran, 61, 110, 146, 187, 207
on Christ's crucifixion, 210

Quratul Ayn, Tahirih, 41, 120
Qutb, Sayyid, 228

Rabbani, Ruhiyyih Khanum, 137, 138, 139, 148, 150, 178, 256n42
The Priceless Pearl, 150, 150
Rabbani, Shoghi Effendi, 15, 17–18, 58, 68, 95, 103, 104–6, 137, 147, 148, 166, 177, 182, 188, 204, 205, 207
on Arab Buraq revolt, 1929, 140
Britain, British, 138, 178, 179–80, 181, 225
Christianising, 62–6
correspondence with royalty, 139
on Gobineau, 57
Guardian of Baha'i faith, 39, 138
infallible interpreter, 199, 225
and Kemalism, 43, 198
modern, anti-modern, 44, 157
and orientalism, self-orientalising, 21–2, 120, 172, 176, 182, 183, 184, 185, 198, 225, 233, 268n32
at Oxford University, 179–80, 198, 225
New World Order, 17, 44, 156, 169, 197, 199, 200, 201–2, 205; 'world order letters', 198, 199, 204
on Pahlavi Iran, 194, 197
on Palestine Administration, 140
racism, nationalism and communism, 171, 201, 228
and Zionist leaders, 139, 198
establishment of Israel, 149, 150, 151
writing: *The Dawn-Breakers*, 56, 58–62, 97, 100, 102, 105, 140, 194, 232; *God Passes By*, 15, 57, 58, 59, 95, 97, 103, 104, 105, 107, 140, 149, 194, 195, 232; *The Promised Day is Come*, 185; *World Order of Baha'u'llah*, 199, 204, 206
Ransome-Kehler, Keith, 174, 189–93, 194, 196, 197
letter to Reza Shah, 190–1
on Babi-Baha'i martyrs, 192, 194, 195
Rashti, Sayyid Kazim, 3
Rawlinson, George, 80, 162

Rawlinson, Henry Creswicke, 80
Reagan, Ronald, 1, 237n1
Remey, Mason, 132, 165, 166, 167, 172, 173
Rémusat, Charles de, 47
the Renaissance, 25
Renan, Ernest, 22, 45, 48, 67, 68, 84, 94, 103, 162, 164, 222, 230
  on Arabs and Islam, 52, 74, 75, 79–80, 81, 89
  on Aryanism and Semitism, 70, 71–3, 75–8, 79, 80; Indo-European, Semitic languages, 72–4, 75–6
  on Bab and Babi martyrdom, 69, 70, 81–3, 121, 261n48
  and Baha'ism, 90
  and colonialism, 263n75
  and Jamal al-Din 'Afghani', 89–90
  on Jews, Judaism, 17, 32, 55, 75, 78, 79, 104
  on modernity and religion, 71
  and Palestine, 79
  on Persia, 80–1
  and philology, 72
  writing: *The Apostles*, 69, 82, 83, 85, 92, 103; *Averroes and Averroism*, 75; *General History of the Semitic Languages*, 74, 76, 77; *History of the People of Israel*, 75; *Life of Jesus*, 69, 76, 78, 83, 84, 94; *Origins of the History of Christianity*, 69, 75, 83;*Studies of Religious History*, 76, 77
Renan, Henriette, 69
Review of Religions, 109, 111, 112, 118, 209
Rida, Muhammad Rashid, 110
Rippin, Andrew, 2, 8, 112
Rohingya Muslims of Burma, 234
Roman Empire
Romantic Orientalism, 47; *see also* Orientalism
Root, Martha, 186–8
Rosenberg, Ethel, 165, 166
Ross, Sir Denison, 180
Rostam-Kolayi, Jasmin, 197

Roy, Rammohun, 20
Rozen, Baron Viktor, 9, 50, 96, 125, 128, 129, 130, 136, 175
  archive of, 125
  school of orientalists, 126, 157, 158
Ruhi, Husayn, 141–3, 224
Ruhi, Shaykh Ahmad, 99, 100, 162
  Hasht Bihisht, 99, 100
Russia, 202, 221
  imperialism, 22, 33, 123, 126, 159
  Tsarist government, 108, 124; policy toward Baha'is, 131
  Soviet Union, 124, 126, 196
  Transcaspia and Caucasus, 124, 126
Russian orientalism, orientalists, 9, 58, 124, 126, 127, 128, 157
  and military officers, 127–8
  travellers in Iran, 126–7, 128
  see also Rozen school
Russian revolution, 133
Russo-Turk War 1877–8, 97
Ryad, Umar, 110

Sacy, Silvestre de, 45
Said, Edward W., 26, 29, 45, 49, 73, 97–8, 102, 157, 183
  criticism and revisions of, 158–9, 176, 183
  'filiation' and 'affiliation', 95
  'Saidian paradigm', and Russia 128, 136, 188; *Orientalism*, 18–19, 21, 25, 45, 52, 106, 161, 176, 227
Saint Paul, 37, 69, 79
salafis, 1, 234
Salih, Tayeb, 178
Samuel, Edwin, 141
Samuel, Herbert, 137, 138, 139, 180
Sand, George, 83, 84
Sanskrit, 73
Saraswati, Dayananda, 20
Sassanians, 52, 162, 163; *see also* Greco-Sassanian
Schemann, Ludwig, 48
Schlegel, Friedrich, 73, 74
Schlegel, Wilhelm, 74

Schopenhauer, Arthur, 74
Schwab, Raymond, 49, 74
Sears, William, 151
Semitic, Semite, Semitism (Fr. *semitisme*), 30
Senusiyya movement, 28
Sevea, Terenjit, 154–5
Shadman, Fakhruddin, 227
Shahvar, Soli, 124, 129, 131
   The Baha'is of Iran, Transcaspia and the Caucasus, 125
Sharbrodt, Oliver, 15, 38, 42, 43
Sharett, Moshe, 139
Shariati, Ali, 228
Sharon, Moshe, 8
Shaykhis, Shaykism, 3, 22
Shaykh Tabarsi fort, 114
Shi'ism, Shi'a Muslims, 31, 56, 66, 67, 10, 132, 161, 162, 164, 166, 214, 225, 226, 232, 233, 236
   polemic against Babism and Baha'i faith, 1, 13, 28, 33, 123, 221, 226; conspiracy theory *see* Dolgorukov
   ulama, mujtahids, 5, 13, 31, 104, 105, 156, 197, 202
Shiraz, 54
Shirazi, Ali Muhammad *see* the Bab
Sikh rule, 34, 36
Singh, Ranjit, 34
Sipihr, Lisan al-Mulk, 57
Smith, Peter, 4, 16–17, 94
Smith, Wilfred Cantwell, 40, 41
Société de Scelti, 47
Sohrab, Ahmad, 141
South Asia, 219
Southeast Asia, 234
Spain, 202
Spinoza, Baruch, 84
Spiritualists, 11
Sprague, Sidney, 165, 166–7, 172
Stendhal (Marie-Henri Beyle), 47
Stone, Donald D., 84
Storrs, Ronald, 137, 139, 142
Soviet Union *see* Russia
Strauss, David, 84
Sudan, 29, 178

Sufism, sufis, 154, 214
Suharto, President of Indonesia, 215
Sunnis, Sunni Islam, 114, 202, 234, 236
   polemic against Ahmadiyya, 2, 123
   Sunni–Shi'a faultline, 234
   ulama, 91
   see also Muslim ulama
Switzerland, 46, 181
Sykes, Percy Molesworth, 162
Symes, George Stewart, 138
Syria, 30, 123
Syrian Protestant College, Beirut, 178

Tabriz, 9, 54
Taine, Hippolyte, 48
Tarbiyat schools *see* Baha'i faith
Tarikh-i Jadid, 58, 94, 99, 103–4
Tavakoli-Targhi, Mohamad, 162, 163
Taymurtash, Abul Husayn, 190, 192, 195–6
Taziya, 85, 262n67; *see also* Gobineau, A.
Tehran, 50, 98, 131, 138, 173, 190, 195
Theosophists, 11
Third International Congress for the History of Religion, Oxford, 1908, 165
Tibawi, A. L., 142, 227
The Times (London), 108
Todorov, Tzvetan, 25, 49
Tolstoy, Count Leo, 20
Toqueville, Alexis de, 45, 47, 52
Tolz, Vera, 128
Tory imperialism, 105
Townshend, George, 68, 150, 183, 198
Toynbee, Arnold, 200
Transcaspia and Caucasus, 22; *see also* Baha'i faith; Russia
Tudeh party, 135
Tumanskii, Aleksandr, 127, 129–30, 136
Turkey, Turks, 31, 156, 186, 202, 218
   Young Turks, 30, 173
   see also Ottomans, Ottoman Empire
Turkish reformers, 156
Turner, Richard Brent, 18

Unitarianism, 71, 230
United States of America, 18, 49, 141;
    see also Baha'i faith
Urabi revolution see Egypt
Urquhart, David, 102
Uyghur Muslims, 234

Vahdat, Farzin, 161, 162
Valentine, Simon Ross, 209
Venuti, Lawrence, 63
Vivekananda, Swami, 20
Volkov, Denis, 128, 129
Voll, John, 2

Wagner, Richard, 45
Wahhabis, 41
Walter, H. A., 9, 117, 118, 209
    The Ahmadiya Movement, 9
Warburg, Margit, 31
Warmind, Morten, 204
Wauchope, Arthur, 138, 140
Weber, Max, 4, 16, 18, 44
Wells, H. G., 200
Western orientalism see European
    orientalists
West Indies, 178; see also Afro-Caribbean

Wickens, G. Michael, 97
Wilcox, Andrew, 19
Willey, Basil, 84
Wishard, John, 108
Woking Mosque, 11, 12, 109,
    111, 120.
World War One (Great War), 30, 43,
    108, 222
World War Two, 44, 49, 205

Yazdani, May, 233
Yazidis, 234
Young Ottomans see Ottomans
Young, Robert C., 49, 158
Young Turks see Turkey

Zarandi, Nabil-i, 58, 60, 62, 63
    Tarikh-i Zarandi, 59, 63, 64
    see also, *Dawn-Breakers*
Zia-Ebrahimi, Reza, 161, 162,
    163, 195
Zionism, Zionists, 33, 144–5, 152, 198;
    see also Abdul Baha; Baha'i faith
Zionist Commission, 144
Zoroaster, Zoroastrians, 52, 86, 99, 107,
    127, 162, 163, 166, 189, 226

EU representative:
Easy Access System Europe
Mustamäe tee 50, 10621 Tallinn, Estonia
Gpsr.requests@easproject.com

www.ingramcontent.com/pod-product-compliance
Lightning Source LLC
Chambersburg PA
CBHW050201240426
43671CB00013B/2205